I0880959

From Dead Ends to Cold Warriors

From Dead Ends to Cold Warriors

Constructing American Boyhood in Postwar Hollywood Films

PETER W. Y. LEE

FOREWORD BY CLAUDE JARMAN Jr.

Rutgers University Press
New Brunswick, Camden, and Newark, New Jersey, and London

Library of Congress Cataloging-in-Publication Data

Names: Lee, Peter W. Y., author. | Jarman, Claude, 1934– writer of foreword.
Title: From dead ends to cold warriors : constructing American boyhood in postwar Hollywood films / Peter W.Y. Lee ; foreword by Claude Jarman, Jr.
Description: New Brunswick : Rutgers University Press, [2021] | Includes bibliographical references and index.
Identifiers: LCCN 2020020463 | ISBN 9781978813465 (paperback) | ISBN 9781978813472 (hardcover) | ISBN 9781978813489 (epub) | ISBN 9781978813496 (mobi) | ISBN 9781978813502 (pdf)
Subjects: LCSH: Boys in motion pictures. | Motion pictures—Political aspects—United States—History—20th century. | Motion pictures—Social aspects—United States—History—20th century.
Classification: LCC PN1995.9.B74 L44 2021 | DDC 791.43/653—dc23
LC record available at https://lccn.loc.gov/2020020463

A British Cataloging-in-Publication record for this book is available from the British Library.

www.rutgersuniversitypress.org

Manufactured in the United States of America

For Dino C. Bello

Contents

FIG. 1 Portrait of Claude Jarman, publicity portrait for *Intruder in the Dust* (1949). (Author's collection.)

Foreword

I was at MGM from 1945 to 1950, the final period of the studio system. Movies were still the major source of entertainment, and MGM was at the top. All one has to do is look at the twenty-fifth-anniversary photo taken in 1949. As L. B. Mayer boasted, "More stars than there are in Heaven." There were lots of films about returning veterans, starting with *Best Years of Our Lives* (1946), then later on with *The Man in the Gray Flannel Suit* (1956). I never knew much about the communist debate, but films were beginning to delve into social issues with *Gentleman's Agreement* (1947).

It has always amazed me that MGM agreed to make *Intruder in the Dust* (1949). Only Clarence Brown could convince Mayer to let him make that film. Mayer got the last word when he buried it after it was made. In those days the studios could tell the academy which picture they would like to be nominated for Best Picture. Because *Intruder* had won awards in Europe, there was a movement to have *Intruder* nominated. MGM insisted that *Battleground* (1949) be nominated (lost, of course).

In 1950 the double whammy hit the studios—arrival of television and antitrust legislation forcing studios to sell movie theaters. It all died when Mayer, Zanuck, Warner, and others were fired or forced to resign.

As Janet Leigh once said, "Nothing will ever be like that again."

Claude Jarman Jr.
2020

Abbreviations

AMPAS	Academy of Motion Picture Arts and Sciences
AMPTP	Association of Motion Picture and Television Producers
ARMS	United Nations Archives and Records Management Section
BO	*Boxoffice*
BOBG	*Boxoffice Bookin Guide*
CCF	Core Collection Files, Academy of Motion Picture Arts and Sciences
CD	*Chicago Defender*
CSM	*Christian Science Monitor*
DV	*Daily Variety*
FD	*Film Daily*
HR	*Hollywood Reporter*
LAT	*Los Angeles Times*
MHL	Margaret Herrick Library
MPD	*Motion Picture Daily*
MPH	*Motion Picture Herald*
NYT	*New York Times*
PCA	Production Code Administration
UCLA	University of California, Los Angeles
USC	University of Southern California
VW	*Variety Weekly*
WBA	Warner Bros. Archives
WHS	Wisconsin Historical Society
WP	*Washington Post*
WSJ	*Wall Street Journal*

Chronology

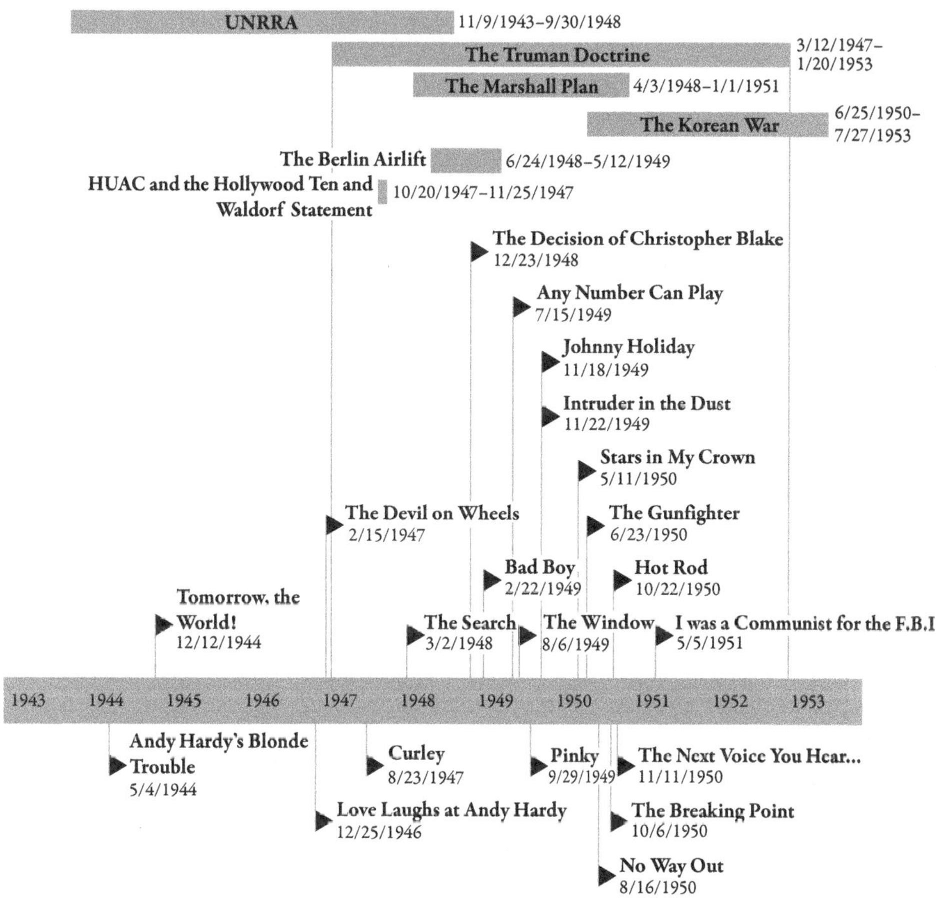

UNRRA 11/9/1943–9/30/1948
The Truman Doctrine 3/12/1947–1/20/1953
The Marshall Plan 4/3/1948–1/1/1951
The Korean War 6/25/1950–7/27/1953
The Berlin Airlift 6/24/1948–5/12/1949
HUAC and the Hollywood Ten and Waldorf Statement 10/20/1947–11/25/1947
The Decision of Christopher Blake 12/23/1948
Any Number Can Play 7/15/1949
Johnny Holiday 11/18/1949
Intruder in the Dust 11/22/1949
Stars in My Crown 5/11/1950
The Devil on Wheels 2/15/1947
The Gunfighter 6/23/1950
Bad Boy 2/22/1949
Hot Rod 10/22/1950
Tomorrow, the World! 12/12/1944
The Search 3/2/1948
The Window 8/6/1949
I was a Communist for the F.B.I 5/5/1951
1943 1944 1945 1946 1947 1948 1949 1950 1951 1952 1953
Andy Hardy's Blonde Trouble 5/4/1944
Curley 8/23/1947
Pinky 9/29/1949
The Next Voice You Hear... 11/11/1950
Love Laughs at Andy Hardy 12/25/1946
The Breaking Point 10/6/1950
No Way Out 8/16/1950

From Dead Ends to Cold Warriors

Introduction

Are the Kids All Right?

In 1953, a motley collection of celluloid motorcycles rumbles into Small Town, USA. After they laugh at the law and harass the civic bluenoses, the leather-jacketed lot swarms a barroom. A local blonde asks their leader, Johnny, what the letters BRMC etched on their jackets stand for. When told he leads the Black Rebel Motorcycle Club, she asks what he rebels against. Johnny mumbles, "Whaddya got?"[1]

What they already "got" was the past fifteen years of American history. On the surface, this exchange, from Stanley Kramer's 1953 movie *The Wild One*, represented the symbolic birth of juvenile unrest in 1950s American film. As Johnny, actor Marlon Brando embodied the seething resentment and discontent lurking under domestic containment during the American Cold War. Although Johnny ultimately repents his wild ways in the final reel, Brando struck a chord among audiences. *The Wild One* spawned a genre of imitators rebelling without causes, rocking around the clock, and living out their dangerous years on celluloid. However, Johnny's query also tapped into underlying fears and anxieties from the past two decades of American history. Johnny's antisocial behavior and outlook challenged the relative postwar prosperity that would lead later generations to characterize the 1950s as a decade of materialism, mobility, and middle-class life. But in questioning the good life at risk, Johnny also "got" that the comforts of the American Dream could easily dissipate, with the country backsliding into the economic and social hardships of the Great Depression and World War II.

The early postwar years, from 1945 to 1950, constitute a unique moment in history, as Americans basked in the glow of V-Day right before hunkering down to the Cold War. The markers of the Cold War that signified escalating U.S.–Soviet Union relations took place in this period: Churchill's "Iron Curtain" speech (1946), the Soviet Union's detonating an atomic bomb (1949), the "loss" of China (1949), and the start of the Korean War (1950). Domestically, the growing civil rights movement questioned the status quo, while suspected subversives and "dupes" undermined the American way from foreign shores and, more alarmingly, at home. Accordingly, the idea of "containment culture"—the promotion of capitalism, the nuclear family, and idealized gender roles—reflects a wary public clinging to the American Dream during an uncertain time.[2]

While this historiography benefits from hindsight, the social and cultural boundaries of domestic containment did not arise solely due to the so-called Red Menace at home and abroad. Rather, in looking back, the public also drew on past experiences; with the United States victorious over fascism, the public feared a national return of hard times. In 1944, the American Federation of Labor predicted up to twenty million workers would lose their jobs once the war ended, leading to a "deadly depression" worse than the stock market's fall in 1929.[3] Indeed, from May to September 1945, employment declined by over three million people.[4] An editorial for the *Christian Science Monitor* agreed, declaring, "Preventing a depression in America can be even more important to national defense than preserving the secret of the atom bomb. The self-discipline which tries to hold down wages and prices is more genuinely patriotic than any hurling of epithets at another country."[5] While the statistics for prices and employment figures waxed and waned, the fear of a return to lean times revived.

The United States proactively sought to prevent the Depression's return by maintaining the wartime production boom. Congress passed the Employment Act of 1946 to assure the public of the government's "continuing policy and responsibility" to "foster and promote free and competitive enterprise," which would "promote maximum employment, production, and purchasing power."[6] American leaders publicly associated free enterprise and free trade with freedom in general through programs like the Marshall Plan, in which the United States created international outlets for its surpluses.[7] At home, the ideology of a "consumers' republic" promoted private ownership and accumulating stuff as signs of social mobility.[8] Houses, of course, were more than storage lots for personal possessions; their inhabitants—the nuclear family—were key to postwar security. As Leonard W. Mayo, the president of the Child Welfare League, proclaimed, "The status of children in a nation is probably the best reflection of the culture and maturity of that nation" in the way "the nation considers them its future and its hope."[9] Threats to the family, notably divorce, chipped at this cornerstone of the nation's foundation.

Family tensions, however, made for excellent melodrama. The film industry cashed in on the national yearning for normality by depicting the household under siege, figuratively and literally. Such story lines were not new; since the medium's inception, movies showed the dangers of parental negligence and fears concerning juvenile delinquents. Coming-of-age tales, where boys figuratively or literally grow up before the audiences' eyes, remained a popular story trope. Childhood, especially father-son themes, permeated multiple genres after World War II, from *Atomic City* (1952) to *The Yearling* (1947). Despite a triumphant United States immersed in "Victory Culture," social guardians worried about the fleeting nature of childhood—and the short window fathers had to raise their sons. In 1949, drama critic John Mason Brown sentimentalized this special bond when taking his son to the movies: "If ever there was a father-son movie, at least in its theme, *The Yearling* is that film." The picture, about a boy and a fawn, was an apt choice, Brown observed, pointing out his son "will himself be a yearling," who "cannot know, any more than any young son can, what strange tugging at the heart he causes as the days go by" as he ages rapidly.[10] As a result, the "period is brief" when a son idolized his dad, and the father "walks the earth a sage, a chief justice, a guide to undreamed-of vistas, a center of trust, and a friend whose word is not questioned even if his authority is. Yet, brief as that period is, it is glorious."[11] Filmmakers honed in on childhood, using boy characters to explore the country's adjustment to postwar life.

However, portraying postwar life on the silver screen caught Hollywood in a crossfire between social, economic, and political forces. The industry had a history of public criticism regarding its portrayal of sex and violence, particularly how these vices impacted the nation's supposed movie-made children, or catering to political radicalism.[12] During the war, the studios scored public relations points by flag waving, and ticket sales reached new heights. But the industry sank into a long decline in 1947, while critics blamed the movies for promoting "un-American" subversion. Hollywood, long a target for anti-leftist sentiments, was among the first industries to feel the heat of Cold War anticommunism. The House Committee on Un-American Activities (HUAC) hearings in 1947, the official blacklist that extended into the mid-1960s, and the beginning of the studio system's demise all took place in the five years after the war. Outside the local bijous, the blacklist captivated moviegoers as a makeshift studio production in itself while troubled filmmakers, less enthralled, initiated an exodus of talent from Southern California to Europe to find relief from HUAC—and to find tax shelters. Postwar money troubles hammered Hollywood, with intense labor strikes, rising production costs, the Iron Curtain descending on half the European market, and the breakup of mass urban audiences for suburban paradise and television sets expedited the end of the studio system. To make matters worse, the 1948 Supreme Court case *United States v. Paramount Pictures, Inc.* (334 U.S. 131) ended the industry's vertical integration system. Studios no longer had a guaranteed distribution network for their films, leading to fewer productions and a gradual emphasis on "blockbuster" hits to fill their ledgers. To drive up ticket sales and to prove their patriotism, studios defensively waved the

Stars and Stripes through scenes of marriage, nostalgic interpretations of history, and anticommunism as anchors of domestic containment.

Youth played a central role in the formation of postwar America, on and off the movie screen. Historians have generally characterized young adults or "man childs" (physically grown men who lack social maturity) of the mid-1950s as those who first subverted domestic containment. The usual suspects include actors Marlon Brando in *The Wild One* (1953) and James Dean in *Rebel without a Cause* (1955), who, in their late twenties when they starred in their iconic roles, certainly struck a cultural chord. However, Brando and Dean inherited the screen legacies of "real" filmic boys in their tweens and teens who addressed the turbulent shifts in the United States. Americans had pulled together during the wartime effort, but small fissures along generational lines were already apparent to returning soldiers. Even *The Best Years of Our Lives* (1946), the pre–Cold War film that scholars herald as the go-to representation of postwar adjustment, shows a weak father-son relationship. Teenage youngster Rob Stephenson (Michael Hall) has one real scene with his returning war hero dad (Fredric March), a moment fraught with tension as he informs his father that a valued samurai sword war booty came from an honorable people, not an axis of evil (figure 2). This troublesome teenager disappears in favor of his older sister's whirlwind romance,

FIG. 2 The awkward years in *The Best Years of Our Lives* (1946), with returning GI Fred (Fredric March, right) failing to impress his son Rob (Michael Hall, left) with his war booty. Wife and daughter (Myrna Loy and Teresa Wright) witness the generation gap. The snipe notes, "But they have lost touch with each other, find it difficult to get back on the old footing." (Author's collection.)

wedding bells, and the presumption of baby carriages that ends the film. Nevertheless, the ubiquity of nonconformist youths and the tensions that emerged during production and reception indicate long-standing familial rifts from the past fifteen years.

For the Sake of the Children

Every generation has its form of youth disobedience, but social guardians grew increasingly worried during the twentieth century. The transformation of American kids from economic contributors in the nineteenth century to sentimentalized youngsters needing protection and guidance in the following century was inconsistent in ideology and implementation. Adults, however, continually shared common cause over how to raise the next generation. In the 1920s, youth craziness escalated; despite President Warren Harding's campaign promise to "return to normalcy," such desires never materialized. Grown-ups freely labeled their children the "lost generation," while novelist F. Scott Fitzgerald simply called himself and his peers the "damned and the beautiful."[13] In the 1920s, children regarded their parents as outmoded; in the Depression, those children came of age, often unable to provide for their own kids. World War II further fragmented families: fathers went to war, mothers went to work, and children became "latchkey" kids. Although many "made do" in the name of the war effort, the dearth of parental supervision, critics argued, created breeding grounds for juvenile maladjustment.[14]

World War II ended with the United States poised on prosperity. Still, the public feared backsliding into an economic crisis. Fears over juvenile delinquency and worries over the shift to white-collar work later culminated in the "crisis of masculinity," described by contemporaries and accepted by historians.[15] The popular image of the "organizational man" who measured his manliness in paychecks and material goods affirmed the United States as a "peoples of plenty" when compared to the gulags behind the Iron Curtain.[16] Many who made it to suburbia found the bland facets of conformity stifling and unfulfilling, but parents reminded themselves that their children's safety and security came first.[17]

The boundaries of Cold War containment idealized American youth through cookie-cutter solutions prescribed by child experts. Searching for signs of national recovery, many venues of popular culture expressed stability via family togetherness. If father "knew best," as one television program headlined, he needed to reconnect with Junior. The prior turbulent decades led many to believe maladjusted juveniles correlated with absent fathers.[18] As a result, postwar social guardians fretted over boys who defied their parents and regarded them as deviants and perverts, not as participants in separate youth subcultures.[19]

With such high stakes for youngsters, many child experts set rigid parental guidelines to raise children. Several historians suggest girlhood took precedence over boyhood as homemakers, consumers, and moral agents.[20] Nevertheless, as future breadwinners, businessmen, team players, soldiers, and political leaders, boys projected fortitude, independence, and risk taking as ideal traits. Failure to do so risked public and peer perceptions of them as "soft" and "wishy-washy," susceptible to "un-American" indoctrination. Should this ideal of boyhood fail, the public feared postwar boys would turn into a "sissified" generation, unable to protect the ideals of American democracy against political radicalism.[21] Even a fantasy picture like *The Boy with Green Hair* (1948), about a war orphan whose jaded locks heralded a simple message that "war is bad for children," had trouble at the box office.[22] The Cold War was bad for peace and kids who advocated replacing the arms race with universal brotherly love.

Historian Victor D. Brooks describes the 1950s as a decade of "kid-watching," where dads and sons dressed in matching attire and parents catered to Little League and scouting demands.[23] Through this family togetherness, adults guided youngsters into adulthood, countering the legacies of the Depression and World War II. Kid watching extended to the movies. Cinematic messages varied and, at times, contradicted each other as filmmakers reconciled their prewar ideologies with the postwar environment. As Americans envisioned a Red Menace infecting the body politic, this search for stability led to the "containment culture" of the 1950s: white-collar social mobility, defending the home, rugged masculinity and abolition of "sissiness," and obedience to parents, particularly fathers.

Movie-Made Screen Children

Just as producers, moviegoers, critics, and social experts disagreed about the ideal way to raise a child, celluloid kids of the screen also underwent a transformation. As they have always done, talent scouts sought "fresh" new faces to boost ticket sales. According to *Photoplay*, "the new look" for actors, like the virile Marlon Brando and sensitive Montgomery Clift, were "boys trying to do a man's work. Most of them are adolescent, and this applies regardless of age. These heroes include boys who'd like to be men."[24] These "boy-men"—grown men who retained a boyish charm and immaturity—fit with postwar Hollywood's swing into the teenage market, but also underscored the blurring boundaries between childhood and adulthood.

Alongside the changes in leading men, Hollywood's "moppet" pool of child actors was not a homogenous lot. In 1956, the *New York Times* reported, "The days of the kiddie star in Hollywood—the precocious, doll-like, Shirley Temple type moving about a peppermint-stick world—seem over. Of late, children are used more naturally in movies, playing roles that spring with some genuineness from life-like situations. None of these new child actors is a star, which seems right, since few children 'star' in actual life."[25] By 1957, industry gossip Hedda Hopper announced, "Child stars are scarcer than they used to be." The shortage of young thespians did not stem from a lack of driven stage mothers. Rather, as

Hopper explained, "When a child role crops up these days it seems to call for more than the usual amount of know-how."[26] This know-how, the ability to portray multiple character parts, reflected the malleability of postwar children. Unlike the precious Shirley Temple, a plucky Mickey Rooney, or a precocious Margaret O'Brien, no single child actor dominated postwar Hollywood.[27] Film historian David Dye notes the "major child-films of the fifties portrayed the confusion" of the industry in general.[28] Even as the public gradually left the image of the postwar child to the Beaver and assorted "sons" of what became the golden age of television, the potential for youth rebellion remained in the public consciousness.

Chapter 1 provides a broad sweep of American history from the 1920s to 1945. The chapter focuses on the cultural and social effects of the Depression and World War II on the family, youth delinquency, and national identity. MGM's Andy Hardy series, produced from the mid-1930s through World War II, captures the idealized, eternal small-town environment that represented familial and societal stability. Andy's small-town utopia visualized the popular myth surrounding family life and boyhood, effectively erasing the "wild boy" image from earlier films. However, not even the Hardys were immune to changes in the outside world, and Andy faced generational, societal, and economic tensions that later informed postwar American cinema.

Chapter 2 looks at the nuclear family, with an emphasis on father-son relationships. The early postwar years, with the threat of an economic backslide to chaotic depression, idealized the two-parent household in a suburban neighborhood as the norm (even if not so for many families) as a foundation for security. Not every family unit was perfect; melodrama required conflict as boys grew up and marriages fell under strain. Civic leaders argued that an "incomplete" family did not prepare boys to come of age, leading to immaturity and delinquency.

Reconciling individual ideals with the real world forced boys to wake up. The family unit always came first. *The Decision of Christopher Blake* (1948) addresses Hollywood's supposed threat to the nuclear family's reconstruction and the HUAC hearings to root out subversives from the film industry. The movie upholds marriage, but its ending rang hollow, unable to reconcile the "Hollywood ending" typical of the Dream Factory with the grim reality of postwar concerns over divorce. In contrast, *Any Number Can Play* (1949) successfully presents a threatened nuclear family pulling together through fatherhood. The Great Depression required a father to be a "tough guy" to withstand the emasculating sense of failure, and World War II films confirmed this image as a patriotic necessity. Actor Clark Gable built his career playing this archetype, and in *Any Number Can Play* his values override those of a moralizing son who questions his rugged lifestyle. The ending allows the family to retire to the suburbs and live respectably.

Chapter 3 builds on the nuclear family via juvenile delinquency. The studios acknowledged juvenile delinquency existed, but in films such as *Johnny Holiday*

(1949), the industry blamed environmental factors: modern city life and bad parenting.[29] Markers of growing up, such as raising and losing pets and learning to drive, became educational tools to prepare children as they came of age and entered adult responsibilities.

This chapter focuses on automobile culture, gun culture, and the militarization of youth to correct delinquency. Cars and firearms had dual roles; critics linked gun violence and car culture to delinquency, but adult guidance, usually a lawman, could harness these subcultures to support law and order. Children could express their natural aggression by pulling triggers and careening down the streets while displaying patriotism and vigilance against threats. Guns and cars in the "wrong hands" led to tragedy, but both were rites of passage for a boy into responsible adulthood. *The Gunfighter* (1950), released at the outbreak of the Korean War, defies this message and portrays gunslingers as lonely, alienated, and tragic, which audiences rejected.

Chapter 4 looks at boys and race relations. Hollywood retreated from wartime-inspired, leftist "social message" pictures of the previous fifteen years, lest critics accuse them of supporting subversive agendas. Many "race pictures" toned down their messages; boys of color sought social advancement, but remained marginalized. *Intruder in the Dust* (1949) and *Stars in My Crown* (1950) are set in small southern towns with the same actor, Juano Hernandez, as the victim of prejudice. The earlier film presents a hard-hitting attack on bigotry, continuing the social progressivism of the 1930s, but met public disfavor for upsetting social norms, especially during the Korean War. In contrast, *Stars in My Crown* affirms the small-town values and backhandedly whitewashes slavery. The film appeals to a sentimental nationalistic narrative set in post–Civil War Reconstruction as the "true" answer to the race question. The failure of the former movie and the monstrous success of the latter highlight the limited progressive stance Hollywood and the public took to race relations.

Chapter 5 looks at the international context concerning the United States' role as a postwar leader. *Tomorrow, the World!* (1944) addresses the rehabilitation of European children through internationalism. *The Search* (1948) highlights the need to support internationalism and cooperation to prevent future war orphans. Director Fred Zinnemann's picture did everything "right" in terms of social containment: a good American father figure, a glorification of American socialization, and an effective use of American ideals of progress. However, the film did not appeal to audiences who rejected the United States expanding its role in international affairs, even for children's sake. Only when the context segued from internationalism to embracing the Truman Doctrine's imperative to combat communism wherever it existed did the movie become a smash hit. Audiences ultimately viewed the film as a representation of American values and the need to promote anticommunism, not the internationalism Zinnemann intended.

Historians have generally categorized the twentieth century into decades, with demarcation events defining each period. World War I, the Roaring

Twenties, and the Depression neatly oblige, and the Second World War *is* the 1940s; even though World War II ended in 1945, scholars have included the end of the 1940s as part of the "Long Fifties" and the Cold War between the United States and the Soviet Union. Certainly, by 1950 Hollywood fully embraced anticommunism. The industry, unsurprisingly, maintained its innocence from all charges of subversion; one pamphlet, "Hollywood Against Communism, publicly declared "only 200 out of 25,000 Americans" fell for the communist party line, while the overwhelming majority found it "stupid, unworkable, subversive, and contrary to all democratic convictions." The defensive tone extended to its products, underlining that "not a single film has been named in which subversive propaganda reached the screen. There never was a chance for it to get in and there never will be."[30] Pictures such as *Bad Boy* (1949) and *I Was a Communist for the F.B.I.* (1951) set a standard for youth containment, with *My Son John* (1952) preaching how young people must reject liberalism lest they end up traitors executed by their patriotic parents.

But the Cold War was not just about containing communism overseas and at home, nor did it originate with the United States preserving the free world from Stalin's bloodlust for world conquest. What became the Cold War began as a domestic response to the historical timeline and public memory of the past two decades. This search for security coalesced into the Red Scare, McCarthyism, and the blacklist. The Hollywood films produced during the five years between World War II and 1950 grappled with the legacy of depression and war, which later erupted via juvenile delinquency, rock and roll, and sex as teenagers with disposable income started taking over the box office.[31] While adult Cold Warriors armed citizen boy soldiers to shore up the American way against the tentacles of the Red Menace, the mixed messages and reception of these pictures indicated American boyhood was still in transition—figurative growing pains that linger to this day.

1

The Family in Trouble, 1920–1945

For its ten-year anniversary issue in 1946, *Life* magazine visualized upcoming trends in American middle-class lifestyles. Titled "Dreams of 1946," the issue detailed the hopes of servicemen and women. "During the war years G.I.s and war workers dreamed of a brave new postwar world that would be full of air-conditioned peace and electronically controlled plenty," the article proclaimed.[1] "The war, which kept a great many American dreams from coming true, also made the dreams more roseate and wondrous."[2] Now, the downfall of Hitler brought those fantasies within reach. Large photo spreads showcased a "Family Utopia": moving vans delivering televisions, new wardrobes, washing machines, baby carriages, and private helicopters to new homes.[3] These images supposedly proved how prosperity lay right around the corner.

Life's description of Americans and their "dreams" of material goods underscored the legacy of the Great Depression and World War II. The economic austerity and the social plights of the Depression and global war left psychological scars on the public.[4] Having known economic, political, and social hard times during the past fifteen years, Americans envisioned a stable postwar world, lest the Depression return. In popular myth, signs of success included family solidarity, social mobility, suburbia, and conformity. However, then-recent history remained burned into the public consciousness, including a "depression mentality": making do with less, building nest eggs in preparation for future hardships, and finding security in the family.[5]

Building Carvel

This dream of security reflects the cultural and social impacts of the Great Depression and World War II. This instability stemmed from the "boom" years of the 1920s. The Roaring Twenties elided presidential candidate Warren Harding's "return to normalcy" campaign slogan that had evoked pre–Great War ideals of late Victorian gentility and propriety. In their landmark 1920s study of typical midsized American towns dubbed "Middletown" (represented by Muncie, Indiana), sociologists Robert S. Lynd and Helen Merrell Lynd observed and documented the generation gap. Here, young people dreamed of "petting parties in the purple dawn" filled with flivvers and flappers, all of which violated traditional, respectable middle-class sensibilities.[6] Movies about "flaming youth" with titles like *The Plastic Age* (1925) and *The Godless Girl* (1929) connoted the artificiality and spiritual dearth among young people infatuated with consumption and new sensations. The slang that characterized "bohemians" and "sheiks" spoke to how the Lost Generation shied away from the traditional social mores of genteel America.

While the Jazz Age placed strains on family ties, the Depression shattered family solidarity and security. By 1935, the median family annual income dropped to $1,600—far below the $2,500 necessary for a comfortable standard of living, and many families made do with a shoestring $500.[7] Those who could not make do found themselves adrift, either on the road for greener pastures or lost in an identity crisis. Studies presented anecdotes about fathers abandoning their wives and children as the emasculating crisis challenged their roles as breadwinner and provider.[8] Nor were the fathers the only ones who left their families behind. The U.S. Children's Bureau confirmed "hundreds of thousands" of "roving boys," not wanting to burden their families, ran away in search of work and to fend for themselves.[9]

Director William Wellman's *Wild Boys of the Road* (1933) effectively presented restless youths during the Depression. The picture features middle-class boys hitting the road to relieve the burden on their families when their dads lose their jobs. Hollywood's self-censorship body, the Production Code Administration, fretted over these teenagers encountering dangers outside the comforts of home; chief censor James Wingate asked Warner Bros. to tone down the roving boys' encounters with streetwalkers, who, employed in the oldest profession, had some sort of job security. Wingate also objected to a railroad brakeman raping a girl hobo; he preferred the assault "be rather an attack in which Lola has been rather badly beaten." Even worse, Lola's lost virtue was shared by all; a younger lad asks what happened, and an older, knowing boy responds, "Aw, don't be so dumb."[10] In retaliation, the kids attack the rapist, beat him, and kill him when they force him from a moving train (figure 3). The censors understood Warner Bros. wanted "to retain as much punch as possible" for box office purposes, but they warned

FIG. 3 Teenage wasteland. *Wild Boys of the Road* (1933) exploits the "roving boy" crisis of the early Depression with sex, violence, and the "agony of today's forgotten youth!" The hero (Frankie Darro, right) leads the boys in revenge on a railroad brakeman (Ward Bond, center) after he rapes one of the group. (Author's collection.)

the studio against obtaining "such dramatic quality at the cost of too much horror."[11] The "horror" was Depression-afflicted kids who lost middle-class security.

The Production Code could not sanitize the "horror" completely. Warner Bros. placated Wingate with a sympathetic judge who rises to the occasion to protect America's youth under the Blue Eagle of the New Deal, and he sends them home with assurances that their families have recovered. Wingate conceded "it would be hard" to gauge public reaction, but he predicted "the picture will meet with a minimum of difficulty," thanks to the turnaround of kindly, sympathetic political officials.[12] But he was wrong. Local censors snipped objectionable shots, including boys peppering police with produce and eggs. In Canada, censors inserted a disclaimer noting the film portrayed "conditions in the United States," but they admitted that "in our own country the patience of our economically disinherited youth is sadly tried in common with all nations of the earth."[13] What happened south of their border could happen in British Columbia. Quebec censors simply banned the picture for one reason: "Featuring vagabond boys on the road—soliciting, etc."[14]

These rowdy youths—from the Roaring Twenties and their younger, lawless, "wild" brothers—needed a strong parental hand. *Wild Boys of the Road*'s judge sitting under the Blue Eagle shield stood in for President Franklin Roosevelt.

Roosevelt projected a grandfatherly image whose "fireside chats" and speeches evoked a folksy, down-to-earth assurance.[15] The First Lady, Eleanor, wrote a "My Day" column where she described meeting people and listening to their problems.[16] The Roosevelts inspired desperate Americans of all ages to seek advice, relief, or a sympathetic ear.[17] Many tales centered on family life, with stories of emasculated men in identity crises, overtaxed women struggling to find food, and children wanting to help, but not knowing how. One father's letter represented the national plight, begging Roosevelt to help him "save my home for my family." He detailed how he and his wife taught their four children to "live to be proper Americans who love their country, and if needs [*sic*] be give their lives for it."[18] The key to national salvation, he asserted, lay in familial well-being.

Young children symbolized this yearning for family stability, and Hollywood complied. Public pressure against unsavory, hard-hitting pictures that glamorized spice and vice led to the Production Code's strengthening in 1934. Fittingly, the renewed code was embodied not by troubled teenagers but by a six-year-old Shirley Temple. Temple, with her precocious charms, ringlet curls, and adorable baby face and voice, projected innocence mixed with wisdom. Her screen characters resolved plotlines dealing with families breaking up and economic distress that stumped the adults around her.[19] Her pictures ended happily, with Shirley winning the hearts of a collective nation that stood up and cheered her on. As Temple aged, her screen persona matured unevenly, her box office waned, and another youngster, Mickey Rooney, succeeded her.

Mickey Rooney projected a teenage enthusiasm and lust for life rooted in a close-knit home life. His famed "Andy Hardy" persona, presented in fifteen MGM films from 1937 to 1946 (plus shorts, radio broadcasts, public service announcements, and a revived attempt in 1958), celebrated wholesome family togetherness in a midwestern small town, Carvel, created on MGM's carefully manicured backlot. The films focused on Andy's troubles with girls, his money to treat girls, and the material pains of growing up and wooing/impressing girls. Stories ended with young Hardy seeking "man to man" advice from his father-judge, and together they promoted piety, patriotism, and generosity (figure 4). The series, cheap to produce and enormously successful, presented an idealized image of American stability that elided large segments of the public outside theaters.

Andy's success lay in consistency and formulaic storytelling. Anticipating what Hollywood now calls a "cinematic universe," studio writers intimately knew Carvel's continuity. In 1941, series screenwriter Katharine Brush explained, "The trouble is that the movie public knows its Hardys like its next-door neighbors and if you make the smallest mistake in characterization, or in dialogue, or in material detail—if you let the slightest off-note creep in anywhere at all—the public protests violently, and swamps the studio with outraged letters."[20] Brush listed specifics: the Hardy family's income and mortgage remained unknown (so Depression audiences could not make comparisons), kept addresses and phone

FIG. 4 Man to man in the New Deal in *Judge Hardy's Children* (1938). As the title implies, Andy Hardy (Mickey Rooney, second from left) gets advice from his father (Lewis Stone, left), who presides over the teen's socialization into manhood. Andy's sister (Cecilia Parker, right) watches the maturation process. (Author's collection.)

numbers consistent, and built a family tree going back five generations. Such attention to detail strengthened the series' characters and tone, while inviting audiences to partake in a growing family saga. Moviegoers could know the Hardys as closely as they knew their neighbors.

MGM recognized the public regarded the Hardys as role models, especially to thwart potential "wild boys." Brush pointed out how the studio took "infinite pains" to keep the Hardys "precisely average," lest the "public cries out bitterly—most recent complaint being from parents who say the Hardys travel too much, interrupting school year and thus setting bad example to Young America."[21] These complaints reinforced how moviegoers saw the movie family as their ideal stand-in. Brush continued, "All examples must be good, of course, and the studio has abundant proof in letter-files that not only do parents send their children to see these pictures—'Why can't you be as nice as that?'—but the children send their parents for the same reason." Through their pictures, the Hardys socialized youths and their elders through these supposedly timeless tales of middle-class Americana. But for audiences in the Depression, MGM warily stayed away from one topic: money. Brush noted, "Any and all financial troubles suffered by Hardy's must be of some unusual kind—here it seems we depart from the average, and the family is never shown harassed with ordinary little everyday debts, of the sort that people go to movies to escape from."[22] Lest the Hardys' predicaments seem too much like the lives of their fans, Andy's problems remained outlandish, outrageous, and ultimately inconsequential.

Carvel existed outside the Great Depression, but, as Brush noted, the Hardys left their small town to venture out west, to New York, and later met world troubles when Andy shipped out to the front lines during World War II. Fans complained when the family left Carvel not just because Andy missed school but because reality threatened to taint his small-town sensibilities. In early production stages, MGM writers, on the lookout for story material and hoping to top each installment, turned to "real life" for inspiration, and facets of the Great Depression and World War II seeped in. For *Andy Hardy's Blonde Trouble* (1944), scriptwriter Agnes Christine Johnson interviewed college students and observed their obsessions with social prestige, money, and sex, and even thought about combining all three with a pregnancy scare, with the potential parents worried about another mouth to feed. Johnson noted previous installments dealt with death and rhetorically asked, "How can you top it by anything stronger, unless you are equally daring—and what could be stronger than having to do with life?"[23] This idea was perhaps too daring, and no newborns resulted from the blonde trouble Andy found himself in, in either this or any of his pictures. Nevertheless, sex, money troubles, and social prestige remained foremost in Andy's social circles. Andy and his sister Marian (Cecilia Parker) consistently encountered youth problems evoking their "wild boy" counterparts, including joblessness, theft, starvation, suicide, rape, intoxication, and prostitution.

As early as the original film, *A Family Affair* (1937), the Hardys face a crisis when the eldest daughter Joan (Julie Haydon) returns from the big city with bad news: she wants a divorce. An unhappy marriage drove her to another man—one of many "affairs" afflicting the title. Joan had good company. Marriage rates dropped during the first half of the Depression as did divorce rates—the latter because many people could not afford lawyers or alimony and simply broke up.[24] Either way, divorce, desertion, or delayed marriage spelled trouble for family solidarity and the nation's morals at large. In Middletown, folks darkly joked one of the few "good" things about the Depression was the dropping divorce rates, and the town now "beat Hollywood's 1934 divorce rate of 25 per 100 marriages."[25] Many movies featured couples who get even with philandering spouses by embarking on their own dalliances or single out traumatized children "going wrong" due to divorce. The opening title card for *Let's Try Again* (1934) unspooled, asking audiences, "Is divorce the only way out? Over 300,000 married Americans found it so last year. But . . . if the home goes to smash, the country goes to smash. Perhaps we need an N.R.A. for matrimony."[26] *Divorce in the Family* (1932) depicts an unhappy boy who learns to appreciate having two fathers, rather than one (or none) during the Depression. *Wednesday's Child* (1934) featured a boy suffering a nervous breakdown before his father overcomes his selfishness. In *What Becomes of the Children?* (1936), parents reconcile to save their kids.

For *A Family Affair*, Joan likewise resolves her irreconcilable differences by the end and leaves Carvel, never to return, lest she remind audiences about her troubled married life. But Joan's departure came too late, as this social ill incubated under the façades of Carvel's suburban streets. In *The Courtship of Andy Hardy* (1942), for instance, Judge Hardy enlists his son to help reunite a divorcing couple. Andy, of course, succeeds, but troubled households remained the norm in this idyllic small town.

Even if marriage endured in Carvel, other issues threatened to ruin young people's morals. In *Love Finds Andy Hardy* (1938), love troubles plague Marian Hardy when her boyfriend Wayne has "an illicit sex relationship, presumably with a prostitute," and Marian's father, Judge Hardy (Lewis Stone), "minimizes and condones the act" as a teenage boy's indiscretion.[27] Chief censor Joseph Breen underlined that "Wayne's illicit sex relationship is <u>unacceptable</u> from the point of view of the Code." When MGM insisted on deflowering Wayne, censor Islin Auster met with studio representatives and "expressed the opinion that the general flavor was different from the previous story, and that the story was more sophisticated. I said that while the story was satisfactory as far as the Code was concerned, they might find public reaction toward the scenes of the adolescent children kissing and hugging, etc., would be unfavorable. I said I thought such reaction might badly effect [*sic*] box-office reaction to this series."[28] The idea of morally compromised children was nothing new, as the Lost Generation in the 1920s and the then-contemporary "wild boys" were aware of the pitfalls of wine, women, and song. But the Hardys' status as role models for parents and their children required them to stay on the straight and narrow. Auster's lecture persuaded MGM to preserve Wayne's virtue by dropping him—and any mention of prostitution—from the series.

Unfortunately for drama's sake, Marian's taste in men did not improve. Four years later, in *The Courtship of Andy Hardy* (1942), she and boyfriend Jeff (William Lundigan) have a spat, this time involving alcohol and the possibility of rape. Again, industry censors pressured MGM to excise the story line, with Breen entering lecture mode: "Our concern is that such a direct reference might be interpreted as an over-pointed reference of rape, which might very readily give offense to mixed audiences. We know your concern in avoiding any such offense in the pictures of this series and respectfully regret that you reconsider these lines." The warning underscored not only the film's dollar value but its reputation. The PCA warned, "In a picture of this type, appealing directly to youthful audiences," the studio had to assure moviegoers that "nothing serious has happened."[29] When the studio opted to keep the sequence, the PCA strongly suggested including "protection shots" as alternative takes. "We have taken this special caution of reading this script carefully, even to the point of mentioning lines contained in a previous script but not called to your attention, because we know how concerned you are about avoiding any slight flavor that might offend your family audience."[30] Breen's predecessor, James Wingate, had passed the rape scene in *Wild Boys of the Road* back in 1933, but sexual assault involving teens had no place in the movies a decade later. By 1942, the hint of impropriety was taboo in a small town under the purview of a grandfatherly judge—and a grandfatherly president. Andy's various bouts of spring fever charmed moviegoers, but more serious teenage drinking and sex hit too close to home. MGM got the message and dropped the troublesome boyfriend after the next installment (*Andy Hardy's Double Life*, 1942), leaving Marian without a beau and a diminished screen presence as her brother took center stage.

Delinquency was not the only reminder of social ills in Carvel. In *Judge Hardy and Son* (1939), the judge helps family friends save their home from foreclosure, while in *Andy Hardy Meets Debutante* (1940), the Hardys aid Carvel's orphaned children from exploitive administrators. In *Life Begins for Andy Hardy* (1941), "life" consisted of graduating high school and exposure to unemployment. Andy meets Jimmy (Ray McDonald), an unemployed bellhop who sleeps in a park. Jimmy's starvation and hopelessness lead him to commit suicide. An alarmed PCA sent their "unanimous opinion that the suicide of an eighteen year old boy, Jimmy, should be omitted from this picture. We feel that Jimmy's death should be <u>accidental</u>, possibly resulting from his being hit by an automobile due to his starved condition. This is especially important since the Hardy family series has been so well established as entertainment for the entire family. This change will necessitate a further change in the dialogue by Andy."[31] For the sake of the Hardys and their moral outlook, screenwriters obligingly swapped suicide for a heart attack. Even though Jimmy remains jobless and is clearly in distress, the film downplays the psychological trauma of a desperate young man caught up in hard times. A relieved Breen reminded MGM that "gruesomeness should be avoided at all times. It is still our thought that the death of Jimmy, which Andy and others first believe is suicide, will probably occasion unsatisfactory audience reactions, especially in a family picture of this sort."[32] Breen was right; the *Motion Picture Herald*'s review, with a headline reading "The Hardy Series Goes Adult," warned exhibitors that the series had turned "away from the broad field of good, clean fun for the whole American family and into the narrower audience band of adult entertainment." The trade journal wondered if exhibitors would want "the House of MGM" to "divert the series from the wide channel of universal family-interest into a numerically smaller audience-bracket."[33] The turn reflected Rooney's—and his fan base's—aging, but at a calculated risk of the series losing its small-town charm and box office appeal. Nevertheless, Andy's inevitable maturation forces him to experience "life," and he slowly emerged from Carvel's umbrella to face a real world.

The adult entertainment angle shadowed Andy's entrance into manhood. The PCA and MGM prolonged Andy's innocence as much as possible by consistently emphasizing family togetherness and patriotism as national strengths. MGM aired public service announcements, such as the radio broadcast "Good News of 1939" (1938), a Thanksgiving-themed special with Judge Hardy expressing thanks for "a great, free country, a country where democratic government shall never perish from the earth."[34] They ended the year with a short Christmas greeting, espousing messages about solidarity and generosity during lean times. In *The Hardys Ride High* (1939), the family becomes swell-headed when they think they inherit two million dollars, only to come back down to earth humble and appreciative for their middle-class lifestyle, but in *Andy Hardy Meets Debutante* (1940), Andy learns about class lines demarcated by money when he goes to New York. Film critic Bosley Crowther spotted the theme: "Now that all good Americans have taken to talking and thinking a lot about democracy, it was to be expected that Metro's Hardy family would get around to the subject, too." Democracy manifested itself when Andy falls hard for "America's No. 1 debutante." But before class snobbery can upend the small-towner in the Big Apple, young Andy realizes "that 'debs' are mere folks just like any one [*sic*] else," and, therefore, Crowther concluded, "democracy is proved."[35]

All good Americans certainly needed reminders about democracy during hard times. The public turned sour on civic institutions when President Herbert Hoover initially reiterated a conservative government stance, arguing relief measures would destroy American self-reliance. As the crisis worsened, presidential inaction fueled disenchantment, and many dubbed the long-heralded American experiment in republicanism a failure. The jaded public, in turn, glamorized outlaws who bucked the system. The legacy of Prohibition, with gung-ho gangsters trouncing the law, took on a symbolic heroism. Impressionable children and their disillusioned parents regarded antiestablishment figures as working-class heroes who got ahead by trumping the rules.[36] Standing up for the little guy also meant combating corrupt businessmen and politicians. In films such as *Washington Merry Go Round* (1932), *Gabriel over the White House* (1933), *The President Vanishes* (1935), and *Mr. Smith Goes to Washington* (1939), the protagonists employ extreme measures—even dictatorship and abolishing Congress in *Gabriel over the White House*—to save the country from a broken system.[37]

Alongside vigilantism and fascism, socialism reached an apex. President Franklin Roosevelt capitalized on his grandfatherly image, while policies, such as union empowerment, Social Security, unemployment relief, job placement, and agricultural assistance, pulled socialists into the New Deal coalition.[38] The Hollywood Left especially supported the New Deal, while some pictures outright praised Roosevelt. In *Heroes for Sale* (1933), one "forgotten man," facing a bleak future, lamented "the end of America," but the hero (Richard Barthelmess), another forgotten man, corrects him: "It may be the end of us, but it's not the end of America. In a few years, it'll go on bigger and stronger than ever. That's not optimism. That's common horse sense. Did you read President Roosevelt's inaugural address? He's right. You know, it takes more than one sock on the jaw to lick a hundred and twenty million people."[39] He knows that Roosevelt would restore the nation for future generations—including the young son he has abandoned but who still idolizes his absent father. Other films gushed over

Roosevelt. *Footlight Parade* (1933) features a musical sequence where drunken, brawling American sailors sober up and line in formation, forming the Blue Eagle and then a portrait of FDR, figuratively ushering New Deal order to a chaotic pre-code America. In 1939, Mickey Rooney and Judy Garland impersonated the first couple in a grand finale, in which they refute fascism and celebrate the United States as "God's Country." Two years later, for the song "How About You?" in *Babes on Broadway* (1941), Garland crooned how Roosevelt's looks thrilled her. The George M. Cohan biopic *Yankee Doodle Dandy* (1942) featured the president as a stand-in for a grateful public, patriotically celebrating the rise of the American century through musical theater as the nation entered war. Many other pictures conveyed activist messages or criticized social ills. *Our Daily Bread* (1934) praised farm collectivism and social cooperation, while *I Am a Fugitive from a Chain Gang* (1932), *Fury* (1936), and *They Won't Forget* (1937) slammed the unthinking, uncaring mob while making heroes of those who stand up for individual rights.

The Hardys did their part to wave the flag. As a judge, the Hardy patriarch gives criminals second chances to make good (*Andy Hardy Gets Spring Fever*, 1939), orders schoolboys to write twenty-thousand-word essays on American freedoms for daring to revolt against their superintendent (*Judge Hardy's Children*, 1938), and fights political corruption (*A Family Affair*, 1937). He also closes loopholes that endanger the town's orphanage's funding (*Andy Hardy Meets Debutante*, 1940), demonstrating that not every child has a home, even in a warm-hearted small town like Carvel. But more typically, the judge plays a father figure for the entire town, inspiring his son to follow in his footsteps, such as in "Andy Hardy's Dilemma: A Lesson in Mathematics—and Other Things" (1940), a public service short where Andy urges moviegoers to donate to community chests. In *Andy Hardy's Private Secretary* (1941), Andy helps a poor immigrant family fit into Carvel's social scene, stymieing any chance of their bucking the system. Their son shows off his gratitude and newfound Americanness by winning the school's coveted American flag as a reward for his attention to the responsibilities and civic duties expected of all high school boys. Of course, the newly Americanized boy thanks Andy, who bursts with pride in doing his part to assimilate potentially restless Others under the Stars and Stripes. Nor was the family saga serial an MGM monopoly: Paramount responded with their own family, the Aldrichs (also based on a play, centered on a teenage boy, and which spawned radio, eleven films, and television adaptations), Twentieth Century-Fox kept up with the Joneses (seventeen pictures, predating the Hardys by a year), Republic Pictures had the Higgins (seven films from 1938 to 1941), and Columbia Pictures featured the Bumsteads, based on Chic Young's popular comic strip *Blondie*, boasting twenty-eight pictures between 1938 to 1950 and a television show. These amusing, wholesome nuclear families provided hours of entertainment throughout the later Depression and war years. Equally important, their box office successes empowered the Production Code to further sanitize the silver screen and to jealously guard the censors' position as purveyors of good taste during hard times.

The Wild Boy Contained: Liberating *Boy Slaves*

With the Hardys on the front lines of American morals, the Production Code shielded youth from the unsavory aspects of life. Emboldened, Hollywood's censors shaped other productions that vied for a more sensationalistic angle. When Warner Bros. rereleased *Wild Boys of the Road* in 1936, an emboldened Joseph Breen ordered the rape scene excised entirely.[40] A greater problem, however, was an original production ripped from headlines, not a three-year-old, outdated movie.

In 1938, RKO started a new "wild boys" picture centering on vagabond kids in a sadistic turpentine camp.[41] The film's title switched from *Saints without Wings* to a title that conveyed how life was not wonderful: *Boy Slaves*. Under any name, the production was a nightmare for the Production Code Administration, as RKO insisted on punching up the exploitation value. Breen took a personal interest, cautioning RKO to "avoid the inclusion of any scenes of undue brutality."[42] He listed the usual offensive words such as "punk," "sissy," and "dirty little wee wee" and singled out lines such as "I'm hotter than a firecracker in L," "like that guy in the Bible," and a reference to Eleanor Roosevelt's "My Day" column. The kids wrote her for help, but the maternal First Lady never responded (figure 5). Cut off from a protective government, the boys fend for themselves by taking the law into their own hands.

The studio did not listen. After Breen tentatively approved the initial plot, producers started submitting rewrites, each draft intensifying the gruesomeness of a vagabond life or further damning the police and various civic institutions. Two weeks later, Breen had enough. He blatantly ordered, "Avoid adding any sequences that would build up the flavor of wrong-doing, or crime, on the part of your young leads. It seems to us that the original script contained about all of this flavor that would be acceptable, and that any serious additions thereto may result in the picture being unacceptable from the standpoint of the Production Code."[43] Any further sensationalism, Breen indicated, would be not only condemned, but a waste of the studio's time and resources.

RKO changed the title to *Pure in Mind* to imply the kids were good at heart, and perhaps to jab at the strict censorship guidelines. Not amused, Breen told the lads to watch their language, and not say "dirty little copper lover" or refer to the "good men in jail before me."[44] The lines spoke to the inability of authorities to dispense justice or be trusted. Given his headaches over cinematic public enemies, Breen told RKO to make sure crime did not pay. He highlighted two issues: the boys making a false police report and a bad authority figure, a judge, who ends the picture with a searing indictment "toward society, the boys, and the criminals, who operate the camp."[45] Simple script changes could address the

FIG. 5 "My day." The vagabond runaways of RKO's *Boy Slaves* (1939) turn to Eleanor Roosevelt for aid, but they ultimately take matters into their own hands. (Author's collection.)

police report. But the judge, as an enforcer of American law, was much more problematic. This guardian figure was unacceptably "ashamed of his robes; accusing the state of cruelty and murder; his statement that there is no law, under which [camp supervisor] Albee can be prosecuted; and his appeal to the boys to 'forgive us.'" This hapless magistrate was no benevolent Judge Hardy; Breen made an "earnest recommendation" for a rewrite "to get away from its present—to us—definitely anti-social flavor." Since the "boys are ether criminals, or potential criminals," Breen suggested "they be sent to a reformatory and not to any 'state farm, where the state may have a chance to pay its debt' to them."[46] As criminals, the boys find rehabilitation in which the government—a friendly judge or institution—provides a happy ending. Breen took the final step of personally screening the finished cut. He passed the film, but with a neatly typed caveat that "the picture, to be put into general circulation, will be exactly as we saw it, yesterday afternoon. It is on this basis of this understanding that the certificate is issued."[47] Editors, then, could not change a single frame.

At this point, RKO gave in. The Production Code Administration may have passed the picture, but more stringent local censors and the foreign market would freely snip away. Indeed, British Colombia eventually rejected the picture as it had *Wild Boys of the Road*, calling the film "not suitable."[48] Producer J. R. McDonough proudly informed the PCA he was "even further carrying out

Mr. Breen's idea to a different conception of the story."[49] The studio removed scenes of the boys breaking the law (they sneak into a boxcar—not unlike *Wild Boys of the Road*—and steal watermelons), cut sequences of interracial harmony such as the boys singing "negro spirituals" to comfort themselves, and eliminated casual references to branding, murder, and a mother who beats her son and calls him a "tramp."

Concerning the disagreeable and disillusioned judge, RKO made him more like Andy Hardy's dad. McDonough even dubbed over the word "state" with the word "society" wherever "a meaning derogatory of the state could be construed," thereby removing any suggestion that the judge was condemning the government he served.[50] Even Albee finds redemption under Breen's guidance. The studio replaced the judge's original line, "Get out of my court, Mr. Albee—before I commit murder myself," in which Albee goes free, to studying the works of Abraham Lincoln while sitting in jail. Presumably, Albee would leave the slammer a better man. With malice toward none and charity for all, the judge rehabilitates delinquent boys and men.

Caught between older wild boys and Carvel, *Boy Slaves* did not set the box office on fire. RKO played up the grittiness of the Depression, only to give in to the censors to save its salability. One critic applauded Hollywood for "actually standing up on its hind legs and stating that something is wrong with the world," but also found it "not at all convincing" with the "'little tough guy' comedy of the juvenile road gang, which has become a stereotype of screen misbehavior."[51] The Bowery Boy–esque buffoonery appeased Breen, perhaps, but countered the grim realism for public consumption. The title remained the most sensational part of the picture; one exhibitor reported, "'Boy Slaves' title got some business" and the programmer "got by nicely and pleased," in which the movie sold tickets, but the film was hardly the searing indictment of political and societal corruption that RKO had originally aimed for.[52]

A New Deal for the Traditional Boy

The Production Code Administration's success in turning boy slaves into boy citizens spoke to the New Deal's role for youth. The New Deal co-opted more extreme political and social radicals by channeling popular anger and disenchantment into teenage pep, pluck, and patriotism, all of which were barely contained in the nation's idealized teenager: actor Mickey Rooney. Andy Hardy—and the actor who played him—captivated the public with his unflagging exuberance and optimism, mixed with a fierce loyalty to his parents, God, and country. Unlike the beleaguered, rebellious child laborers of *Boy Slaves*, Andy may have addressed social ills, but he never raised a fist against his father. While Rooney later recalled that portraying Andy exhausted him, and he did not like playing the part off screen, he toed the studio line.[53] In a whirlwind tour in 1939, the carefree teenager told reporters, "I don't like serious things," then corrected himself with a more appropriate answer: "I like Kipling and Shakespeare—I really do."[54] An accompanying studio rep and handler elaborated that Rooney, like Andy, "is so representative of American middle-class family life." When the reporter observed the actor had "a tremendous feeling of responsibility to young America," Rooney agreed. Lying on his back, the actor "solemnly recited, his eyes half closed with fatigue" that "I try to live up to what they expect of Andy Hardy. I try to be as close to Andy as possible. I really do."[55] MGM exploited Rooney's image, assigning him other archetypes of American boyhood, including *Huckleberry Finn* (1938) and *Young Tom Edison* (1940), the latter featuring a foreword that the atypical inventor had "the courage and triumph of a typical American boy," ala Andy. That year, 54 million Americans voted Rooney as the top box office draw; two years earlier, Rooney did not even place in the top one hundred.[56] One reporter attributed Rooney's rise to a "wholesome reaction" to the "saccharine children of the screen"—a rebuttal of Shirley Temple—and a "refreshing taste of salt and pepper after a diet of custard and treacle." In every film, Rooney gave "veracious portrayals of an awkward, nervous, sometimes puzzled and frustrated, but always triumphant adolescent, an idealization of youngsters they knew." This "zing-diggetywhamdam" burst of energy was a refreshing wave of zest for Depression audiences.[57]

At times, Rooney's boundless energy could land the actor in trouble. The public's typecasting Rooney made MGM cautious; should the actor skirt on the edge of risqué behavior, the studio went into damage control to protect not only their contract player, but Andy Hardy's image. Rooney's ascent into the top star of Hollywood's firmament placed him under even greater scrutiny. Even as the press lauded his achievements, they noted how Rooney, armed with a sixty-five-dollar allowance, "goes to night clubs because that's where the best swing bands are apt to be. They say he smokes a little, in private, drinks not at all, and is careful to be chaperoned when he goes out with girls."[58] Rooney's private life—made public in the press—was a perpetual potential dash of cold water on the clean living the Hardys presented on the silver screen.

Furthermore, the Hardys' righteousness limited their character growth and plot developments, and the series risked wearing thin as time progressed. Studio writer William Ludwig recognized the risk that the Hardys might end up looking like "mere puppets," reenacting the same scenes in each film.[59] Screenwriter Agnes C. Johnson kept notes about potential story lines that never came to pass, such as giving Andy a friend who is a juvenile delinquent (a "poor boy" who resents his poverty) or giving the family's lived-in spinster, Aunt Milly, a stronger presence in the household by losing her job or showing Judge Hardy and wife coping with a family crisis. "I know the Hardys are a somewhat '<u>idealized family</u>,' and the Judge and Mrs. Hardy, after all these years, have brought the 'art of marriage' to more or less perfection," Johnson wrote, but she hoped to create a squabble between husband and wife: "something connected with health, finances, or his career, so that he is seriously concerned about his family. An effective scene would be one, which has occurred in every family, in which the parents are worried to death—but haven't told the children."[60] As Johnson noted, the scenario of concerned parents shielding their kids from economic burdens was certainly no stranger to Depression-era audiences, and Johnson singled out one plot idea where "parents like the Hardys, no matter how carefully they budget their money, still have to 'give up something' in order that their children may have education and advantages."[61] But no matter how moviegoers might relate to real life woes of familial unemployment or making sacrifices, MGM refused to budge. The Hardys remained righteous, generous, and pious as they maintained their faith in democracy, individuality, and a perpetual upward social mobility.

Johnson and other screenwriters recognized that success spoiled Andy Hardy. Their ideas to expand the series never came to fruition, and at times the Hardys' hyperwholesomeness could become a satire of its own formula. In an unusual misstep, MGM's anthology picture *Ziegfeld Follies* (1945) originally featured "Andy Hardy Meets Maisie," a sketch where the small-town boy meets a sassy big-city gal from another MGM series. The episode dripped with sexual innuendo and mocked the Hardys' middle-class lifestyle of abundance—Mrs. Hardy breaks the fourth wall to tell audiences that her large meals did not come from a wartime black market ("This is before rationing"), and Aunt Milly boldly proclaims she sticks around because the pictures are "real wholesome. And the pay is good." When the judge demands a "man-to-man" talk with his son for associating with the brassy Maisie, Maisie interjects, "Say, ain't it about time you stopped playing that old record? Everybody knows that man-to-man routine of yours by heart."[62] Maisie's line may have cut close to the truth for moviegoers who, by the end of World War II, had followed the Hardys for fourteen films in eight years. The studio caught themselves in time and dropped the completed sketch from the final print.

The risk of satire and typecasting hurt Rooney's career in later years, but his immense popularity in the years leading up to World War II made him bankable at the box office. His short stature enabled him to play filmic teenagers for over fifteen years. During that time, Rooney celebrated American boyhood with a patriotic zeal. He wrote a letter to publicist and gossip Hedda Hopper, stating he was a "lucky guy to be in America. It never occurred to me that one fellow is any different from another but I guess from what people tell me there aren't very many places left where you can think so." He reiterated, "I've always been proud to be an American. And when I look at the papers these days I'm prouder than ever."[63] Such statements, disseminated to moviegoers, reinforced the idealized image of the American boy: respectful, patriotic, and grateful for the privileges of being an American. Rooney—and Andy Hardy—bolstered the system, not as boy slaves, but as citizen-soldiers, and his reputation as an ideal American youth won support from young and old alike (figure 6).

FIG. 6 America's boy. On tour in New York in 1939, Mickey Rooney "is cheered by an honor guard of Boy Scouts who turned out to greet him," the accompanying snipe notes. Rooney's screen persona neatly fit with the First Couple's reputation. Mickey "will be honorary co-delegate with Mrs. Franklin D. Roosevelt at the American Youth Congress." (Author's collection.)

By 1942, after thirteen pictures in five years, Andy Hardy became a man. He started college in *Andy Hardy's Double Life* (1942) and went to war, around the same time Rooney married and enlisted. Even as Rooney/Andy confessed he knew little about "world affairs," he was soon caught up in them. One critic approved Judge Hardy casting his son loose: "The world that moves outside of Carvel, the family's home town, has seen some change. The Hardys, who have become symbolic of the plain (?)[*sic*] American family on the screen, are confronted with certain realities which they can no longer get around."[64] The interrogative around "plain" was significant, as the reviewer recognized that Carvel was an ideal; the "plain" Hardy family did not really exist outside the silver screen. The reviewer hinted as much when Andy leaves Carvel: "Andy can't go on being a girl-crazy college boy, and he certainly can't run home to papa every time a little problem comes up."[65]

Andy's maturation mirrored the United States' growing involvement in global politics. As a celluloid cultural ambassador, the Hardy series propagandized American values abroad. Prominent author Pearl S. Buck compiled a list of pictures to "convey to Asiatic audiences an authentic reflection of life as it is lived in this country, rather than as it is seen through the lenses of Hollywood's glamorous cameras." The first was "Andy Hardy," not a particular film, but the idealized boy that represented American life.[66] Indeed, as the Hardys reaffirm American democracy over class snobbery in *Andy Hardy Meets Debutante*, *Variety* grinned, "Metro has an answer for theatre-goers who have been crying for something to make them forget—for a few minutes at least—war jitters, defense talks, and presidential bally" and the picture "contains a bit of flag-waving and a few words of preachment in behalf of American ideals, but it is all so cleverly handled that it serves to increase, rather than detract from the story values."[67] The *Motion Picture Daily* called it "the type of picture showmen of the nation over have been watching for in order to forget, with their patrons, the war and other troubles."[68] One treatment, "Andy Hardy Discovers America," had Andy patriotically partaking in sugarless meals and giving up roast beef on Saturdays.[69] But the real action comes when Carvel's girls adopt visiting soldiers to make them feel at home. Andy impresses all by selling bonds and putting on the usual show-stopping bravura. But when Mickey Rooney went to war, the project ended.

Attention: All Joe Smiths, Americans

Andy Hardy comforted audiences during the Depression and provided a bridge to the postwar world. World War II ended the economic aspects of the Great Depression, but the war continued concerns over familial instability and uncertainties about the country's future. The public objected to the army drafting men with dependent children, but the urgency for manpower prevailed, and men who had kids but were not employed in war work were eligible for service by 1943.[70] By 1944, the *New York Times*, covering the public anticipation of D-Day, reported over 200,000 families "already felt personal shock and pain through the death, wounding or capture of a relative." To bolster morale, the writer turned to "such homely matters as tomato plants and cutworms."[71] By tending to victory gardens and economizing, the home front did its part to ward off regrettable telegrams from the War Department.

The war effort bathed the war-torn family with stiff-upper-lip patriotism. Films such as *The Fighting Sullivans* (1944) highlighted the sacrifice young men gave to their countries, while *The More the Merrier* (1943), *The Doughgirls* (1944), and *Since You Went Away* (1944) featured the home front coping with housing shortages and disrupted domestic life and love. A more optimistic look was *Joe Smith, American* (1942), which, released three months after Pearl Harbor, featured a father and son learning the importance of keeping secrets (Dad's bombsight; Son's Father's Day necktie) and staying true to principle (figure 7). The kid idolizes Revolutionary War hero Nathan Hale, who had regretted having only one life to give to his country, translates phrases like "e pluribus unum," and recites the Pledge of Allegiance. Dad reciprocates; after he foils a Nazi plot

FIG. 7 Family solidarity under the shadow of war. In *Joe Smith, American* (1942), the everyman dad (Robert Young) works in a war plant and presents the fruits of his labor to his son (Darryl Hickman). Homemaker/wife (Marsha Hunt) completes the family unit. (Author's collection.)

masterminded by a high-level traitor, Smith brushes off his heroic feat, saying any of the 135 million American citizens would have done the same. "All of us guys are the same way. We got hopes, we got wives, we got kids. We got things to have guts for, and we don't like anybody who pushes us around."[72] The script ends: "This is the best, then, of the Americans: sitting down with their friends to a safe, happy, joy-filled Sunday dinner—knowing in their hearts that no one can push them around."[73]

The "best" characteristics of the American home—the virile, unpushable masculinity embodied by Smith and son—ensured the nation's survival. But critics were not certain that Americans still had the right stuff. During National Family Week in 1944, J. Edgar Hoover reported youth craziness and crime increased since the Depression. "An appalling wave of juvenile crime which threatens to engulf the flower of American manhood" was under way, the FBI director warned.[74] Despite the appealing visuals of Johnny Smith saluting the flag and knowing his American history, outside the theaters reports of intense battles overseas desensitized boys into becoming "thrill seekers" via acts of "hoodlumism." Even patriotic boys became delinquents when they ran away from home to enlist, lied about their ages, or quit school to get war jobs. The lack of parental supervision—with dad in the service and mom performing war work—left children directionless. Hollywood cashed in with B movies like *Where Are Your Children?* (1944) and *Youth Runs Wild* (1944), confirming the causality between fractured households and delinquency.

Even the Hardys had trouble with postwar maladjustments. In *Love Laughs at Andy Hardy* (1947), Andy returns from the home front, as plucky as ever. *Variety* nodded in approval: "This pic doesn't vary much from the basic formula used in the numerous predecessors in the Hardy family saga, but why should it? More than ever now in this era of atomic jitters, the secure, comfortable, middle-class dream world of the Hardy domicile is guaranteed a powerfully favorable audience reaction." The reviewer concluded, "It's everyman's escape into adolescent nostalgia."[75] But happy days were not quite here again, as Andy wasn't content to go back to being Judge Hardy's son. At one point, he accidentally breaks a street lamp off-camera due to heartbreak over a broken engagement, and the Production Code censors fretted about Andy's overaged delinquency as the young man worries over his future: "We believe this would be particularly objectionable in this type of story," Breen wrote.[76] However, unlike the rapes, drunkenness, unemployment, suicide, and prostitution that the Production Code had successfully excised from Carvel in previous years, this time the objectionable content remained—even if audiences did not see shattered glass. The broken street lamp was apt, as it indicated a darker side of American victory culture. MGM placed a hiatus on the series (and Rooney would leave MGM two years later, after suffering mixed box office results in three subsequent pictures). The studio would not produce another Andy Hardy picture for a decade, preserving Carvel in the public imagination as the idealized prewar town of family harmony. Outside Carvel's celluloid tomb, however, family anxieties signified deeper shades of postwar blues.

Postwar Upsets

Throughout World War II, the family unit remained central to solidarity. The marriage rate rose as people, seeking stability in creating a home life before the war tore the social fabric apart, rushed to the altar. Looking back from 1947, actress Linda Darnell commented that women feared "being 'old maids' and also because there was so much emotion in the air."[77] For Darnell, the heavy atmosphere contained more than just romance. Becoming an "old maid," without family support and security, was first and foremost on the minds of Hollywoodites and their fans.

Even as World War II's end approached, many Americans worried the brief window of prosperity was already closing. The wartime boom provided a foundation for economic stability, but potential depression threatened to bring the nation back to 1929. The Servicemen's Readjustment Act of 1944, popularly known as the GI Bill of Rights, provided veterans with job help, housing, unemployment compensation, education, and medical assistance (in *Love Laughs at Andy Hardy*, a discharged Private Andy notes that the GI Bill enables him to continue college). The bill reflected the public need to build nest eggs against potential future hard times. Congressman William Lemke insisted on the bill's expedition, saying businessmen and veterans "are convinced that the only way to prevent another depression after this war is to put the returning servicemen on their feet and help them get re-established in our civilian economy."[78] Approximately 7.8 million GIs took advantage of the bill to attend higher education programs and find housing.[79] Indeed, when Andy steps off the train at Carvel, he walks away from his mother's embrace to dreamily look at advertisements for wedding rings and furniture. "Bride and Groom Special. $109.50."[80] Cut to an alarmed Mom Hardy; her son may be home, but he already plans to leave the roost.

However, permanent stability seemed illusory, as threats from home and abroad threatened to abort the American Dream. Communism especially shadowed projections for prosperity. "Everyone knows that Communism is for state ownership of all property, including your house, your farm and the factory, the shop the office in which you work," New York governor Thomas Dewey declared in 1944, as he accused "reds" of infiltrating the New Deal.[81] For fifteen years, the American Dream eluded the Depression/war-torn public and the public guarded its hopes and aspirations.

In this context, the House Committee on Un-American Activities' insisting "commies" spawned in the film industry took on renewed vigor. Hollywood promoted friendlier relations with the Soviet Union during the war and propagandized social progress, but the public now read those messages as subversive. Self-declared leftists, such as screenwriter John Howard Lawson, the "number one" of the Hollywood Ten, publicly refused to recant his support for labor rights and "the complete equality of the Negro people of this country and I feel passionately about it."[82] By continuing to upset American social mores, Lawson and his ilk convicted themselves in the public eye. Their guilt stemmed not solely from their supporting communism but for undermining the nation still reeling from economic and social change.

Throughout the Depression and the war, the family remained the main bulwark of the American Dream. In 1945, *Life* documented the formal end of the war in Europe, giving President Truman a full-page photo as he announced V-E Day.[83] But the issue's main article, and the cover, focused on teenage boys in the postwar family. Boys, when "faced with war, they are just the same as they have always been."[84] Readers saw adolescents engaged in daily life: pretending to shave, "fooling around" with jalopies and girls, and consuming large piles of food—just as Andy Hardy had done since 1937, and which *Life* projected as the norm for all. But the article, like the Hardy series, elided contemporary history. The magazine deliberately ignored the Depression in photographs and text as if it never happened, just as the Production Code censors had shielded family audiences from seeing the ugliness of hard times on the screen. Teenage boys, *Life* alleged, were never "roving boys" and CCC workers in the 1930s or delinquents during the war. Instead, the article's tribute to the resiliency of teenage boys "as they always have been" underscored the public's continuing search for stability; these kids were middle-class suburbanites, as if all teenagers and their families resided in Carvel. These anxieties later transitioned into anticommunism, conformity, social mobility, and patriarchy. But in the immediate aftermath of World War II, these values rebutted the legacy of economic depression and global war, with the immediate impact centered on the construction of the postwar family.

2

Gable Is Able

Re-creating the Postwar Family

"He was small for his age. The world he lived in was small, too. Or rather, one of them was. He lived in two worlds at once. One of them was a small, drab, confined world—just two squalid rooms in the rear of a six-story tenement, 20 Holt Street."[1] Thus begins writer Cornell Woolrich's "The Boy Cried Murder," a short story published in *Mystery Book Magazine* in 1947, which RKO adapted as *The Window* (1949).

The filmic boy in question is Tommy Woodry (Bobby Driscoll), an imaginative youngster whose second world was an escape from his seedy New York surroundings. Despite the popular image of the postwar boom and bright, sunny suburbs, *The Window* offers a peek at how the other half lives, with dad working the nightshift, the family stuck in the lower rungs of the social ladder, and murderers for upstairs neighbors (figure 8). To compensate for how disappointing the American Dream turned out, Tommy spins tales about moving west to a horse ranch. Children have certainly used urban spaces as a form of agency; film scholar Pamela Robertson Wojcik points out Depression-era films have depicted runaways, street urchins, and working-class kids claiming city streets as makeshift playgrounds and as "their" turf.[2] But in a time of supposed postwar prosperity, Tommy's lies land him in trouble with his friends, who eye his tiny apartment as a step up from their own dwellings, and the police. His parents, already overburdened with the economic hardships of making do in the big city, worry over the seductive power of Tommy's daydreams, preventing their son

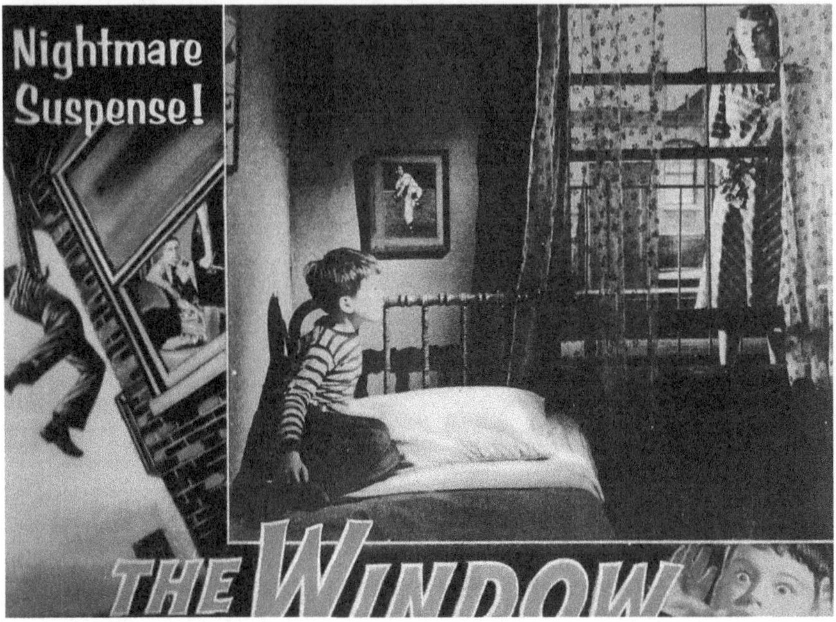

FIG. 8 Peeping Tommy. In this lobby card for *The Window* (1949), Tommy Woodry (Bobby Driscoll) recognizes danger, death, and decay in American victory culture in the form of the upstairs murderess, Mrs. Kellerson (Ruth Roman). (Author's collection.)

from maturing. In a man-to-man talk, his father (Arthur Kennedy) tells him, "I have a lot of nice things planned for you when you grow up . . . and I want you to live up to them by being decent and honest now . . . a father wants to be proud of his son, Tommy . . . why, there's nothing that would give me more pleasure than to be pointed out someday as 'Tommy Woodry's father' but if you're going to get all mixed up like you're doing now . . . well . . . I just don't know what we're going to do about it."[3] Tommy's inability to face reality not only spoiled his manhood but brought shame upon the family name.

Thankfully for Tommy, the picture ends when the boy hero exposes the killers and earns the praise of the police. But the film's real victory is the solidification of the Woodry family. Dad, ashamed of his imaginative son, not only is proud but predicts that when the family arrives at the police station, "a lot of guys will point at me and say, 'There goes Tommy Woodry's father.'"[4] Tommy smiles in a close-up as the picture ends. He gives up his fantasies for the greater satisfaction of paternal approval. In Hollywood fashion, an unsatisfactory working-class life can lead a child to escapism, but love holds the family together. Dad's pride is the only thing Tommy needs. RKO made $210,000 off this low-budget sleeper.[5]

That Mr. Woody proudly brings Tommy up to face a grim and gritty world speaks to the social priority placed on strong father-son bonds. Historians point to an idealized "hard" masculinity as the "normal" gender role for 1950s men to prove modern life did not make them "soft." Indeed, film critics certainly praised the look of *The Window* for its location shooting among urban decay. However, a broader historical context suggests the world outside Tommy's window was nothing new. The boy's witnessing murder and squalor in the noir-esque underbelly of the Big Apple evokes the Depression-era gumshoe and foreshadows the hard-boiled Mike Hammer archetype.[6] Furthermore, inattentive mothers, absent fathers, and pinchpenny living and other hallmarks of a struggling family unit were carryovers from the Great Depression and World War II. In February 1944, J. Edgar Hoover warned law-abiding citizens of how juvenile delinquency simmered under decades of family disruptions: "Admittedly, the causes of this situation [juvenile delinquency] are not new, but they have been accentuated many times over by the changed conditions brought on by the war. Juvenile crime flourishes where the home ties have been weakened by divorce, separation, the desertion of a parent or the ignorance, carelessness or indifference of fathers and mothers. Our homes are not the sanctuaries of family life they once were."[7] Social guardians, reformers, and psychologists responded in kind, continuing to champion a narrow projection of remasculinized manhood to rebuild the family unit and thwart these social ills.

This chapter examines *The Decision of Christopher Blake* (1948) and *Any Number Can Play* (1949). The two movies, released one year apart, highlight the reconstruction of family solidarity in the postwar period. *The Decision of Christopher Blake* responded to the divorce crisis through a boy's eyes, but the film failed by not adequately addressing the public's concerns about a troubled nuclear family. In contrast, the father-son relationship in *Any Number Can Play* renews patriarchy as the family unit's salvation. Charley Kyng's Depression-era background endows him with a strong backbone, empowering him to succeed economically and correct his son's passivity. While scholars generally attribute Kyng's "tough guy" image to postwar anticommunism, these movies demonstrate how this centered patriarchal persona represented a source of stability after two decades of economic and social uncertainty.

Manning Up

From the late nineteenth century to the end of World War II, industrialization, urbanization, and enculturation redefined familial relationships. In the immediate postwar period, the nuclear family remained a top concern, especially the reintegration of the father as head of the household. The 1950s have a reputation as a time of close family ties, but contemporary studies confirmed how returning soldiers and their kids had difficulty adjusting to one another.[8] Child experts, notably Benjamin Spock, believed that absent dads during the war and the Depression led to an upswing in juvenile delinquency and "sissiness" in sons. In *The Common Sense Book of Baby and Child Care* (1946), Spock thought it necessary to tell parents, "A boy needs a friendly, accepting father."[9] After years of familial troubles due to economic hardship and war, Spock's statement underscored the urgency to reconstruct father-son bonds. Indeed, *The Window*'s gritty realism shows that struggling households like the Woodrys had figurative absent fathers, where dads worked the graveyard shift to make ends meet, but were not there for their sons. The result: junior's detachment from reality breeds untrustworthiness and antisocial tendencies.

The child who lives in his own fantasy was a cause for concern. A daydreaming youngster signified a lack of emotional maturity and an inability to face harsh realities. While fantasy functioned as an escape mechanism in which children could create their own worlds, child experts preferred that children not do so alone. Rather, "wholesome" forms of play and recreation socialized the child among peers and his environment. By 1951, one textbook on adolescent psychology cautioned, "Only the idle, daydreaming child who indulges in fantasy instead of wholesome play activities wastes his time."[10] The reason: by interacting with others, a boy learns the value of teamwork and can face adversity, not run from it. In contrast, "extreme introversion and daydreaming or antisocial tendencies are quite likely to arise when there is a failure in the socialization process."[11] Tommy Woodry's inability to separate fact from fiction prevented him from growing up.

The political backdrop made such masculine socialization a necessity. In 1948 and 1949, Czechoslovakia and China fell to the commies and the Soviets acquired the atomic bomb.[12] "Military, economic or political destruction of Western civilization and of our American way of life are definite possibilities if the danger from the East is not met boldly, imaginatively, and with united effort," the *New York Times* warned.[13] While Americans like Tommy Woodry lulled about in what the newspaper called a "never-never-land" of wishful thinking, the communists shouldered arms for world conquest.[14] Other voices urged for a masculine preparation for an inevitable World War III, with fathers at the helm. Public figures, such as the Venerable Fulton John Sheen, took to the airwaves, urging an aggressive form of fatherhood as an essential part of the postwar family and national defense. The two-parent household was ideal, Sheen argued, asserting the current "instability of man" was "due to a flight from fatherhood."[15] Presumably, faith, as a spiritual strength, translated into hardened physiques and built positive character traits like self-reliance and confidence. This "muscular Christianity" was a staple of twentieth-century manhood, and this heightened religiosity reemerged in the postwar years, propelling preachers like Sheen and especially Billy Graham into national prominence.[16] The United States even projected this image abroad; when screening candidates to represent the "average" American man and woman, the U.S. Information Agency rejected applicants if they had divorce records.[17] Divorce signified a perceived moral failing in the eye of God and country. Muscular Christianity steeled its nerves in the face of family troubles, notably divorce. Since the birth of the industry, the movies tore families apart by unraveling the knots between couples. Marriage breakups, whether on-screen or in scandal-ridden Hollywood, incurred the wrath of moralizers. The industry had felt congressional charges of "un-Americanism" since the 1930s, and the pressure heightened in the postwar years. In particular, the House Committee on Un-American Activities (HUAC) charged the Dream Factory with subverting national norms and morals with dirty fantasies about infidelity. Although the Hollywood Ten has attracted most of the scholarly attention, the supposed loose living among Hollywoodites fueled critics' rhetoric over how Hollywood undermined American values. Rising divorce rates in the immediate postwar years especially intensified scrutiny into Tinsel Town. In response, the industry scrubbed its image by embracing the reconstituted nuclear family with its virile, masculine father figure knowing best.

Not Hooraying for Hollywood

While Americans basked in Hollywood's Dream Factory of home front heroism and romance during World War II, the war's end brought a rude wake-up call. During the war, couples rushed to the altar in hopes of creating a home life, but the postwar years witnessed a rise in the divorce rate as spouses realized they were not compatible.[18] In 1946, one out of every fifty-five wedding knots unraveled.[19] Although the divorce rate was numerically small, it generated widespread concern about the continuing familial strains from the past fifteen years. Pictures such as *My Reputation* (1946) acknowledged family dissolution existed, but kept marriage intact at all costs, even if death did them part. Already a period piece set two years back into the war, *My Reputation* asks if a widow would run away with an officer on leave and expect her two adoring sons to understand. Mom would not; she must sacrifice love and happiness rather than live in sin. Indeed, Joseph Breen wanted to eliminate dialogue such as the officer's line, "I don't want marriage," and the widow's reply, "I'll take what you want to give me, Scott. Even if it's just for a day or a week."[20] With marriage out of the question, so was their future together, as the Production Code mandated. The widow's last line, "I'll never be lonely again," speaks to her resolve—and resignation—to keep her family intact: two sons, her dead husband's spirit, and her reputation.[21]

Social critics agreed that the family came first. In September 1946, columnist Malvina Lindsay considered the economic impact if families broke up: "It will definitely mean that more mothers will have to work outside the home, more children require day or institutional care."[22] Such conditions existed during the war, and the majority of women workers in 1945 wanted to keep working, but Lindsay believed family was more important. "The social trend of the day is toward a more feminine role for women," she insisted, and she feared divorces would lead to "a decline in the birth rate."[23] In 1947, *Life* noted that "most social scientists" claimed the "family system is undergoing the Greco-Roman style of dissolution."[24] The fall of classical antiquity had "almost universal corruption and disregard of the marriage agreement," a declining birth rate, sloppy parenting, and "juvenile delinquency and adult delinquency."[25] Supposedly, Pax Americana was doomed to repeat this history if people did not learn the lessons from previous civilizations. The family unit remained as "troubled" as it was in the Depression.

The legacy of the Depression found a cinematic home in film noir pictures like *The Window*. Film historians have documented the emergence of film noir in World War II and its heyday in the postwar period. Despite the French label, film noir spoke of American pessimism and dark social forces from the late 1920s onward. Depression-era pictures like the prison genre (*The Big House* [1930], *Hell's Highway* [1932], *The Mayor of Hell* [1933]) or urban squalor (*Dead End* [1937], *Hell's Kitchen* [1939]) used deep shadows, low-key lighting, and low-life characters to explore the ugly side of American abundance and prosperity. Postwar pictures like *The Window* offered peeks into families trying to make ends meet in an unfriendly city. Other films, such as *The Naked City* (1948) and *The Cry of the City* (1948), pointed to the sad decay of the urban environment. In the aptly titled *Mr. Blandings Builds His Dream House* (1948), the patriarch sets his sights on the countryside, and the mounting expenses and bickering contractors still beat living in a cramped New York apartment. Both Tommy Woodry and Mr. Blandings knew the city was a rough place to raise a family.

The emergence of film noir's antisocial themes of crime and disillusionment further threatened to dissolve family ties during a time of supposed "Victory Culture." Certainly, not every psychologist viewed increasing divorce rates with alarm; in 1948, psychologist Joseph Kirk Folsom believed that the "freedom" gained through divorce signaled a healthy American democracy as partners realized they were no longer chained to each other. When they did find true love, their emotional bonds would be much stronger.[26] However, Folsom was drowned out by alarming reports of divorce rates exceeding prewar rates and that the nation was "headed toward Sodom and Gomorrah."[27] Signs of the end times were relayed through press anecdotes covering the blasé attitudes of adults and their children who apparently held little respect for the sanctity of holy matrimony.[28] These sensationalistic reports of distraught children and outraged relatives found a cinematic counterpart in pictures like *Chicken Every Sunday* (1949), *The Marrying Kind* (1952), and *And Baby Makes Three* (1949), the last about a bride who, when walking down the aisle, realizes she is pregnant with her first husband's child and must decide which man makes the better father. The idea of marriage remained sacrosanct even if couples split, as in the case of *My Foolish Heart* (1949) and *Payment on Demand* (1951), both cases in which a wife regrets her rash divorce; in the latter, she leaves a candle burning for her ex-husband to return. One producer complained about the pressure to uphold marriage at all costs meant that "divorce never can be shown as a solution to a domestic problem. Thus a major factor in the life of the United States can never be shown in the movies."[29] But such edicts did not stop productions from skirting around the edges.

In the 1940s, the powerful Catholic pressure group Legion of Decency classified half of Hollywood's output as "B"—"objectionable in part"—for featuring a "light treatment of marriage," and audiences responded.[30] In 1946, RKO remade the Depression-era *Wednesday's Child* (1934) as *Child of Divorce*, with a glum ending showing the neglected child in a settlement house, resenting the melody "Home Sweet Home" and waiting, "like many other lonesome children of divorce."[31] One reviewer nodded, "Honest, intelligent little pictures are rare and should be cherished, even celebrated in Hollywood."[32] Still, public disfavor made the story unsalable. Despite a lean production cost, RKO lost $20,000.[33]

According to guardians like the Legion of Decency, these "light treatments" of marriage reflected Hollywood's attitudes regarding their moral responsibility to public taste. Since the medium's birth, critics blamed the movies for the nation's perceived moral failings.[34] Texts like *Movie Mad America: An Utterly Frank and Revealing Expose of the American Movie* kept up the attack: "Hollywood is a divorcing set!," screamed the author, describing how, even as he wrote, actress Hedy Lamarr secured a divorce and "Heddy being Heddy [*sic*], the radio had to blast this forth as the news of the day."[35] The dalliances of celebrities, their outlandish lifestyles, and their cavalier transgression of public taste burned the airwaves and ears of self-appointed social guardians. Fan culture, especially movie magazines, routinely fueled the public's fascination and fantasy for movie glamour by featuring Hollywoodites who held nothing sacred concerning the bonds of matrimony. Meanwhile, socially conservative citizens fumed.

The emphasis on family life, however, required Americans to take their wedding vows seriously. The blend of faith and family played out as "muscular Christians" exercised their vocal cords against "un-Americans" who abandoned their marriages. Religious leaders vigorously led the crusade against a morally lax Tinsel Town. In 1947 *Motion Picture Magazine* published "What Does Your Church Say about . . . Divorce in Hollywood." In the article, Catholic, Protestant, and Jewish leaders demanded Hollywood stop "being what it is now popularly regarded as being—the very front and center of the attack upon sanctity and integrity of American home life."[36] Allegedly, celebrity divorces correlated with broken homes, juvenile delinquency, and outright criminality—all of which spoke to the *noir*-ish textures of the American landscape. One reader claimed, "The latest Hollywood marital cavortings have left us feeling disgusted, and we haven't seen a movie since."[37] Actor John Garfield spoke out, writing a rebuttal in the magazine. He defended his peers' wedlock statistics, arguing the divorce rate was only 30 percent among his colleagues. He lamented, "Hollywood actors and actresses live in a small town which is spotlighted by more than 400 newspaper and magazine writers who write and print all the rumors."[38] Unfortunately for Garfield and the movie colony, the polemical article gained circulation when the *Los Angeles Times* featured it on the front page.[39] The controversy intensified when industry representatives demanded the magazine withdraw the material, and publisher "Buzz" Fawcett refused. Instead, Fawcett made his case on radio, asserting his magazine "has done its proper job" in exposing "the lightness with which Hollywood people seem to take marriage . . . and we wanted it corrected from within before the movie public became aroused and perhaps would take matter into their own hands."[40] The "public's own hands," in the form of HUAC, were already a public relations nightmare.

Motion Picture Magazine needed the studios' cooperation to survive and ultimately apologized.[41] But the scandal it caused showed that the association between marriage, religious faith, and anticommunism impacted Hollywood in the postwar years. While not as widely studied as anticommunism, the Hollywood family—on and off the screen—inflamed the public eye. On November 26, 1947, *Variety* reported the formation of a new watchdog group to "scan cast lists for names of divorced players and take action."[42] The trade journal did not specify the repercussions, but studio heads worried. RKO's Dore Schary publicly spoke about the "tide of hysteria," asking, "How many organizations are we going to permit as monitors for the industry?"[43] One week later, on December 3, 1947, the Motion Picture Association of America's president, Eric Johnston, answered Schary with the so-called Waldorf Statement. Named after the New York hotel where he, Schary, and other executives met, the industry officially disavowed the Hollywood Ten and promised to fire anyone who "advocates the overthrow" of the U.S. government.[44] The Waldorf Statement set the stage for the blacklist.

While Hollywood divorced itself from communism, marriage troubles continued to play out in the movies, Hollywood, fan culture, and the general public. When Eric Johnston succeeded Will Hays, many disgruntled moviegoers took the opportunity to demand reform. One fan complained how the "appearance of divorce in motion pictures has sharply increased in the last two to three years."[45] Another took the opportunity to play moviemaker and pitched a story: show the "average family, portraying the causes leading up to divorce and then immediately portray the same family under the same circumstances showing how the same pitfalls are avoided, [and] the production would receive the blessings of God and the appreciation of all the people."[46] While this compare-and-contrast approach to filmmaking did not materialize, the studios realized they had to address the general concerns about divorce, specifically, toward Hollywood. Warner Bros.'s answer was *The Decision of Christopher Blake*.

The Nondecision of Christopher Blake

The Decision of Christopher Blake (1948) reflects the popular view of divorce as a national crisis through a child's eyes. The failure of the play and film adaptation highlights the public's attitudes toward divorce's impact on children. Playwright Moss Hart had recently married and, although childless, found the topic a timely "change of pace" from his usual satires.[47] The protagonist, twelve-year-old Chris, says as much: "It's always in the papers about people getting divorced. Nearly every single day."[48] Hart staged the boy's daydreams, allowing viewers to peer into his subconscious in visions of abandonment, revenge, and delinquency due to his parents' splitting.[49] Like *The Window*'s Tommy Woodry, Chris uses daydreams to escape postwar anxieties. Tommy envisions a better, exciting life for his family, only to realize there is no place like home, even if it is a figurative dump. In contrast, Christopher Blake enjoys the good life Tommy yearns for—he has a private lab in a garage and gets a new bike for Christmas—but his daydreams render such luxuries inconsequential without mom and dad.

But Chris's parents have irreconcilable differences. His dad becomes chummy with a sculptress, and his mother's fundamental unhappiness foreshadows a "disease" Betty Freidan identified a decade later. Mrs. Blake thought domesticity would satisfy her, but with her son near adolescence, she prefers to end the façade. Chris accepts his mother's need to start over and chooses to live with his father. Chris leaves his nightmares behind, but audiences rejected the final divorce. The play received mixed reviews and lasted 114 performances on Broadway, much to Hart's disappointment.[50]

Christopher Blake flopped, but Warner Bros. studio chief Jack Warner liked the play and offered $305,000 for the rights.[51] To adapt the Broadway disappointment, screenwriter/producer Ranald MacDougall suggested exploiting "whatever little selling value is left in the memory of the play," such as renaming the work with sentimental titles such as *The Innocent Heart of Christopher Blake* or *This Small World of Christopher Blake*.[52] For the title role, MacDougall chose veteran Ted Donaldson, convinced Donaldson's perceptive reading would convey Chris's tough decision.[53] One treatment described Chris's "sensitive face that reflects dignity somewhat beyond his years. He is very serious about nearly everything and gives the impression of continually wondering about things. . . . He is growing up."[54] Even with a good lead, Warner Bros. conservatively estimated a cost of $4,622,500 (with a camera negative cost of $2.5 million) and hoped to gross $5 million for a tidy $337,500 profit.[55]

MacDougall's main job was to succeed where Hart's play failed. The production took its cue from popular opinions; one critic thought children from divorces "are often unwanted, dissatisfied, unhappy, starved for attention and love." They "are the people who will crowd our courts and fill our prisons tomorrow [and are] so poorly equipped to face life and dissatisfied, are fertile ground for that sinister evil communism or something even worse."[56] Accordingly, MacDougall faulted Hart's ending. "Divorce is on the upsurge in the U.S.," which was a sign of "the result of uneasy times in which we live," he wrote a week after the *Los Angeles Times* reprinted *Motion Picture Magazine*'s exposé. Referring to the article, MacDougall lamented the "currently popular [trend] among the clergy and the laity, to blame the situation on Hollywood" in shameless publicity plugs. He wanted to show "Hollywood is as conscious of the moral and human implications of the divorce problem as any other segment of the population." Some "certain changes in the basic structure of the play" would create "a high engrossing picture that will meet great sympathy and do a certain amount of good." By producing an "interesting, entertaining, box-office, and a 'clean' picture" about family solidarity and resiliency against disruptive forces, *The Decision of Christopher Blake* would defend the industry.[57]

The first step in changing the play's "basic structure" consisted of revamping the parents. MacDougall called Hart's married couple "rather selfish and unpleasant people, almost entirely preoccupied with themselves," which, he thought, made for unsympathetic characters. "Neither of them should be placed in the position of insisting upon a divorce," he wrote. "We should feel that if there were any way possible to avoid it, or prevent it, both of them would do everything possible to stop the proceedings."[58] MacDougall acknowledged the contemporary concerns about divorce, but he ignored the historical context in which couples saw marriage as a form of security, even if matrimony itself proved unsatisfying. Hart's version of Mrs. Blake especially reflected the Depression. She gave birth to twelve-year-old Chris in 1935, the middle of the Depression. Her child and her husband came from a desire for family stability, not romance: "I married Dad because I was frightened and alone, and I wanted what every girl is brought up to want—a husband and something called security."[59] With the war over and Chris on the cusp of adolescence, she wants to move on.

Mrs. Blake echoed the public sentiment about family togetherness, but her open confession countered the rhetoric of a happy home. MacDougall rejected her marrying "for security, and down through the years has shuddered to herself every time it became necessary to go to bed with him." He acknowledged some women did this, but thought this happened "only rarely, and such a woman is a psychiatric case rather than a human problem."[60] Indeed, some social experts traced divorce to "the personal freedom of women, which can and does cause innumerable tragedies," which was allegedly "the real cause of juvenile delinquency and other social ills."[61] MacDougal wanted Mrs. Blake to morph into "a woman of great worth and sterling ability, who has consciously and with full knowledge of the sacrifice it entails, given up an independent existence for love of her husband and son." Familial commitment, not a cold calculation for security during economic and social hardships, became the new backdrop.

While Mrs. Blake received the majority of attention (actress Alexis Smith has top billing), Mr. Blake fared less well. Hart's Mrs. Blake's initial desire to find security from economic conditions made her the dominate spouse. Her husband suffers by comparison, coming across as a nice guy. However, Mrs. Blake's unhappiness makes him unhappy, which leads to his initial infidelity. Blake realizes his mistake, but remains puzzled why his wife insists they divorce. His clinging to the romance of an ideal marriage, rather than face reality, persuades Chris to choose to stay with his father. The boy realizes Dad cannot go on without a family.

While Hart's Mr. Blake lacked a masculine demeanor, MacDougall's version fared no better. Blake cannot even talk to his son without fumbling. When Mr. Blake haltingly brings up sex education, for instance, Chris bluntly tells his father the school system has informed him of the basics, even if he did not believe it. When Mr. Blake approaches the topic of his adultery (defined as nightclubbing and theater), Chris takes charge, asking his father what his intentions are toward his lover. Later, Mr. Blake tells his wife he "made a mess of things" trying to explain the divorce to their child and wants to call the whole thing off. All the while, Blake nervously scrunches his hat, which his wife comments on. She then rebukes him, reminding him that he asked for divorce and she's giving it.[62] The film switches the roles in the divorce suit, revealing Blake, not his wife, originally wants out. But he flip-flops while his hurt wife remains firm. Although Blake is a successful breadwinner, judging by the family's spacious house, he lacks a masculine demeanor and a literal "hard" body to guide his son.

To avoid public apathy, MacDougall's revisions inverted the play's ending. He determined to avoid accusations of furthering Hollywood's "light treatment of marriage" and avoid reprimands from industry executives. "Our entire story hinges upon not having an objection from the [Eric] Johnston office to the question of adultery and the eventual forgiveness of him [Mr. Blake] by Mrs. Blake," the producer wrote.[63] She finds forgiveness easier, as an "adjustment to each other becomes imperative to the continuance of life together." This premise led to the "most important of all the changes . . . that I consider vitally necessary there should be no divorce." MacDougall underlined his position, arguing the disintegration of the family unit "would be a resounding flop at the box office, and a target for every moralist and clergyman in the country," who, as *Motion Picture Magazine* demonstrated, had a ready audience. He wanted the parents to discover "their true feelings" and "Chris will stay with both of them."[64]

To help publicize MacDougall's view, Warner Bros. studio publicist Marty Weiser ordered promotional stills to emphasize family togetherness. Weiser posed the actors with Donaldson in the middle, to visually anchor the parents together (figure 9). He instructed photographers to "point out how a child is the strongest link between husband and wife," noting, "We do not know who they are but they represent the average American family."[65] Publicity also avoided the plot, circulating articles about Alexis Smith hearing wolf whistles and Robert Douglas's ordeal posing as a statue for his movie son's daydreams.[66]

MacDougall's treatment reflects contemporary political tensions and the family as a source of stability. Like Tommy Woodry, Chris fantasizes—but unlike Tommy's yearning for a better life, Chris fears his nuclear family's atomization. His dreams tie divorce and family disintegration with the continuing threats from abroad. With tensions between the United States and Soviet Union increasing and predictions of World War III in the press, Chris develops a "super atomic bomb" and a world peace plan.[67] In his dreams, Abraham Lincoln awards Chris a "super-duper badge." But when Lincoln learns Chris's parents are splitting, Honest Abe regards this domestic calamity as a national disgrace, and he orders the Blakes reunited. Unlike Tommy, however, Chris has limited agency to shape his dreams; an assassin targets the Great Emancipator and Chris takes

FIG. 9 The carefully composed nuclear family. In *The Decision of Christopher Blake* (1948), Chris (Ted Donaldson) binds mom (Alexis Smith) and dad (Robert Douglas) together. Producer Ranald MacDougall believed this portrait would bolster Hollywood's image as a city of "clean" family living. (Author's collection.)

the bullet, cementing the family's destruction (figure 10). The boy genius's demise is tragic, but, worse, his death leaves the United States unable to either use the super atomic weaponry or implement the plan for world peace. The family unit literally acts as the backbone of the nation's strength. The harsh reality of divorce denies Chris a future, even in his daydreams.

To emphasize the family unit, industry censors played down the theme of divorce. Concerning the Lincoln dream sequence, industry censor Joseph Breen described the original script, writing, "Christopher envisions himself as committing suicide publicly in order to bring his parents together." Breen claimed suicide due to broken homes was "a situation which is, unfortunately, so common nowadays" and presented "a very bad and easily imitable example to numbers of unhappy and possibly unbalanced children."[68] He suggested a "heart attack and public collapse and death," a so-called solution that befell the bellhop Jimmy in the prewar *Andy Hardy Meets Debutante.* MacDougall swapped suicide to an outside assassin to threaten the family. Chris saves Lincoln, but his death leaves his family, and his nation, bereft of leadership.

To soften the subject more, MacDougall took a hatchet to his production without motivation from Breen. Stills advertised Chris's worst nightmare: a "howling, hostile mob and a cruel-looking Judge who tries to force a decision out of the whimpering witness." The court rules "the divorce is the boy's fault and

FIG. 10 One with the ages. Divorce leads to the destruction of the nation in *The Decision of Christopher Blake* (1948). The parents and maid (Mary Wickes, far right) witness the dissolution. (Author's collection.)

that his parents never wanted him."[69] Divorce made Chris a thief, arsonist, and poor student—just as critics had argued a lack of family structure created delinquents (figure 11). Indeed, educational classroom shorts such as "Angry Boy" (1950) traced psychologically disturbed children to family tensions; the titular "angry boy" expresses his frustrations by stealing from his teacher, tripping little girls, and throwing darts at the friendly doctors trying to help him. Film editors denied this outlook to Chris, eliminating his worst dream and ultimately reducing the running time to seventy-five minutes, relegating it to half of a double feature.

The studio's cuts removed the "bite" from the picture, diminishing Chris's experience. In part, the film's lack of character development came from conflicts on the set. Ted Donaldson recalls the original director, Irving Rapper (who had tested Donaldson for the part of Christopher), was "very serious" about the script and wanted to emphasize the relationship between the Blakes and their son.[70] However, after Rapper had a dispute with the star, Alexis Smith, the studio replaced Rapper with director Peter Godfrey, whom Donaldson noted was "quite uninterested in the character relationships," and preferred the fantasy sequences and showmanship. Donaldson notes Godfrey left the actors to work out their characterizations on their own. Donaldson worked with his dialogue director,

FIG. 11 Deleting delinquency. This cut scene from *The Decision of Christopher Blake* (1948) shows the child of divorce as a lawbreaker, with a stern judge throwing the book at him. (Author's collection.)

Howard Lynn, to discuss Chris's relationships with his parents and his feelings about world events referenced in the movie and developed emotional high points—including his prepubescent voice breaking in two instances (both cut from the final picture).[71] His work paid off, as critics credited Donaldson's good performance and emotional pathos, but despite Donaldson's acting skills, the ending falls flat. He "chooses" his father, and his mother, ashamed, flees the courtroom. Mr. Blake chases his wife, and they reconcile off camera while Chris and the judge share a wink. The reunited family leaves the courthouse together. The end.

This "real-life" solution mocked the issue of divorce by portraying it as a silly spat between parents. Chris's sudden about-face negates the impact of his personal nightmares over the loss of a parent. Picking up on the film's lack of characterization, especially the parents, the *Washington Post* thought nothing "suggests that these people could possibly have been in love with each other; a happy ending does nothing to make you suppose that this time they will be any more compatible." MacDougall rejected Hart's original backdrop for the Blakes, but did not concoct a new backstory, and the critic pointed out the film itself was fantasy: "Had these parents seemed like ordinary human beings instead of polished celluloid puppets" or "their home resembled an ordinary home instead of some plush designer's idea of what a home should be, there might have been an air of actuality about this very real problem."[72] Instead, the picture settled for a contrived ending, passing the silver screen off as reality. "Watch the clever trick he [Chris] pulls! And sure enough, there's the sweetest reconciliation you ever saw," *Modern Screen* scoffed. "Until Pop falls in love again, I guess." The emotional punches were "so far from honest it makes you tired."[73]

Ironically, MacDougall's desire to turn a public service seemed phony, leaving audiences feeling cheated. *Boxoffice* suggested, "If there is a 'Christopher Blake' in your area, invite him as a special guest on opening night."[74] But such strategies contradicted the film's message. Real "Christopher Blakes" need not exist because the film asserts divorcees needed only to rekindle the flames. Bad timing also played a part, as Warner Bros. released the picture around Christmas, and premieres flopped in New York and Chicago.[75] The film flailed in larger cities, with Cleveland reporting an abysmal 42 percent of the average gross.[76] In small towns, the film also struggled. "This show didn't entertain nor did it do any business," complained one West Virginia rural theater.[77]

MacDougall inadvertently sabotaged his own production, but his desire to helm a "clean" production reflected "Muscular Christians" strong-arming the industry with charges of immorality. Moviemakers struggled to juggle the contradictory demands of changing times. In a *Life*-sponsored roundtable, producers addressed sagging box office receipts, bemoaning the "thousands of prohibitions" and catering to the lowest common denominator who "will be the first to desert it for television." One showman thought *The Decision of Christopher Blake* a "reasonably adult treatment of divorce" but had to "double it up with Abbot and Costello to bring in the customers." Another asserted, "Hollywood deliberately confuses fantasy with reality, thereby providing neither the recreation of true fantasy nor the recognition of true experience."[78] Boys could stop make believing; in *The Window*, Tommy Woodry's daydreams ultimately make him a hero, and he wins his father's respect. But the film remained anchored in the gritty New York tenement street scenes, and audiences never enter Tommy's daydreams. But for Christopher Blake, the lack of a "true experience" centered upon the cardboard parents whose troubles came from disillusionment about family life. While MacDougall cut the negative cost down to $1.489 million, the expected earnings never materialized. By 1956, the movie grossed a mere $516,000 in domestic and foreign rentals.[79]

Remasculinizing Fatherly Bonds: "Delinquent" Dads versus "Priggish" Sons

The failure of *The Decision of Christopher Blake* came from many factors. The audience and critics deplored the handling of the divorce plot, but they rejected MacDougall passing off a typical happy ending as a realistic solution. The film removed the parents' underlying reasons that drove divorce, but left the void unfilled. The lack of ideal role models, particularly a strong father figure, belied Chris's screen maturation in the public imagination.

In contrast to Mr. Blake, MGM's *Any Number Can Play* (1949) successfully presented a father figure whose masculinity empowers him to triumph against all odds. The film symbolizes this "high stakes lifestyle" with a casino setting populated with character types, from society matrons to drunken bums. One character, gambling addict Ben Snelerr, was played by none other than actor Lewis Stone, who had stayed in the public eye as Judge Hardy for over a decade. Even though the last Andy Hardy movie, *Love Laughs at Andy Hardy* (1946), premiered years earlier, Stone noted, "I still receive an abundant fan mail from them, you know."[80] Stone reassured fans they would not see Andy Hardy's dad turned into a human derelict; rather, he reminded them he played screen heavies long before he donned judicial robes. With the Hardy series over, he was merely returning to a rich theatrical past. "They accepted me as Judge Hardy after those other pictures," he pointed out. "Maybe they won't hold this against me either."[81] Stone reaffirmed his versatile acting chops while making sure audiences would not place Kyng's casino in Carvel.

But among the many players in this all-star cast, the movie's winner is the house proprietor, Charley Kyng. This father's "hard" masculinity affirmed him as the "king" of his castle: the home and workplace. Appropriately, the movie's protagonist reflected this view in his surname and the actor who played him, Clark Gable, long known as Hollywood's "king" for his rugged masculine screen persona established during the 1930s. Unlike the hesitant Blake, Kyng thrived on challenges, having built his casino from the ground up during the Depression. His success has costs: his doctor urges him to retire due to a heart weakened from stress, and his son thinks gambling is immoral. Despite the strains on his family life and his body, Kyng presses on.

Kyng's masculine occupation unnerved some social critics. The Production Code censors demanded MGM make clear Kyng was not an underworld ne'er-do-well. Joseph Breen believed it "absolutely necessary to indicate definitely that it takes place in a state or city where gambling is legal. Otherwise, the present treatment would be entirely unacceptable."[82] Breen's criticism of gambling reflected a long-standing moral outlook against gambling and betting as sins. In 1949, critics saw gambling as a moral failing for those who wanted to get rich quick, even though nearly half of American adults admitted they gambled as a form of social mobility.[83] Indeed, when reviewing *The Window*, Breen okayed the policemen playing cards in their spare time, but asked "that they not be gambling."[84] Card playing for fun or profit was ubiquitous, even among law enforcement, but had no place in Hollywood's list for clean living.

Actor Clark Gable countered the charges of immorality. "I don't want tripe and I don't want pictures with messages," the King declared. He elaborated, "This picture has no cockeyed message. The guy's a gambler with guts and the picture doesn't preach for or against gambling or making the eight the hard way."[85] Contrary to Gable's publicity statements, MGM screenwriters addressed Breen's concerns by portraying games of chance as a legitimate business through taxes, retail sales, and employment. This also came from the Depression, as cash-strapped local governments legalized horse racing, bingo, and lotteries to raise revenue.[86] Kyng asserts, "If you don't like gambling you might say you're not supporting your city government."[87] *Newsweek* connected legalized betting to character building, noting, "Gambling is presented as a respectable vocation and even, after its rugged fashion, as something of an aid in molding character." A gambler "associates with some of our very best people and is often required to exhibit a high order or moral and physical courage." The result of courage and civic duty: a "pretty-adjusted citizen."[88]

As a masculine, "adjusted" citizen, Kyng seems the ideal father to impart these values to his son. *Variety* noted MGM cast Darryl Hickman as Paul because the young actor was "almost a dead ringer for Clark [Gable] in movement and manner."[89] But similarities were only skin deep, as Paul, a moralizing prude, rejects the violence and aggression that his father used to provide for his family. The teenager, Kyng fears, lacks the male stamina to succeed in the real world as he had. Rather, his son disguises his cowardice with a skewed, ethical outlook, and this "yellow" streak shames the family.

For Paul, the casino's deep shadows belied crime and unsavory characters, not unlike Tommy Woodry's tenement in *The Window*.[90] Although the Kyngs have a brightly lit suburban house, the dimly lit downtown casino remains the focus of Paul's anxieties.[91] Screenwriter Richard Brooks described the seventeen-year-old as "in that awkward limbo between boyhood and manhood" who "'knows all the answers to the world's problems'—except to his own personal problems, of course."[92] Paul, a loner, "speaks softly, adolescently self-piteous. . . . His sensitivity makes him prey to his vivid imagination."[93] This "vivid imagination"—not unlike Tommy Woodry's daydreams—enables Paul to cope with an unsatisfactory home life. Tommy dreams of leaving the slums, while Paul wants his dad to give up a shady profession. Even though the movie explicitly states Kyng operates within the law and the town's elites patronize the casino regularly, Paul deems gambling immoral.

Paul rejects his father's masculine fusion of individualism, capitalism, and all-or-nothing risk taking and instead sees the family fortune coming at the expense of others. He asks his father to "stop the game. Give them back their money."[94] The incredulous father tells his son to wake up. Paul grew up in the latter Depression and war years, but he attended the "best schools" and the "best summer camps" and always received extravagant gifts from his father. Paul directly profited from this lifestyle and knows nothing about hardships. The boy is even reluctant to step into his dad's casino, and a bitter Kyng flatly tells him, "If I'm still around when you've got it—give me the rules and I'll try to live by 'em. But right now I'm living in *this* world—and these rules I know." When Paul continues to protest, Kyng shuts him up: "I don't think you're old enough to judge your father."[95]

Kyng's last statement underscored the hard times he endured. The film does not cite the Great Depression directly, but, as Gable stated, Kyng "made the eight the hard way." He recounts how he started out as a "nobody" who "made a bundle in the roughest, toughest race of them all where you don't get any second guesses."[96] Although Kyng describes his background within the context of his profession, this "gamble" took place in the Depression, when state governments made gambling legal—Paul's age of seventeen and his never recalling poverty suggest Kyng started his career around 1930–1931. His "rules" come from his surviving austerity, and he resents his pampered son's criticizing him for providing for his family and the city. Failing to appreciate his father's struggles, Paul comes across as spoiled, selfish, and childish.

Screenwriter Richard Brooks's take on the Kyngs was opposite that of Ranald MacDougall's approach for the Blakes. Rather than avoid the Depression context as MacDougall did, Brooks refashions history as a positive experience for the characters and moviegoers. Mrs. Kyng (Alexis Smith) survived the Great Depression by supporting her husband. Although she enjoys the family's current success, she looks back on the Depression as a character-building exercise. Unlike Mrs. Blake, who wanted comfort and security, Mrs. Kyng revises the Great Depression as a masculine endeavor that empowered her husband (figure 12). To commemorate those happy years, she redecorated the basement, where she spends her time when she feels down, with secondhand furniture to resemble their old one-bedroom apartment. She knows her husband also lives in the past in his desire for Paul to "man up" and assume the family name. Mrs. Kyng asks herself, in a standoff between her husband and son, whose side she would take. She sides with Charley: "I was a wife before a mother."[97]

However, Mrs. Kyng undermines her husband's masculinity by indulging her son's moralizing against her husband's career. This form of smothering echoed warnings from wartime writers, notably Philip Wylie, about the "sissification" of boys, and which continued in the postwar years. Charley Kyng contributes to Paul's emasculation through detachment—a common form of antisocial behavior contemporary sociologists observed among returning servicemen. Paul's disconnect from his father also originates from the same environment that had empowered his dad. Paul explains the rift started when he ran away during a kindergarten scrap. His father had begged his son to man up, getting down on his knees so he would appear smaller than the boy and ordering him to strike, but Paul refused to swing. Since then, Charley Kyng grew increasingly disappointed with his son in a "rough, tough" world that does not offer second chances.

In a larger social context, Paul's passiveness indicated meekness, timidity, and a lack of masculinity. This behavior had some supporters; one advice columnist told a mother who raised a combative six-year-old that her son would grow up to become a "brute-male in relation to wife and children" and a "bully by habit-reflex" if he resolves his differences through fisticuffs.[98] But many other child experts disagreed. According to one child-rearing guide published in 1949, the

FIG. 12 Nostalgia for the Depression in *Any Number Can Play* (1949), as the Kyngs (Clark Gable and Alexis Smith) fondly recall their younger days during hard times. The Spanish lobby card's caption reads, "Este es mi cuarto de recreo" (This is my recreation room). For Mrs. Kyng, escapism into the past allowed her to cope with present-day insecurities. (Author's collection.)

same year the film premiered, by age seven "boys will fight for their rights if necessary" and a "certain amount of aggressiveness and ability to hold one's own is necessary at this age." The child, "especially the boy, will find it even more necessary to hold his own" when he grows older.[99] A boy's assertiveness, then, indicated maturity. Dr. Spock confirmed, "At the high-school and college level, make-believe no longer satisfies. Organized athletics, games, debates, and competitions for school jobs take its place. All these call for aggressiveness."[100] While Spock made a distinction between "fierce feelings" channeled through "dozens of rules and conventions" and outright bullying, these guidelines mandated a child leave his childhood fantasies behind. Paul's unyielding idealism and refusal to fight from an early age signaled his abnormality. Paul is in the wrong, not his father.

Charley Kyng's only fault was giving up on his son. By throwing himself into his career, he allows Paul to drift toward his mother for guidance. The boy turns to his mom for everything, confiding his concerns with his father and problems at school, and when a fight breaks out among his classmates and the police book him, his mother bails him out. Paul's passivity stems from his moral high ground, but at the cost of his masculine maturation. The script spells out instructions for Darryl Hickman during the fight sequence: "PAUL HAS NOT YET STRUCK A BLOW."[101] A disappointed Charley Kyng leaves child-rearing to his wife, and the audiences witness the tragic results due to an absentee father.

Paul's point of view had merits. The Production Code censors wanted MGM to clarify the legality of gambling, worrying that audiences might see the film as a glorification of a moral vice. In reviews of *Any Number Can Play*, some critics questioned Charley Kyng's gambling, but few defended the boy's ideals.[102] *Variety* reported, "Pic's thesis maintains that gambling is legitimate—if you're a winner. Yarn develops the point via a domestic break between Gable, as the legalized gambling house operator, and his collegiate son who is ashamed of his pappy's profession. But . . . the kid becomes a convert to the rolling dominoes as a character builder."[103] The *Hollywood Reporter* warned exhibitors about the "exaltation of gambling and the holding up of the wheel of chance to a young boy as a fine, sportsmenlike way of life. It could be, but the PTA will have its own ideas."[104] One exhibitor affirmed this view: "Big time gambling is too rich for small town oil men and school kids. They complained. Business was only slightly below average, so I have no grouch over it. I enjoyed it myself and think it should do okay anywhere except in very small or rural communities."[105] While social bluenoses, like the PTA, church groups, and "womenfolk," may have objected to Kyng's family business, the idealized "hard" image of manhood—represented by Gable's rough-and-tumble screen persona—played well.

Audiences may not have approved of Charley Kyng's profession on a moral level, but they agreed Paul needed toughening up to survive in the "real world," just as his dad had done. In the end, Paul becomes a man in his father's image. In the climax, two criminals sneak into the casino.[106] The bad guys rob the town's elite at gun point. Seeing no one support his father (who has, as Paul noted, taken all their money), the boy jumps one gunman, effectively saving the family name (figure 13). The script notes, "As though releasing all the punches he has withheld for many years, Paul starts hitting [holdup man] Sisti with fury, sobbing and crying."[107]

Paul mans up as he enters the real world with Kyng's grinning approval. MGM's story synopsis corrected itself to emphasize the boy's rising to meet his father's expectation: "~~At least Paul realizes his father's worth.~~ In the brawl, Paul also proves his worth by coming to his father's help."[108] By slugging it out, Kyng's "son is finally showing some spirit," the story synopsis notes. "In the brawl, Darryl, now recognizing that his father is a great man, comes to his father's help. Clark is proud of his son."[109] *Film Daily* concurred, calling Paul, not gambling, the problem. The boy "is something not quite the chip off the old block that he might have been. But he improves."[110]

With the family reunited under his terms, Kyng no longer needs the casino to symbolize his hard-won success. He retires, leaving the darkened den for country fishing with his wife and son. Kyng transfers his tough-guy persona into the

FIG. 13 Like father, like son. In *Any Number Can Play* (1949), Paul (Darryl Hickman) matures as the spitting image of his father. He sheds his passivity to defend the family, just as his father's "guts" allowed him to succeed during the Depression. Dad (Clark Gable, standing second from left) grins in approval. (Author's collection.)

suburbs, his son at his side (figure 14). Kyng's last act is to cheat at cards—the first time he has done something shady—but he loses deliberately to give his gambling house to his associates. Moviegoers approved; the film grossed $3.205 million against a large $1.363 million cost, netting $763,000 in profits.[111]

Although Paul leaves for college after the film ends, he earns a more useful education outside the classroom. He learns his former moralistic fantasy outlook on life did not take into account his father's life experience, whose "guts" empowered him during the Depression to establish a prominent place in the community. The same parenting guide from 1949 affirmed this maturation process, claiming daydreaming adolescents must "fit into a realistic situation, translating the day-dreams of childhood into the actual possibilities of real life."[112] Paul finally accepts this lesson—just as Tommy Woodry did, both boys appreciating family solidarity as the ideal means to thrive in the *noir* environment around them. The *New York Times* praised Kyng as an honest and dedicated family man: "The pious intention is to show that gambling is rough, particularly on a fellow who has heart trouble and a priggish son."[113] By battling quasi-illegality, his weak heart, and his son's misguided ethics, Gable wins the town over. Society widows throw themselves at him and the town's business tycoons shoot craps,

FIG. 14 Kyng of his castle. In *Any Number Can Play* (1949), Kyng cheated "only once" to retire to a life of fishing. Paul's (left) accepting the card suggests he has tempered his absolutist morals. Gable (center) stands out from his family with his lighter-colored coat, and the gambling house's name "Charley's," above Gable, affirms the father's dominance over his wife and child. (Author's collection.)

transferring their boardrooms to the casino tables. Kyng, the self-made casino operator, supports them with taxes and projects a masculine demeanor they all admire. In this environment, prudish Paul grows up. Just as Kyng's guts led him to success, Paul will leave his childhood home able to defend his family and country against subversive forces.

Growing Up in a Man's World

Given the concerns about the Depression and the war and fears about the return of both, the movies suggested no price was too great for family solidarity. Boys grew up, leaving their daydreams behind. Millions of parents lined up behind Dr. Spock's commonsense advice: "If a child is living largely in his imagination and not adjusting well with other children, especially by the age of 4, a psychiatrist should be able to find what he is lacking."[114] Boys who did not receive psychiatric help, like Tommy Woodry, risked shaming their fathers. Christopher Blake tried using fantasy to cope with his family's breakup. Reality intervened, turning each dream into a nightmare.

Manning up was not easy. But, as the Kyngs demonstrate, hard times could be "good" years in that they hardened men to meet the practical demands of the real world and conditioned them to survive. With a third world war seemingly around the corner and depression looming, families could not afford to become lax and start questioning the hard living that drove Charley Kyng. Privately, Clark Gable the man was not Gable the image; as Darryl Hickman recalled, before takes, prop men continually offered the King towels to wipe his nervous, sweaty hands. However, before the cameras and the public, Gable played the part.[115]

In contrast, Christopher Blake's failure to make a decision irked moviegoers. The issue of divorce implied the failure of the family as the country faced turbulent international crises ahead. The unfolding arms race and predictions of World War III—with Chris "one moment devising a plan for world peace, the next, building a whizzer of an atom bomb"—reinforced the need for families to stay homeward bound.[116] Producer Ranald MacDougall thought a happy ending appropriate; his judge ends the picture by ordering the Blakes to "keep out of my court. I hate divorces!"[117] The public did too, but MacDougall's decision to save marriage at all costs did not work. The *Hollywood Reporter* lamented, "Not even the best efforts of such superior artists can make Christopher Blake anything more than a bad dream dramatically and a worse one artistically."[118] Unlike Paul Kyng, Christopher Blake never really woke up.

In and about the Dream Factory, divorce scandals continued to make headlines. In 1950, MGM production chief Dore Schary confirmed actor John Garfield's statistics that divorce among Hollywoodites occurred in only 30 percent of marriages, and Schary added an optimistic caveat, noting the industry was settling down to be "a little more dignified, a little more reserved, a little more fitting to their position in the public eye."[119] But the producer's words were drowned out by more sensational headlines. America's former sweetheart, Shirley Temple, ended her first marriage in 1949 and never looked back. The following year, Ingrid Bergman's fling with director Roberto Rossellini spawned speculation over her child's fate.[120] A distraught Joseph Breen even begged Bergman to return to her husband to save her (and Hollywood's) reputation.[121]

More publicly, an outraged senator Edwin C. Johnson proposed a "Movie Clean-Up Bill"—another attempt to license the movies for interstate commerce in which films featuring actors "convicted of a crime involving moral turpitude" would never leave California. Johnson directly referred to Bergman: "When she feels an urge to go on an immoral binge . . . she should have respect enough for her chosen profession to retire from it forever and forever remain in retirement."[122] With the family idealized as a source of national strength, those who chose to forsake it lost their privilege to appear in the public eye.

As Johnson and others believed, the nuclear family under a strong father gave boys the moral guidance to become citizen-soldiers. Such soldiering required militarized discipline to keep kids on the straight and narrow. Scouting, military schools, and ROTC were rites of passage for boys to toughen their bodies and hone their minds. When the Depression worsened in 1930, the War Department refused to defund Citizens' Military Training Camps, citing their contribution to civic character development.[123] In 1936, General John J. Pershing declared, "Good citizens cannot shut their eyes to the possibility of wars," and "they owe it to all that is sacred to make ample preparation against an evil day."[124] As U.S.–Soviet Union tensions intensified, it seemed the "evil day" arrived, with families on the front line. Hollywood, under scrutiny for its supposed disregard of the sanctity of marriage and home life, crafted masculine father figures to steer sons straight. Militarism helped make men out of boys.

3

Curbing Delinquency

Hot Rodding and Hot Rods

On April 15, 1954, Dr. John Otto Reinemann, the director of probation at the Municipal Court of Philadelphia, testified before the Senate Judiciary Subcommittee on Juvenile Delinquency. Reviewing the "last fifteen years," Reinemann observed the tense times "have created what may be called delinquent youths in a delinquent world." He clarified that "the uncertainty of the future, the expected draft into military service, the threatening possibility of another war and its predicted and widely publicized destructiveness" had a deleterious impact on kids. Accordingly, "some adolescents" now have a "last-fling attitude" where they flout the laws and social mores in times of prosperity. "To this we can—at least partly—attribute the growing instances of hot-rod driving, of vandalism, of the use of illegally purchased or homemade guns in gang fights," the officer lamented.[1]

Reinemann's testimony struck a chord with the public. In April 1954, six months after the Korean War ended in stalemate, many Americans wondered if its current crop of young men had what it took to commit to a protracted engagement against communism. Reports of communists brainwashing POWs, the high numbers of men turned away from service for mental and physical deficiencies, and the hysteria over the Red Scare and "duped" government officials had led the public and grandstanders like Senator Joseph McCarthy to call into question the country's manhood.[2] Furthermore, postwar jitters over masculinity coincided with the mounting concerns over juvenile delinquency. As Reinemann made clear, teenage boys channeled their anxieties concerning the draft and military service into antisocial behavior, ranging from vandalism to murder. In doing so, they undermined a long-standing connection between militarism as a rite of passage for boys. Masculine traits of bravery, valor, and patriotism figured heavily in twentieth-century gun culture, while automobiles connoted a man's mobility, independence, and technical prowess. Now, hot rods and hot rodding became hallmarks of juvenile delinquency as boys shirked their obligations and directed their energy into a devil-may-care, "last-fling attitude."

Child experts and the public fretted over this development in youth culture.[3] As Reinemann pointed out, the past fifteen years took a toll on the family. On the same day that Reinemann testified, Judge Herbert Millen, an associate judge with the Philadelphia Municipal Court, also testified for the subcommittee, tracing the upswing in problematic youth to a general moral decline that originated with parents from the past: "Since the war and since the depression, these parents presently are the products of that, and there was a gradual letdown. After any war it seems to me that there is a gradual letdown in the moral strata of a community."[4] Millen singled out the "heavily populated districts which are crowded." Cities, Millen implied, were breeding grounds for gun violence and road-raging teenagers. Left unstated was that the recently ended Korean War could lead to another decline among jaded parents and their children.

Within this context of moral panics and lingering war jitters, social guardians actively refashioned children as citizen-soldiers by redirecting the conversation around guns and cars. As Millen asserted, part of the fault lay with poor parenting; those who went through the Depression and World War II were now determined to maintain their current, more prosperous standard of living. In doing so, parents neglected their offspring. The chairman of the subcommittee, Senator Robert C. Hendrikson, put it bluntly: "War uproots the family, usually."[5] But just as drag racing and gangsterism could corrupt urban youth, these subcultures, under proper guidance, could acculturate them. That the Senate subcommittee turned their attention toward popular culture and pointed fingers at show business showed that Hollywood, the longtime whipping boy for corrupting children, remained on the front lines. For their part, the movie industry cashed in on screaming headlines of youth run amok (figure 15). Hollywood's exploitation of the front page under the veneer of providing a public service only raised the ire of social guardians who called the industry out for making bucks off the bangs of gun- and car-crazy kids.

Kids and crime did not mix in the movies. Pictures like *Wild Boys of the Road* (1933) showed youth in political, social, and moral revolt, but the strengthened Production Code explicitly laid down the law: "Pictures dealing with criminal activities in which minors participate, or to which minors are related, shall not be approved if they incite demoralizing imitation on the part of youth."[6] During the latter Depression and war years, the Production Code censors diligently kept kids clean on the silver screen and prevented "demoralizing" messages from seeping into impressionable tykes in the dark. When reviewing *Boy Slaves* (1939),

FIG. 15 Ripped from the headlines. In this detail from *Johnny Holiday*'s (1949) pressbook cover, the star (Allen Martin Jr.) contemplates his exploitation as a sign of the times. (Author's collection.)

for instance, Joseph Breen cautioned RKO that, even when striking out for freedom, these underage outlaws had to obey a strict hands-off policy for guns. Breen sweated bullets with an on-screen tally: "Only two shots will be fired by the boys, and at no time will the boys be actually shown firing guns. We feel this is important, particularly from the standpoint of political censorship generally, as any use of fire arms by boys, or adolescents, is extremely questionable. Unless this scene of violence is kept down to the absolute minimum necessary to carry the story it may make the whole picture unacceptable."[7] No matter that the boys targeted abusive camp supervisors who beat and starved them or that their shots went wild. The sight of juveniles taking aim at authority figures during the Depression raised red alerts. Accordingly, RKO producer J. R. McDonough agreed: "All business of the boys shooting at anyone was eliminated. The only shots fired now come from offstage and only from the men surrounding the house."[8] While scrubbing a firefight between bad adults and desperate kids potentially lessened the film's punch, McDonough, like Breen, preferred to avoid a public backlash over arming children.

With the industry under public scrutiny for supposedly undermining the family through scandal and subversion, studios closely supervised bad boys through militaristic appropriation on hot rods and firearms. Police and civil defense stood ready to turn speed demons in *The Devil on Wheels* (1947) and *Hot Rod* (1950) into proud citizen-soldiers, while strong father figures in *Johnny Holiday* (1949) and *The Gunfighter* (1950) steered boys from crooked paths to become figurative straight shooters.

A Detour into Kids and Cars

"Our best bet is the boy," one bicycle manufacturer proclaimed in 1888. The bicycle industry, regaining a second wind after the initial fad faded among adults, found a marketing angle by passing the bike off as an eternal rite of passage among children.[9] For the boy, the bike connoted power and independence from his parents. Bikes enabled boys to exercise and find jobs as couriers and spurred their interest in mechanical experimentation as they customized and maintained their bikes.

The bike segued to the first autos. Fittingly, the film *The First Auto* (1927) featured a young man who leaves his father's horse carriage shop to build roadsters. Early racing pictures, such as *Speedway* (1929), *The Crowd Roars* (1932), and *High Gear* (1933), emphasized how men of good character and unwavering discipline possessed the requisite sobering minds and quick reflexes to finish in first place, impressing sons and younger brothers alike. Car sales and hot rods already signified social mobility and status during the 1920s and 1930s. As one historian notes, car manufacturers did not produce an economy-sized "depression car," but instead promoted installment plans and installing luxury add-ons to existing models to persuade consumers they were getting more value for the same price.[10] Nevertheless, the Great Depression stalled car consumption as people turned back to bicycles. One reporter commented on the increasing number of cyclists: "If you look closely you will see that the bike boom began in 1931, the bluest of the depression years," as consumers started cutting back on gas and garage expenses.[11] But the automobile remained a staple in American life; one 1935 survey noted that over three-quarters of respondents affirmed the car as a necessity, while one cheery report even claimed that "the automobile is actually pulling America out of the depression."[12]

While the car industry may have fantasized about singlehandedly wheeling in prosperity, the wishful thinking conveyed the automobile's high position in the public imagination, especially among youths. Many boys were too young and too poor to own cars, but they could satiate their inner speed demons and fulfill their impending manhood by building substitute roadsters. *Boys' Life* asserted that "keen American boys who are sportsmen enough to have a will to win and a smile should they lose" could direct their energy and knowhow toward soap box racers.[13] The "All American Soap Box Derby," the magazine contended, was "the greatest competitive event offered the American boy," in which the child customizes a basic model while following official "Rules and Regulations."[14] The car made the man; the design work and craftsmanship became bragging rights and signaled maturity for the studious, industrial youngster. In 1930, General Motors inaugurated the Fisher Body Craftsman Guild, a corporate educational club for teenage boys to hone their automobile know-how. The guild started as a competition for boys to build Fisher's signature Napoleonic Carriage models, but soon expanded so boys could design and construct original automobile models from scratch. The prizes consisted of college scholarships ranging into the thousands and, more importantly, the promise of a bright future from hard times.[15]

The automobile signaled a filmic boy's coming of age. In *Wild Boys of the Road*, the boys tearfully sell their beloved roadster to ride the rails across the country. In Carvel, Andy Hardy bonds with his car as much as he does with his father (figure 16). He struggles to come up with the twelve-dollar down payment for a wreck (*Love Finds Andy Hardy*, 1938). He remains at risk of losing his wheels as he persuades his father he is mature enough to drive and maintain it. In later installments, Andy cautions his sister to be careful with his clunker as he lacks auto insurance ("Good News of 1939," 1938), tempers his dreams about buying a new car in an economic downturn ("Andy Hardy's Dilemma," 1940), pays off the balance (*Judge Hardy and Son*, 1939), and sells it (*Andy Hardy's Double Life*, 1942). The troublesome jalopy finally finds a permanent owner in *Andy Hardy's Blonde Trouble* (1944). In the Depression, Andy's car and money troubles were hardly unique, but he has the requisite happy endings under his father/judge's sound advice. The judge rewards his son's high school graduation with a new Plymouth convertible, equipped with an automated top. Andy was growing up and moving up.

Most boys did not have it as good as Andy. The masculine attributes of auto racing and car ownership could guide boys into becoming responsible men, as Andy learns, or they could lead kids astray. The two were not mutually exclusive. During the Roaring Twenties, speed demons, customizers, and carjackers got their thrills from eluding the police.[16] But the Depression frustrated teens

FIG. 16 Man to man to wheels. Andy Hardy (Mickey Rooney, right) and his dad (Lewis Stone, left) have one of their "famous 'man-to-man' talks right on the running board of Andy's jalopy," reads the accompanying snipe, while flexing their mechanical know-how in *Judge Hardy and Son* (1939).

from following their tracks. In 1941, "Coffin on Wheels," an episode of MGM's *Crime Does Not Pay* series, warned youngsters about unscrupulous car dealers who gave bargains too good to be true. Tommy (Tommy Baker) thinks he landed a great deal on a coupe, but does not realize the shady salesman lined the brakes with asbestos. Tragically, the brakes fail at the pivotal moment and Tommy ends up in the hospital while his younger brother (Darryl Hickman) ends up in the titular coffin. Other boys were not willing to bargain or count pennies, as Tommy did. Instead, they stole cars for fun or profit.[17] As the press noted, these maladjusted youths ended up behind bars, in the reformatory, or dead on the streets.[18] Even in Carvel, children were victims of careless drivers, and teenagers—like Marian Hardy's boyfriend Jeff (William Lundigan)—drove while intoxicated, leaving Judge Hardy in *Andy Hardy's Double Life* to sort out the emotional and legal issues. In any case, cars—and their symbolic speed, status, and independence—were the manly stuff of dreams. When Andy graduated high school in *Andy Hardy's Private Secretary* (1941) and audiences ogled at his new convertible, *Variety* predicted a backlash. "The final and complete junking of Andy's streamlined jalopy roadster in favor of a new model runabout with push button toplifter might prove disconcerting to many youths who have followed young Andy's auto experiences in previous pictures. But Andy's blossoming forth with a new car will also give the kids plenty to worry about."[19] Fans may mourn the loss of the decrepit lemon whose "adventures" they followed for several years, but, as the trade journal hinted, Andy's new Plymouth would take its place among car-crazy kids. Andy's penchant for trouble would certainly drive future plotlines involving maintaining, damaging, or wrecking the vehicle.

After World War II, prosperity enabled suburban Americans to not only consume new cars but hop them up for added horsepower. In 1947, the same year that *The Devil on Wheels* premiered, *Popular Mechanics* informed young readers, "Winning the 1947 All American Soap Box Derby is not just something to dream about—it's going to be done by some boy with ingenuity, initiative, skill, designing ability and a willingness to compete with the best the field has to offer in a spirit of four-square sportsmanship and fair play."[20] These male attributes rendered auto racing and car ownership as a boys-only club. The first hot rod organization, the Southern California Timing Association (SCTA), explicitly "discouraged the weaker sex from racing the souped-up cars," *Popular Mechanics* reported, leaving in the organization only one woman—the wife of a record holder and whose duties included editing their monthly magazine.[21] In films like *The Devil on Wheels*, a teenage hot rod club refuses to admit girls even as spectators for fear that their loose lips would expose their illegal street racing. In *Hot Rod*, girls are mischievous enablers, urging boys to show off, which leads to crack-ups. The male domain of automobile know-how even made for novelty sales gimmicks; poverty row studio PRC used gender reversal ballyhoo to produce and promote *Blonde Comet* (1941, about a woman race car driver) and *Danger! Women at Work* (1943, a wartime comedy about female grease monkeys and truckers). But aside from novelty acts and parodies, the automobile was a manly art.

While boys took to joy riding and racing as a form of self-expression, as they did with makeshift soap boxes and clunkers, the resulting traffic tickets, smash-ups, and fatalities led naysayers to regard the postwar hot rod as a dead end for youth socialization. A car gave its owner mobility, but the immature boy made for a poor driver. As the American Automobile Association stated in 1948, "show-off and childish driving of any type" made for reckless driving and reflected badly on the "sportsmanlike" character of the man behind the wheel.[22] Critics pointed out how reckless adults passed their habits to their kids. To address these concerns, studios released shorts such as MGM's Oscar-nominated "Traffic with the Devil" (1946), in which LAPD officer Charles Reineke describes how rude and careless driving killed over one hundred people and injured twenty-four hundred others per day. Speeders, tailgaters, horn honkers, distracted drivers, and confusing traffic signs all contributed to road-kill pedestrians and smash-ups. Vivid newsreel footage of roadway carnage and hospital infirmaries confirms his points. "Stopping cars won't stop reckless driving," the sergeant admits. "That's up to the driver, and too many had to learn the hard way."[23] Learning the hard way became plot boilers like *The Devil on Wheels*, while *Hot Rod* centered on the father-son generation gap behind the wheel.

Postwar Hollywood continued to depict the relationship between a boy and his wheels, in which youngsters came of age via automobile culture. Historian Gary Cross observes a class divide when it came to cars, with wealthier kids driving new vehicles and "greasers" and working-class youths customized hand-me-downs and jalopies.[24] However, on film, the "hot rod" epidemic applied to all boys in the form of unchecked masculinity run amok. Filmmakers jumped in; *Film Daily* declared the "irresponsibility of kids at the wheels of stepped-upped cars is something that must be curtailed" as immature boys "sport around with girls, all for male vanity."[25] Male vanity was a cross-generational issue. In *The Devil on Wheels* (1947), young Mickey Clark (Darryl Hickman) wonders, "What's the use in hopping up a car if you can't ever give it the gun?"[26] Mickey's gunning the throttle stemmed from his dad's bad behavior. His dad, John (Damian O'Flynn), resents his wife's backseat nagging and disregards speed limit signs. The elder Clark's repeated insistence that he has driven for twenty-five years points to his maturity during the 1920s and 1930s. Like *Any Number Can Play*'s Charley Kyng, John Clark is confident and brash, but while Kyng's casino worked within the law and benefitted his community through taxes, Clark elided his responsibility. Moral decay seeped into their suburbia through alcoholic neighbors (Breen ordered their removal, complaining that liquor was "unnecessary for the telling of this story and therefore cannot be approved under the special regulations re[garding] drinking and drunkenness in motion pictures"), hints of teenage sexuality, and, of course, road rage (figure 17).[27] John Clark's blindness to his own poor driving habits was a sign of a failed man, now transferred to his son.

Mr. Clark's hypocrisy reflects the car as an agent of masculine socialization. On the surface, he acts the part of a responsible citizen and father. He allows Mickey to buy and work on a hot rod, just as kids built soapbox racers for the past two decades prior, but he refuses to let the boy race in unsupervised, unregulated roads. His justification: he knows that every boy needs a car, but he draws the line at illegal speeding. Clark also sees cars as status symbols; his dialogue suggests that once wartime rationing ended in 1945, Clark signed up on a wait list for a new car, even though he could not afford it. Two years later, his new coupe arrives—and he promptly gets into a fender bender. When he witnesses an accident in which a reckless driver kills his own daughter, Clark readily volunteers to testify before the police. "For the sake of other children!" he snarls in righteous anger, before proceeding to weave, tailgate, and hog the road.[28]

The law catches up to the wayward Clarks. Mr. Clark gets in an accident with the local judge and then mouths off at him. For his part, the judge, like Andy Hardy's father, shows leniency and understanding and lets Clark go with a suspended sentence. Clark promptly considers himself exonerated and remains a public menace on the streets. Mickey gets in worse trouble; in the climax, his

FIG. 17 Teenagers' (left to right: Sue England, Darryl Hickman, Jan Ford, and Robert Arthur) need for speed in *The Devil on Wheels* (1947) leads to crack-ups, death, jail time, and psychological scars. Here, the kids contemplate breaking into a morgue after hours to identify a friend who died in an accident. (Author's collection.)

roadster's smash-up kills his best friend and leaves his mother in critical care. The glum ending, with Mickey facing time behind bars and his mother hospitalized, not only leaves the family torn apart but also deprives the Clarks of their car keys.

Not all the Clark males are car fiends. Mickey's older brother Jeff (James Cardwell), a navy graduate who flew fighter planes during World War II, is the family's moral center. Mickey worships Jeff; the film's first line has Mickey praising Jeff's automobile know-how ("My brother Jeff says that new camshaft will give me a higher lift valve"), and Mickey impresses his girlfriend with Jeff's war tales "that will curl your hair."[29] Jeff's maturity manifests in filmic tropes; he holds a fatherly pipe (but never puffs), is soft-spoken, and is girl shy. He attributes his careful driving to his military discipline and training, and he occupies a middle ground between his father and the law, urging Clark not to settle fender benders with brawls. Jeff's law-abiding do-goodery becomes formalized as he woos the judge's daughter, of whom Mr. Clark eventually approves. Jeff serves as a stabilizing force for the family, staying calm under fire; when Mickey starts sobbing after his big accident, his brother tells him to rein in his emotions: "You've got to be a man!" Likewise, when Mr. Clark considers banishing his youngest son, Jeff tells him to cool down lest he do something he regrets. He chastises his dad's failed masculinity through a misuse of automobile enculturation: "You were one of the best fathers two boys ever had. You gave us everything we ever wanted. Bought us cars when you couldn't afford them. Taught us how to drive them. Told us all the things we shouldn't do, told us over and over again. And then went out and did those things yourself. Mickey believes in you. You're a great guy to him. Who could be more right than his old man?"[30] A bit old-fashioned, Jeff is uneasy with Mickey's expertise in the opposite sex, but while he is a bit colorless compared to his kid brother, Jeff's wartime experiences make him a mechanic and the moral center for the family.

Mr. Clark's failure to raise his boys correctly reflected Hollywood's stance on juvenile delinquency. The industry deflected public criticism from the movies by targeting misguided institutions. In the postwar years, a deluge of letters flooded the Motion Picture Association of America (MPAA), complaining about the perceived moral downfall in movies. Hot topics such as divorce worried producers like Ranald MacDougall, who defended the industry with pictures like *The Decision of Christopher Blake*. One concerned moviegoer, Mrs. Esther Hart, pointed out other worrisome issues, such as rampant drinking, smoking, and lovemaking, which, among other supposed "low standards" long prevalent in the movies, perverted Hollywood from becoming "good influence for young people."[31] She bluntly stated, "Boys and girls as well as adults must be taught the right way to live thru motion pictures and the home."[32]

MPAA president Eric Johnston forwarded Hart's letter and other complaints to the Production Code Administration for responses. Joseph Breen signed his name to a generic form letter, stating the industry was doing all it could to clean up its act while delivering top-notch entertainment. Breen also addressed specific points of contention, reminding adults that they, like John Clark, had parental duties. "The motion picture screen is always a red herring for problems of this sort, and merely saying that there is a connection between movies and juvenile delinquency does not make it so," he lectured Mary W. Robinson after she complained about the usual gruesomeness being shown to innocent children. "We do not claim that all pictures are fit subject material for children," Breen continued. "Some pictures by their very nature are mature in theme and as such are directed at an adult audience." Faulting adults for not employing viewer discretion when advised, he concluded that the family unit should not use Hollywood as a babysitter. The Production Code Administration did not, and should not, "police the theatres"; rather, family togetherness began at home.[33]

The failure of the family unit, Breen lectured, created juvenile delinquency. "It is, unfortunately true that young people seem to resent authority nowadays," he acknowledged in 1946, "but I wonder if the motion pictures are to blame, or is it the parents again?" Breen elided the generation gap from the interwar period, which studios had readily presented on the silver screen. Rather, Breen deflected the issue from the legacy of the Lost Generation and wild boys toward long-lived social institutions, especially the beleaguered household still reeling from over a decade of social and economic turmoil. Children, Breen continued, who are "taught a proper respect for authority at home, at school, and in the churches, would take little harm from what is presented on the picture screen in this respect." While he did not have all the answers, Breen suggested people should "allocate the source of juvenile delinquency to where it belongs."[34] He meant the decline of civic values came from the home, not the movies.

As in *The Devil on Wheels*, Breen praised the law not only for serving and protecting, but for recognizing where the true blame lay. He informed one critic that J. Edgar Hoover "has studiously avoided mentioning the motion pictures, while pointing the blame at the home, the school, the radio, and other familiar sources" that cause delinquency. For good measure, Breen added that the "same thing is true of [Attorney General] Tom Clark in his several recent important utterances."[35] Through Breen, the industry used the law—and wise veterans such as Jeff Clark—to project their pictures as civically responsible. In early 1947, after a year of answering letters, Breen testily told the representative of the Washington State Federation of Junior Women's Clubs, "So many people write to us complaining of the undesirable effects of certain films on children, without exhibiting any willingness on their part to take action in the matter themselves."[36] With the war over and economic prosperity—which allowed children and their parents to buy and service cars—seemingly at hand, it behooved them to live up to their civic and familial responsibilities.

In *The Devil on Wheels*, Mr. Clark accepts blame. Inspired and humbled by Jeff's admonishment, Clark delivers a courtroom confession: "I am equally guilty as my son. I set him the example. I gave him 'good advice.' But like so many parents, I seldom practice what I preached. Why is it that the best of us become greedy, bullying beasts the instant we have the power of a hundred horses in our hands? The power for good, for progress? Why do we use it to cause fright and unhappiness? To main and to cripple? To kill?"[37] Clark's questions go unanswered, but he learns, too late, that a vehicle connoted a man's power and position in society, but only in the hands of mature men who did not have a "last fling" attitude. Lacking Jeff's discipline and restraint, Clark pays the price and literally loses his family.

The judge agrees. He tells Clark, "I wish it were possible for you to share the legal responsibility of this charge."[38] But Mickey bears the brunt of the law alone and, hopefully, will emerge from his sentence a more mature man. In this regard, Mickey's prison time is a blessing in disguise. The final shot flashes forward in time, and a recovered Mom Clark sits behind the wheel, picking up her son from prison. Her husband, riding shotgun, enthuses that Mickey took his sentence "like a man." But for the Clark patriarch, old habits established after twenty years of driving die hard. He starts complaining that this "snail's parade" will prolong their one-hour trip to the jailhouse to three. Mrs. Clark chastises her husband, saying Mickey will not mind waiting.[39] The boy's patience outpaces his father's, as Mrs. Clark reiterates how she has repeatedly admonished her husband for micromanaging her driving. Clark continues to gripe until a police siren wails in the background. He closes his eyes, remembers the past hour of cinema time, and tells his wife to take it easy as the screen fades. The devil may no longer be behind the wheel in this household, but the traffic cops know that many more families will succumb to temptation.

The heavy-handed preachment resonated with the public. *Variety* optimistically noted the production "rates strongly as exploitation subject and accomplishes its goal—namely to make audiences conscious of the peril of such hopped-up autos" and the "current hot-rod craze among juv America which is causing so many thousands of deaths annually."[40] But *Motion Picture Daily* found the picture more than a blanket condemnation of unruly boys. The picture provided "welcome relief from the jive-talking youngsters who have only dares and dates in mind." While the reviewer found the flimsy plot inconsequential, the message rang clear: "Suffice it to say that the youngsters of the town, with their home-built autos, are a problem and that the parents, in their own laxness, are responsible in part for consequences."[41] The Clarks' suburbia was no paradise, with plenty of blame to go around.

Authority figures like Jeff Clark helped guide a younger boy's automobile enculturation, but mixed signals from peers and parents might compromise the youngster. Mickey tries to obey his father's command about not racing, but his girlfriend openly compares Mickey's reluctance with his military brother, who has "courage and guts and everything." Mickey, full of hero worship, tries to follow Jeff's image, which leads to trouble. Even lawmen might err in their good intentions. *Hot Rod* (1950) shows speeding *can* be channeled into civic duty. However, an intolerant Judge Langham (Art Baker) associates hot rods with murder; a quarter of his court cases involve teenage speeders. Like Joseph Breen and Judge Latham, Langham attributes delinquency to parental failure. He admonishes two aged mothers for their teenage sons' driving habits: "You parents may well be grateful that today you attend a trial instead of a funeral. Court adjourned!"[42] According to Langham, hot rods wreck families, turning kids into liars and sneaks. This includes his younger son, David (James Lydon), whom Langham allows to buy a car to deliver newspapers but is insulted when David hops it up behind his back. David taunts his dad to keep an open mind when his father clearly has no interest in doing so. Although he briefly considers sponsoring a speedway in the Los Angeles desert for teenagers to race the clock rather than each other, he concludes that "such hot rods have no place in our community!"[43] Cut to a crestfallen and shamed David.

David proves the adults wrong. The film's opening narrator contextualizes David's point of view, telling audiences that "real" hot-rodders consider their craft "educational as well as exciting." Stock footage shows SCTA experts testing and timing cars in the desert. A narrator notes that SCTA members even hated the term "hot rod" due to the public stigma. The SCTA no doubt appreciated this cinematic boost; as one media report claimed, "Traffic police, educators, social workers, and juvenile authorities are behind hot-rod racing—properly controlled and regulated. It's a fine outlet for youthful drive and enthusiasm. And in the mass-produced world of the future, young minds and hands that understand machinery will be a valuable asset to the United States."[44] Such authoritative views were embodied by David's brother, Joe, a police officer who—like Mickey Clark's navy vet sibling—tells his father to be "sensible" over the hot rod issue. Joe winks conspiratorially to David, arguing, "Racing by the clock has been approved by every police department I know of."[45] But their close-minded father refuses to listen.

The judge changes his mind when David's speed racer catches a hightailing burglar in a Cadillac. Officer Joe joins his kid brother as they speed down rural Los Angeles without having to worry about pedestrians, other vehicles, and gunfire. Cut to a full police escort taking David home. The cops approach His Honor and—in a long shot out of earshot—persuade Langham that speeding pays. The judge accepts his mistake, and a fade-in shows him breaking ground on Langham's Straightaway Hotrod Heaven. The police and kids cheer, and David enthusiastically kisses his girlfriend to end the picture. By making hot rodding acceptable under adult purview, David wins his love interest from a rival hot-rodder, Jack (Tommy Bond), and romances her under his dad's watchful eye. The studio's synopsis cheekily commented, "Once influenced by Jack's racy hot rod, [she] now has attention only for David."[46] Like Mickey Clark's girlfriend, who had taunted him into speeding, David's sweetheart also encouraged him to "open it up" when he plods along at thirty-five miles per hour on suburban roads. Now, the teens can go the distance under the eye of the law.[47]

The Devil on Wheels and *Hot Rod* tell similar stories, even using the same footage of aged jury-rigged Depression-era jalopies speeding past a motorcycle cop. "This is similar to *Devil on Wheels*. Business and comments on it were both good," reported one Arkansan exhibitor.[48] Both films show adults who fail to practice what they preach or preach too hard. PCA censor C. R. Metzger summarized the message for *The Devil on Wheels*: the judge and John Clark "realize that older people are to blame in part for the troubles of the younger people."[49] The movies did not blame car manufacturers; after all, the public had long regarded cars as essential in times of depression, war, and peace. Judge Langham says as much ("Automobiles, yes; hot rods, no!") and divides respectful from reckless driving. When David openly reads a hot rod magazine, his father does not opt for censorship, since "I never heard of anyone being killed by a magazine."[50] For his part, David declares the magazine is clean-cut: "They only deal with legal hot rod racing." The only problems were those on either side who went too far. *Variety* approved how the "hot rod driving by the nation's teen-aged mechanically minded" now do so under adults who "supervise of timing tracks, where youth can work off its penchant for speed, rather than use city streets or highway with accompanying danger to all motorists."[51] An Iowan exhibitor agreed, calling the picture "a natural for any town or any place. We had to cancel this

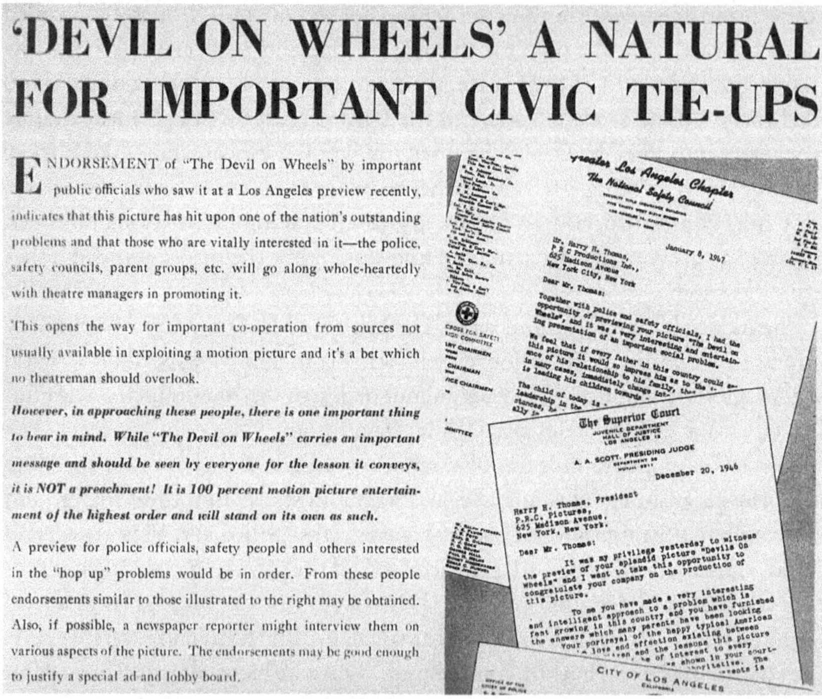

'DEVIL ON WHEELS' A NATURAL FOR IMPORTANT CIVIC TIE-UPS

ENDORSEMENT of "The Devil on Wheels" by important public officials who saw it at a Los Angeles preview recently, indicates that this picture has hit upon one of the nation's outstanding problems and that those who are vitally interested in it—the police, safety councils, parent groups, etc. will go along whole-heartedly with theatre managers in promoting it.

This opens the way for important co-operation from sources not usually available in exploiting a motion picture and it's a bet which no theatreman should overlook.

However, in approaching these people, there is one important thing to bear in mind. While "The Devil on Wheels" carries an important message and should be seen by everyone for the lesson it conveys, it is NOT a preachment! It is 100 percent motion picture entertainment of the highest order and will stand on its own as such.

A preview for police officials, safety people and others interested in the "hop up" problems would be in order. From these people endorsements similar to those illustrated to the right may be obtained. Also, if possible, a newspaper reporter might interview them on various aspects of the picture. The endorsements may be good enough to justify a special ad and lobby board.

FIG. 18 Seal of approval for *The Devil on Wheels* (1947), bestowed by officials in Los Angeles for turning speed demons into responsible drivers. PRC ballyhooed these testimonials in their press book. (Author's collection.)

one out before, and I ran into a lot of trouble with the public, so it was rebooked fast. This is one of the best pictures I've seen come from Monogram, and you won't go wrong on this one, as business was way above average."[52] Such high demand paid off; the National Safety Council credited radio, magazines, and movies "with a safety theme," singling out "Traffic with the Devil" and *The Devil on Wheels* for reducing traffic fatalities.[53] Studios quickly exploited such praise in hopes of selling their films as a makeshift public service. In Los Angeles, a successful preview led to endorsements from the city's Superior Court and various officials on the "reckless youth" and their joyriding—the colloquialisms, the testimonials, and the exploitation angles of entertainment and education date back to the car-crazy Lost Generation (figure 18). Journalists also lauded responsible hot rod clubs, like the Kegs in Southern California, who defied the stereotype of "crazy kids driving through town." Mickey Clark and David Langham lament how parts are scarce, and the Kegs dared not risk their $1,500 investments. Rather, the club stressed responsible driving, no traffic tickets or "rowdiness and horseplay."[54] Incorporating kids' hobbies into the grown-ups' expectations led to safer results.

Some civic guardians went further, deputizing speedsters as part of civil defense. Filmic authority figures, like Joe Langham and Jeff Clark, recognized the attributes of hot rods, and real-life civic officials considered recruiting would-be delinquents as junior lawmen. One California proposal suggested enlisting hot rod racers as part of a Highway Patrol Corps, where they would "be used primarily to handle traffic in an evacuation," or "man the patrol's radio network 24 hours a day and provide a motor pool and messenger service." Their youth, energy, and stamina "for long hours on duty in all kinds of weather" made them prime military material.[55] By 1955, the Senate subcommittee investigating juvenile delinquency learned how local communities successfully made hot rods mainstream. "As a last resort we dropped the idea of trying to 'beat' the hotrodders and decided to 'join' them, gain their confidence, and by so doing lend responsibility to their sport," one civic official testified. "The alliance between the police and hotrodders has caused the young drivers to use more consideration in their driving habits toward the public, and the public has responded by taking a keener interest in the hot-rod program." The result: Sunday drag races "on a well laid-out, properly-supervised drag strip," just like Langham's Straightaway Hotrod Heaven.[56] Under the SCTA, the police, or civic authorities, the hotrodders followed the law. Adult and government approval rendered car customization an acceptable and safe hobby under the auspices of family togetherness.

Suburban kids sped for fun and exercised their mechanical know-how, but their urban counterparts saw cars as vehicles to escape city blights. One 1949 study observed that "to a slum boy, a car represents something mighty remote, like a hundred-dollar bill or a cruise to South America." The urban environment enticed kids to simply escape: "What harm in borrowing it for a while, ditching it when the gas runs out?"[57] The kid's rhetorical thinking leads to a life of crime. Those who lacked proper guidance, such as "slum kids" who presumably had poor family environments and no outstanding older cop-brother, channeled their car craziness into becoming big shots. For wannabes who had delusions of grandeur, car culture coincided with shooting their way to the top.

Gunning Down Delinquency

Like car culture, gun culture had a close relationship with boyhood during the postwar juvenile delinquency scare. As with automobiles, this relationship grew out of decades of militarism used as a socializing agent to usher boys into manhood. Guns, proponents claimed, empowered boys to release their natural aggressiveness and served as a rite of passage to protect their families, country, and patriotic values. As with cars, controversy abounded. Critics contended guns contributed to the country's growing urban crime rate, and parents expressed alarm over their children's war games, toy pistols, and, of course, the "inappropriate" movie content reinforcing this culture.[58]

Two films highlight this relationship between boys and firearms. Pictures such as *Johnny Holiday* (1949) featured good male role models who instruct boys to bolster the arsenal of democracy. As with the case of hot rods, cooler heads who worked in law enforcement or the military prevailed in teaching younger boys to partake in the masculine traits of self-reliance, individualism, and patriotism. Movies contesting this ideology, notably *The Gunfighter* (1950), fared less well. These films drew upon militarism from the Depression and World War II as a defense mechanism to train youth as citizen-soldiers. Magnified by the Korean War, gun culture eventually coalesced around anticommunism as the primary threat to the United States.

The issue of masculine social "decay" worried reformers, educators, and the public throughout the nineteenth century. Industrialization and urbanization reduced men to emasculated wage slaves, critics alleged, which led to alienation and criminality. In response, social reformers, especially Progressives, romanticized farm labor and the "strenuous life," as Theodore Roosevelt phrased it, in rural environments to build children's morals and physiques.[59] Early prolabor movies directly reflected these concerns, with factories transforming bright-eyed youngsters to downtrodden laborers, prone to disease, disfigurement, and early death.[60] Other films showed the moral "ruination" that befell naïve youth who mingled with the wrong crowds. The first all-talkie film, *The Lights of New York* (1928), ended with a disillusioned cop telling an ingénue and her beau to trade the Big Apple for the great outdoors. The youngsters respond, "We'll fly!"[61]

Child savers promoted country living and its accompanying strict discipline and regimentation to rehabilitate criminal boys. For instance, the Indiana Boys' School—the setting for *Johnny Holiday* (1949)—dates its origins to 1867 as a "House of Refuge" for delinquent youths.[62] In the early 1900s, paramilitary groups like the Boy Scouts, with their ranks, uniforms, and rituals, reminded members of their civic duties as citizens and as men. Concurrently, early twentieth-century education experts, such as G. Stanley Hall, believed raising boys was an evolutionary endeavor, in which a child grew up physically and mentally to attain the highest level of manhood. Americans subscribed to a popular belief in a global social Darwinist hierarchy of races and nations, and Hall advocated that rigid discipline could channel a boy's natural primitivism and aggression into service for the state. Fittingly, Hall singled out military schools, with their marching and drilling, as "a great promoter of national health and intelligence."[63]

However, not everyone lauded the connections between firearms and children. Social critics claimed fascination with guns led to desensitized, violence-prone kids.[64] Congress passed the first federal gun control measures in 1927 to limit access to mail-order pistols, and again in 1934.[65] During Prohibition and the Depression, reformers worried over children growing up with the wrong impression about weapons. As social order tottered, gangsters became working-class folk heroes who rose to the top. Movies like *The Public Enemy* (1931) and

Manhattan Melodrama (1934) opened with impoverished boys who shoot their way through competitors and lawmen to hit the big time. Guns and cars went hand in hand; from 1930 to 1933, Hollywood released seventy-eight gangster pictures rife with car chases, drive-by shootings, speedy getaways, and other automobile tropes connoting the corruption and fast living of city living. A year later, the genre halted due to a public outcry fueled by the Legion of Decency, which led to the enforcement of the Production Code.[66]

In 1934, coinciding with Prohibition's repeal, Hollywood's Production Code censors deglamorized the gangster. However, the industry relied on firearms as visual props to intensify drama, and opted to retool guns to emphasize law and order. Notably, the tommy gun became an exclusive weapon for law enforcement personnel.[67] J. Edgar Hoover jumped in, promoting government agents, the "G-men," to co-opt the gangsters' fan culture. In 1937, the FBI director told parents "to let children play with toy guns."[68] In a publicity stunt, he also gave Shirley Temple a toy machine gun so America's Sweetheart could yield deadly force under proper guidance, namely, the nation's top lawman.[69] Hoover's savvy inspired a generation of "Junior G-men" in movies, radio, comic strips, and pulp novels, which legitimatized gun usage for kids through patriotism and heroism.[70] This cooperation between Hollywood and the bureau enabled Joseph Breen to cite Hoover when deflecting claims that the movies corrupted kids. Accordingly, guns alone did not create juvenile delinquents, and there was no such thing as a "bad boy," to paraphrase Spencer Tracy's Academy Award–winning portrayal of Father Flanagan in *Boys' Town* (1938). The filmic Flanagan knew little tough guys merely needed good guidance to transform into idealized citizens. Boys who resisted positive influences—such as Mike Davis (Darryl Hickman) in *Fighting Father Dunne* (1948), another biopic about a child reformer—inevitably landed on Death Row. More positive cinematic gangs, like the urbanized "Dead End" kids, morphed into clean-cut stars in "reform school" pictures by battling crooked politicians and celebrating their working-class, ethnic heritages.[71]

Reformers believed sending boys and young men away from crime-littered cities to the "great outdoors" symbolically and physically revived their civic pride. During the Depression, work camps for young men echoed this discipline, hard work, and spiritual rejuvenation.[72] The New Deal's Civilian Conservation Corp channeled this ideology for restless men who had slim job prospects. One former "roving boy" and CCCer even named Franklin Roosevelt his "all-time hero" for taking "a multitude of young men off the road and keeping them on the straight and narrow." He added, "We were under military discipline. When World War II came, we made good soldiers."[73]

World War II heightened the patriotic gloss concerning gun culture and militarism. After the Japanese bombed Pearl Harbor, many boys revised their Christmas wish lists to include military hardware and accessories to avenge their country's honor and dead, replacing conventional toys.[74] In 1943, President Roosevelt praised the Boys' Clubs of America for their work as Victory Volunteers.

"I have always advocated the plan of citizenship training sponsored by your organization through its programs of physical training in the manual arts," the CCC founder proclaimed, especially when the country was "beset with enemies who would destroy our way of life and who would destroy us."[75] The Boy Scouts continued to do their part, earning Marksmanship Merit Badges, and Winchester's 1944 "Every Boy Has His Hero" campaign applauded boys for "writing new and unforgettable chapters in the moving history of America."[76] "On guard for America since 1866," the company's motto boldly proclaimed, connecting its past with "the historic Seventh of December," and former scouts who, as men, mentored the current scouting generation.

American demobilization did not end military preparation. The Truman administration proposed universal military training, in which all teenage boys, upon turning eighteen, would undergo one year of basic military training.[77] Secretary of State George C. Marshall called the program part of the "democratic traditions," with citizens actively engaged in the country's defense.[78] Echoing the rhetoric of the Civilian Conservation Corps, Marshall advocated a "school of democracy" to foster strict discipline and skills for survival.[79] The advent of atomic weapons escalated the stakes for preparation.

Universal military training failed. The proposal stalled under President Dwight Eisenhower, who thought the program too costly, and his "New Look" prioritized air power over ground troops.[80] Universal military training also reminded critics of a Nazi-styled "cheerful obedience to the will of the leader."[81] Opponents contended the army "*is no youth movement*" designed to teach kids how to "clean their teeth [or] do 3rd grade arithmetic" because "the meaning of true discipline [came from] our homes and our schools."[82] While critics conceded youth needed strict guidance, they wanted parents, not the army, to impart these civic values.

The outbreak of the Korean War on June 25, 1950, heightened the tensions over manhood and militarism. The United States "lost" China to communism in 1949, and the country dared not "lose" Korea as well.[83] But civic leaders wondered if American GIs could contain communism, citing how World War II recruiters rejected high numbers of draftees due to psychological and mental immaturity.[84] In 1950, with the country once again in combat, reports warned about an emasculated "creampuff army" due to the "babying of soldiers."[85] As the so-called police action dragged, opportunists, notably Senator Joseph McCarthy, mugged the cameras. According to McCarthy, emasculated troops reflected incompetent, weak-willed men in the State Department. He singled out Secretary of State Dean Acheson, whom McCarthy branded a "pompous diplomat in striped pants with a phony British accent," as if the secretary snobbishly took on foreign airs.[86] McCarthy's self-aggrandizement at the expense of the top echelons of government reflected the intersections between masculinity and militarism, now retooled for anticommunism.

The potential "delinquency" of government officials reinforced the need for proper male role models to guide boys into American manhood. This fear complemented the reformation of the nuclear family. The movies promoted fathers who surmounted the hardships of the past two decades, such as *Any Number Can Play*'s Charley Kyng, as ideal masculine figures to mentor their sons. Gun culture, like automobile culture, enabled boys and fathers to bond. In 1946, child expert Dr. Spock told parents not to worry about their boys play acting and "shooting you dead." The lad is "just passing through the necessary stages in the taming of his aggressive instincts that will make him a worth-while citizen."[87] The film *Johnny Holiday* (1949) drew upon this legacy of militarism and gun culture to address postwar delinquency.

Johnny's Country Holiday

Roland W. Alcorn wanted to make a movie. Alcorn, a former juvenile delinquent and reform school graduate, made a fortune in South American and Kansan granaries before his thirtieth birthday. He envisioned a biopic based "on my experiences as a boy in reform school—the Indiana Boys' School in Plainfield, Indiana."[88] Alcorn invested one million dollars and dedicated his film "to the youth of America."[89]

As a novice to Hollywood, Alcorn quickly learned he could not simply produce a film about a "fallen" boy who makes good. The topic of juvenile delinquency had hurdles; the *Hollywood Reporter* noted juvenile delinquency stumped producers who wanted to punch up their melodramas: "First, because people don't like to be preached to, and, second, because unless the subject is handled with intelligence and restraint, something very hard or very maudlin is inevitably the result."[90] Producers balanced sentiment and violence; even the word "delinquent" connoted crime. In 1946, RKO producer Dore Schary planned a film tentatively entitled *Delinquent*, and he turned to local policemen for advice because many movies "have appealed to sensationalism and have lacked the objective educational point of view that is important when approaching this kind of problem."[91] Even with his precautions, the MPAA cautioned Schary that titles could not "be sensational or attempt to cater to an irresponsible audience" for it could "quite easily lend itself to the sort of exploitation that gets the industry into trouble."[92] Forewarned, Schary dropped the project.

In contrast, Alcorn depicted a real, successful reform school. A guest appearance by Indiana's governor lent authenticity, not exploitation.[93] The biopic's happy ending (as evidenced by Alcorn's example) and a Christmas sing-along from popular songwriter Hoagy Carmichael reinforced the family-friendly tone. Most critics approved; *Variety* noted the film avoided the "preachment" stigma with a "warmly human picture that will send the customers home in hearty agreement with the Abraham Lincoln–inspired theme 'A man who never made a mistake never made anything.'"[94] The trade journal later clarified its initial enthusiasm: "Its grosses potentially in the key city first runs is [*sic*] dubious, but it will undoubtedly score in the subsequent runs and the sticks." The reviewer believed "tie-ins with the public schools, PTA, etc., should be naturals."[95] The trade journal's observations reflected the movie's theme; only "in the sticks"—the same rural and small-town theaters that embraced *Hot Rod*—would boys find rehabilitation from the corrupt city.

A training camp "in the sticks" reflected the old belief of a controlled primitivism, where boys' "natural" ruggedness flourished under adult guidance. The Civilian Conservation Corps, and paramilitary institutions in general, lingered in public memory as an effective means of checking delinquency. "The boys who were in the CCC became happier men, better citizens, better workers, and better soldiers because of their CCC experience," recalled one newspaper reader, fretting over the "shocking accounts" of "criminal gangs of boys and girls" in "crowded city areas."[96] The reader proposed a federal "Conserving American Boys" movement in which "good citizenship should prepare the boys for military service."[97]

Johnny Holiday thus draws from decades of urbanization, youth crime, and militarism. The film opens with a noir-esque urban night scene that *The Window*'s Tommy Woodry would find familiar. Here, in an underworld of squalor and vice, children become budding criminals. Older teen Eddie Dugan (Stanley Clements) and his younger accomplice, Johnny Holiday (Allen Martin Jr.), fence hot goods to Eddie's father, Barney (George Cisar). Barney Dugan suspects the boys of holding out and roughens them up. Eddie responds by drawing a gun on his father.

Even in the opening, the behind-the-scenes interplay reflected the issue of gun culture, boyhood, and delinquency. The Production Code Administration's chief censor, Joseph Breen, calmly explained to the rookie filmmaker their responsibilities as purveyors of public taste: "It is not good, we feel, to suggest on the screen that a sixteen-year-old boy would threaten his father with a gun. We must ask that there [*sic*] use of a gun be eliminated entirely in these scenes—possibly some less lethal prop could be substituted which would suit the purposes of your storyboards. Further, the brutalizing of the boy [Johnny Holiday] by Barney is unacceptable and would have to be toned down considerably."[98] A father as criminal accomplice was objectionable itself, but Breen allowed the minor character to remain. Nor did he mind young Dugan threatening his father for dramatic purposes. However, he drew the line at giving Eddie a firearm with which to do so.

Alcorn insisted on staying "true" to his life story. PCA staffer M. E. Hohenfield summarized a "lengthy discussion" and "a number of alternate suggestions" with associate producer Frederick Stephani before they agreed Dugan would "merely reach for a gun, but before he could get his hands on it, Barney, the boy's father, would grab him." Hohenfield clarified, "At no time would Eddie actually have a gun trained on his father." Perhaps sensing Eddie's inability to directly threaten his father lacked drama, Stephani opted to dump the gun entirely, "provided it would be acceptable for Eddie to draw a knife on Barney. We told him that, under the circumstances, this would be acceptable."[99] A knife was certainly lethal, and the PCA routinely urged caution for knife fight scenes, but the censors compromised. Given a choice, they selected knives as the lesser evil.

The authorities catch Johnny and send him to Indiana Boys' School. A kind of summer camp in the bright outdoors, not unlike Roosevelt's CCC, the reform school has a machine shop, a shoe shop, a bakery, and, for Johnny, a farm to revitalize his masculine virtues.[100] "Life in the reform school never looked more inviting," the *New York Times* observed, pointing to the fenceless, "rolling, green country," unbarred windows, and how "occupational therapy is liberally and wisely employed."[101] The boy wises up when a gruff ex-cavalryman, Sergeant Walker (William Bendix), takes a shine to him. Walker's military credentials affirm him as a good model to reform undisciplined boys, and he has his old service revolver and Jeep as reminders of his authority. Employing a "soft touch," Walker assigns Johnny to a mare, Nellie, and the boy falls in love with the animal (figure 19).

Walker's giving Johnny an animal rekindles the boy's own humanity. Indiana Boys' School's country setting and working farm aligned with child-rearing.

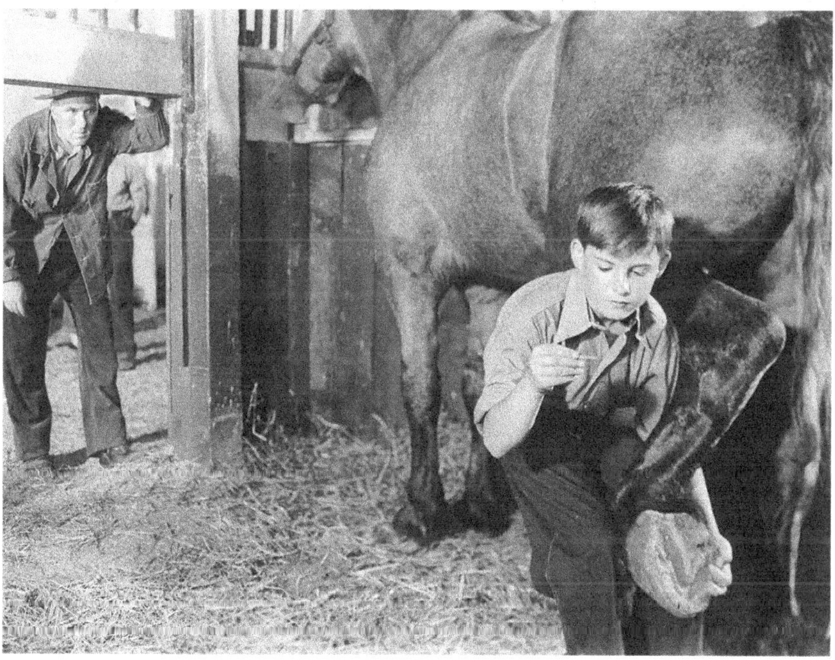

FIG. 19 My friend, Nellie in *Johnny Holiday* (1949). A juvenile delinquent (Allen Martin Jr., right) finds redemption by looking after his horse. A father figure (William Bendix, left) watches the boy's rehabilitation. (Author's collection.)

In the nineteenth century, middle- and upper-class reformers established humane societies to care for neglected waifs and dumb animals alike, hoping to rehabilitate what they perceived as moral decay as the United States industrialized. Stories like *A Dog of Flanders* (1872; filmed 1924, 1935) sentimentalized children and pets by playing up purity and innocence in rustic settings. Dogs, like the various "Petes" in the *Our Gang* shorts, got into mischief alongside their owners, while horses in *Thoroughbreds Don't Cry* (1937), *Stablemates* (1938), *National Velvet* (1945), *The Red Stallion* (1947), and *The Story of Seabuscuit* (1949) gave disillusioned teenagers of both sexes chances to make good, riding their steeds just as their suburban counterparts maintained and drove cars.

Animal companions enabled the innocent children to mature. "Today, most boys, sooner or later, own a dog," *Boys' Life* informed its readers in 1947.[102] The magazine provided tips on house-training puppies and teaching dogs to have good etiquette inside and outside the home. The reward for dog socialization: the Dog Care Merit Badge, equating canine care to civic duty. "He can help you to add another Merit Badge to your sash," the magazine gushed, in which a boy would sew the patch alongside his marksmanship badge. "What a pal!"[103] Even without merit badges, children "palled" around with pets. Novels from *My Friend Flika* (1941; filmed 1943) to *Old Yeller* (1956; filmed 1957) and *Where the Red Fern Grows* (1961; filmed 1974) depict children entering adulthood by raising, then burying (or preparing to bury), their pets. Movies starring Lassie (starting with *Lassie Come Home*, 1943) or Rusty (eight films between 1945 and 1949) and shorts like "A Boy and His Dog" (1946) showcase the closeness between boys and pets. The dog allows the kids (including girls, as in *A Boy, a Girl, and a Dog*, 1946) to find a place in their otherwise unfriendly families/communities made up of overly stern fathers, unsympathetic mothers, and indifferent townsfolk.

In the end, the pet is a catalyst to the boy's reconciling with his community, transferring his sense of responsibility to civic duty (and, presumably, owning a car). The boy completes his entrance into manhood by sacrificing his pet. He mourns but accepts his tragedy. For instance, in *The Yearling* (1947), young Jody (Claude Jarman) executes a beloved fawn to save his family's crops. As MGM's synopsis notes, "Forced to kill his pet, Jody runs away from home, to return after suffering, grown a man in spirit."[104] Throughout the late 1940s and 1950s, films such as *The Sun Comes Up* (1949) and *Good-bye, My Lady* (1956) use separation as the climax; the latter film's theme song, "When Your Boy Becomes a Man," confirmed the point.

Nellie also makes Johnny Holiday grow up. The horse's pregnancy excites Johnny, and he eagerly awaits her colt's birth. The boy's relationship with his horse takes an appropriate military slant. Walker wants to name the colt after World War I general John J. Pershing. Johnny prefers a contemporary reference, "Eisenhower." Getting into the spirit, Johnny drills with the other inmates, wearing uniforms and shouldering rifles. When Indiana governor Henry F. Schricker drops by, the boys parade in his honor. Schricker tells them this strict discipline "should and I know will, make good citizens of all of you. When you leave here, your slate will be clean."[105]

Schricker's message of mixing militarism with the creation of good citizenship reflected World War II patriotism and the popular memory of the CCC camps. Although the CCC ended in 1942, as early as 1944 officials considered reviving the program for demobilized troops to boost employment and promote "the interest of national defense," the *Washington Post* reported.[106] A permanent CCC would maintain national parks and ensure "adequate supplies of lumber and pulp wood should another war develop."[107] This connection between paramilitary camps, national interests, and citizenship continued throughout the postwar period, and guns played a central role in this association. In 1948, *Boys' Life* featured advertisements for "A Complete Home 'Shooting Gallery,'" promoted as "safe fun for the kids."[108] Toy ads and television shows relayed how military hardware toughened boys to defend democracy on the home front, in the "wild frontier," or in outer space via ray guns.[109]

In *Johnny Holiday*, the Indiana governor's speech also sets up Johnny's fall in the second half of the film. During the parade, the police bring in Eddie Dugan. The school's matron calls Eddie a "bad boy" beyond redemption. Since Hollywood shied from depicting innately "evil" children, the resident psychologist corrects her: "No, he's a sick boy" with a "big shot complex."[110] Eddie's urban "big shot complex" defies the rural rehabilitation and good parenting. As a "big shot," the teenager feels he has no need for a father figure, and this delusion renders him a "sick boy" in the eyes of experts. Indeed, when Johnny first spots his former mentor while parading for Governor Schricker, he distractedly breaks formation and trips over his rifle. Eddie grins in victory and Sergeant Walker groans in embarrassment. For his part, Eddie resents the gruff, but loveable, ex-cavalry sergeant for rehabilitating Johnny, and he tries to murder Walker before Johnny's eyes.

Walker himself wrecks his relationship with Johnny when Nellie has complications giving birth. The sergeant chooses to save the newborn colt rather than lose both horses and shoots Nellie with his service pistol. To Johnny's horror, Walker not only kills a defenseless animal, but his use of lethal force against a boy's best friend undercuts the societal expectations of an officer's duty to serve and protect. Nellie's death is the most violent scene in the film. This betrayal drives Johnny from Walker completely.[111]

Eddie exploits Johnny's trauma to accelerate his great escape. His breakout includes taking everything Walker values: "Walker's car, Walker's boy, and Walker's gun."[112] By stripping the sergeant of his masculine attributes—his army weapon, his military transport, and his symbolic son—Dugan compounds Walker's failure to redeem Johnny and pervert the state's arsenal for criminal purposes (figure 20). Eddie forces Johnny to hotwire Walker's car, as he plans their getaway. Although the film does not establish if Eddie drives, the casual reference to Johnny knowing how to hotwire a car speaks to automobile know-how

FIG. 20 Urban corruption in *Johnny Holiday* (1949), as Eddie Dugan (Stanley Clements, left) plans to take Walker's (William Bendix, center) gun, car, and boy (Allen Martin Jr., right) to the city. (Author's collection.)

among the juvenile set. Audiences readily accept that Johnny knows his cars. A concerned Joseph Breen, worried that savvy kids in the audience might get some ideas, even recommended the "actual details of what Johnny is doing to the car should be masked from the audience."[113] Fittingly, Eddie gives Johnny the tools to tinker with the car rather than do it himself: "Whatsa matter, you ain't forgotten how to make a connection, have ya? Do it!"[114] Eddie's lack of mechanical skills underscored his immaturity. Unlike teenagers Mickey Clark and David Langham or prepubescent Johnny, Eddie's delinquency had no redeeming values. The Dugan household was marked by theft, a failed father, and casual violence. Eddie hopes to fulfill his "big shot complex" by taking Walker's masculine attributes as his own, and take the car, gun, and boy to the corrupt big city. Walker intercepts the two boys, and in the final showdown, Johnny spurns Eddie and calls for help. Eddie turns the gun on Johnny, but Walker goads the big-shot wannabe into plugging him instead. The good inmates burst in and haul Dugan away.

Dugan stealing Walker's gun and shooting the ex-sergeant gave the Production Code Administration pause. Joseph Breen approved various incarnations of good guys—lawmen, GIs, and cowboys—who used guns effectively while the villains often missed or superficially wounded their targets. Relegating the "bad guys" to poor shots saved the lives of filmic heroes and robbed the villains of their masculinity. Their failed socialization included an improper introduction to guns and their inability to defend themselves, and the bad guys always lost.

When Ronald Alcorn wanted Eddie to fire six bullets into Walker, Breen balked. The censor condemned the shooting, even for melodrama's sake. Even though Eddie stood point-blank next to his target, Breen refused to allow him to hit Walker, writing, "We cannot approve having the boy deliberately pump six bullets into the man. Some means will have to be found to limit this to one or two." To make the point clearer, Breen wanted to remove the "juvenile delinquent" aspect entirely, recommending "in all seriousness that this boy [Eddie] be older than sixteen. This, in our opinion, is most important."[115] Dugan's final age remains undisclosed, although actor Stanley Clements's moderately hairy chest connotes an older age than the script's designation. PCA censor M. E. Hohenfield confirmed Alcorn's agreement to tone down the climax: Dugan "will not actually pump six bullets into the man; five of the shots will go wild, the sixth will hit and wound Walker."[116] Even though he is a legal-aged adult, Dugan's poor shots demonstrate his lack of maturity, and his downfall is swift. The final scene shows a scrubbed-clean Johnny thanking a cane-wielding Walker—the sergeant's injury in the line of duty gives his wound a heroic air. The boy promises to drop by and care for his colt, Eisenhower. As he departs, a new kid with a surly attitude enters Indiana Boys' School. An exasperated Walker appeals to the heavens: "Here we go again!"[117]

Walker's last line underscored boyhood socialization as a protracted process. Eddie Dugan failed to appropriate the retired sergeant's boy, car, and gun for criminal purposes. Still, reformers worried, without a good adult's guiding hand (i.e., not Eddie's father), boys, guns, and cars contributed to delinquency. Eddie's poor aim demonstrates how Hollywood symbolized immaturity. But outside theaters, naysayers feared trigger-happy kids could develop "big shot" complexes and defy adult efforts to discipline them.[118] One news report called the toy pistol an "equalizer," meaning the child, "in his imagination, [is] on a par with an adult world that is forever telling him what to do and what not to do."[119] For delinquents with delusions of grandeur, the "equalizing" agent of guns refuted the moral outlook father figures upheld. Fathers, too, might deem the links between firearms and children corrupting. *The Gunfighter* (1950) presented one such troubled father who believed gun culture turned kids into hounded outlaws. The movie's disappointing box office returns suggest the public disapproved of revisionism of gun culture and its ties to social maturation as the United States entered the Korean War.

Addressing Gunfighters and the Cowboy Mythos

Johnny Holiday presented Indiana Boys' School as a microcosm of the "good" reform schools. However, gun culture and youth socialization extended beyond the social woes surrounding urbanization and industrialization. Rather, the public read gun culture in the fabric of American history, especially the "Wild West." The western frontier reigned in the public imagination as a refuge where boys underwent the "strenuous life" and transformed their soft city bodies into hardy men. Popular amusements capitalized on dime novels, circus acts, and Wild West extravaganzas, where Manifest Destiny played out before audiences. The West took the form of rugged cowboys, dashing cavalry officers, daring outlaws, and even women sharpshooters who "civilized" the wilderness from "savages."[120] During the Great Depression, cowboys championed individualism, self-reliance, and folksiness on par with the pioneers they protected.[121] Antagonists came in the form of outsiders: Native Americans, Mexican bandits and outlaws, and bankers—the latter, corrupt "money-men" from the East, resonated with Depression-era audiences.[122]

Westerns enjoyed greater popularity during the postwar years.[123] The everyman cowboy continued into the postwar period as gunslingers championed family, hard work, community, and private property as the traits that tamed the American frontier, and which delinquents like Johnny Holiday came to value in rural boys camps.[124] In 1950, a poll conducted among boys listed the western as their favorite genre, capturing 36 percent of the vote, with 25 percent favoring comedies and 18 percent preferring mystery/adventure tales. The "average boy attends motion pictures approximately once a week" or "3.6 times a month—and enjoys Westerns more than any other type of film fare." The article used these statistics as a guide, noting "movie attendance has slumped off appreciably since the advent of television," which also had an abundance of westerns.[125]

Gun culture, as a historic force in the American western mythology, became a source of stability during the postwar years. Studios relied on these high-noon showdowns as low-cost, bankable sources of income, accounting for nearly a quarter of films in 1948.[126] In 1947, film critic Leonard Spinrad, looking back at the genre's evolution, observed that westerns, "expressed in simplest terms," highlighted "Good meets Evil, Good fights Evil, Good beats Evil."[127] Gun enthusiasts connected this moral maturation with the rustic frontiers of the past. In 1950, *Boys' Life* sponsored a Daniel Boone Target Shoot, where Scout Troops or members of the National Rifle Association's Junior Rifle Club showed off their marksmanship and won rifle accessories.[128]

Firearms figured heavily into this youth socialization, but as the negotiations between *Johnny Holiday*'s production team and the Production Code Administration showed, gun culture remained controversial. As postwar concerns over juvenile deviancy escalated, lurid headlines added to the anxiety.[129] In 1947, Albert B. Hines, executive director of the Madison Square Boys Club of New York, stated, "Delinquency has changed for the worst."[130] Tracing juvenile delinquency from the club's founding in 1884, Hines observed that "physical violence has decreased while stealing with guns has increased."[131] In 1952, psychologist Vera Emanuel saw a correlation between letting children pump an "enemy full of lead," even in play acting, violence in the media (including "casual gun talk"), and the country's rising crime rate.[132] Some law enforcement officials agreed, noting clever teenagers modified cap pistols to shoot real bullets.[133] Gun culture, they argued, contributed to delinquency, not thwarted it.

Films critiquing gun culture as a form of youth socialization played into this controversy.[134] Twentieth Century-Fox's *The Gunfighter* (1950) explicitly challenged gun culture and the hailed image of the mythic heroic cowboy. The plot, loosely based on real-life "bad man" John Ringo, presents Jimmie Ringo (Gregory Peck), a weary figure who wants "to forget his sanguinary past" as a "top gun."[135] Outdrawing him becomes the "top prize" for fame among young, trigger happy teenagers. Ringo tires of these fame seekers hounding him and yearns to settle down with a schoolmarm wife, a white picket fence, and a quiet life with their son. Unfortunately for him, "the young, foolish 'squirts' in every bar-room won't let him peruse his peaceful way" because they all want the honor of killing Ringo.[136] Producer Darryl Zanuck hoped this reversal of the heroic lone cowboy trope would spark box office revenue, by placating critics who blamed movies for encouraging violence and attracting fans wanting more than singing cowboys and simple plots.[137] He believed the movie had the potential of a "real classic" by turning the gunslinger into a "pathetic figure of a lonely man who realizes his mistakes too late in life and tries in vain at the last moment to free himself from the mess of his own making."[138]

Ringo's son Jimmie (B. G. Norman) plays the most crucial part in this revisionist narrative. All the kids idolize Ringo, and Jimmie has bragging rights when he learns the famous gunman is his father. Ringo rejects the kids' enthusiasm and promises the boy's mother their son will not follow in his footsteps. The Production Code's film synopsis notes that when Jimmie asks his father to name "the toughest person he ever met, Ringo names [the sheriff], since he wants the child to get the right impression about outlaws," namely, killers like himself.[139] Ringo further orders Jimmie to keep his distance and to clear out other congregated youngsters "hoping to catch a glimpse of the famous killer" from the grounds where the film's anticipated showdown will take place.[140] Young Jimmie does so, using his newfound authority as the famed outlaw's son to carry out father's wishes.

The idea of a disenchanted gunslinger telling his son not to follow his footsteps challenged the conventional western. Zanuck stressed Ringo's disdain for gun fighting would generate buzz: "It will probably startle and horrify certain dyed-in-the-wool Western fans who expect Roy Rogers to end up harmonizing with Burl Ives but these are the very things that will make it great."[141] Zanuck deliberately countered the "folksy" cowboy with historical accuracy. Some reviewers also appreciated the preaching against guns; the *Los Angeles Times* reported Peck's "moralizing" speech at the end, where a lifetime of gun-slinging inevitably leads to death, "is not too hard to take."[142]

Unfortunately for Zanuck's hoped-for profits, *The Gunfighter* did not connect with audiences. Another critic for the *Los Angeles Times* explained the "novel

FIG. 21 $25,000 error in the making in *The Gunfighter* (1950), as Gregory Peck hoped to go for realism in the Old West, but audiences refused to accept his mustache or his message. (Author's collection.)

idea" of a gunfighter's regret was "precisely its weak point."[143] The "tall, gaunt, very convincing gunfighter" who refuses to fight flew in the face of audience expectations and their perception of cowboys as historic figures and as role models for boys. Ringo did not even play a role in his son's upbringing; the boy did not even know his father's identity until Ringo identifies himself. In hindsight, Zanuck recognized he violated too many motifs and moviegoers, mainly women, hated the aesthetics of a peace-toting gunfighter, symbolized by Gregory Peck's walrus moustache. Zanuck recalled women complaining, "If they wanted an ugly man, why didn't they take an ugly actor? Why waste Peck?" He later sighed, "I would give $25,000 of my own money to get that moustache off Peck."[144] For his part, Peck said the mustache was his effort to make Ringo "like the people in daguerreotypes of the early West" (figure 21).[145] But audiences rejected this revisionism, clearly preferring the "handsome" heroes in the mythic West, even if this image flew against historic authenticity.

Even worse than Peck's facial hair, *The Gunfighter* premiered two days before North Korean troops crossed the thirty-eighth parallel.[146] With headlines about "pampered" soldiers and wishy-washy statesmen, coupled with the lack of immediate military success, the film's message went against public sentiment right

FIG. 22 Wannabe in *The Gunfighter* (1950). Surly teenager Hunt Bromley (Skip Homeier, center, standing) wants to be the top gunfighter of the Old West. Ringo (Gregory Peck, seated left) would gladly give him the title. (Author's collection.)

when Americans worried over the fate of the free world. Ringo's ideology clashed with the cowboy's and the country's mythology as a protector of innocent townsfolk. Instead of Ringo drawing his six-guns in a thrilling climax, he lectures his young son about the evils of being a "tough guy." He then plans to settle down in domestic bliss rather than ride off into the sunset.

Even in retirement, Ringo fails. A teenage gunslinger wannabe, Hunt Bromley (Skip Homeier), shoots him in the back just as Ringo prepares to flee. Bromley, like *Johnny Holiday*'s Eddie Dugan, has a "big shot complex" and sees gun play as his claim to fame just as Eddie wanted ex-sergeant Walker's gun, car, and Johnny. The gunslinger, tired of facing young "squirts," tells Bromley the image the teenager subscribes to is that of a "cheap, no-good bar-room loafer."[147] Hunt is initially not a delinquent; regardless of his surly personality, he breaks no laws until he murders Ringo (figure 22). When the teenager shoots the gunfighter, he takes his place, becoming the same hounded gunslinger. In *The Gunfighter*, justice and retribution did not come from the law, but from wannabes bumping each other off. Indeed, the sheriff, whom Ringo told his son was the "toughest guy" he knows, does not arrest Hunt, but kicks Bromley out of town to meet his fate. One reviewer commented on the "irony of [Ringo's] situation," noting "his reputation as bad man supreme" made every "happy young trigger finger full of bravado and ready to take him on" to be like him.[148] Gun culture, the film implied, made for a lifetime of loneliness.

Audiences rejected the message alongside Peck's ugly mustache. The picture earned above average grosses in the first run market, but the returns disappointed Zanuck, given the production's budget and big-name stars.[149] He called the premiere "miserable" and predicted Peck would help "make a profit although not as much as *Yellow Sky* (1949)," a more traditional and violent western he produced two years earlier (also starring Peck), but he thought was inferior.[150] He attributed the lower earnings to the violation of "so many true Western traditions that it goes over the heads of the type of the people who patronize Westerns, and there are not enough of the others to give us the top business we anticipate."[151]

Zanuck's observation was correct. The long-lived legacy of the western hero, from tall, silent horsemen to guitar-twanging singing cowboys, dominated the public imagination. Attempts to alter this narrative met resistance. One critic sarcastically predicted the "members of the Society of the Preservation and Promotion of Western Pictures" would form a posse to stop further pictures of the sort. *The Gunfighter* "is so subversive to the whole way of life that has been developed so beautifully by the cowboy pictures that it threatens to overthrow the concept of pioneer Western life as handed down by our fathers." The critic thought the movie "may alienate a large segment of the nation's moppets," even if serious adults might appreciate the unusual story line.[152] In 1947, one naysayer even dared to suggest violent westerns contributed to delinquency, and Joseph Breen shot her down cold: "We thoroughly disagree with you that cowboy pictures make murderers of our young boys. We think that this is a gross overstatement of the facts and would like to invite you to prove your claim. I am sure you cannot, not even remotely."[153] A confident Breen based his claim on his job as a diligent protector of public taste and the reputation of the cowboy as an outstanding pioneer and lawmen. When the mustachioed Ringo said otherwise, western fans worried the film alienated the "moppets," and the public went up in arms.

The theaters were caught between Zanuck's message and the wary public. One showman thought the film was a "small town natural" simply because it was a western, but another noted it lacked "the hard-rising, fist-fights, and gunplay that the ordinary western has, but when things do happen, they happen fast." The exhibitor stated his audience appreciated the novel ideas about a disillusioned gunfighter, but he was "sorry to say that I just broke even on the show."[154] Another exhibitor added, "My only comment on this picture is that it is different from the superwesterns," although this "difference" did not pay: "we did below average business on this one."[155] Another described *The Gunfighter* as "a western with a good moral and suspense but not much action. It is not worth anywhere near the top bracket that I paid for it."[156] He concluded with a warning to Twentieth Century-Fox to stop "misallocating pictures" or skip his Lansing, Iowa, location altogether.

The Gunfighter's debunking a glorified gun culture did not appeal to audiences during the Korean War. At a time of crisis, moviegoers wanted a renewed commitment to hard masculinity, which gun culture provided during the Depression (with cowboys as the symbols of individualism and patriotism) and World War II. For some critics of gun culture, this glorification of firearms amounted to a conspiracy between the media and government. One critic in the journal *Film Sense* pointed out how "the films of violence and sadism" met "with the needs of the Defense Department, the State Department, and the industrialists who benefit from a staggering 'defense' budget."[157] Accordingly, the "Mickey Spillane mentality on celluloid" desensitized moviegoers to the horrors of atomic war.[158]

But the real world mandated vigilance and preparation for such horrors. As the Korean War progressed, Americans emphasized the connections between guns and youths with appropriate adult supervision. American psychiatrist and father Sidney Green countered Vera Emanuel's "foreign" interpretation of gun culture with a male, native-born perspective. Green claimed that "the emotionally healthy child who plays at killing with guns today is pretty sure to grow into a considerate adult, a person who uses good judgment and restraint with an irritable boss and who can control his temper when everything goes wrong."[159] Guns helped build character, just as militarism did for CCC workers in the Great Depression and Ronald Alcorn / Johnny Holiday in Indiana Boys' School, or, by extension, law enforcement did for speeders. Green, like Dr. Spock, argued boys used guns to release their natural aggression; the boy who blasted make-believe villains had a fantasy safety valve should an "irritable boss" make unreasonable demands.[160]

More important, guns protected the nation and its ideals from harm. Ringo made his son vow not to take up firearms, but the Korean War and anticommunism made this promise seem shortsighted. *The Gunfighter* took place in the mythic West, but in contemporary melodramas, the average American family also recognized the necessity of firearms, should dangers surface. The Korean War represented such an outside threat. Rather, the tensions concerning delinquency from earlier decades played out in the Korean War.

Soldiering On

Hollywood had a mixed relationship with firearms and automobiles. Throughout the twentieth century, guns and cars gave boys a sense of power and mobility they otherwise lacked. But for critics, family crack-ups during the Depression and World War II led directly to juvenile delinquency in the form of smashed cars and itchy trigger fingers. Even amid postwar prosperity, father-son relations remained strained, leading to mismanaged upbringing for children. Boys wanting to ascend into manhood only became juvenile delinquents; in quiet suburbs, hot rodding turned boys into devils on wheels, speeding down streets and mowing down pedestrians. Other boys saw guns as a means to garner respect and power. *Johnny Holiday*'s Eddie Dugan wanted to steal Sergeant Walker's boy, car, and gun to satisfy his "big shot complex." He failed because, as the Production Code Administration insisted, the bad guys were not real men.

Reconciling automobile and gun cultures for youths remained an issue in the postwar years. The specter of communism threatened to upend the stability of American life, including education. As the House Committee on Un-American Activities made clear, the commies planned to take a child "from the nursery, put him in uniform with the hammer and sickle flag in one hand and a gun in the other, and send him out to conquer the world."[161] American boys needed to step up as citizen-soldiers, if and when the "red" invasion occurred. Guns served to toughen a boy to resist such mental infiltration. Cars, under the right guidance, turned boys into agents of civil defense.

Cars and guns remained ubiquitous in the movies. Drag racing, from Poverty Row productions like *Born to Speed* (1947) to the more prestigious *Rebel without a Cause* (1955), spotlighted the hot rodding subculture that had captivated boys since the days of the horseless carriage. Like youngsters and their roadsters, firearms became familiar accessories for screen kids. In *Close to My Heart* (1951), one beleaguered dad wonders why anyone would want kids, as his three boys shoot up the living room with cap pistols, screaming bloody murder. *The Trouble with Harry* (1955) had Arnie's (*Leave It to Beaver*'s Jerry Mathers) play-time shoot-'em-ups introduce the story about a lively corpse, while *On Our Merry Way*'s (1948) Edgar Hobbs (Donald Whorf) terrorizes two conmen with a BB gun. In *Cause for Alarm!* (1951), Hoppy (Bradley Mora) imitates his namesake Hopalong Cassidy to compensate for his emasculating eyeglasses and suburban life. *Little Fugitive* (1953) centers on a boy who thinks he shot his brother and flees to Coney Island. At the end, the lad casually shoots blanks at the TV screen. More notably, *Suddenly*'s (1954) pacifist mother learns that guns are essential to safeguard liberty and should therefore allow her young son to have toy pistols. When a disgraced GI sharpshooter becomes a mercenary and tries to assassinate the president of the United States, mother and son pick up arms and end the threat. The ubiquity of toy guns in the movies and daily life could create a blasé parental attitude. In 1954, one parent noted not every kid who played with a gun "will grow up to be either a cop or a criminal."[162]

Even though some parents seemingly shrugged off firearms, their presence in the public and popular culture stemmed from decades of social messaging. In the postwar years, advocates of gun culture and militarism looked to the past. These eras included the Old West, "child-saving" scout programs in the 1910s, "junior" G-men and work camps in the Great Depression, and the patriotism during World War II. Delinquents like Eddie Dugan or wannabes like Hunt Bromley represented failed men. Without a father figure, the troubled boy—budding delinquent Johnny Holiday or firearm fan Jimmie Ringo—might fall into delinquency as well. Along the same lines, misguided fathers, such as bad driver John Clark or stubborn Judge Langham, could inadvertently fuel their sons' car craziness, leading to smash-ups. Thankfully, elder sons who faithfully upheld the law had the foresight and discipline to correct their fathers and the younger brothers. As the postwar period entered the 1950s, gun culture and car culture centered on communism as the threat to the social order.[163]

The "reds" were not the only source of social agitation in the late 1940s. The civil rights movement challenged the reconstruction of white, middle-class stability. The *New York Times* noted civil rights leader A. Philip Randolph demanded complete desegregation in the armed forces to "prevent negro draftees from entering into a campaign of civil disobedience."[164] When President Harry Truman ordered army desegregation in 1948, ROTC programs incorporated African American enlistees. The *New York Times* explained, "More Negro youths may receive the military training and acquire benefits from such training."[165] Militarism socialized African Americans in the same manner as white delinquent boys, soothing the uneasiness such racial agitation generated. The next chapter looks at the end of the postwar "social message" race cycle through the lens of American boyhood.

4

Whitewashing the Race Cycle in 1949

In 1949, MGM lined up three race-centered movies. One project, *Lost Boundaries*, based on William Whyte's account of Dr. Albert Johnston and his family "passing" as white in a quiet New Hampshire hamlet, did not make the cut. MGM shelved the story due to budget concerns and because it had already greenlit "two films already dealing with other Negro questions, *Intruder in the Dust* and *Stars in My Crown*."[1] The three pictures also shared a central theme: white (or light-skinned) boys coming to grips with racism in their communities.

An independent production company, Film Classics, picked up *Lost Boundaries*. Whyte's book focused on the teenage son's identity crisis, and while the film broadens the plot to include the parents and their white community, the boy's story arc remained central. Although the teenager abandons his upper-middle-class community for the urban slums to experience "black life," he eventually accepts that his life remains the same. Screenwriter Charles Palmer stated the teen's new outlook "has the glimmering of a realization that his life isn't exactly down the drain, that perhaps he can live as a colored man and get something out of it." Despite this message, Palmer avoided the label "race picture" because "sociologists who hope to see it come out as a clinical study of the racial problem. Audiences will not go to see a picture of that sort. This must be the story of a <u>man</u>, who happens to be a negro." Palmer even suggested classifying *Lost Boundaries* a "spy" thriller, situating one man "among enemies, where one false move may bring ruin," or a "blackmail" plot involving a "guarded secret." Either way, "this sort of picture will be more powerful than a clinical study. And it will be entertainment."[2] From a censor's standpoint, Joseph Breen found the picture "reasonably free from any likely difficulty from the standpoint of political censorship."[3] He thought it "contains little, if anything, to which anyone might find offensive."[4]

Breen was wrong. After an initial run in the northern circuit, *Lost Boundaries* made its way south. Notorious censors who had long resisted pictures with race themes banned the movie. In Atlanta, censor Christine Smith bandied her authority to protect the public from material that "adversely affect the peace, health, morals, and good order of the city," in this case, blacks passing for white.[5] Her Memphis counterpart, Lloyd T. Binford, found the film's blurring racial boundaries a form of "social equality between white and Negroes in a way that we do not have in the South."[6] In an interview with *Variety*, the eighty-year-old Binford "exploded" with rage, calling the "lead character, a Negro passing as a white, was an imposter and a liar. The people of his New Hampshire home town resented him until the minister in the film smoothed it over."[7] Binford's comment wryly turned the film's tagline against itself; lobby cards had invited audiences to see the "lie" unfold on-screen (figure 23). Film Classics attempted to overturn Binford on First Amendment grounds, but the Tennessee Supreme Court refused to hear the case and the ban remained.[8]

FIG. 23 Liars not allowed in the South. Memphis censor Lloyd Binford banned *Lost Boundaries* (1949) with the excuse that blacks who passed for whites were immoral liars. In this lobby card, teenager Howard Carter (Richard Hylton) reconciles his skin color with the content of his character. (Author's collection.)

Binford's and Smith's outrage toward *Lost Boundaries* demonstrated the resistance toward Hollywood's cycle of social messaging. This chapter looks at MGM's two other pictures, *Intruder in the Dust* (1949) and *Stars in My Crown* (1950). Made concurrently, the films feature white boys responding to racism in their small southern towns. *Intruder in the Dust*'s financial failure and *Stars in My Crown*'s monstrous success highlight audience apathy regarding civil rights and Hollywood's withdraw from activism. Like Binford, one civic group, the Citizens' Councils, viewed civil rights as an attack on "southern values" and worried over the "softening" of children's sectional pride due to "integrationists" and "race-mixers."[9] This fear of children overturning the status quo led the public to reject *Intruder in the Dust*, in which a white teenage boy does just that. In contrast, *Stars in My Crown* used nostalgia and a revised historical narrative, especially post-Reconstruction, to present a "true" solution to racism, one rooted in small-town solidarity, simplicity, and religiosity. *Stars in My Crown* garnered public and critical acclaim and, by appealing to mainstream white sentimentality and downplaying civil rights activism, reinforced the hardening stance against communism.

Intruder in the Dust and *Stars in My Crown* complicate the traditional narrative surrounding Hollywood's brief social message cycle after the Second World War. Historians traditionally point to World War II movies as the catalyst for this genre by promoting an idealized racial "melting pot."[10] Compared to the rhetoric of the "master racists," Hollywood ballyhooed the ethnically diverse casts of studio-made combat units as microcosms of democracy. Army segregation notwithstanding, interracial camaraderie among celluloid GIs and civilians in pictures like *Bataan* (1943), *Sahara* (1943), and *Lifeboat* (1944) showcased diversity as an American strength. After the war, a "race" cycle, including *Gentleman's Agreement* (1947), *Pinky* (1949), and *Home of the Brave* (1949), battled prejudice, culminating in Sidney Poitier's ascent as a "distinguished" black actor.[11]

This narrative ignores continuities from the Great Depression. During the economic crisis, unskilled whites vied for jobs in traditionally black-dominated fields, such as construction and domestic work. White workers also urged employers to fire black workers first, leading to higher unemployment rates for blacks. Black activists responded, but national and regional unity eluded them. Nationalists competed with socialists, militants, communists, trade unionists, and religious figures, all of whom had different political strategies. New Deal programs also resisted integration. Civilian Conservation Corps (CCC) officials, for instance, discouraged black enrollment, and such discrimination led blacks to make up a mere 5 percent of the program.[12]

Any New Deal aid to African Americans led critics to accuse Roosevelt of political and religious subversion. In 1928, the Soviet Union had heralded a purge of "white chauvinism" from its ranks and advocated "self-determination for the Black Belt."[13] In response, conspiracy mongers, notably red-baiter-isolationist-anti-Semite Elizabeth Kirkpatrick Dilling, called the "Jew Deal" an attempt to imitate "mongrel Russia" in the United States.[14] "The New Deal is not only Communism but it is black Communism," she declared, bemoaning a "Negro Supremacy" movement.[15] On a local level, white supremacy groups linked civil rights to civil unrest. One Alabaman Ku Klux Klan bulletin warned, "Paid organizers for the communists are only trying to get negroes [*sic*] in trouble." The flyer assured the state "is a good place for good negroes [*sic*] to live in, but it is a bad state for negroes who believe in SOCIAL EQUALITY."[16]

Klan sentiment endured after World War II, as whites feared backsliding into the Great Depression. Postwar civil rights threatened white stability in the same way black activism did during the 1930s and the "Double V" campaign had during the war. Critics believed communist masterminds manipulated African American "dupes" to upset social norms.[17] In 1947, Congressman John Rankin, chairman of the House Committee on Un-American Activities (HUAC), reiterated the conspiracy between blacks and reds: the "racial disturbances you have seen in the South have been inspired by the tentacles of this great octopus communism, which is out to destroy everything."[18] Two years later, Albert Canwell, chairman of the Washington State Legislative Fact-Finding Committee on Un-American Activities, agreed, "If someone insists that there is discrimination against Negroes in this country, or that there is inequality of wealth, there is every reason to believe that person is a Communist."[19] Hollywood, ensnared in the same tentacles, struggled to free itself by severing its ties to the "social message" cycle.

Orthochromatic Blacks and Whites

From the birth of the movies, African Americans countered stereotypes from older stage traditions, especially blackface minstrelsy and caricatures, like the sassy mammies and accommodating "Uncle Toms." But producers often lacked funds and quality equipment, and they competed with studios' technically superior "race" pictures catering to segregated theaters and minority neighborhoods. Due to studio dominance, the majority of African American roles remained limited, even in mainstream films about race, such as *Imitation of Life* (1934, 1959) and *Show Boat* (1929, 1936, 1951). Only in the underworld, such as *Bullets or Ballots* (1936), or in those set in prisons did black and white adults maintain a crude equality, as characters actively undermined respectable mainstream mores.

Filmic portrayals of children differed from those of grown-ups. Not yet fully integrated into adult sensibilities, screen children questioned social prejudices. Juvenile delinquents drew strength from a universal brotherhood in *The Mayor of Hell* (1933) and *Boys' Town* (1938). Outside reform schools, children shared race-neutral friendships in movies including *Skippy* (1931), *The Champ* (1931), and *Penrod and Sam* (1937). The *Our Gang* series (1922–1944) featured inclusiveness in the title and the kids accepted each other as equals.[20] White children extended this relationship to black adults, most famously Shirley Temple tap dancing with

FIG. 24 White tutelage. In *The Beloved Brat* (1938), an interracial friendship between children leads to social uplift for a black family. (Author's collection.)

Bill Robinson in *The Little Colonel* (1935), reprised in three subsequent pictures. In contrast, white adults struggled with their children's idealism. In *Personal Maid's Secret* (1935), a young boy constantly asks white elites if they have black children and openly wishes his family associated with blacks. His mother awkwardly explains she once had a "colored" servant, and her son now has an interest in African studies. In *The Beloved Brat* (1938), the friendship between a rich white girl and a poor black boy makes her parents and white servants uneasy. They eventually compromise by hiring the boy's parents as new servants, dressing them in white, and promising to educate their child (figure 24). Some scenes were more poignant; in *Zenobia* (1939), young Zeke (Philip Hurlic) stops the plot to recite the Declaration of Independence by heart as the entire cast looks on. The reminder that all men are created equal shames a snooty white dowager to allow her daughter to marry a poor suitor. Even in *Boy Slaves* (1939), before Breen ordered the producers to tone the picture down, the child laborers band together in racial harmony, with the white children singing "negro spirituals" in solidarity with their fellow black prisoners.[21]

During World War II, Hollywood constructed a "New Negro" in the spirit of racial tolerance. This figure appeared more "natural" than the shuffling caricature of old, but remained largely confined to maids, porters, and passers-by.[22] The *New York Times* noted "all-Negro" pictures like *Cabin in the Sky* (1943) and

Stormy Weather (1943) "are following the desires of Washington in making such films at this time." The "official expression" mandated "increased employment of Negro citizens in certain heretofore restricted fields of industry [and] would be helped by a general distribution of important pictures in which Negroes played a major part."[23] Ethnic characters appeared as "crowd filler" to demonstrate integration; their ubiquitous presence connoted social progress. *Secret Command* (1944), for instance, took place in a navy construction yard and featured an integrated work force of black and white women and men. Even in Carvel, the Hardys are amazed with their new doctor, Lee Wong How (Keye Luke), who promptly reassures them he is Chinese, not Japanese. In *Andy Hardy's Blonde Trouble* (1944), Lee not only cures Judge Hardy's cold but also buys and repairs Andy's old, broken-down roadster, even installing automatic doors and an antitheft alarm. Lee's Brooklyn background and medical and automobile know-how (along with his mocking the stereotype of a Confucius-quoting Asian) signified his underlying Americanness.[24]

The wartime "New Negro" complemented and reinforced the color blindness screen children shared. In *Mokey* (1942), the boy hero (Bobby Blake) runs away to his friends and passes himself off as their cousin, preferring the close-knit African American shantytown home to his broken middle-class family. In the *Our Gang* short "Baby Blues" (1941), Mickey (Bobby Blake) learns that every fourth child is Chinese and thinks the stork will bring an Asian sibling. Mickey gradually accepts a new Asian brother, but his mother gives him twin sisters; the "other" reflects gender, not race. Frank Sinatra, no stranger to slurs about his Italian heritage, starred in the short "The House I Live In" (1945), dissuading Anglican boys from ganging up on a dark-haired Jew. After the war, enlightened veterans pointed out how times have changed; after watching a reissue of the Depression-era film *The Champ* (1931) in 1946, one "Wounded Ex-GI" wrote to the Motion Picture Association of America, complaining how the lead boy character uttered "anti-racial terms such as 'chink,'" and commented how "these types of remarks" should not have been acceptable "at the time of production and [were] surely not now."[25] The same year, another protestor commented how one animated short about barn animals gave a pig a "negro accent. This is not only an insult to 13,000,000 Americans, but it is fascist propaganda in true Hitler style."[26] Not every American had their consciousness raised to the same level; the Sleepy Lagoon murder case in 1942 and the Zoot Suit Riots in 1943 demonstrated racial tensions simmered just below the surface. Still, Hollywood and enlightened activists presented tolerance as essential to good government.[27]

Despite the accolades of progress, actual reform, either in studio sound stages or on Main Street, faced enormous challenges. The race issue played into the increasing antagonism between the Soviet Union and the United States as the two superpowers competed to expand their political and economic spheres in Europe and, later, newly decolonized nations. The United States could not simply impress impoverished civilians with displays of material goods, cultural exchanges, and the Marshall Plan. To counter charges of bigotry and xenophobia at home, the United States circulated statistics and articles showing "the situation of blacks in America never stopped improving" due to "the capitalist system's constant ability to adapt to change."[28] In a capitalistic Hollywood, studio admen milked such "situations." For *Any Number Can Play* (1949), MGM's publicity department spotlighted Caleb Peterson, a "noted Negro actor" who played Charley Kyng's "loyal friend and employee" in his gambling casino (seen on the far left in figure 13).[29] Peterson's presence and camaraderie with the picture's hero connoted colorblind progress. MGM pointed out Peterson's part was not a one-off engagement; he had roles in other studio productions. Such integration in popular culture prompted one reporter to even claim segregation all but over, predicting "the good times will roll forever," symbolized by Jackie Robinson's ascent into Major League Baseball.[30]

Despite these accolades, Hollywood's "New Negro" declined after 1949. Social critics, drawing from the association between "reds" and "blacks" during the Great Depression, clamped down on industry leftists, notably the Hollywood Ten, for promoting social equality. Intensified government investigation and heavy studio pressure persuaded progressive filmmakers to selectively embed messages to avoid outright critiques of social norms.[31] In one "all-color" production, *Bright Road* (1953), the opening narration described a harmless "fantasy" and "make-believe" rather than explicitly address inequality. Still, the movie faced wary audiences who disliked potential messages, and the film lost money.[32] Other films featured minorities as troubled kids needing white tutelage to "make good." Delinquents of color find rehabilitation through private institutions (*The Quiet One*, 1948) or government social workers (*Navajo*, 1952; "Give Us the Earth!," 1947). While such films garnered critical acclaim (*The Quiet One* received two Academy Award nominations), audiences remained lukewarm. The *Washington Post* reported one theater double-billed *The Quiet One* with *Tomorrow's a Wonderful Day* (1949), a film about a boy's future in the then-new Israel, and the preachment wore thin: "No matter how much you may admire the aims of both pictures, by the time you've seen them together, you've had all the elevation you'll want for a month."[33]

On the surface, Hollywood paid lip service to its images of tolerance. In 1947, actress Hattie McDaniel extolled the progress she witnessed during her fifteen years in Los Angeles.[34] Nevertheless, such progress remained limited. That same year, NAACP executive Thurgood Marshall blamed the "damn" HUAC for harassing progressive moviemakers and urged for the committee's "abolition."[35] With HUAC investigating charges of communist propaganda and the public calling "message pictures" un-American, Hollywood folded rather than play the race card.[36] The studios, selectively drawing from earlier associations of communism and civil rights activism, rejected children as agents of change as the social message cycle came to a close.

Unwanted Strangers: *Intruder in the Dust*

When crafting *Intruder in the Dust*, director Clarence Brown adapted William Faulkner's 1948 novel and added his own recollection of lynch mobs when growing up.[37] Producer Dore Schary had a reputation for his progressivism, and he and Brown overrode studio chief Louis B. Mayer's objections.[38] The film pleased Faulkner, who initially feared a bowdlerized adaptation, and he worked with Brown to ensure the message remained.[39] Less satisfied, exhibitors noted the theme put off moviegoers. "'When is this cycle to end?' was the general trend of the comments," reported one North Dakotan. "It is a good story that Metro sold to us right by our customers [who] were not having any lecture films—before, now, or later."[40]

Early on, MGM warily avoided a "lecture." During preproduction, the studio confined racism to the South and advocated a "hands-off to the federal government." Studio reader Irma E. Lowe explained, "The negro problem is one that must be faced and solved by the Southerners themselves. And this story is aimed to show that there is a nucleus from whom the solution will, in time, come."[41] Director Clarence Brown agreed, "It would do a lot to set the South right in its thinking. That thinking must come from within themselves—and they're doing a hell of a good job of it . . . without antilynch laws from Washington."[42] Lowe concluded the picture showed a positive, "seldom-seen side of the Southern white—decent, compassionate, and humane. With the proper handling, this could make a terrific film."[43]

These disingenuous statements concerning a federal "hands-off" policy underscored the political tensions the issue of civil rights generated in postwar America. Contrary to what MGM believed, the developing civil rights movement consistently demanded federal intervention. On July 26, 1948, President Truman desegregated the army with Executive Order 9981. In response, disgruntled southerners formed a "State's Rights Party," later called the Dixiecrats, and a platform around states' rights and resistance to integration. Party leader Strom Thurmond connected African American advocacy with communists, who had "their designs upon our national security."[44] In their view, attacking the longstanding racial hierarchy undermined the heart of American national identity. For MGM's purposes, crafting a film promoting a "states' rights" methodology, whereby the South does not need federal laws, sidestepped the political tensions. It also deflected further charges from HUAC of "anti-Americanism" and subversive Hollywood attempts to undermine the status quo.

On a local level, Oxfordians in Mississippi resented the Hollywood intruders airing their racial problems. According to Faulkner, his fellow townsfolk complained they "don't want no-one comin' into our town to make no movie about lynchin'."[45] Although Brown supported a hands-off approach for the federal government, he drew the line here. The director pressured Oxford's leaders to welcome his cameras or he would film the picture in MGM's soundstages and depict them however he saw fit. Fearing inaccuracies and seeing the chance to boost their economy, local businessmen endorsed the project.[46]

MGM intended a "proper handling" to limit an antiracist message geographically and politically. By depicting racial troubles as a peculiar institution confined to a small southern town, the studio implied the message lacked relevancy elsewhere, such as urban cities, or small towns in the North. The picture premiered in Oxford, but, as *Motion Picture Daily* reported, the "green light to an all-out campaign . . . in the Tennessee, Louisiana, and Mississippi areas" required the "approval of picture by Memphis censor Lloyd T. Binford."[47] Binford notoriously resisted antiracism in the movies, banning movies such as *Lost Boundaries* from screening in his jurisdiction. However, Binford had less success banning *Curley* (1947), a light comedy about grammar schoolkids playing pranks on their teacher. The censor had argued that scenes of integrated classes and playtime went against the southern creed of social inequality between the races. While Binford correctly pointed out that this mild picture defied Jim Crow, the Tennessee Supreme Court overruled him, stating Binford had "no authority to ban the motion picture *Curley* because of the presence of Negro actors in the cast."[48] Even if the court denied First Amendment protection to the movies, Binford could not literally whitewash the screen to suit his tastes.

To avoid similar legal entanglements, MGM shrewdly selected Oxford for the gala premiere (including sending the film's star, Tennessee native Claude Jarman on a promotion tour) to open the southern market.[49] The studio paid thirty-four film reviewers to cover the premiere on newsreels.[50] The message about the South's ability to solve its own problems also appealed to local pride.[51] Binford gave in to this marketing blitz, commenting, "It doesn't live up to Southern ideals, but it will be all right to show in Memphis."[52]

Binford's tactful admission underscored his growing concern over civil rights. In an interview with *Variety*, the censor accused Tennessee's Supreme Court of playing politics. Specifically, he connected the court's decision to President Truman's desegregating the armed forces and Truman's wider support for civil rights, including antilynching legislation. "Truman controls it [the court]," he glowered, backhandedly condemning the president's "recent actions" as the military desegregated. Recognizing the court effectively denied him power to ban race-themed pictures due to casting, Binford admitted he passed *Intruder in the Dust* and other race-themed movies because he had "an inkling of what the court's attitude probable would be," if he tried to ban them as he did *Curley*.[53]

Not taking chances, MGM heavily emphasized the film's unique local color as a selling point (figure 25). The press book ballyhooed the 112-year-old town as a ready-made set with five hundred citizens portraying themselves, including a bit part for the mayor, and glossed over the townsfolk's initial hesitance.[54] But even as MGM encouraged exhibitors to set up contests to "catch your own intruder" (with cut-out footsteps for would-be sleuths to follow), the marketers

FIG. 25 Blacked out. This ad mat for *Intruder in the Dust* (1949) demonstrates how MGM showcased the "sensational" picture through local color while avoiding the theme of race. (Author's collection.)

danced around the central point. Aside from a few taglines ("A White Man is Murdered—and a Negro is Accused"), MGM avoided the race issue in its marketing or its poster.[55]

The movie opens by telling audiences not to confuse location shooting with reality. MGM modified its usual disclaimer about the film's fictional elements, emphasizing that, despite the film being shot on location, "none of the events took place in Oxford or its vicinity or any other actual place," and any suggestion otherwise was "purely coincidental."[56] The scene shifts to Lucas Beauchamp (Juano Hernandez), accused of murdering local businessman Vincent Gowrie. Beauchamp tells Chick Mallison (Claude Jarman) he wants to see the boy's lawyer/uncle, John Stevens (David Brian). Chick's parents do not want to get involved, and Chick initially saves face, telling his mother, "They're gonna make

FIG. 26 Grudging admiration. In *Intruder in the Dust* (1949), Lucas Beauchamp (Juano Hernandez, right) strips Chick Mallison (Claude Jarman, left) of his racial assumptions. Aleck (Elzie Emanuel, center) obeys both. The accompanying snipe calls Beauchamp "insufferably proud and considers himself the equal of any white man, asking no favors of anyone, and accepting none." (Author's collection.)

a nigger out of him once in his life, anyway."[57] But his conscience bothers him, and a flashback shows Beauchamp saved Chick after the boy fell into a stream, nursed him to health, and refused payment for services rendered (figure 26).

Chick realizes he carries a heavy moral debt and tries to buy Beauchamp gifts. Beauchamp reciprocates, and this builds mutual respect, even though Chick denies it.[58] Nevertheless, the boy urges his uncle to defend Beauchamp.[59] Stevens grudgingly accepts the case, but he is resigned to the status quo, believing the expected lynching has "nothing personal on either side" because it merely restores the racial norms. Indeed, the town's black population all but disappears as white hatred brews. Brown contrasts Beauchamp's dignity with more submissive extras, inserting shots of wary African Americans keeping vigils at night, watching from windows and doorways lest they share Lucas Beauchamp's fate. The Mallisons' maid directly tells her son Aleck not to get involved. Studio reader Irma Lowe underlined this southern code regarding turning proud blacks to passive observers, an ideology to which Stevens adheres: "We got to make him be a nigger first. He's got to admit he's a nigger. Then maybe we will accept him as he seems to intends [*sic*] to be accepted." Beauchamp violates this code when he says "'sir' 'master' to you if you're white but who you know is thinking neither and he knows you know [but] he doesn't even care."[60] Stevens openly blames Beauchamp for upsetting social order: "If you even just said 'mister' to white people and said like you meant it, you might not be sitting here now."[61] He plans to beg the court for mercy.

Beauchamp ignores Stevens and turns to Chick because the youngster is not fully indoctrinated in these social norms. Chick demonstrates his openness by offering to testify on Beauchamp's behalf and, when Stevens leaves, resigned to the inevitable lynch mob, Chick directly asks Beauchamp what he wants him to do. Beauchamp says, "You ain't cluttered. You could listen."[62] Chick listens, enlisting Aleck (Elzie Emanuel) and elderly Miss Habersham (Elizabeth Patterson), the latter defying the town with her independent spinsterhood. The trio persuades Stevens of Beauchamp's innocence. Gowrie's father, more interested in justice than blind racism, joins them. Meanwhile, the townsfolk gather for the lynching turned festival. The camera pans over the spectacle, with music blaring over loudspeakers, kids eating ice cream, women slathering makeup, and men urging Vinson's brother, Crawford (Charles Kemper), to set fire to Beauchamp's cell. Habersham blocks the door, using the social veneration of southern womanhood to keep them at bay while the men unearth evidence. They eventually apprehend Crawford for killing his brother. Stevens moralizes that Crawford's scheme "should have worked by every reason of geography and psychology and two hundred years of this county's history."[63] But he failed to consider a boy's outlook toward a black man who saved his life. The crowd disperses in shame.

Prejudice does not die easily. The next day, Beauchamp visits Steven's law office and invites Chick over, which the boy readily accepts. Beauchamp then pays his legal fees in coins, and Stevens suggests his former client should pay Miss Habersham a visit to thank her, and then inquires why Beauchamp did not trust him as he did Chick. Beauchamp casually rebuts the grown white man: "Would you have believed me?"[64] Irritated at his earlier prejudice being called out, Stevens figuratively dismisses Beauchamp as he sweeps the loose coins into an open drawer and picks up a book to read. But Beauchamp lingers, expectantly, as if waiting for a reply to his question, and the lawyer finally explodes in pent-up anger, asking him what he wants now. His former client, looking down at the seated lawyer, calmly responds, "My receipt" to conclude the business transaction, and Stevens realizes he, too, must overcome his own racism.[65] In the closing shot, Chick wonders why the townsfolk, including blacks who come to town in broad daylight now that the danger is over, ignore Beauchamp the day after. His uncle explains the town's struggle to incorporate their new sensibilities; they now see Beauchamp "the same as I do. They always will. . . . Proud, stubborn—insufferable: but there he goes: the keeper of my conscience." The script notes, "Stevens has been looking down toward the crowd but now he looks up, INTO CAMERA, as if toward the invisible audience" as he delivers the last lines: "—our conscience."[66] The finished film gives the last two words to his nephew (who looks at Stevens, not the camera) to indicate a transfer across generational lines. Chick Mallison represents white youth's recognition of black dignity.

The idea of white youth, unburdened with "two hundred years" of racial baggage, as the new hope for the America's race relations did not excite the public. Some critical acclaim came forward; *Parents* magazine approved of a white boy who "learns a Negro has a right to personal dignity" in a town full of "racial tensions Beauchamp didn't create."[67] NAACP secretary Walter White preferred the movie to Faulkner's book for its removal of the author's "pseudo-science about 'characteristic Negro odor'" in its portrayal of Lucas Beauchamp. White urged fans who had a "profound conviction that something must be done about race hatred" to write producer Dore Schary a note of congratulations.[68]

White's enthusiasm aside, Chick's challenging southern norms and, by extension, American racial identities did not sit well with crowds who saw the film as an attack on southern values. Historian Jennifer Ritterhouse points out children learned racial codes at early ages, with etiquette and respectability centering on white dominance and enforced through coercion and threats of violence.[69] For Beauchamp to call Chick "uncluttered" connotes local values as a pejorative mess—"clutter"—and signifies Chick as an agent of change. Film reviewers took exception to this view. One critic wondered if the film should "necessarily brand ALL Southerners, or even a majority as suggested by this incident, as bigoted and prejudiced human beings?"[70] Another claimed the picture "fails to come forth with a coherent viewpoint" and thought the concept of "the Negro [as] 'the keeper of the white man's conscience' and that Southerners are 'running away from themselves' in the treatment of the Negroes" ludicrous.[71] Critics found these social role reversals, with dignified blacks and prejudiced whites stewing in their own societal disorderliness, unsettling.

The critics' defensiveness drew from the South's long-standing perceptions of outsiders—usually the North—intervening in their deep-rooted values. Such values included familial honor, social grace, and community solidarity as the basis of their way of life. This sectionalism existed since the birth of the nation, tore the country apart during the Civil War, and continued as the South struggled economically when compared to the North. One biographer notes Faulkner never referred to the Great Depression by name, partially because the economic crisis "was simply more of the same and deeper."[72] But Faulkner also hated the New Deal for its "undermining" the "individuality and freedom of his plain folk."[73] In Depression-era Memphis, for instance, one newspaper criticized the New Deal, accusing "professional agitators and adventurers" of attacking "southern customs, southern traditions, southern institutions."[74]

MGM, aware of this larger context, attempted to mollify critics. The film emphasized southern agency in lieu of federal intervention. Critics, including social progressives, attacked the film anyway. At Twentieth Century-Fox, Darryl Zanuck felt Brown did not go far enough. Zanuck, having produced *Pinky*,

Home of the Brave, and *Gentleman's Agreement* and preparing the anti-cowboy film *The Gunfighter* (1950), believed, "*Intruder in the Dust* was a flop because it did not have the courage to say anything. It compromised up and down the line and sacrificed realism for pictorial beauty."[75] Another compromise involved Elzie Emanuel, who played Chick's friend Aleck. Emanuel told *Ebony* magazine Brown ordered him to act bug-eyed and tremble "in the best Stephen Fetchit manner" during moments of superstitious fear. Emanuel stated he resisted, but "was finally forced to do the stereotype" (figure 27).[76] Even as Brown pushed mainstream racial boundaries, he never fully broke free of social conventions—especially the racial codes long perpetuated in show business.

Race films like *Intruder in the Dust* sparked commentaries, but irked the public. *Variety* noted the race cycle turned off large segments of the audience: "One of the difficulties of this type of message pic is that it does not play as many contracts as other top-grossers." The trade journal compared race pictures to fluff like *Mr. Belvedere Goes to College* (1950), where the "lighter fare gets many repeat dates that the Negro pix do not, plus the fact that some few houses in the South skip this type of product."[77] Industry commentator Bert Briller suggested the public grew tired of message pictures nitpicking supposed societal faults. He observed how succeeding movies tried to top previous "message" pictures by piling on condemnations. "What next?" he asked. "Where do you go after *Home of the Brave*, *Pinky*, *Intruder in the Dust*, *Lost Boundaries*, and *No Way Out* (Negro themes)—*Gentleman's Agreement* and *Crossfire* (anti-Semitism)," and other messages? He suggested studios direct the genre to "specialized audiences" and "their particular needs and preferences."[78] Indeed, one exhibitor in McMinnville, Oregon, commented, "A picture of this type is not entertainment. It should be left to the lecture platform or the public forum." His patrons complimented the film's technical merits, but "this was a subject that did not appeal to them. They wanted entertainment and relaxation."[79]

These controversial topics divided audiences, and many chose to stay away. *Intruder in the Dust* elicited opinions varying "from disappointing criticism to rare unreserved praise," but carried little middle ground.[80] Like Zanuck, one moviegoer expressed disappointment, finding Brown's film "rather cold . . . I was almost forced to react with a 'So what?'"[81] The *Washington Post* noted such audience indifference killed the movie's distribution. One local theater had "an abbreviated booking [for *Intruder in the Dust* and the film] hasn't been seen since." The paper wrote "to exhibitors it's a problem, because it has no stars and because it happens to concern the relationship of whites and Negroes."[82]

This relationship between the "whites and Negroes" deteriorated in the postwar environment. Many American servicemen returned with ideas about a universal brotherhood.[83] But postwar adjustment coincided with fears of backslide into the Depression. During the Depression, communists and civil rights activists, jointly and separately, promoted labor unionization and assorted "don't buy

FIG. 27 Not quite there in *Intruder in the Dust* (1949). Aleck (Elzie Emanuel), bug-eyed and superstitious, provides the sole comedic relief in an otherwise hard-hitting picture. Clarence Brown detested racism, but he also indulged in ethnic stereotype. (Author's collection.)

where you can't work" campaigns for African Americans.[84] After World War II, the Congress of Industrial Organizations promoted full employment for black union members.[85] However, a backlash against labor unions and civil rights coalesced into anticommunism; in the Southern Baptist Convention in Knoxville, for instance, Reverend A. A. Haggard accused communists of making "definite plans to take over America this year, using 'organized labor and the Negroes.'"[86] Referencing God and country, Haggard urged his followers to resist, warning that "all fundamentalist preachers are first on the communist death list." Presumably, preachers' followers—the plain southern folk—followed next. This wariness against social agitators solidified support for the status quo.

Audience apathy toward *Intruder in the Dust* reflected the perception of civil rights as a communist movement. Desegregation in the armed forces seemingly hampered American military strength during the Korean War. The *New York Times* reported one "major problem" in the army concerned "the best use of Negro troops."[87] Integrated support personnel, like truck drivers, "did well," the newspaper conceded, but "in combat units, particularly in the infantry, it is an understatement to say they did considerable less well." The columnist concluded "despite the peacetime social problems involved" desegregation failed, and "many in the Army" now advocated integration "in small numbers" only. Although international tensions did not appear in *Intruder in the Dust*, the public kept the "social problems" in mind. One exhibitor expressed his disgust: "This one took the cake. If we have many more poor nights, we'll ship [MGM mascot] Leo to Korea."[88]

The exhibitor's wisecrack about deploying the studio's pet lion to Korea underscored the picture's rocky reception. The heart of the movie featured a boy questioning social values during a time of crisis. Just as *The Gunfighter* fizzled with audiences because of its anti-gun message as GIs headed into a potential World War III, *Intruder in the Dust* similarly challenged social norms. Actor Claude Jarman recalled MGM "didn't know what to do with it [the movie] because they were dealing with a subject matter that they weren't ready to deal with."[89] Jarman stated the studio instead promoted *Battleground* (1949), another of Dore Schary's pet projects, and according to Jarman, the war film "wasn't very good."[90] But artistic merits aside, *Battleground*—about the Allied winter campaign in Bastogne—fittingly allegorized the GIs in Korea.[91] By representing World War II with American soldiers battling for the principles of democracy and freedom, the studio scored public relations points and good box office results.

With *Battleground* and reissues of older World War II movies doing well, Hollywood revived the dormant war combat genre.[92] In 1951, industry commentator Ivan Spear noted World War II and Korea served as settings for over forty titles detailing battles, the home front, biopics, and comedies.[93] In 1953, blacklisted screenwriter Michael Wilson accused Hollywood of promoting an unpopular war: "Conceived militarily, the tactical mission of film producers has been to make an unpopular war palatable to the American people."[94] Public apathy, due to "the known facts of the misery, confusion and cynicism of American troops in Korea," led producers to revive World War II as a Korean parallel. These "skillfully revived combat stories of Normandy and Okinawa" played "upon the patriotic memories of a middle-aging generation while feeding the glory dreams of a younger generation born too late to take part in the crusade against German and Japanese fascism—*provided* the stories were stripped of anti-fascist content."[95] Indeed, *Battleground*'s Nazis are minor players compared to what the American screen chaplain called a lager mission: "We must never again let any force dedicated to a super-race . . . or a super-idea, or super-anything . . . become strong enough to impose itself upon a free world."[96] By 1949, the super nemesis was no longer Nazism but the commies who erected the Iron Curtain.

Intruder in the Dust's challenging the American/southern character held little appeal as the United States cemented its leadership of the free world. MGM studio chief Louis B. Mayer justified his initial reluctance to okay the project, explaining race pictures struggled overseas because of the "danger inherent in the foreign exploitation of such pictures."[97] Mayer singled out the communists in Eastern Europe who, "with thinly disguised glee," projected the plight of Great Depression–era Okies in *The Grapes of Wrath* (1940) under the irony-laden title *This American Paradise!* to politically naïve audiences.[98] As for *Intruder in the Dust*, Mayer expressed "dread to anticipate the probable reaction to so faithful and undistorted a picture of mob violence and race hatred." While the mogul thought "enlightened" people could see democracy's "incalculable privilege of self-improvement through self-criticism," the "less-understanding" folks would not. "Abetted by a little Communist prompting, [they] only see in them the failure of our institutions to live up to the high ideals we profess."[99] The studio's tepid exploitation angle reflected their meager earnings overseas. *Battleground* made over $1.5 million in the foreign market, whereas *Intruder in the Dust* grossed a tenth of that amount abroad.[100]

Given the Korean/postwar context and MGM's lackluster promotion, *Boxoffice* reported *Intruder in the Dust* underperformed in large cities, playing 99 percent in Atlanta, but flopped in other cities.[101] In Atlanta, censor Christine Smith did not ban the movie outright, but she excised content that she believed went "above the head of the average moviegoer."[102] Her edited film "played largely on the peculiarities of southern whites," such as family honor and the Gowrie patriarch's seeking justice for his son.[103] *Boxoffice* agreed selective marketing and editing successfully toned down the "emphasis on lynch law and its blood lusts." The "best chance to please audiences lie in its scattered moments of suspense and some action—not in its message."[104] The "racial discrimination question" could appeal to "special screenings for religious and educational groups, service clubs, school children, etc.," but not the general public. The savvy exhibitor could also sponsor "an essay contest on 'Democracy at Work' or some similar topic."[105] The trade journal implied that to simply expose audiences without a filter seemed like an attack on the social fabric, not showcasing democracy "at work."

In Memphis and Atlanta, censorial edits made the movie palatable for local tastes.[106] In other locations, audiences just stayed away. In Los Angeles, MGM gave a sneak preview during a reissue of *The Wizard of Oz*. *Variety* reported "only two patrons objected" to the theme, "and both of these admitted they were from

[the] deep south [*sic*] and therefore prejudiced."[107] In regard to the questionnaire's crucial question, "Do you like this type of picture?," the audience responded, "This is the type of picture we should get more often." The trade journal concluded an "absolute acceptance of Negro theme" and hoped for good returns.[108]

The preview audience paid lip service to racial reform, but their sentiments did not translate to box office figures. Los Angeles's Four Star Theater optimistically booked an extended run of over one month, but then struggled to pull in customers. *Variety* reported "despite a hyped opening," the movie failed to gross even a weak $4,400 in its first week.[109] The Thanksgiving holiday boosted attendance, but the "forced run" did not earn much more. By the time Four Star's booking ended, the film grossed $800 in its final three days.[110] The poor returns made industry commentators uncertain if studios would continue to take chances. The U.S. Supreme Court's decision to end block booking (where theaters booked a studio's yearly output in advance to have access to a few choice selections) in 1948 deprived studios of a guaranteed distribution network for their products. *Variety* wondered about future risky projects once "producers and distributors are divorced," or if studios would simply turn to mediocre, and risk-free, quality, like the aforementioned *Mr. Belvedere Goes to College*.[111]

Outside the big cities, small-town theaters rejected the movie outright. One complained the "pat little sermons" did "no credit to the spectator's intelligence."[112] The *Los Angeles Times* admitted, "We still don't want to concede that any large segment of our population is that ruthless. We feel that its [*sic*] undermining to our general spirit in the eyes of the world in general." Finally, the film "isn't helped one whit by pretty final speeches about conscience."[113] One Michiganian regretted, "When we first studied this picture, we decided that we could not play it, and we should have stayed with that decision. We believe that this is not good small town material."[114] A North Dakotan, catering to a "rural and small town patronage," complained, "Leo, you are giving us some headaches lately. This picture fell flat and definitely did not meet the rental asked." He concluded, "It's a problem picture," summarizing the film's content and salability.[115]

White resistance to Brown's movie was clear and vocal, but some African Americans also disliked the film. One Arkansan reported, "Our white patrons enjoyed it very much, but I don't think the colored people understood it enough to enjoy it." The exhibitor shrugged off this assessment as inconsequential because "not a single one came to see it the second night." When he asked an African American patron why more blacks didn't attend, the customer replied, "We wants [*sic*] to be left alone. We liked westerns."[116] The respondent may have disliked the film, but his response hinted at a deeper fear. Rather than stir up agitation, the black community preferred to remain silent, invisible, and out of harm's way—just as the black community in Beauchamp's town refused to get involved. Instead, they found comfort in the frontier myth; through the Cowboy and Injuns stuff, they safely participated in the national narrative celebrating individualism and national expansion. Even the *Chicago Defender*'s reviewer wished "two or three somewhat righteous lines near the end might have been omitted" to avoid the "soapboxes with patent messages."[117] While the newspaper hailed Brown's film as a serious step in progressive social messaging, the reviewer observed a fine line between entertainment and preachment, with *Intruder* veering close to the edge.

These African Americans distancing themselves hinted at the civil rights movement as an attack on the "southern way of life." This perceived persecution had long roots; since the Constitutional Convention, the South maintained a defensive posture as they witnessed their institutions assaulted by meddling abolitionists and various congressional compromises in the antebellum period, the devastating Civil War, and decades of sharecroppers, near poverty, and troubled race relations.[118] In 1951, book critic Nash K. Burger noted the shift in southern historiography, describing a time, "not so many years ago, when every schoolboy knew that the antebellum South was a land of gentlemanly slave owners who spent their mornings under the dueling oaks and the rest of the day on pillared porches bemused with mint juleps, while faithful Negro field hands worked and sang in the cotton rows." However, Nash noted, "It has become even better known that the Old South made up of a minority of arrogant, miscegenating plantation owners, mobs of tobacco-chewing poor whites and many Negro slaves, all of whom were busily engaged in escaping on the underground railway."[119] In response to this paradigm shift, southerners reconstructed a "New South," projecting prosperity and modernity without federal interference. White supremacy remained one of the few proud legacies from a troubled past. Brown challenged this makeover by puncturing the foundational racial values of small towns from which the New South traced its origins. This past shadowed the film's production and reception. The association between communism and civil rights in the public mind, mixed with Hollywood leftists and HUAC in the headlines, contributed to the industry's retreat from social messages. MGM lost $614,000 on *Intruder in the Dust*.[120]

Heaven Sent: *Stars in My Crown*

Intruder in the Dust continued the prewar filmmaking motif of using children to explore race relations. The film's adolescent hero, Chick Mallison, saves a black man's life and serves as the voice of generational change for Oxford. When the movie failed, screen children lost much of their agency as social crusaders. *Stars in My Crown* (1950) signified a shift in the construction of a child hero from a social activist to a champion of the status quo.

By mid-1950, independent theaters pulled the flagging *Intruder in the Dust* from circulation and embraced MGM's *Stars in My Crown* in its stead. Director Jacques Tourneur adapted Joe David Brown's novel about a white boy's upbringing in small-town Alabama with his grandfather preacher (the film de-ages the preacher into an uncle). Juano Hernandez repeated the role of a wronged victim due to racial tensions, and the films even begin with similar exterior shots of the local church. But while Oxford's bell chimes gave way to a police siren and the ensuing race troubles, Tourneur conveyed a more spiritual setting. Evoking Christ in the title, *Stars in My Crown* uses religion and celebratory history as its framework. The picture does not end with a black man the keeper of white morality. Rather, an upbeat tone ensures small-town American values remain unchallenged and timeless, regardless of the changes in the outside world. This message of universal Christian brotherhood reaffirms the image of the United States as a nation of racial and social harmony; the country's "crown" contained no thorns.

While MGM's publicity stretched its marketing ploys for *Intruder in the Dust* to attract moviegoers, *Stars in My Crown*'s salesmen had an easier task. Advertisements briefly tapped into the nation's gun culture; posters ballyhooed a pistol-packing parson whose "sermons were spoken with bullets, his prayers were said with his fists!"[121] The poster exaggerates a one-minute scene where preacher Josiah Doziah Gray (Joel McCrea) sermonizes among the local saloon's patrons at gun point with the tag line "Take your choice.... Either I speak... or my pistols do!" As with *Intruder in the Dust*, the marketing angle for *Stars in My Crown* ignores race. Instead, Gray becomes a masculine, virile hero in the best gunfighter tradition.

MGM's admen mixed the poster's implied violence with another facet of American mythology: the utopian small town. One showman stated, the "biggest hits are those that tell the best stories about real people," and this film was set in "a U.S. town called Walesburg—very much like the one we live in."[122] Tie-ins glorified small-town life. MGM suggested contests to "find the family with the most interesting pioneer history or antecedents." *Stars in My Crown* boasted a "Dean Stockwell American Boy Contest," inviting schoolboys to compare themselves to the film's child star: "A sure-fire promotion for family picture patronage. Judges select winner on the basis of being 'most typically American school-boys.'"[123] By valorizing the "typical" American boy and his community and not airing social problems, the film struck box office gold.

MGM studio reader Alice Goodman praised the story as "a nice, clean piece of Americana simply told." The plot revolved around "a boy's memories of his Grandpa, a fine old parson who preached the Golden Rule and won to religion those who scoffed."[124] The *Hollywood Reporter* also favored the nostalgia angle: "to be brutally mercenary, there's an almost untapped source of revenue in this section of the potential film audience, the over-35 group who have stopped going to movies."[125] Accordingly, older folks, tired of the controversial films, wanted escapism, and glorifying childhood worked. Imitators should use "the same simplicity, single-mindedness and sturdy values that have distinguished this one."[126]

Stars in My Crown constructs the American character through small-town roots. Film scholar Chris Fujiwara notes the picture contains almost no shots outside Walesburg, and "the idea of community is already present in every scene."[127] Unlike *Intruder in the Dust*'s Oxford, the fictional Walesburg existed in novelist Joe David Brown's book, in MGM's soundstage, and, most importantly, in popular memory, especially the former Confederacy. The screen treatment identifies the year as 1880, post-Reconstruction. The story thus eliminates the meddlesome agenda of the Radical Republicans, but the narrator's name, John Garfield Kenyon, indicates a reconciliation of sorts, evoking a Union general who later became president.[128]

The Civil War, like the Korean War's use of World War II, became a means of providing racial stability for post-1945 by eliding the Great Depression entirely. The Civil War's legacy shifted in public memory as the "bloody shirt" faded into history. As early as the 1880s, civil rights pioneer Frederick Douglass urged a healing across the Mason-Dixon line, but he worried reconciliation would come at the expense of the freedmen, as whites would relegate Emancipation a "blunder" and "failure."[129] Douglass was right; by the fiftieth anniversary of the "Lost Cause" in 1915, the birth of the movies had romanticized loyal "darkies," heroic cavaliers, and spunky belles.[130] Depression-era films ranging from *The Little Colonel* (1935) to *Gone with the Wind* glorified the South "rising again" from the Civil War and contemporary hard times.[131] After World War II, *The Romance of Rosy Ridge* (1947) brings a northern schoolteacher into a southern home and bridges the gulf between the blue and the gray through education and the boy-girl stuff indicated in the title. Ostensibly about the Civil War, the film suggested people should be judged not by the color of their trousers but by the content of their character. *Rocky Mountain* (1950) showcased Confederate and Union cavalries teaming up to battle "reds"—the Indians. During the Civil War's centenary in the 1960s, historical fiction writers concocted scenarios whereby a triumphant Confederacy reunited with the Union to "make common cause" under "the original American Dream" and defeat Soviet invaders.[132]

For *Stars in My Crown*, an adult John Garfield Kenyon looks back at his childhood self (Dean Stockwell). The grown-up's nostalgic narration reflects a longing to return to this idyllic small-town life. Just as Depression-era audiences basked in Andy Hardy's relatively wholesome, modern small-town setting, the same moviegoers could project Carvel backward to circa 1880, before twentieth-century industrialization took hold. Young Kenyon plays the part, not undermining social norms as Chick Mallison did. Rather, the boy's name signified unity for the reconstructed nation. Kenyon's uncle, Parson Gray, idealizes the status quo. After he proves his shooting skills, as shown in the movie poster, Gray settles down among the congregation.

Tourneur brings the audience directly into this atmosphere. The screenplay instructs the camera to simulate the effect so "the movie audience feels itself to be part of the congregation on the screen."[133] As Gray speaks, "we see various SHOTS of the town that help to create an atmosphere—the peace and nostalgia of times long ago."[134] The narrator, Kenyon's adult voice, says as much: "There's a city of gold right here on earth for all of us—the city of our youth. Walesburg is just one name for it . . . Walesburg, not as it is now, but as it used to be," and concludes, "I'm always a boy in Walesburg."[135] Through Kenyon's recollection, timeless values—Walesburg "as it used to be"—remain the bedrock to rectify modern-day troubles. The plot centers on two story arcs. In the first, a young doctor moves in and tries to prove medicinal science trumps religion. His fancy medical degree belies a lack of sympathy for his patients, but he wises up, woos the schoolmarm, and helps end a typhoid epidemic.

The other theme involves race, in the form of white supremacy. MGM reader Alice Goodman described the "saving of the old Negro from the Night Riders is one of today's problems and should go well with Southerners who are appalled at what is going on."[136] The "Night Riders" obviously stood in for the Ku Klux Klan, but MGM dodged a libel suit by renaming their celluloid clan. Indeed, the Klan resurged during the civil rights movement as a prevalent force in the white "backlash" during the later 1960s.[137] One Klan spokesman vowed, "If the Supreme Court can't maintain our Southern way of life then we *are* going to do something about it."[138]

Stars in My Crown masks the Klan's ideological racism through the Night Riders' economic agenda. Uncle Famous (Juano Hernandez), an elderly ex-slave, enjoys his retirement teaching young Kenyon how to fish (figure 28). But he finds his property rights under siege by miner Lon Backett (Ed Bagley), who wants to tap a rich mineral vein. When Famous refuses to sell, Backett forms the Night Riders to lynch him. Early screen drafts resolve Famous's ordeal in the middle of the story, but the finished film moved this sequence to the end, replacing the typhoid epidemic as the film's climax.[139]

MGM released *Stars in My Crown* in May 1950, six months after *Intruder in the Dust*. Although the financial debacle of Brown's film may not have outright influenced Tourneur's project, the studio brass recognized fairly early they needed to tone down the virulent racism. Shortly before Brown's movie premiered, the studio reshot one confrontation between Uncle Famous and Backett. The miner originally offers to buy Famous's land. The former slave declines, and in response, "Backett stares at the old man in furious silence. He opens and closes his mouth a couple of times, but no sound comes. Then he gives his horse a stinging cut with the whip. The horse plunges down the road, the buggy rattling behind." Cut to Juano Hernandez: "Famous's face is creased with worry. He shakes his head."[140]

In the retake, Backett's fury simmers, but does not boil over. Instead, after Famous declines, Backett merely urges, "Think it over, Famous."[141] He calmly rides away, and Famous's concern does not appear. The villain's race hatred transforms into a cordial warning. Along similar lines, earlier drafts had Gray pleading his parishioners to leave Famous alone. The final print excises his rhetoric, such this denunciation of the Night Riders: "You're sick men, every one of you—sick with greed and hate—and if you're let, you'll spread your sickness until there isn't a whole soul or a healthy conscience left in Walesburg!"[142] Gray originally called the men "sick" with "greed and hate," which will lead to murder. This

FIG. 28 Saying uncle in *Stars in My Crown* (1950). Congenial ex-slave Uncle Famous (right) bonds with John Kenyon (Dean Stockwell, center), teaching him how to fish in this idyll community while his uncle (Joel McCrea, left) approves. (Author's collection.)

and other deleted lines left any mention of "sickness" strictly in connection with the typhoid epidemic.

Ten-year-old Kenyon knows his uncle will stand up to the Night Riders alone. Worried, he hides under Famous's front porch to provide support. But the boy is helpless to act; typhoid leaves him weak and he passively observes the confrontation. Kenyon need not have worried for his uncle, since the film preserves the town's utopist community. Outsiders to "normal" Walesburg, like the young doctor, must conform to these eternal values, not contaminate them with cold science. The doctor recognizes small-town optimism as a superior cure-all, while Gray defeats the Night Riders with a fond recollection of slavery.

When the Night Riders demand Gray hand Famous over, Parson recalls the antebellum days, when Uncle Famous faithfully served them and their fathers. Without uttering the word "slave," Gray reads Uncle Famous's will, which leaves the old man's meager possessions to his killers (figure 29). For instance, Parson singles out one Night Rider whose father once owned Famous. Famous bequeaths him a gift because "I couldn't go out of this world without leaving something to old Mr. Cumberly's son."[143] This sentimentality works, and the "mob is a mob no longer but forty of fifty bitterly ashamed men in long white sheets, stumbling . . . faintly ridiculous."[144] These Klan members, the filmmakers suggest, are buffoonish men who simply need a lecture about how their actions disgrace their family legacies and southern values.

FIG. 29 Side-stepping the Night Riders. Parsons Gray (Joel McCrea, right) and his nephew John Kenyon (Dean Stockwell) confront the Night Riders in this misleading production still. This shot never appears in the film, as the status quo of historical memory triumphs in Walesburg. (Author's collection.)

Through a veil of heavy nostalgia, the film rebuts the necessity for civil rights. In the 1930s, the Ku Klux Klan warned blacks not to fall for communist lines about phony "social equality" and urged African Americans to accept subservient social positions. In the postwar years, critics of civil rights revived this argument, warning would-be dupes that social angst played into communists' plans. *Stars in My Crown* validates this rationale by providing a historical moment predating twentieth-century civil rights activism and political radicalism. Walesburg survived the Civil War and Reconstruction by adhering to a romantic view of slavery as proof of racial harmony. The film positions this older tradition as the "true" and ideal bond between blacks and whites, which civil rights agitators and their "commie" allies sought to undermine. Gray urges the Night Riders to restore this ideal, and when they do, racial tensions vanish. The historic small-town model, with the adult Kenyon's fond recollection, serves as the framework to answer postwar racial anxieties.

Actor Juano Hernandez's Uncle Famous is hardly the same man as Lucas Beauchamp. After the Night Riders depart, young Kenyon emerges from hiding and learns his uncle pulled the sheet over their eyes. Famous's "will" is merely blank sheets of paper. Famous is illiterate, unseen, and reliant on a white man's glorifying the very traditions that condemned him. Indeed, audiences cannot tell if Gray's words reflect Famous's feelings, or if Gray made them up to play on the Night Riders' emotions. Either way, the film renders Famous irrelevant to his own rescue, as he gives in to his inevitable lynching and bequeaths everything to his murderers. *Stars in My Crown* reinforces the status quo, leaving blacks stripped of their possessions, their agency, and their lives.

Intruder in the Dust's Gavin Stevens wanted to throw Beauchamp on the mercy of those who would execute him. Here, Gray does this, appealing to the lynchers' respect for a collective past. The use of public memory, such as the loyal slave who tended to his masters' whims, motivates the mob to disperse. The audience, already basking in the adult Kenyon's fond recollection (and the debunking of modern medicine in favor of folksy charm), affirms their small-town roots and traditions as sources of strength. Afterward, the scene shifts to the finale, where the local atheist, who had resisted Gray throughout the picture, stumbles in and converts. The congregation sings the title song, and the closing shot, featuring the church, repeats the opening shot. Fujiwara suggests this repeat symbolizes a "closed universe."[145] Walesburg remains eternal.

The studio's shuffling dialogue and scenes toned down the race stuff, placing Uncle Famous's ordeal within acceptable narrow boundaries. The Production Code Administration also recognized the family-oriented theme required a softer touch. The censors gave *Intruder in the Dust* freer rein in dialogue, but Breen had wiser words for Tourneur: "The word 'nigger' is particularly offensive to Negroes, and we must ask that the word be omitted."[146] The slur appears in Brown's film as a summary and condemnation of southern race relations. Such controversial words had no place in Walesburg, and MGM assured the censors "the objectionable word above referred to is definitely out."[147] With the stamp of approval, *Stars in My Crown* contained little objection (or objectionable material) to American tradition or history.

This careful adherence to the racial boundaries paid off at the box office. Mrs. Dan Frankhauser, writing for the Synodical Women's Guild in Nebraska, praised the picture for its cleanliness. "Our America needs more of this type of fine picture, those which portrays the moral and ethical value of our Christian faith," she declared.[148] Reviewers lauded the wholesomeness while ignoring the race angle.[149] One Ohioan grinned, "The church people are our best friends since we gave them the chance to see and place their OK on this one in advance."[150] The glorification of small-town life appealed to locals: "Best picture ever made in Hollywood for a small town. Broke house records. Brought in the mayor's wife and one woman who came to a movie for the first time in 30 years, so must be good," an Illinoisan reported.[151] "Give me room, my friends, on this one," gushed one showman in a two-paragraph report detailing "one of the biggest grosses of the year, plus one for our all time big grosses. . . . The story is so wholesome that nearly everyone who came out make it a point to ask why we can't give them more like it." He concluded, "Every theatre should play this great picture and every manager should beat the brush to get them in. This is real public relations."[152]

Black critics did not share this enthusiasm. One reviewer called the film a "sentimental costume picture" with "adroitly works in a few sequences of Ku Klux Klan activity in the border states." The reviewer questioned the sentimentality for hampering the narrative: "It hardly seems possible that men who have been friendly all their lives, from boyhood on, with a kindly old man could don hoods and robes and march on his home."[153] The Night Riders' boyhood friendliness toward blacks—not unlike young Kenyon—underscored the gentle characterization of Uncle Famous. The passive, folksy demeanor of this "uncle" signified his helplessness—Hernandez disappears from the remainder of the film—and tapped into the motif of the friendly manservant who raised white children to become respectable citizens.

Uncle Famous's name and genial characterization alluded to the post–Civil War storybook character "Uncle Remus," the narrator of writer Joel Chandler Harris's collection of folktales published in 1881, a year after *Stars in My Crown*'s period setting. In his original incarnation, Remus told stories to morally uplift young white boys in the same way Uncle Famous taught young Kenyon how to fish.[154] On the surface, these kindly "Uncles" echoed movie children's ability to form friendships with black characters, but critics attacked these "Uncle Toms" for catering to white audiences.

When Walt Disney adopted Harris's Uncle Remus in *Song of the South* (1946), white mainstream audiences denounced the project, leading to mediocre returns. One newspaper reader, "White Texan," told the *Washington Post* the "simple and clownish characters" with "arrested mental stature" were outmoded and offensive.[155] Black and white demonstrators picketed theaters with signs referencing the Double-V campaign: "We fought for Uncle Sam, not Uncle Tom."[156] One disgruntled moviegoer wrote the Motion Picture Association of America, complaining how *Song of the South* perpetuated the stereotype that all blacks were "ignorant, servile people who are cast from a different mold than the rest of us."[157] Blacks were not united; actress Hattie McDaniel, who performed in *Song of the South*, snapped, "What do you want me to do? Play a glamour girl and sit on Clark Gable's knee?"[158] She pointed out actors of color took whatever work available. While *Song of the South* conflicted with postwar advocacy for improved race relations, by 1950 the backward projection of nostalgia and fears of communist agitation made *Stars in My Crown* an accepted part of the national narrative.

Through nostalgia, a portrayal of a glorified, united country after a devastating conflict, coupled with a poke at the Ku Klux Klan to show that Americans could address social problems, *Stars in My Crown* won accolades. The film won the Freedom Foundation's first place prize for the promotion of "political and economic rights which protect the dignity and freedom of the individual."[159] General Omar N. Bradley praised the picture for showcasing America's

Table 1
Exhibitor survey

	Excellent	Above average	Average	Below average	Poor
Intruder in the Dust	n/a	1	2	1	6
Stars in My Crown	74	29	15	5	n/a

SOURCE: "Independent Film Buyers Report on Performance," *MPH*, October 7, 1950, 48.

"righteous crusade" that would win the "global struggle for freedom's eternal survival."[160] The image of close-knit communities like Walesburg became selling points for international moviegoers. Army films such as "A Town Solves a Problem" (1950) informed the former occupied European countries how American small towns foster the roots of democratic freedoms.[161] John Kenyon's adult voice-over echoed the theme, demonstrating how the unbroken heritage of American values from the Civil War to 1950 resolves all problems. The film acknowledges the problematic Ku Klux Klan, as the ornery townsfolk *do* don white robes, but sentimentality and history trump bigotry.[162]

Stars in My Crown's mainstream appeal generated monstrous box office for MGM. *The Motion Picture Herald* tallied independent exhibitors' assessments of the two films (table 1). A North Dakotan summarized public opinion on *Stars in My Crown*: "When two of your regular patrons . . . say, 'That is the best movie I have ever seen in my life,' you know it has something. Then when another customer, who is a very irregular attendant, says, 'If they had more of this type of picture, I would go to the movies more often,' you are more convinced of its value."[163] Such verdicts gave MGM $225,000 in profits.[164]

Containing Race in the American Century

During the 1930s and 1940s, Hollywood movies showed all children experiencing the same hardships afflicting the country. Economic troubles, fragmented families, and wartime uncertainties encouraged them to form friendships and group solidarity on screen. The postwar "social message" pictures used the same motif; as Lucas Beauchamp tells Chick Mallison, young people "aren't cluttered" and could become agents of reform. Looking back, Jarman noted, "If we tried to film *Intruder* ten years later, it would have been impossible. But at that moment in time, in the early spring of 1949, it all came together."[165]

But critics associated civil rights with communist subversion. For example, one spokesman for a local citizens' association in Washington, D.C., deplored "certain organizations" for disrupting the "natural state" of segregation in restrictive housing covenants.[166] Tracing the historical black migration northward, the spokesman claimed "unscrupulous agitators" took advantage of "uninformed Negro" migrants, exploiting them to promote "social democracy, which is but another name for communism."[167] The "nefarious plan" would place the "Nation's

Capital [in] the same condition that befell France and other European countries." In this view, the communists duped ignorant and innocent African American into pawns for world conquest.

The film industry caved under pressure. The Hollywood Ten vocally supported racial equality, which proved their supposed un-Americanism. This pressure encouraged Hollywood to stifle children's voices. White screen youth had a history of racial tolerance and even friendships, but such film content now played to empty houses. The *New York Times* praised *Intruder in the Dust* for not catering to "the lowest and most juvenile of popular tastes" and the "educational impact . . . has been wholly positive."[168] The public, caught in the beginning of the Korean War, rejected this form of education. Director Clarence Brown returned to the soundstages for his next project, *To Please a Lady* (1950), a Clark Gable vehicle about "midget autoracing." Brown shrugged, "Essentially, it's a studio picture."[169]

Stars in My Crown avoided such troubles by setting the clock back to a romantic, rustic 1880 to present an idealized harmony between blacks and whites. The *Los Angeles Times* observed the picture "'looks back' on an older America, rich with the triumph of right over wrong, and filled with pastoral charm."[170] This nostalgia satisfied white audiences who wanted to see their small-town heritage hailed, not hissed at by leftists. By 1959, critic Bosley Crowther observed, for each "dramatic subject in which Negroes are prominently involved," marquees advertised "fifty white society dramas, family comedies, Walt Disney animal pictures, Westerns, and monster films." He lamented, "Few of the pictures about the problems of the Negroes have done well at boxoffices in this country, or, especially, abroad." He characterized "one of the best [as] a financial disaster. That was *Intruder in the Dust*."[171] Ten years after the movie premiered, Crowther recognized Brown's film as the apex of the "social message" cycle—and its failure marked the genre's decline.

In 1949, the *Chicago Defender* optimistically predicted Hollywood found a "black gold mine" with race pictures. With four pictures released that year about racism and two more in development at the time of publication, the writer thought the "once-feared films about race" now made for sure-fire box office hits.[172] Six months later, the same writer expressed dismay, noting the only success from the 1949 "experiments" was Juano Hernandez's career.[173] In 1957, the newspaper recalled 1949 as a golden year for promoting racial equality, but the potential languished unfulfilled. Noting that tensions over desegregation had the earmarks for a first-rate melodrama, one columnist hinted "the Hollywood touch" was key to "shaping American attitude" about race.[174] Hollywood did not respond.

Even in silence, a quiet moment could pack a punch.[175] After *Stars in My Crown* wrapped, Juano Hernandez contemplated a remake of the century-old *Uncle Tom's Cabin*. This symbolic continuation of Uncle Famous did not materialize.[176] Instead, he signed up for *The Breaking Point* (1951), as sidekick Wesley

Parks to fisherman Harry Morgan (John Garfield). The duo battle human traffickers and Morgan loses an arm while Parks loses his life. In the end, a sympathetic crowd whisks the wounded star away so "the Morgan family can face the future again, secure."[177] Morgan trades an amputated limb for his wife's embrace and a stable future. In contrast, the last shot leaves Parks's young son alone and unnoticed on the pier, waiting for his father who will never come back. The races that have and have not the public eye become the film's final impression as the screen fades to black.[178]

The falling curtain on the social message cycle mirrored the descending Iron Curtain in Europe. The public readily connoted Hollywood's social message cycle as subversive when the United States needed to project strength as the superpower of the free world. One disgruntled moviegoer, hearing about Darryl Zanuck's *No Way Out*, starring Sidney Poitier, wrote the producer, condemning the "government sponsored movie [that] won't do anything but make me hate niggers and nigger lovers more."[179] He called integration a disaster because "America has always been 'the strongest' segregated. Now with this form of degeneration going on, anything may happen," and he doubted foreign nations would "respect a 'mongrel race' or hordes of malatoes [*sic*]. Is that a good advertisement for democracy? How about these thousands of black bastard babies left in Europe. That's one good reason why democracy is making <u>no</u> headway in Europe."[180] Breaking down the color line allegedly wrecked international relations, with the American mission—democracy in Europe—faltering.

For domestic filmgoers, even race-free internationalism proved a hard sell. After *Intruders in the Dust*, Dore Schary produced *The Next Voice You Hear* (1950), a film about a modern suburban family reevaluating their lives when God unites humankind through faith. Schary saw his picture as "part of a larger pattern, a pattern that will eventually make one world, a United Nations World."[181] The film flopped; even with a low cost of $421,000, it lost $65,000.[182] Schary later admitted he "had no idea that we would be caught up in the Korea situation."[183] The Korean War changed the audience's context to anticommunism—a similar shift that flummoxed *The Gunfighter* and *Intruder in the Dust*. Exhibitors advised Schary to imitate *Stars in My Crown* and reach out to "ministerial associates, PTAs, etc." and "tell people if they liked the former they will like the latter."[184] The strategy failed; one North Dakotan dismissed the film as "a midget in comparison to *Stars in My Crown* at the boxoffice."[185] The eternal small town, isolated from global tensions, appealed to audiences in the proverbial sticks, not "bigger picture" issues like race and world affairs. The political upheavals in postwar Europe similarly shaped *The Search*, discussed in the final chapter.

5

The International Picture

The February 1949 cover of *Boys' Life* featured a troop of youngsters standing at attention near the Statue of Liberty's base, with the world's flags unfurled before them. "Strengthen the arm of liberty" ran the tagline under the boy parallel of the United Nations. The article described how "a war orphan just arrived from Europe" and "was so impressed he joined a Scout Troop." The boy fled from an unspecified "dictator's government" that crushed its Scout program. "Boy Scouts aren't wanted in a dictator country," the writer explained. "They are considered enemies of the state because they represent individual resourcefulness, courage, and honesty."[1] By channeling common American values, any boy who joined the Scouts became a solider in the front lines against statist totalitarianism.

Boys' Life portrayed the Americanization of foreign kids as crucial to creating a stable postwar world. The youngsters who came of age in the late 1920s and 1930s saved the world from fascism. Now their children continued the mission, facing dysfunctional families, juvenile delinquency, and the "race question." To address these concerns, Hollywood emphasized patriarchy, paramilitarism through groups like the Boy Scouts, and the "whitewashing" of social messages. The end point for this process created the citizen-solider who protected his home and promoted these values abroad.

President Franklin Roosevelt hoped the United States would serve as the chief postwar international policeman.[2] A projected American involvement abroad would sustain the wartime economic recovery and prevent the country from backsliding into the Depression.[3] The rhetoric of the "American way" as an ideal lifestyle and form of government justified the country's role as an international guardian.[4] Children played the role of innocents who needed the protection a policeman offered. Contemporaries called the Second World War as a "war against children" due to the high involvement of youngsters in mobilization and as casualties. The "lost children" of Europe became a means for the United States to refashion the world in an idealized American image, thereby ensuring international stability and assuaging anxieties at home about future wars.

However, the war orphan's joining the Boy Scouts did not make him an automatic American, nor did Americans necessarily embrace the part of global policeman. Despite *Life* magazine's cover showing boys creating a symbolic world community, the public rejected the "one-world movement" and criticized the United Nations for superseding American identity. Journalist John Gunther published observations after a cross-country tour, describing a renewed isolationism: "Once the war is over, its backwash smears over us, and the nation succumbs to greed, dear, ineptitude, fumbling of the morning hopes, shoddy dispersal of the evening dreams" as the people jealously guarded against a backslide to a depression.[5] The United States promoted itself as the defender of the free world, but the long-term commitment to the reconstruction of Europe proved a hard sell. West Germany especially became a contentious battle ground. After the massive propaganda campaign to demonize the Third Reich, Americans now scrambled to protect Germans from falling behind the Iron Curtain.

Hollywood's depicted postwar internationalism through the rehabilitation of European youth. The wartime picture *Tomorrow, the World!* (1944) provides an early example of public apathy toward internationalism. Despite a massive publicity campaign, *Tomorrow, the World!* met box office disappointment. Internationalism met increasing public hostility during the late 1940s. Hollywood's visualization of American involvement in Europe mirrored the changes in public taste.

This chapter primarily focuses on *The Search* (1948), a picture in which an orphaned Czech boy reconstructs his identity with an American soldier in postwar Germany. Swiss producer Lazar Wechsler and MGM director Fred Zinnemann collaborated on the project to highlight the suffering in Europe and galvanize the American public to action. In terms of filmmaking, they did everything "right" in crafting the rehabilitation of a lost boy into a potential American citizen under a military father figure. The film displays strong family ties through father-child bonding on the individual and national scenes. The producers inserted a happy ending and played up emotional hokum to appeal to American audiences. The film won praise and awards for its message, and the United Nations endorsed the project with enthusiasm.

But *The Search* failed to entice the public to embrace a wider American involvement. The film's initial poor reception demonstrated social progressivism did not ring the box office, which *Intruder in the Dust* confirmed a year later. As Hollywood turned defensive due to HUAC, the industry embraced anticommunism to encourage ticket sales. Concurrently, the industry distanced its filmic rhetoric from themes of "one world" government and brotherhood prevalent in pictures from the Great Depression and World War II. By the 1950s, the industry's self-policing promoted internationalism, but through a political filter of containment. By the end of the 1940s, Hollywood's American boy was firmly cast as a Cold Warrior.

Past and Present Fears: *Tomorrow, the World!*

After World War I ended, the United States largely retreated from world affairs. The Republican presidential administrations of the 1920s vowed to "seek no part in directing the destinies of the Old World" as a repudiation of Wilsonian internationalism.[6] Their position drew support from popular views of the Great War as a European bloodbath, doubts whether the Versailles Treaty could prevent an "inevitable" war, and the perception of the League of Nations as a check on American freedoms. In 1937, the twentieth anniversary of the U.S. entrance into World War I, one poll noted nearly 70 percent of the public believed involvement in the war was wrong.[7] "In a large sense," one newspaper commented, "the 1929 depression may be attributed to war causes; the end is plainly not yet."[8] Congress's repeated Neutrality Acts (1935, 1936, 1937, 1939) gradually allowed President Franklin Roosevelt expanded powers to support the Allies, but the acts also reflected the public resistance toward entering another war.

The "Day of Infamy," when the United States declared war on Japan after the attack on Pearl Harbor, changed this outlook. Historian Melvyn Leffler points out that "only after the cumulative impact of world depression, totalitarian aggression, and universal conflict, did American policy makers come to believe that European stability was vital to American well-being."[9] As early as 1942, Raymond L. Buell, former president of the Foreign Policy Association, warned that a renewed isolationism would lead to "a colossal internal depression and World War III."[10] He urged the "war effort at home" to suppress Americans' "natural inclination" to indulge in domestic luxuries and ignore "devastated foreign countries." "Postwar America," he lectured, must "subordinate immediate desires for enlightened self-interest." The Kansas Institute of International Relations noted the "isolationist Midwest" vanished after December 7, 1941, and many citizens believed "that world events and problems growing out of this war imposed a collective responsibility on the citizens of democracy to prevent a third world war."[11]

Hollywood's wartime melodramas urged audiences to join the Allied effort. As scholars note, noninterventionists such as the America First Committee rejected U.S. involvement, and prominent Firsters like Charles Lindbergh preferred peace with Hitler rather than endure hardship, famine, and mass death tolls. To counter isolationism, the film industry criticized the Third Reich and promoted the war as a fight for American democratic values.[12] American Firsters, critics alleged, were Nazi supporters, closeted commies, and anti-Semites.[13]

In contrast, internationalism rebutted the legacy of isolationism. The docudrama *December 7th* (1943), a Department of War–Hollywood collaboration, glorified a postwar international fellowship. In a closing conversation between a dead, disillusioned World War I doughboy and a casualty from Pearl Harbor, the elder soldier tells his younger counterpart the world has learned nothing from the massive slaughter in no man's land. The sailor disagrees, prophesying the Day of Infamy created a global coalition based on brotherhood. He allegorizes the war with the national pastime, predicting Team USA would usher in a "world series of peace."[14]

The European war orphan became a celluloid symbol of greater U.S. involvement abroad. Americanizing foreigners made the world safe for democracy and prevented future wars. The movies presented foreign children adopting American values and sacrificing themselves accordingly. Chinese (*China's Little Devils*, 1945), Filipino (*Back to Bataan*, 1945), and Russian (*The Boy from Stalingrad*, 1943; *Song of Russia*, 1944) kids battled the Axis powers to the death (figure 30). Young siblings of German American descent in *Watch on the Rhine* (1943) boldly intend to follow their father into Germany as resistance workers should the war continue past their eighteenth birthdays, and Mom reluctantly agrees. European war orphans in *The Pied Piper* (1942) and *Journey for Margaret* (1942) characterize the United States as a haven for the world's tired, poor, and war-torn refugees. *Babes on Broadway* (1941), released less than a month after Pearl Harbor, trotted out British teary-eyed orphans in a show within a show to galvanize the public on and off the screen to buck up Anglo-American solidarity. Charities, such as the March of Dimes, appealed to the public by using "modern science" to turn kids into "normal, happy, useful citizens."[15] Postwar media coverage of orphans elided the horrors they witnessed in favor of the exciting possibilities of a bright future under American care.[16] A U.S.-led peace and prosperity, these programs implied, would prevent a third world war and depression. In 1943, the *Los Angeles Times* worried, "There will be depression following this war; there will be disruption of family life and consequent broken homes."[17] Preventing this "disruption" involved civic duty; one child expert claimed the "most patriotic thing a mother can do is to rear her children to be good citizens" because "no good can come from homes where neither parent is in charge for long days or nights."[18] The idealized parent came in the form of strong patriarchs like *Any Number Can Play*'s Charley Kyng or through military-style discipline.

Postwar Germany became the contested grounds between children, international stability, and rehabilitation. The Nazis presented a youth-centered movement, and the United States countered Third Reich youngsters.[19] The movie *Tomorrow, the World!* (1944) played upon child redemption and the fate of Hitler Youth. The story centers on a German orphan Emil Bruckner (Skippy Homeier), sent to live with his midwestern American uncle. The boy terrorizes his adopted household, taking the American family to the brink of disintegration as he breaks up his uncle's engagement, beats his cousin to near death, exploits his aunt's anti-Semitism to sow discord, and tries to erase the memory

FIG. 30 "They stopped the Nazis cold!" in *The Boy from Stalingrad* (1943), in which American audiences saw child soldiers giving their all for the war effort, even at the cost of their lives. (Author's collection.)

of his "good" German father who had opposed the Nazis (figure 31). Thankfully, the melting pot—an ethnic-themed wartime solidarity—wins him over. After his uncle nearly strangles him, his classmates shun and beat him up, and officials threaten him with reform school, Emil starts to appreciate the United States. But the film's mixed reception presents the difficulty of rehabilitation.[20]

Critics recognized Emil as a microcosm of postwar German children and Europeans in general. Unfortunately for internationalists, rehabilitation met

FIG. 31 Crashing the happy American household in *Tomorrow, the World!* (1944). Homeschooled rehabilitation does not come easy for Nazi Youth Emil Bruckner (Skippy Homeier, left) or his American hosts. (Author's collection.)

resistance, partly from anti-German sentiment that had persisted throughout the twentieth century, magnified largely by World War I,[21] from sensational pictures such as *Hitler's Children* (1943), with a notorious scene featuring Nazis whipping an American schoolgirl, and the self-explanatory *They Came to Blow Up America* (1943), based on Germany's failed Operation Pastorius. Director Ernst Lubitsch's black comedy *To Be or Not to Be* (1942) features Nazis using children to unwittingly squeal on their parents' anti-Hitler witticisms, while Walt Disney's animated short "Education for Death" shows Nazi education at work, stripping boys of all compassion and turning them into goose-stepping automatons that march into the grave. *Tomorrow, the World!*'s Aunt Jessie (Agnes Moorehead) voices this sentiment, proposing a final solution for her "Aryan" nephew: "If it were up to me, I'd exterminate the entire German race!"[22] But she wises up when Miss Richards (Betty Field), a Jewish schoolmarm / child psychologist / Emil's prospective aunt, optimistically predicts everyone can learn from each other to become good friends.

Critics accepted the film's premise that "twelve-year-old Germans can be cured with patience and kindness" and expressed hope "if little Emil Bruckner is multiplied by 12,000,000, the venom of Hitlerism eventually may be washed away."[23] Publicity material recognized film as a medium to remove Nazi indoctrination, but offered no details.[24] In a Los Angeles Unified School District survey, kids expressed uncertainty, with one claiming, "If we don't run the world right after this war, there will be a World War III."[25] Another echoed Aunt Jessie's outlook: "Re-educate the German people . . . until they can prove that they are capable of joining the family of nations. If this fails, kill them all."[26]

The characters' mixed views underscored public aversion to social "preachments," anti-German sentiment, and doubts about the United States' role in the postwar world, even if with the family at stake. This view became clear to child actor Skippy Homeier, who played Emil. Homeier recalled that the public confused him with his character: "It was difficult taking heat as a twelve-year-old from people on the street who would give me static for being a Nazi, which was about as far from my upbringing as you could throw a rock."[27] The press also confirmed Homeier's Americanism. "Mrs. Homier observes that her family has been talking American for 300 years," the *New York Times* reported.[28] While on tour, Skippy disavowed his screen persona, stating, "I do hope the citizens of Springfield [Massachusetts] will not think of me as the mean kid I portray in *Tomorrow, the World!*" and claimed he would play a likeable fellow in his next picture, *Boys' Ranch* (1946).[29] He ultimately played the villain.

Homeier's typecasting underscored the American ambiguity toward the film's message of postwar rehabilitation. Despite the optimistic ending, animosity on both sides indicated a rough, or even undesirable, healing process. A Chicago exhibitor complained, "This failed to draw," adding, "Propaganda pictures seldom do well here."[30] The Office of War Information (OWI) even banned the film in North Africa and occupied Europe because officials deemed Emil's redemption "too sympathetic" and inferred a "soft peace" for Germany when many wanted revenge.[31] The OWI refused to export the film to those "who have lived alongside of Nazi terror."[32] Such reports endangered the picture's salability. *Variety* reported the OWI ordeal "raises the question that if an American family is unable to cope with a single Nazi-indoctrinated youngster, then what will be the approach in handing the millions of little mobsters in Germany after the war?"[33] Distributor United Artists countered, instructing publicity agents to enlist some "educational delegates" for the film's San Francisco premiere: "Get a couple of representatives from European and South American countries to shoot off their mouths to the effect that the picture should be shown to all the liberated countries contrary to the O.W.I. rulings."[34] The premiere was successful but failed to reverse the OWI's position or to sustain the box office.[35] Producer Lester Cowan remained dissatisfied and considered withdrawing the film until V-E Day.[36] With internationalism and rehabilitation stalled, Emil Bruckner took the world after all.

The postwar years witnessed a mass exportation of American culture to rehabilitate the "twelve million Emil Bruckners." Historians point to what Rheinhold Wagnleitner called the "Marilyn Monroe Doctrine," in which American popular culture saturated war-torn Europe to sway people from Soviet influence.[37] In 1948, celluloid diplomacy worked in Italy when the U.S. Information Services screened MGM's anti-Bolshevik satire *Ninotchka* (1939) as a smear campaign against communist candidates and helped win a parliamentary election.[38] Garbo not only laughed, she got votes.

The rhetoric of international democracy made for good advertising as officials, including President Truman, discouraged a return to isolationism, which, they claimed, caused the "'30s Depression."[39] Idealists, taking advantage of the wartime enthusiasm for "social messages," envisioned a new one world government placing global citizenship above nationalism. These internationalists, notably Wendell Willkie, believed the wartime alliance could transition into a permanent world government. Willkie hoped to "unify the peoples of the earth in the human quest for freedom and justice."[40] His treatise, *One World*, sold over 1.2 million copies in the first two months.[41]

Willkie's idealism initially fit in with Hollywood's postwar "social message" cycle. Willkie served as chairman of the board at Twentieth Century-Fox, a ceremonial position he earned by refuting the Nye Committee's 1941 accusations that Hollywood was a Jewish front to instill war fervor.[42] Willkie sold the rights to *One World*—the "hottest selling book," according to *Variety*—to the studio, hoping actor Spencer Tracy would play him, with the planned film dubbed in eight languages.[43] Twentieth Century-Fox never produced the picture. A former New Dealer, Willkie switched to the Republican ticket as the GOP's 1940 presidential candidate and lost. But his internationalism generated a backlash among conservative politicians, who eyed the coming 1944 primaries and resented

"Willkie propaganda."[44] The thought of re-antagonizing Congress gave Twentieth Century-Fox pause, matched by the Catholic diocese's moral qualms. They labeled *One World* "Not Recommended to Any Class" for its "false premise" in promoting the "obvious and criminal tyranny of an ally," namely, the godless Soviet Union.[45] Accordingly, the powerful Catholic Legion of Decency condemned the film adaptation of such blasphemous work. Willkie's death in 1944 and the failure of the studio's internationalist-themed epic *Wilson* (1944) probably dampened production chief Darryl F. Zanuck's interest in the project.[46]

Willkie's passing coincided with a renewed isolation as the war ended. The threat of backsliding into the Great Depression encouraged industry leaders to focus on economic conditions back home. The American Federation of Labor, worried over the scaled-down wartime production, turned protectionist and isolationist, stating, "America is now getting too little [resources for] reconversion," and "it may be too late to avoid a major postwar depression."[47] In 1947, journalist John Gunther observed the country's "somewhat faltering steps to justify its new station as a mature world power."[48] He quoted Missouri congressman Dewey Short, who denounced the United States subsidizing UN appropriations: "I am against it with all my heart and soul." Short accused cash-strapped London and Moscow of not selling their crown jewels, which would be "enough to run any government for quite a while," and instead took "bread and bacon, cornpone and sowbelly out of the mouths of my poor people."[49] Referring to the Depression and its impending return as reasons, Short even rejected the Marshall Plan, asserting "the average American is not willing to bond his children and his grandchildren to save these countries that are not worth saving."[50] Instead, he preferred to pass the cost of rebuilding Europe to the United Nations, which would allow the United States to withdraw from Europe.

In the face of this neoisolationism, the Hollywood left clung to the social progressive messages they used to rally the public in pictures such as *December 7th*. By the war's end, Harry Warner officially announced his studio's position in this scheme:

> The motion picture industry would be shamefully remiss if it were not looking ahead to its task in the postwar world. The essence of the task can be stated in a single phrase, "To interpret the American Way." . . . One of our chief aims now in the postwar world will be to show Americans how millions of Chinese, Icelanders, Indians, Eskimos, and Russians live. I can think of no clearer, surer way to achieve a community if nations—and certainly of no clearer, surer way to show the world what our democracy means. Once the world understands the blessings of democracy, the results are beyond question.[51]

Even while Warner spouted good faith, other one worlders slowly lost enthusiasm at the prospects of global harmony and forgiveness. During one screening of *Tomorrow, the World!*, producer Albert Margolies noted how Walter

Lippmann, a one world supporter, "got up and left the room in a hurry but not before he expressed strenuous objections to the ending. . . . He said that the picture makes Americans all 'look like saps,'" which caused a buzz "and of course there was the usual difference of opinion."[52] The "usual difference of opinion" pointed to the divisiveness of the German question; even some supporters, like Lippmann, who believed in global government, thought the message of universal friendship and understanding made Americans look foolish and naïve. As the war ended, United Artists also hoped to exploit the public debate and "revise [the] campaign on *Tomorrow, the World!*, dependent on the territory, when the European war is over." The distributor aimed to showcase "the angle of now that we have licked Germany, what are we going to do with all the Emils that we will have on our hands."[53] Other films focused on internationalism among children. Dore Schary's *The Boy with Green Hair* (1948) focuses on a boy who pleads for universal disarmament. When Schary moved to MGM, he produced *Intruder in the Dust* (1949) and *The Next Voice You Hear* (1950). All three films flopped.[54]

The Search (1948), produced by Switzerland's Praesens-Film and distributed by MGM, demonstrates producer intent and audience antipathy concerning internationalism. The project, tagged "The Children's Film" during production, urged the United States to commit its resources, personnel, and time to aid traumatized Czechoslovakian children.[55] *The Search* highlighted the rehabilitation of war-torn Europe under the American flag to refute Depression-era isolationism, but the film's production and reception showed the transition of internationalism from "one world" to anticommunism.

Hegemony as Stability: *The Search*

Director Fred Zinnemann embraced a project on postwar Germany.[56] Later known for movies like *High Noon* (1952), *The Nun's Story* (1959), and *A Man for All Seasons* (1966), Zinnemann started with fare such as *My Brother Talks to Horses* (1947), a boy-and-pet tale that, according to actor Peter Lawford, the director found beneath him.[57] In addition to his desire to make prestigious pictures, Zinnemann lost family in the Holocaust and wanted audiences to never forget.[58] His research files contain clippings deploring "our obsession with the Russians and our seeming disinterest in the country which has started the last two wars in which large numbers of our fellow citizens were killed."[59] Political commentators worried over occupied Germany, in which exploitation, misdirection, confusion, and inconsistency among the Allied policy makers "were really provoking and protecting, and not discouraging, the worst kind of German nationalism" as aggressive factions, determined to reunify their nation, turned back to fascism.[60] As a result, leftover Nazis, "whose power is increasing more and more each month," could initiate another world war.

Drawing Americans into a proactive, internationalist global dialogue became Zinnemann's goal in *The Search*. In an article to screenwriters, he reiterated his intent to reconcile the "generosity innate in most Americans and their lack of comprehension of the extent of human suffering abroad."[61] His "primary concern" was to "dramatize contemporary history for the large American audience and to make them understand in emotional terms what the world outside looks like today."[62] He teamed with Praesens-Film A.G., a Swiss studio headed by Lazar Wechsler.[63] The American film actors newcomer Montgomery Clift and veteran Aline MacMahon—and Zinnemann's home studio, MGM, guaranteed a wide U.S. distribution

According to Zinnemann, the producers "unanimously agreed that the picture was primarily destined for the American market and that it must reach as many people as possible."[64] To achieve their goal, Praesens hired photojournalist Therese Bonney—whose photo book *Europe's Children* (1943) depicted these young victims with emotional appeal for American sentiment—as a technical consultant. Screenwriter Peter Viertel declared, "To state bluntly, I should say that in many ways America is the hope of Europe today. We have food, materials, and a general welfare which exists nowhere else." While public figures, such as Dewey Short, worried over economic depression in spite of this abundance, Viertel urged Americans not to turn inward: "We cannot be satisfied to be Sir Galahads in shining armor, who kill the dragon and then go home, to forget the battle, for we have learned that this is one world and if disillusionment and cynicism spread again the children who today scurry through Europe's gutters will become new fuhrers [*sic*], new scourges of humanity."[65] With this framework, Viertel created a relationship between a boy and a GI as a public stand-in / father figure. Understanding American apathy to long European entanglements, he acknowledged the soldier was "not a permanent solution to their lives," but would "show the tragedy of our army of occupation, how they are only a bunch of homesick children themselves, not equipped for the job that have [*sic*] fallen on them."[66] This relationship provided an allegorical foundation for the youth's socialization into international Americanism.

Zinnemann agreed with Viertel. He informed Wechsler they would "make a film about displaced European kids—and the world as it appears to them—including their friendship with a young G.I.," the latter initially "reluctant and disinterested in Europe" but "who grows to understand what is at stake through his friendship."[67] He specified the danger of repeating history "when the first peace was sold out from under the nose of a fat, dumb, and happy America, that wanted nothink [*sic*] but to go to sleep again, just like today."[68] A more colorful view in Zinnemann's file, undated and unsigned, reads, "Maybe we could scratch that thick, slick, complacent hide of America and . . . tell them that their Allies had locked the Jews of Europe, in together with their murderers, and ask what about it. Maybe we could tell them that America is an island of prosperity surrounded by an ocean of human degradation that won't work and that the lid will blow off again unless they wake up soon. And maybe a few people here and there will sit up and take notice."[69] The memo darkly characterized the typical

American as a callous ignoramus whose approach to world affairs was to proclaim, "Isn't it too bad about them foreigners, how they never seem to know what they want. Why don't they get together among themselves. Well, hell, we can't do anything about it so let's go get drunk."[70] Publicly, Zinnemann announced he "softened the truth" in the picture because "the American audiences would have lost any desire to face it, used as they have been through the years to seeing a sentimentalized world."[71] Indeed, one moviegoer complained about "the happy ending, which the American audience must have. Must it?"[72]

Zinnemann's happy ending answered her in the affirmative, although he and Praesens wanted to capture the reality of a devastated Germany to justify a protracted international commitment. *The Search*'s producers turned to the United Nations for support. Even in its infancy, the UN already recognized the importance of film. In 1947, UN liaison Mogenn Skot Hansen went to Hollywood to shape dialogue and "turns of plot that might condition audience to accept the U.N. as part of their daily lives."[73] Hansen knew he faced high odds, and his best opportunities were influencing the early stages of script development, not when a production was well under way. Offering free advice, Hansen distributed pamphlets about relief programs. He succeeded in inserting references to the UN in the melodramatic *Storm Over Tibet* (1952) and the comedic *Here Comes the Groom* (1951). The UN made occasional screen appearances; *When Worlds Collide* (1951), for instance, featured an emergency session as the earth neared doomsday.

The United Nations Relief and Rehabilitation Administration (UNRRA), whose displaced persons program centered prominently in *The Search*, welcomed Zinnemann's story. According to the organization's historian, the agency "suffered from the unreasoning and implacable hostility of nationalists and isolationists of all types who saw in international organizations at best futility and at worst mortal danger."[74] UNRRA was painfully aware of the press's mocking "UNRRA the Unready" and its inability to interest the public in its unsexy relief work.[75] The agency struggled to not seem like they were stealing "bread out of U.S. mouths"—a clear reference to the fears of a postwar depression, which Congressman Dewey Short accused them of doing.[76] Zinnemann answered these charges by centering on displaced children who "had really been in a concentration camp," including the protagonist, a Czech boy named Ivan Jandl, filtering the real tragedies of war through Hollywood make-believe (figure 32). When the director instructed them to respond to the UN's uniformed officers, "the terror that they registered on their faces was incredible."[77] *Life* reported the setting was "convincing enough to cry about."[78]

An American Innocent Abroad

The Search centered around a nine-year-old Czech holocaust survivor Karel Malik (Ivan Jandl) and his mother (Jarmila Novotna) trying to find each other. In the interim, American GI Ralph Stevenson (Montgomery Clift) cares for Karel.

FIG. 32 Lights, camera, UNRRA in action for *The Search* (1948). Director Fred Zinnemann mixed real concentration camp survivors with the Hollywood way. (Author's collection.)

Mrs. Malik finds her calling working with UNRRA under the supervision of sympathetic officer Deborah Murray (Aline MacMahon). The camera tracks over the destitute charges, leading to whom a narrator introduces as a "little boy with the sad face and the big eyes, you have eaten with your fingers for so long you're forgotten how to eat with a spoon."[79] Here was Karel.

Even in this introductory shot, *The Search* reflected creative and commercial tensions. Zinnemann hated the narration and wanted the sentimental hokum removed, but doing so would add extra cost for redoing the soundtrack in the first reel.[80] Although the narrator disappears, for Zinnemann this layer of sentiment jarred with the picture's tone. In contrast, MGM executives had concerns over the realism, especially lengthy dialogue sequences in non-English. Producer Arthur Hornblow Jr. objected to subtitles because he felt subtitles, along with the location shooting, connoted an "'education' factor into the film at an early point." Audiences, he believed, would think they were "being submitted to a lecture."[81] Hornblow recommended deleting these passages entirely, stating there did "not seem to be much need for all the foreign length footage that is presently in the picture for the point to be established."[82] The scenes remained, albeit with an English interpreter included. The contentions between realism and audience salability on the American side, however, paled to Zinnemann's conflicts with his European partners.

Americanizing the film and Karel Malik became a battleground between the American and European filmmakers. Zinnemann intended to promote UN efforts, and the film focuses on UNRRA as an American-led effort. Historian Tara Zahra notes the producers' casting a Czech child reflected the belief Czechs were the most "western" and "cultured" of Central Europeans, which Czech nationals emphasized as a common heritage with their American benefactors.[83] Rather than find an "exotic" Ukrainian or Pole or even a Jewish Czech, the filmmakers cast an "Aryan"-looking boy who enjoyed a middle-class lifestyle before the war. His rehabilitation would show the need to rebuild an American-style Germany.

To contextualize Karel within the U.S.-led efforts, UNRRA provided Zinnemann with statistics and studies about Czech children needing guidance to re-create a national identity. Czech kids like Karel struggled to "unlearn German, the only language they know, and re-learn Czech, the language they have forgotten."[84] In Karel's case, reeducation comes directly from Americans. The boy runs away and meets Ralph "Steve" Stevenson, a GI. Steve kindly gives the kid a sandwich and later takes him to his flat. The locked iron gate scares the young refugee, but Steve shows him "he's with people he can trust" and leaves the door open.[85] The boy immediately flees, but, seeing Steve not pursuing, comes back. The camera, situated behind Steve, records Karel ascending the stairs back to his American benefactors. One Londoner loved the scene: "I thought the two best sequences were the boy's return to the Americans' home when he realizes that he is among friends—this was so beautifully done—and, of course, the end, which I found extremely moving."[86]

The camera's framing and anticipated audience sympathy segues into Steve raising the boy himself. His roommate, Jerry Fisher (Wendell Corey), is skeptical. Fisher, a pencil pusher with the Allied Military Government, knows adoption takes months of bureaucratic red tape. When Steve balks, Fisher retorts, "All of Europe will be in America if we didn't have all the rules." His comment backhandedly supports the necessity of a prolonged U.S. presence, if only to keep "all of Europe" from swarming American shores. Fisher pointedly observes Steve "used to make cracks about all the filthy DPs [displaced people]."[87] Steve admits the boy has awakened a renewed sense of duty to see this mission through. Karel shakes the GI from the neoisolationism and inwardness Zinnemann deplored.

The picture segues into Steve's attempts at fathering. Since he does not speak German, his only recourse is to acquaint him with the American way of life. The solider begins with language, explaining words like "okay" are universal. Steve teaches Karel that "tomato" refers to an American pinup, and says Karel "must know" Abraham Lincoln. The boy also learns to call an image of a fawn "Bambi," and sees photos of metropolitan New York (figure 33).[88] Steve, not knowing the boy's name, rechristens him "Jim," and even after Karel becomes conversant in English, Steve never asks his real name. Karel repeats the name of Steve's home

FIG. 33 Americanization at work. In *The Search* (1948), Karel (Ivan Jandl, center) learns a girl is a "tomato." Steve (Montgomery Clift, left) and Jerry Fisher (Wendell Corey, right) teach the lessons. (Author's collection.)

country, and the scene ends on the connection between the refugee and the land of the free.

Zinnemann's projection of an American hegemony created a feud with his European partner. Praesens-Film clearly had a stake in displaying a sympathetic Europe determined to recover and prosper. Zinnemann, however, remained adamant on selling the need for greater American involvement abroad to its target domestic audience, not Europe. The film, he argued, required a U.S. slant. "It is my understanding that you hope this film to be primarily successful in the United States rather than Switzerland, and I am sincerely anxious to help you in this."[89] According to Zinnemann, screenwriter Peter Viertel's draft "lacked inner truth and strength" and was "too remote from reality."[90] He fired Viertel and brought in screenwriters Richard Schwiezer from Praesens to revamp the script and Paul Jarrico from Hollywood to authenticate the American dialogue. Jarrico wanted to Americanize the script further, focusing it "for the American audience so that the collary [*sic*] of the theme is clear: American responsibility for the refugee children in Europe."[91] Jarrico's characterizing Steve as a perfect father figure was not lost on actor Montgomery Clift. Clift later described his role as "so damn saintly that a special prop man would have been needed to polish my halo."[92]

On the European end, Praesens-Film's producer Lazar Wechsler blasted the Americans taking over the picture. He chastised Montgomery Clift for ad-libbing during the "taming of the boy" sequences (Wechsler's phrasing), such as calling Karel "Jim" and "Jack," which Welchsler felt dripped with sentimentality.[93] He accused Zinnemann of muddling the script, such as changing one line between MacMahon to Novolta from "You're really over the worst. Nothing can happen to you now" to "Only good things will happen to you now." Wechsler groused, "The prophecy of 'only good things' has no meaning for the European mother of today" and believed Zinnemann pandered to Americans who wanted happy endings.[94] Zinnemann countered, saying the disagreement over the dialogue delay was "one more example of your organisational difficulties." Since Wechsler resided in another country, the director "did not consider it feasible to stop production for several hours in order to discuss such minor changes."[95]

Despite Wechsler's objections, the Americans dominated. Steve gently persuades Karel to go to UNRRA and wait for clearance to go with Steve to the United States. At UNRRA headquarters, they run into Karel's mother, who has found a new calling working with children. With Steve as a father figure (since he is stationed there for the duration), Karel and his mom become a family again under the watchful guidance of American tutelage.

What Russia Wants?

Despite Zinnemann's efforts, *The Search* faced an uphill battle with domestic audiences. The public's resistance to message pictures coincided with their desire to leave the Depression and war years behind. As noted last chapter, by 1948 World War II largely vanished from American screens until the Korean War revived the genre. A case in point: in 1944, director William Wyler's smash documentary *Memphis Belle: The Story of a Flying Fortress* captivated audiences. In 1947, Wyler's *Thunderbolt*, a follow-up about a different aircraft, found a distributor in poverty row Monogram. The major studios shied away from what actor and Army Air Force colonel Jimmy Stewart sardonically called "ancient history" in his introduction to the picture.[96] The public agreed.

For *The Search*, MGM marketed it through wartime internationalism. In a radio "promotion flash," MGM aired an endorsement from Minneapolis mayor Hubert M. Humphrey, lauding the Americanization of world refugees. "Within the next two years, 205,000 people will come into this country under the Displaced Persons act of 1948," Humphrey declared. "Many of them are women and children who, for the first time, will experience the blessings of liberty which this country will give them."[97] One testimonial touted the film's educational merit with "special tickets for children . . . at the request of school teachers."[98] *Boxoffice* agreed: "Get your civic organizations, service clubs, churches, Boy and Girl Scout troops and schools behind this one and tie them all in with a local newspaper on a campaign to back the United Nations' new drive to help Europe's displaced children. Set up collection boxes for clothing, money and anything else that could help. A factor in the campaign could be a contest in the lower school grades with entrants writing letters on 'Why we should help our less fortunate friends in Europe.'"[99] Social reformers asserted these Americanization programs helped displaced people "become alive" thanks to the efforts in the United States.[100]

Such optimism belied a less idealized reality. *Life* conceded the happy ending was "pure hokum," which "highlights the fact that real displaced-children stories hardly ever end happily."[101] The magazine provided photos comparing "Scenes from the Movie" with "Scenes from Real Life," with the real UNRRA centers populated with more "ragged, hungry, and hopeless" children than those seen in the film.[102] Zinnemann replied, reiterating it was "necessary to soften the truth," otherwise "the American audience would have lost any desire to face it, used as they have been through the years to seeing a sentimentalized world."[103]

Indeed, isolationists warned about the "draining" of precious American resources and stigmatized refugees as the "little people" in Europe who stroked American egos to keep aid coming.[104] The movie's characterizing postwar reconstruction as a protracted process also discouraged the public. In 1946, eighty 80 percent of Americans agreed keeping troops in Europe was "the best thing."[105] Some movies also confirmed the necessity to maintain the wartime commitment; in *Tomorrow Is Forever* (1946), a woman who lost her husband in World War I refuses to let her eldest son, Drew (Richard Long), enlist on the outbreak of World War II. Her youngest son chastises her: "After all, Mother, Drew's old enough to make up his own mind and if a man can't do what he wants, well, well, I'd know how I'd feel. Well, I'd feel like Patrick Henry—give me liberty or give me death!"[106] With Drew, a college history major with dreams of doing his part for world peace, and his younger brother citing American revolutionary heroes, mom has no choice but to tearfully give assent. However, despite the tearjerkers, public sentiment, and poll numbers, many preferred bringing the "boys" home. One reporter added, "The feeling is growing that we have been too sanguine in demobilizing not merely our troops but our wartime resolve."[107] The public wanted to "concentrate on our legitimate home-town affairs," but the projected occupation of "at least 25 and perhaps 50 years" was disheartening.[108] American foster parents also expressed disappointment in war orphans. Contrary to reports about orphans "becoming alive" in U.S. homes, refugee children resisted American culture, missed their parents, and thought themselves second-class citizens in a xenophobic land.[109]

Even worse, internationalism became a harder selling point as political stability in Eastern Europe deteriorated. In February 1948, the "fall" of Czechoslovakia—and the little Karel Maliks who lived there—signified to contemporaries "American power was not considered a match for Soviet power."[110] MGM released *The Search* a month later and expressed dismay over

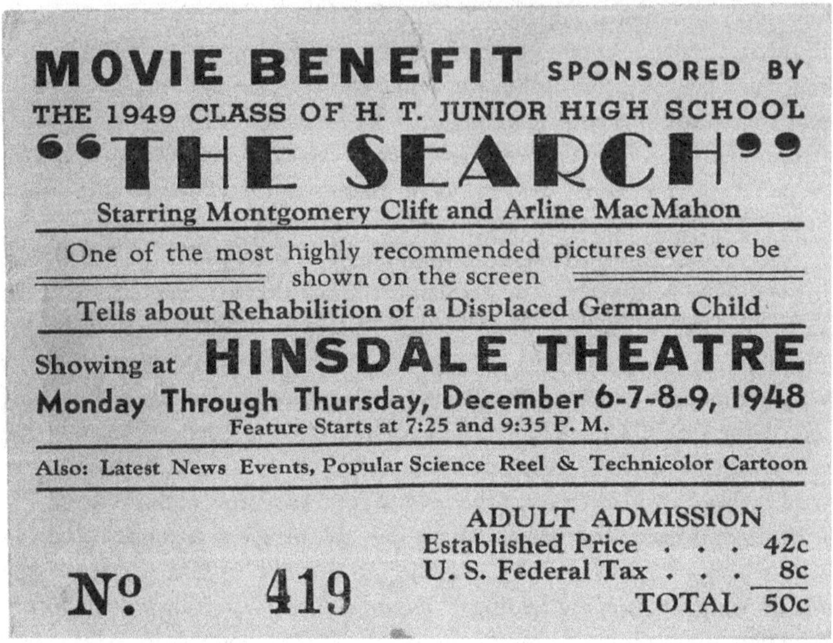

FIG. 34 Selling *The Search* (1948) under the banner of internationalism. Here, schoolkids sponsor a screening promoting German rehabilitation. The education theme included newsreels of local events and science to accompany the "highly recommended" film. (Author's collection.)

the initially poor box office returns. Trade journals emphasized the tough sell. *The Independent Exhibitors Film Bulletin* rated its box office potential as good, with the caveat "for select houses; less generally," although the reviewer cautioned "it will take a lot of intelligent selling to achieve the grosses it merits." He suggested exhibitors should "Hail it as a GREAT film," with its glimpse into "occupied Germany. Bill it a stirring drama, full of throbbing emotion." Should the dramatic buzz fail, showmen could appeal to "teachers, editors and social workers interested in the rehabilitation problem."[111] Some screenings took this approach, with civic-minded sponsors, including schools and church groups, informed audiences that they could see German rehabilitation at work (figure 34).

MGM responded, shifting its marketing angle to downplay internationalism. In February 1948, as Czechoslovakia was "falling," actress Aline MacMahon informed Zinnemann, "MGM [is] fogging on publicity. They are intent on selling the picture as entertainment—and fearful it will be damned as a 'cause' documentary." She characterized the studio's marketing ploy of *The Search* as a tourist excursion (in the same way that *Ben-Hur* [1925] showcased Italy) rather than one with a social or political message. "Well, who am I to criticize MGM?"

Table 2
Preview card tabulation results for *Berlin Express* (RKO, 1948)

Outstanding	Excellent	Very good	Good	Fair	Poor
59	74	75	34	10	9

SOURCE: "Berlin Express, Preview Comments," f.6, Bert Granet papers, MHL, AMPAS.

MacMahon asked rhetorically, concluding, "I hope they're right."[112] MacMahon and MGM had different concerns over *The Search*, with the studio worried about the picture's salability and the actress upset over the misleading advertising. But both had good grounds to protect their investment.

Studios had raced into bombed-out Germany—a readymade film set with the victory of spoils: a shattered people, a political vacuum, and a very long cleanup ahead. Hollywood, sensing the home front's understandable curiosity over the fruits of their four years of labor, produced a small cycle of "rubble films" that made the devastated German backdrop a star.[113] Paramount injected a sense of satirical fun in *A Foreign Affair* (1948), and RKO's *Berlin Express* (1948) touted that the Allies are better together than apart—at least to weed out leftover Nazis stirring up trouble. *Berlin Express* made it to theaters ahead of *The Search* and *A Foreign Affair*, but ran into unexpected hurdles. When RKO previewed the film on March 17, 1948, a month after MacMahon's letter, the majority of respondents labeled the movie "excellent" and "very good," with 164 out of the 262 cards saying they would recommend the movie (table 2).[114] For fans, international fraternity reflected a one world angle (figure 35). Moviegoers even singled out actor Roman Toporow's performance as a young Russian lieutenant who warms up to international fellowship and, when returning to the Soviet zone, breaks from his dour militaristic regiment to wave the American stars goodbye.[115]

But even if the majority of filmgoers respected RKO's efforts to maintain the wartime alliance, many regarded such sentiments as sappy. Respondents were lukewarm toward the obligatory happy ending, the gloomy aftermath of war, and the Hollywood combat units turned diplomats. "Don't you think we've had enough of this type of picture?," one commenter complained, while another groused, "Why make such drab uninteresting war pictures. We are sick of them at this house."[116] Even the spectacular shots of ruined Berlin were not enough to win favorable responses; if anything, the hope-filled finale contrasted sharply with the grim location shoot. One previewer took the time to explain why Hollywood hokum rang hollow. "And of the picture where the 'friends' part was a little drawn out, I think falls so dismally short in many instances. The final scenes, particularly, I felt were terrible due to largely to such bad writing and such ludicrous attempts at 'understanding.'"[117] The end reel, filled with optimistic vows of future transatlantic get-togethers, left American moviegoers cold. One fan, who liked the picture, read a different sort of fear not centered in postwar Europe:

FIG. 35 International train wreck for *Berlin Express* (1948) and marked the decline of the One World movement. Moviegoers singled out actor Roman Toporow (far left) among the international cast of good Germans (Paul Lukas), British (Robert Coote), French (Charles Korvin), and Americans (Robert Ryan) for his earnest performance as the Soviet officer, Maxim Kiroshilov. (Author's collection.)

"I sincerely hope they don't claim this 'Red' just because it tries to put across a message."[118] The sympathetic Russian soldier—with Toporow's breakout performance—and the thinly veiled message of one world fellowship evoked brewing home front wariness about supposed subversion emanating from dupes in the film colony. Images of war-torn Berlin inspired not determination to reconstruct Germany but a cautionary note about lurking un-Americanism at home. Such fears, coupled with the production's high cost, made *Berlin Express* stand still. RKO lost $985,000 on the project.[119]

Berlin Express proved to be a train wreck in terms of box office boffo. MGM similarly struggled over *The Search*. *Variety* noted how the "foreign-mades, even when American technicians and actors have been employed, very often still have an overseas air about them. Result is that they are considerably harder to sell than the Hollywood product, even when rated tops by critics. A case in point is *The Search*. Metro has been forced to aim its whole campaign at scotching the idea this is a foreign picture."[120] Critical acclaim, fine craftsmanship, and strong acting could not overcome the stigma of "foreign" airs. In April 1948, *Variety* reported MGM was "fully cognizant" of the "apparent antipathy of filmgoers outside the key cities against foreign-made films, one of Metro's chief problems is to remove the foreign-made stigma from *Search*" by "spotlighting the appearance in the cast of Montgomery Clift above others with foreign-sounding names."[121] The new emphasis on Clift met with some derision; the *Portsmouth Herald* scoffed, "After promoting a dignified, adult sales campaign for that great picture, 'The Search,' M-G-M is now ballyhooing it with such incongruous lines such as 'Montgomery Clift! Girls, he's from Omaha and he's terrific.'"[122] This ad played up Clift's bobby-soxer appeal, conjuring a farm boy image far from occupied Germany. The studio's press book also emphasized a nonexistent "search" for romance. Such "current advertising of *The Search*" led the *Motion Picture Herald* to mock the press book's ad "Are Press Agents Liars?," before dismissing the tactic as effective showmanship.[123] Despite the misleading ads, Clift's star power rose; one reader said, "I believe one reason for the failure of *The Search* was insufficient advertising. All I had heard or read was that Montgomery Clift was in it. Had he not been in it, I probably would not have seen it and missed a very good picture."[124] The confused marketing annoyed the picture's production crew, who had loftier ambitions. In May 1948, Aline MacMahon wrote Zimmerman again, complaining MGM was "experimenting in a dangerous way with *The Search* and that by now a potential audience is pretty much puzzled here in New York as to what *The Search* is really about. But, Fred and Renee [Zinnemann's wife], dears, whom am I?"[125] MacMahon reluctantly resigned herself to the studio's grab-all approach for attention.

As MacMahon noted, American audiences wanted entertainment, not a "cause" documentary. Exhibitors, commenting on the poor performances of "message pictures," demanded lighter fare. Producer Joseph Mankiewicz wrote an open letter to exhibitors, acknowledging the unpopularity of message pictures, but insisted on diversifying film offerings. "Certainly no one should expect *The Search*, for example, to be as profitable as a 'Belvedere,'" he conceded, using the same comparison that industry commentators had made with *Intruder in the Dust*, but he believed Hollywood had greater potential than churning out formulaic, uncontroversial story lines. Mankiewicz, who would later direct the race-themed picture *No Way Out*, claimed even a "modest but encouraging profit" on pictures like *The Search* encouraged experimentation and secure "a vast, varied, and discriminating world audience," lest they lose audiences completely.[126] With the television industry emerging and audience attendance diminishing, Mankiewicz feared the industry strangled itself by playing it safe.

Facing stiff competition from television, some showmen jumped on the chance to air their civic virtue. One small-town Minnesotan reported, "We did a lot of extra advertising, both by newspapers, special cards to all boxholders, and lots of word-of-mouth advance boosting to the 'solid citizens' . . . when we saw we had lots of repeats among patrons and heard them rave, we relaxed. It deserved our best playing time, some told us."[127] One Canadian reported, "Why can't Metro make a few more of this same caliber. This picture had something most MGM productions lack. It had feeling, understanding, and a story that wasn't padded with unnecessary dialogue. This had more favorable comments than any Metro picture this year."[128] Despite critical acclaim, a September 1949 Gallup poll noted *The Search* "flopped because too few people knew about it."[129] A year and a half after its release, barely 9 percent of filmgoers had heard about the picture, and 4 percent knew something about its plot. Despite these glowing reports, enticing audiences proved difficult.

On a different front, UNRRA regarded the film a public relations coup. As early as 1946, the organization's chief of visual media, William H. Wells, reported Loew's International was "very helpful in providing Latin American distribution for films about UNRRA" and wanted UNRRA to reciprocate concerning the upcoming production of *The Search*.[130] A year later, a pleased Wells wrote Zinnemann, "We are used to knocks that a word of commendation once in a while comes about as a shock." He added, "The project seems to me especially important because it stems from real international cooperation" and hoped for more.[131] Deputy zone director Ralph W. Collins agreed, issuing a blanket directive: "This film will be of great value to the aims of UNRRA and it is requested that every assistance and facility be accorded to Mr. Zinnemann."[132] UNRRA's director of publicity, Leo G. Margolin, also hoped publicity would pressure Congress to pass a bill to allow 400,000 displaced persons into the United States "at a rate of 100,000 a year." He urged "the assistance of every possible media, including what I consider to be the most effective—motion pictures."[133] Herbert H. Meyer of the International Refugee Organization commended *The Search* for showing to world audiences "the true and heartbreaking story of the Displaced and Unaccompanied Children," in which Karel's story represented the work of the International Tracing Service to reunite relatives.[134] In January 1948, two months before the film's release, William Wells wrote Zinnemann, beaming, "Three years ago I tried to explain to people in Hollywood that there was a great feature picture in UNRRA's work. Now you have proved it."[135]

Despite the accolades from the United Nations, Zinnemann doubted lightning could strike twice. In May 1949, Herbert Meyer asked him to consider a follow-up, but the director demurred, citing the film's struggle. "It is very difficult at this point to persuade people here in Hollywood that another interesting film about European children could be made. Most people seem unwilling to follow *The Search* in a film on a similar theme."[136] Zinnemann himself expressed interest in the topic of Germanized children, but he doubted if he could "undertake another film of this kind" and was "a bit pessimistic" about the industry's support.[137] Meyer bowed to the director's expertise and agreed: "Another picture on this subject probably cannot be produced."[138] Despite MGM's promoting the Displaced Persons Act of 1948, Congress selected the most desirable refugees along racial and ideological lines; up to 90 percent of the 205,000 hopefuls found no place on American shores.[139] Two years later, the Subversive Activities Control Act (aka the McCarran Act), designed to root out unfriendly foreign agents, decreased the number further.[140] The stigmatization of refugees took its toll on the box office. *Harrison's Reports* projected the box office receipts as "fair."[141]

1948: Revising the Postwar Narrative

Zinnemann's belief in the poor prospects for any follow-ups to *The Search* reflected fluctuating international politics. When he started *The Search* in 1946, the social message cycle in Hollywood and UN enthusiasm reflected wartime optimism for reform. By the film's release in March 1948, the atmosphere hardened, encouraging the public to shy away from the one world movement. Reporters noted Americans were determined to avoid a repeat of World War I, when the nation's inward turn created "confusion, bitterness and disillusionment."[142] But the rationale for increased international engagement shifted from brotherhood to antagonism. As U.S.-Soviet relations crumbled, policy makers and the public increasingly regarded communism as an ideological enemy. Two weeks before the film's release, Secretary of Commerce W. Averell Harriman warned about "aggressive forces in the world coming from the Soviet Union which are just as destructive in their effect on the world and our way of life as Hitler was, and I think are a greater menace than Hitler was."[143]

These tensions played out dramatically before the public. While Zinnemann filmed *The Search* and MGM prepared their initial marketing angles, the public read about the U.S.-led efforts in the Berlin Airlift, where Soviet cruelty and obstinacy forced American heroes to daringly air drop aid to Germany's war-torn, resource-hungry civilians. U.S. secretary of state Dean Acheson and British foreign secretary Ernest Bevin jointly announced an Anglo-American effort "to resist the use of lawless force" and to unite the occupied German zones "under a real democratic government," which, they implied, was clearly not what Moscow wanted.[144] The airlift scored good public relations points, especially when pilots delivered candy packages specifically for children.[145] Mrs. Roscoe C. O'Byrne, the president general of the Daughters of the American Revolution, proclaimed the airlift proved the need for superior airpower. "If ever America needed a strong national defense, it is now," she told President Truman. "We want smashing air power and plenty of it" so the Cold War would not "become a 'deep freeze.'" She concluded, "We can turn on a little heat if necessary—and we have the fuel."[146] In her view, security and strength came from a projection of military power, even if it meant applying "a little heat" and confronting the Russians.

Fittingly, actor Montgomery Clift returned to Germany for *The Big Lift* (1950). Taking the name from the Berlin Airlift, the film opens with a newsreel explaining the American necessity to save Germany from communism. The "Cold War reaches a new crisis" when the reds withdraw from the joint Allied government in Berlin, blockade the city, and try to "starve the city into submission."[147] General Lucius D. Clay appears before the cameras to confirm the American "right to be in Berlin and we intend to maintain that right."[148] The newsreel establishes this political setting (before segueing into a beauty contest), but this backdrop is almost irrelevant to the story. Soviets appear fleetingly and the airlift appears not at all. Rather, *The Big Lift* lifted American patriotism and internationalism to check a lurking Soviet threat.[149] Its tagline said as much: "Now You Can See It as You Cheered It!"

With the Soviet Union as the enemy, the United States presented itself on the defensive, needing the home front's support to win the peace as effectively as it had won the war. Some naysayers worried the air convoys could become another "Pearl Harbor" by inviting Soviet attacks.[150] Complaints about the airlift's high costs also echoed criticism about the relief efforts draining needed resources to prevent the country from sinking into another depression. The Air Force countered, stating the program's $393,000 price tag was not a "pain in the pocketbook," but an exercise in "peacemaking, propaganda and persistence."[151] This investment in democracy demonstrated a public and political resilience against communism, as the United States was willing to go the extra distance to drop candy bars for malnourished German tykes. Despite public clamoring to "bring the boys home," the United States rejected a Soviet proposal to withdraw all occupation troops from Germany as a scheme to lull the world into a false sense of security, allowing Stalin carte blanche in Europe.[152]

International security required a permanent check against communism. Former British prime minister Winston Churchill delivered his Iron Curtain speech in 1946, calling for an Anglo-American "special relationship" to counter Soviet expansion. Although the United States had little enthusiasm about bolstering the faltering British Empire, the speech clearly worried Stalin, who feared the Allies planned to inhibit Soviet recovery and marginalize him.[153] In 1947, the threatened "fall" of Greece prompted the Truman Doctrine as a defensive measure to save American democracy.[154] A year later, with *The Search* still playing, the "Bamboo Curtain" fell in Asia when China went "red."[155] This twinning of the iron and bamboo curtains saved *The Search*'s salability. Although the public did not accept the film for its message of brotherhood, moviegoers applauded the movie as a patriotic salute to American values against communism.

With countries "falling" to communist oppression, the one world movement became tainted as naïve at best, a subversive movement at worst. Writers, such as news correspondent Joachim Joesten, worried about the fate of a divided Germany. Writing at the close of 1947, Joesten observed, "One has the feeling that the Allies have almost given up the idea of making peace with Germany before starting a new war among themselves."[156] Irreconcilable differences divided the Allies; Joesten pointed out, "Socialism in any form or shape is alien to the American way of thinking and abhorrent to most American politicians," and the socialist turn throughout postwar Europe left American officials "in a state of bewilderment mingled with indignation. Was this a relapse into barbarism or utopian quackery?"[157] To safeguard against such barbarity or political deception, a wary public scrutinized leftist sentiments that potentially weakened a strong

U.S. presence abroad. Even the progressive 1948 presidential candidate Henry Wallace lost credibility when he seemed to advocate a military withdrawal from Berlin, leaving the beleaguered people in Stalin's hands.[158] One newspaper columnist observed the "capacity of Soviet Russia to 'collect' its neighbors" and warned, "Always the question arises: Who's next? And the next question is, When's our turn?"[159] The reporter's answer: "Americans will become more receptive to increased expenditures on national defense and to Universal Military Training" because "Russian tactics inevitably breed warmongers."[160]

The polemical rhetoric against the commies and the American need to rebuild Europe to protect freedoms at home politicized children. As historians point out, throughout the 1950s, children became unofficial ambassadors as they donated books, clothing, and money to UNICEF and relief programs that catered to war orphans in the name of humanitarianism and anticommunism.[161] Hollywood also did its part, releasing pictures like the aforementioned *Tomorrow Is Forever*, where Mom not only reluctantly lets her oldest son enlist to make the world safe for democracy but also has adopted a German war orphan, and *Little Boy Lost* (1953), starring Bing Crosby as an American newsman who recovers his traumatized young son in a French orphanage and rehabilitates the lad through the folksy American charm that Crosby built his career on. A more action-packed offering was *Kim* (1951), based on Rudyard Kipling's poem about a street-smart orphan who enlists as a British spy under Errol Flynn's tutelage to play the Great Game against Russians in India. Comedies also featured cute war orphans and their adorable hijacks, such as Abbott and Costello's *Buck Privates Come Home* (1947), with the duo smuggling a French girl into the United States. *Here Comes the Groom* (in which, as noted earlier, the UN managed to get an onscreen endorsement) has Bing Crosby—playing another foreign correspondent—facing the disheartening news that his readers are not interested in hearing about war orphans anymore. Fortunately, one French boy hitches a ride with Crosby to the United States, just in time for the newsman to fulfill the title's promise of marriage, and the lad conveniently becomes a readymade son for the new family.

The political stakes that war orphans represented played out in *The Search*. Although the film does not mention communism (or the Nazis), preview audiences read the movie as an exercise for democracy. Several preview cards stated as much. "What a lesson in humanity we English-speaking peoples are teaching the German and Russian tyranists," wrote one doctor.[162] Another agreed: "It should be shown to the world to teach them what Fascism and Communism really mean."[163] Looking at the European map, Assistant Secretary of Labor John W. Gibson urged for greater American involvement to aid Europe and win the peace. The fall of Czechoslovakia, he asserted, "hinges on a depression in America, an event which fellow travelers here and abroad fervently yearn for."[164] Supposedly, "the Communist-dominated nations and their leaders are prepared to flood our country with cheap European goods," making the United States an economic dependent. Gibson ended with a "simple" choice: "Either we pay higher taxes to aid European nations now, or we pay with the blood of our sons and daughters within a few years."[165]

This combination of anticommunism with pro-Americanism paid off. After a year in theaters, *The Search* finally clicked with moviegoers. Critics expressed disbelief in MGM's disguising the film to lure in teenage bobby-soxers, but where sex appeal failed, "Americanism" in the face of communism succeeded.[166] "After seeing this, one should thank God he is an American," one Montanan smiled in December 1949.[167] In July 1949, *Variety* reported, "Metro's *The Search*, bewailed as an instance of an adult pic which caught on with the critics but not the public, is now proving to be a big profit maker for the company handling it."[168] The grosses "sparked to a $850,000 domestic take and is still grossing $7,500 weekly in the United States after a full year's distribution," while, abroad, the film "is doing even better with a series of house records shattered behind it." The numbers were "minor" compared to the studio's typical revenue stream, but the trade journal argued *The Search* "has proven a real earner against its cost to the company of less than $300,000" paid to Wechsler for distribution rights. This small expenditure for the rights paid off, and *Variety* predicted MGM "will eventually capture a sensational $1,000,000 profit on a $300,000 investment."[169]

Variety's report underscored Hollywood's uncertainty concerning the shift in public's attitude. The stumped writer confessed, "Metro's homeoffice staffers are at a loss to explain what all the shouting is about," implying even studio marketers did not know why the picture suddenly caught fire.[170] Nevertheless, Hollywood recognized the movie contained a powerful message moviegoers picked up. *Variety* explained the film's initial release "was cited by film industryites as a disappointment to Metro box office–wise when critics' raves failed to bring in the customers." But now, "on the basis of strong word-of-mouth, film is getting plenty of dates at the present time."[171] According to one source, *The Search* ultimately grossed $1.4 million, with a profit of $609,000.[172]

Hollywood's puzzlement over *The Search*'s role reversal within a two-year period reflected the hardening political atmosphere and anticommunism's impact on the industry. By the 1950s, many industry leftists were blacklisted; *The Search*'s Peter Viertel and Fred Zinnemann cleared themselves, but Paul Jarrico fell under HUAC's axe.[173] In contrast, Ivan Jandl's role as the film's Americanized child took on new meaning in an anticommunist light. As a symbol of brotherhood, celluloid character Karl Malik did not click with audiences. As a victim of "fallen" Czechoslovakia, Jandl attracted sympathy. In May 1948, Jandl wrote to Zinnemann (in English), three months after *The Search* premiered. His fame seemed like stepping stones to more work, including broadcasting and two roles in Czechoslovakian pictures before his career ended.[174]

As trade papers noted, the newly empowered communists shortly denied Jandl's working for American capitalists. MGM, sensing Jandl's star potential, wanted to sign the boy to a contract. One insider noted Jandl was studying

English and "would be an asset to any studio." After *The Search* made money, MGM "thinks enough of him to be negotiating to lure him across the ocean. They're very high on the whole picture [*The Search*] down Culver City [MGM's home town] way because all the rest of the country seems to think it's a wow."[175] Unfortunately, Czechoslovakia's fall in early 1948 nixed those plans. *Variety* reported MGM encountered "international complications" because "political conditions in Czechoslovakia have grown too touchy."[176] The "international project" of bringing Jandl over met resistance from "the political coup that brought Red control to Czechoslovakia."[177] The *New York Times* noted the same "political coup which brought Communist control to Czechoslovakia put an end to the plans of Metro-Goldwyn-Mayer's publicity department to bring him here for a visit at the hour of his triumph."[178] Denied a promotional tour and trapped behind the Iron Curtain, Jandl had no future in Hollywood.

On March 24, 1949, Jandl won the Academy Award for best juvenile performance. He missed the ceremony, and Hollywoodites worried "Czechoslovakia's Commie-controlled government would prevent the youth from learning of the award."[179] The industry relaxed when Jandl cabled Zinnemann, thanking him for the notice; the director had notified Jandl directly, avoiding the red channels.[180] Renee Zinnemann assured the press Jandl still received her care packages, "so there's no reason to believe he won't get his Oscar." Even if the communists denied him his prize, she suggested the boy might not mind so much since he wanted to train as an engineer, not an actor, much to his parents' disappointment. She added Jandl wanted to visit the United States and see the country Karel promoted so much, but admitted, "I don't know if he could get a visa."[181] Three months later, Jandl informed Zinnemann he still had not received his trophies (he also won a Golden Globe) and described the press photos the director sent covering the ceremony: "all hold Oscars and me only a piece of bread."[182] A concerned Zinnemann informed the Academy the award would brighten the boy's life, and MPAA president Eric Johnston personally presented the award to Czechoslovakia ambassador Vladimir Outrata in Washington, D.C.[183] *Variety* noted Czechoslovakia, "his own country," did not bother to acknowledge their native son's thespian abilities.[184]

Jandl's Academy Award tainted him as a tool for the capitalist nations. The boy never came to the United States, but he preferred the idealized image Karl Malik spoke about to the realities at home. "If I could fly to Amerika I would fly immediately," he wrote Zinnemann in September 1948.[185] By November 1949, Zinnemann noted Jandl was studying engineering in Prague, but hinted the lad wanted to change careers. One gossip columnist claimed Jandl wanted "to come to H'wood but nobody's bidding."[186] Jandl continued to perform on the stage.[187] But neither the American film industry nor its Czech counterpart had any place for him. In the 1980s, documentarian Oskar Reif informed Zinnemann how Jandl's "American film prize" was a "Kain's sign" prohibiting him from work. For decades, Jandl refused to surrender his awards to the state, and he recalled

The Search "with great pleasure." The former actor worked "as an auditor in Prague's grocery."[188]

Any search for Jandl ended shortly thereafter. Zinnemann, concerned for his former charge, asked if publicity would help: "whether this story of his misfortunes should be kept confidential or whether it could be told to some newspapers here in England [where Zinnemann was then living] or in America."[189] Jandl died three years later, in 1988, and the director later eulogized, "He received an Oscar [which] ruined his life" because "the Communist government considered it a disgrace that he should have accepted an award from a capitalist country."[190] In 1990, documentarian Dagmar Mackova Smržová confirmed Jandl was "persecuted all his life in this country." As the Czech government built "a socialist-communist system, it was announced by the government that [Jandl] is no more allowed to travel abroad or to accept any film contract in the then so-called 'rotten imperialist' countries, including the USA."[191] Even though the Soviet Union had collapsed by that point, for Hollywood, Oscar winner Ivan Jandl was a casualty decades earlier.

Defining the Postwar Hollywood Manner

In 1947, the *New York Times* created a minor publicity crisis for *The Search* by quoting actor Wendell Corey, who played Steve's GI pal. The article, part of a larger story about Hollywood cowering under HUAC, discussed Corey's assertion that the American production crew believed "they would be free of the shackles of commercialism and come face to face with pure cinematic art."[192] Unfortunately, Corey claimed, the "Europeans soon made it plain that they had imported Americans only because they wished to make a picture in the Hollywood manner for sale at American boxoffices." The accusation of crass and mass commercialization at a time when the United States tried to keep Europe open for American consumer goods sent MGM's lion into an uproar. With the industry already suffering from charges of un-Americanism (which included several of *The Search*'s crew) and box office decline (which led exhibitors to want fewer "social message" pictures), MGM drew a line. Vice President G. Muchnic politely demanded an explanation "since this is hardly the type of publicity which will be beneficial to the distribution of the picture in the United States."[193] He added, "It was certainly not our purpose in becoming financially interested in the production to 'make a picture in the Hollywood manner,'" with the pejoratives implied.[194]

Two weeks later, Corey explained the *New York Times* made much ado about nothing. "There is, as you know, a feeling in part of the film industry and public that only abroad do you find art, culture, history, and freedom from the 'shackles of consumerism.'"[195] Defending his craft and career, Corey clarified he only referred to Zinnemann defying the stereotype that American-made products intrinsically lacked European flair. "In the Hollywood manner" applied to technical aspects, he stressed, such as the slick production values and the happy ending, not the message.[196]

Corey's interview underscored the shifting public attitudes toward postwar Europe. *The Search*'s rocky reception reflected this transition from the Great Depression and World War II. Zinnemann supported the one world movement as a means of global stability, and he targeted isolationists who, fearing a return of Depression, accused UNRRA of taking food out of American mouths. The movie trumpeted "the tortured soul of Europe to America and at the same time to reveal to Europe the true nature of America's 'big heart,'" the *New York Times* declared.[197] It presented a healthy father-son relationship between a handsome GI and a luckless orphan. He intended its happy ending in "the Hollywood manner" to satisfy audiences, uplifting them as they left theaters.

But Zinnemann's "big heart" failed to attract audiences. Film critic James Agee snorted, *The Search* "had been made to interest American clubwomen in sending CARE packages—as indeed I wish they would," the latter phrase suggesting the intended audience, and Agee, did no such thing.[198] MGM, wary of the tensions between internationalism and depression-weary isolationism, marketed the film as a "search" for romance, especially for newcomer Montgomery Clift. The Tinsel Town glamour approach did not work. Furthermore, the film featured no villains to hiss—no Soviet or Nazi masterminds, not even an Emil Bruckner who needed a slap for wanting the world tomorrow. Instead of a climatic showdown of good versus evil, the film left viewers with Monty Clift—the "terrific" heartthrob from Omaha—stuck in the midst of a drab cleanup taking him away from home for years.

The film itself did not change, but the context did. While Zinnemann worked between 1946 and the film's release in March 1948, tensions between the United States and the Soviet Union escalated. The public initially harbored isolationist sentiment, but when communism loomed as a threat to postwar stability, the public accepted *The Search*'s glorification of the American mission abroad. The "fall" of Czechoslovakia especially highlighted the Soviet desire to undercut democracy in Eastern Europe. Child actor Ivan Jandl, who took home two top prizes for his role in "American imperialist" propaganda, became a victim. By 1950, the "Hollywood manner," like the public's mood, equated internationalism with anticommunism.

This chapter opened with *Boys' Life* describing an enthusiastic refugee who became an ideal American Boy Scout. However, the lad's enthusiasm led his "crackerjack" peers to initially shun the foreign child with a "cold freeze."[199] The new kid "knew more about the Statue of Liberty . . . and what it symbolizes than all the rest of the Troop combined," the article explained, which made the "native-born" boys uneasy with the war orphan's ultra-Americanism.[200] "His fellow Scouts hadn't had the same sort of experiences. Therefore, they couldn't possible have such strong feelings as he had." They eventually warmed up by adapting the newcomer's hyperpatriotism as their own. By forming a consensus around the rhetoric of antioppression (communism is not named), they thawed their standoff. But Scouts all over needed to duplicate this experience. The writer asked, "Now how about your Troop?"[201]

Director Fred Zinnemann had tried to answer by glamorizing the American mission abroad as "one world," but altruistic internationalism did not entice a depression-weary public. Anticommunism, however, via HUAC and various international crises, reframed internationalism as a defensive show of patriotism. This glorification of American values turned *The Search* into a blockbuster hit. This red-baiting foreshadowed the Red Scare and the solidifying boundaries of containment as the United States vied for hegemony in the domestic and international Cold War.

Conclusion

Revising the "Deanlinquent"

In 1952, a scholastic magazine, the *Junior Review*, published an article titled "Life under Communism" featuring a cartoon Joseph Stalin as a puppet master and the church, factories, government, and mass media as his marionettes. The first sentence, "Dictator Joseph Stalin of Russia wants to rule the world," neatly summarized the content. The writer then detailed the plight of the Potoff family in the Soviet Union, who subsisted in a room of cracked walls, shared a bathroom and kitchen with four other families, and voted in a one-party system. The *Junior Review* no doubt intended the American schoolkids reading about the Potoffs' meager lifestyle would sympathize, but it ended on a cliffhanger that hit closer to home. Next issue: "We shall discuss Russia's world ambitions."[1]

The Potoffs' woes conveyed the horrors should Russia's world ambitions come to fruition globally, and in the United States in particular. Soviet aggression permeated American culture, even everyday language; in the boy-and-dog picture *The Son of Rusty* (1947), a mysterious stranger with a dishonorable discharge and prison time under his belt moves into town, and young Danny Mitchell's (Ted Donaldson) attempts to socialize fall flat. His father (Tom Powers) casually remarks, "Our good neighbor policy doesn't seem to penetrate his Iron Curtain, does it?"[2] Miniature Iron Curtains descended upon the American landscape as suspicion, mistrust, and fear led neighbors to regard each other with a mix of vigilance and wariness. In another boy-and-dog movie, *Talk about a Stranger* (1952), the Red Scare appears via a witch hunt when an inquisitive lad equates an antisocial nonconformist's disagreeableness as a threat to his community—a lesson that *The Window*'s (1949) Tommy Woodry learned firsthand with upstairs neighbors who keep to themselves. By the 1950s, anticommunism absorbed these postwar concerns about familial stability, social institutions, and magnified fears of backslide into hard times. Earl Bunting, the president of the National Association of Manufacturers, warned that "the peace of the world is being stalled by Russia in hopes that our country is headed for a depression."[3] The reason why "Uncle Joey" wanted a new American depression, Bunting explained, was his lust for "total power." What happened to the Potoffs could easily take place in the United States, with Stalin presiding as the ultimate father figure over the state and family.

In contrast, the United States presented itself as a beacon of democracy and capitalism. But economic depression loomed over postwar America, threatening to snuff out prosperity and liberty. "The American people have not lost the fear of insecurity caused by the last depression and are now being assailed by fear caused by the cold war," the *New York Times* commented in 1949.[4] More cheerily, economist Fritz Sternberg rebutted Stalin, informing the public they "won't be selling apples in 1949."[5] The United States will not fall on hard times, assured Sternberg, because "the American productive apparatus is now finding its markets in a fat foreign-aid and armament program."[6] The European Recovery Program and checking Soviet aggression—in which Stalin's push into Eastern Europe galvanized the Americans into action—has "almost certainly eliminated the possibility of a large-scale deflationary depression in 1949."[7] Although the economist could not guarantee "that there will not be recessions" in the future, Stalin's supposed hopes for an American economic slump did not materialize.

Children played key roles in ensuring American productivity would marshal on. Ideally, boys took after their fathers as they trained to move up the corporate ladder, network with peers in socially constructive teamwork, and achieve material success. In 1949, the Business Historical Society linked this social mobility with protecting national values: "The lad who wants to engage in social service, and win the approval of his fellows, can go into business with the assured feeling that he is entering the greatest social service yet devised." In short, the society concluded, "He who fights for private business fights for democracy and for freedom."[8] Free enterprise and freedom of expression worked in tandem under the Stars and Stripes. Under this model, boys grew up as productive citizen-soldiers, not delinquents or "dupes" susceptible to communism or subversion.

The postwar reconstruction of family, the workplace, and national ideals became hallmarks for anticommunism. But that rhetoric drew from earlier decades. The fifteen years of depression and war made stability a paramount priority after V-J Day. The United States emerged as a superpower in 1945, emboldened to lead global rehabilitation efforts, but the potential for instability remained burned in public memory. By 1945, middle-aged Americans born at the turn of the century experienced the Great War, the Roaring Twenties, the Depression, and the Second World War. Armed with hindsight of the past decades, Americans constructed the building blocks of "cultural containment" to ensure a brighter future for their children.

Hollywood, with its mixed history of sex and violence on and off the screen, remained a battleground of postwar anxiety. During the 1930s and 1940s, progressives clamored for class and race reform, reflecting the crises of the times. But such activism became treasonous after 1945, as the Hollywood Ten found out. In addition, in 1948 the U.S. Supreme Court ruled the studios' block booking and vertical integration of theaters constituted an illegal monopoly, stripping the studios of guaranteed distribution for their products. As urban audiences started migrating to suburban single-family homes and television sets, the studios retreated from risky social message pictures. By 1952, Eric Johnston, president of the Motion Picture Association of America, declared an end to Depression era motifs: "We'll have no more *Grapes of Wrath*, we'll have no more *Tobacco Roads*. We'll have no more films that show the seamy side of American life. We'll have no pictures that deal with labor strikes. We'll have no pictures that deal with the banker as villain."[9] Not everyone bought this ballyhoo; in 1955, evangelist Robert L. Sumner sneered, "It is impossible for one to be a 100% American and a devotee of the silver screen at the same time. Hollywood is a 'Red' Menace!"[10] Hollywood countered these charges of treason with polemical anticommunist pictures that vigorously waved the flag. The early archetype, *I Was a Communist for the F.B.I.*, highlighted the transitional relationship between fathers and sons, juvenile delinquency and discipline, and American goals in the international arena. By the mid-1950s, even films such as *Rebel without a Cause* and its brand of James Dean–inspired "Deanlinquents" projected domestic containment as "traditional," historically timeless as the American way.

Why *I Was a Communist for the F.B.I.*

The Cold War family became part of the arsenal of democracy in Warner Bros.'s *I Was a Communist for the F.B.I.* (1951). The real-life espionage activities of Matt Cvetic, an American civilian counteragent, became the basis of a radio series, a literary serial, and a movie, all having variations on the same title.[11] The exploitation of then-current events even led to an Academy Award nomination for Best Documentary, confirming the content's authenticity. The picture shows Cvetic (Frank Lovejoy) as a typical American, "an average sort of guy about thirty-eight years of age."[12] Originally from Slovenia, the Cvetics "came over to this country forty years ago—became citizens," signifying their assimilation.[13] Unfortunately, Cvetic's public persona as a communist shames his family, who regard his subversion as betrayal of their adopted country.

As a double agent, Cvetic's job is maintaining the status quo. With clandestine operations lurking under the surface, any challenge against postwar America helped communism. The producers depict the commies as masterminds of deception; they complain about class inequality but enjoy champagne brunches while mocking workers. Their greatest feat consisted of exploiting civil rights and anti-Semitism, hoping the American melting pot will boil over into a race riot.

After urging African Americans to stand up for their rights in a rally, the main villain privately refers to them as "niggers." Cvetic, standing in for the audience, asks, "Don't you mean 'negroes?'" and his boss dismisses the Soviet propaganda about race equality as bunk.[14] Race-based red-baiting resurfaced in other films; MGM's *Trial* (1955), for instance, features the commies exploiting a white girl's alleged sexual assault and death at the hands of a Latino youth to stir up race hatred. To affirm "true" American race relations as harmonious, *Trial* casts Juano Hernandez—previously a victim of white supremacy in *Intruder in the Dust* (1949) and *Stars in My Crown* (1950)—as a dignified, respected judge who helps expose the Soviet plot. Hernandez's casting also provides an opportunity for dupes to spout off slurs in open court, thus revealing that the "real" racists are the communists.[15]

I Was a Communist for the F.B.I. contextualizes the civil rights movement within an anticommunism framework, but its main plot centers upon Cvetic's family. The assimilated Slovenians call the United States home, and their children vigilantly guard their status as Americans. The strain between a "red" dad and his "red-blooded" boy plays out via Dick Cvetic (Ron Hagerthy), "his sixteen-year-old son," who avoids his father's gaze.[16] Matt Cvetic's triple life as civilian, spy, and counterspy makes him an absent father, and he observes Dick is "getting taller every time I see him."[17] Postwar pictures had addressed the nuclear family's reconstruction from the threat of divorce and poor father-son relations. Here, the commies place party loyalty above kinship. Cvetic misses his mother's birthday and later learns she died heartbroken. Appropriately, Cvetic's siblings shun him, and his ashamed son disowns him.

Cvetic mourns his mom, but the film places greater concerns for the young generation. An encounter with a neighborhood boy shows why. Young Jackie (Erik Nielsen) asks Cvetic how to bunt a baseball bat, and the spy cheerfully complies. Jackie's dad (Roy Engel) intervenes, telling his son to go home because "baseball's an American game."[18] An uncomfortable Cvetic retreats under the watchful eye of the boy's father (figure 36). As a communist, Cvetic has no right to teach budding youths the national pastime, a character-building sport to participate in a democratic citizenry.[19]

Jackie's batting average does not compare to Dick Cvetic's profound disappointment in his father. When Matt Cvetic receives a note about his son fighting at school, he learns Dick fought "one hell of a scrap" to protect his father's reputation.[20] In addition, Dick, nearing draft age, will soon battle the ideology his father supposedly supports. Young Cvetic says, "When I was a kid, about nine or ten, I use to tell myself I want to grow up to be my dad." Now he would "rather drop dead" and tells his father to "never come near me again."[21]

Torn between his son's shaken faith in him and his job as an FBI agent, Cvetic places the family above country. He decides to end his cover by writing a letter to his son, even though doing so jeopardizes his mission. The script describes the scene with as Cvetic's photo album "shows snapshots of his boy recently taken.

FIG. 36 Defending childhood and pastimes. In *I Was a Communist for the F.B.I.* (1951), Matt Cvetic (Frank Lovejoy, left) is ostracized from mainstream Americans. The wary father (Roy Engel, center) shields his son Jackie (Erik Nielsen, right) from subversive elements. (Author's collection.)

As his hand turns the pages, going backward in time, each succeeding snapshot shows the boy at a younger age—and always grouped with his father—at the beach, in the park with a dog, at a baseball game."[22] These memories elide the Great Depression and World War II for happier moments of family solidarity. Such imagery also hints how communism rips the fabric family unit regardless of economic or social crises. Despite the communist rhetoric of elevating the downtrodden masses, their true aim is severing father-son bonds to undermine the state. The movie superimposes Dick's hurt expression as Cvetic flips through his photo album. By blowing his cover to his son, Cvetic knows his son will understand he was a communist for the FBI and for family: Dick and Uncle Sam alike.

Thankfully, the government steps in. The actual Senate subcommittee caused Hollywood much grief, but Warner Bros. demonstrated the industry's submission with HUAC portrayed as upstanding political figures. The film's commies take the Fifth Amendment, like the Hollywood Ten did in 1947, but Cvetic names names and, while his family sits in the audience, exposes the Soviet scheme to turn America into a Russian slave colony. The script instructs Dick to stand up, "applauding like mad, as tears of joy run down his cheeks."[23] In the coda, Dick runs up. Dressed as a seaman, Dick is not a legal-age adult, but the teenager readily joins his father to protect American values (figure 37). He begs his father for forgiveness, and Dad says he is proud of his son's patriotism throughout this ordeal: "Even when you hated me, I loved you for it."[24] "The Battle Hymn of the

FIG. 37 The teenager at stake in *I Was a Communist for the F.B.I.* (1951). While testifying before HUAC, Matt Cvetic (Frank Lovejoy, right) cements the father-son bonds under anticommunism. The accompanying news snipe reads, "Dick (Ron Hagherthy, second from right), especially, is overwhelmed by his father's patriotic heroism and a reconciliation ensues." Cvetic's staunch anticommunist brother (Paul Picerni, second from left) and sister-in-law (Ruth Kramer, far left) look on. (Author's collection.)

Republic" plays on the soundtrack, and as the Cvetics exit, the camera irises in on Abraham Lincoln's bust, to show that Americanism goes marching on.

Buoyed by Cvetic's real-life adventures and celebrity status, *I Was a Communist for the F.B.I.* enabled Hollywood to counter its critics. For Warner Bros., Jack Warner issued a statement, claiming the picture will "help halt the march of those who are trying to undermine the foundation of our democratic structure and destroy the fabrics of our lives."[25] Warner had previously produced the pro-Russian picture *Mission to Moscow* (1943) during the war, which personally landed him in trouble before HUAC. Now, he redeemed himself with an updated look at the Soviet Union, adding, "Mr. Cvetic's activities on behalf of his country are, in my opinion, worthy of our nation's gratitude and a decoration for civilian heroism."[26] One reviewer agreed, "It will at once dissipate unfortunate impressions that may have been carelessly formed about the industry and at the same time enlighten the film-going public on the nature of homegrown Communism."[27] To this extent, Warner Bros. courted the press and the government, even donating sixteen-millimeter prints to Washington, D.C., for "government use."[28] The public responded positively, and one fan wrote to the Vatican, stating, "It is a picture like this that help [*sic*] enlighten the world" and "help us learn the truth and teach us how to better human-beings."[29]

The picture's anticommunism and hyperpatriotism reflected the public need to train potential troublesome children. Governor John S. Battle of Virginia endorsed the picture, declaring, "Somewhere a youngster may be turned from thoughts of crime by the grim lessons which are portrayed here. It may well be that this picture will save the life of someone in this audience."[30] One showman affirmed the picture's educational value: "This is one picture that should be made in 16mm and shown in every school in the United States and Canada [for] free."[31] As a documentary, the film had greater value than mere entertainment. The exhibitor believed anticommunism was now requisite in the Cold War classroom.

Dick Cvetic accepts his duty to battle the Soviets, dressing as a seaman in the final scene. This uniform was an old plot device in pictures like *Johnny Holiday* as a means of visually bestowing discipline to youths. Another movie, *Bad Boy* (1949), specifically connects militarism in youths to national defense. The film cast World War II hero Audie Murphy as Danny Lester, a hotheaded teenager who lashes out against society through a fascination with guns. In a last-ditch effort to save him, the courts ship the delinquent off to the Variety Clubs' Boys Ranch, described as "forty-two hundred acres of wide open Texas space," to rehabilitate.[32] Like the inmates at Indiana Boys' School, Danny finds redemption among paramilitary figures and "good" boys, including Stanley Clements, who had played baddie Eddie Dugan in *Johnny Holiday* (figure 38). Danny learns to channel his gun craziness to civic duty; the last scene shows Danny at Texas A&M, drilling in uniform as he and other soldiers prepare for war.

FIG. 38 The soldier-star. Juvenile delinquent Danny Lester (Audie Murphy, center) embraces the cast in *Bad Boy* (1949), establishing a film persona matching Murphy's real-life role during World War II. Among the notable cast members are "good boys" Stanley Clements (far left), the heavy in *Johnny Holiday* (1949), and James Lydon (far right), who played David Langham in *Hot Rod* (1950). (Author's collection.)

Bad Boy blurs history, creating a fictional biography for Murphy, which not only confirmed his credentials as a citizen-soldier but established his screen persona. Murphy launched a second successful career with this first starring role and later played cowboys and gunfighters. Guns and kid-cowboys continued to thrive in films, from *Shane* (1953) to *Gun for a Coward* (1957) and *The Cowboys* (1972)—the last film about tweens who take up arms to avenge their slain father figure, played by none other than John Wayne. Like Wayne, war hero Audie Murphy's screen career glamorized gun culture for youths (figure 39). *Bad Boy* highlights Murphy as the ideal citizen-soldier model for real-life "bad" boys. Moviegoers agreed; one exhibitor exclaimed, "Audie Murphy is really hot now."[33] In 1950, when Dore Schary cast Murphy to play the reluctant hero in *The Red Badge of Courage* (1951), gossip columnist Hedda Hopper nodded approvingly: "It's about a youth who develops courage under fire. With so many untried youths going to Korea, we can do with this kind of story."[34] In a biographical sketch, Hopper noted Murphy started as a "poverty-stricken youth"—Murphy, born in 1925, came of age during the Great Depression—and "could easily have fallen for the Commie line. But I know of no more loyal American."[35] She emphasized how Murphy has "always been bitterly so opposed to everything that smacked of Joseph Stalin's philosophy, and he who gave so much to retain our way of living

FIG. 39 Taking aim for youth. Audie Murphy coaches Brandon de Wilde (who had earlier idolized a gunfighter in *Shane*, 1953) to shoot straight in a publicity still for their production *Night Passage* (1957). (Author's collection.)

is ready to go back to the front to preserve what so many of his comrades died for."[36] As relayed in the press, Stalin hoped the United States would collapse into depression, but, as Hopper asserted, young men like Murphy stood ready to guard the American way of life. As a genuine war hero, Murphy's persona became a poster boy of sorts for promoting militarism among youth on and off the screen, whether as hot-rodders for civil defense at home or as soldiers on the front lines abroad.

Militarized socialization for "bad boys" like Danny Lester empowered them to protect the United States. Americans retreated from isolationism, but they also rejected ideas about "one world" internationalism as foreign policy. Political developments, especially the Korean War, impacted receptions of *The Gunfighter* (1950) and *Intruder in the Dust* (1949). Warner Bros. originally intended to tie Korea to *I Was a Communist for the F.B.I.* Screenwriter Borden Chase wanted to start the picture with American troops in Korea struggling with faulty supplies and weapons, thanks to communist sabotage. Newsreel footage would "dramatize and bring the subject matter up to date. Should late developments in Europe or the Orient offer a better frame, a change can be made during the cutting of the picture or prior to its release."[37] Chase also wanted to cast HUAC senator John S. Wood and red-baiter Richard Nixon as themselves, who awaken Dick Cvetic to his father's heroism. In an early draft, as Seaman Cvetic ships out, straight-shooter Nixon tells him, "Your father deserves a Congressional Medal of Honor—but instead he must take the heartfelt thanks of a grateful nation."[38] While neither Korea nor Nixon appeared, the overt patriotism's link to the nuclear family shines through. This theme of older mentorships extended to a public relations stunt, where actor Frank Lovejoy gave studio tours to San Pedro High School students to commemorate Boys' Week. Warner Bros. played up the filmic "Cvetic" guiding the future leaders of democracy through the studio soundstages.[39] These father-son dynamics paid off; *I Was a Communist for the F.B.I.* grossed $1.754 million against a small $0.684 million budget.[40]

"Tearing Me Apart!" Revisiting the Rebel

Many film histories characterize domestic containment as firmly in place by 1950. They point to *Rebel without a Cause* (1955) as the first instance of resistance, with actor James Dean embodying the nation's collective teenage angst chafing under adult expectations. When Dean's character, Jim Stark, famously screams to his parents, "You're tearing me apart!," this exclamation supposedly symbolized the first display of youth agency against the Cold War consensus and simmering counterculture that would erupt in the 1960s.[41]

However, Stark's cry says less about teenage rebellion than his worrying over his parents' role reversal. His domineering mother and wimpy dad, complete with the patriarch wearing a Mary Petty apron, fuel their son's daydreaming for a "normal," stable family life. Worse for Jim, his parents are fine with this arrangement. The family's inability to set down roots highlights their nonconformity; when the going gets rough, the parents simply pack up rather than adhere to community standards. His emasculated father is neither a protector nor a provider, unable to shield Jim from bullies or a henpecking mother (figure 40). Their son is different; Jim Stark just wants to fit in with the high school crowd, and he, his girlfriend, and a dependent son figure attempt to rebuild a nuclear household in an abandoned mansion. Their makeshift family ends in tragedy, but Stark rejoices when his newly masculinized father promises to do better in the "dad"

FIG. 40 Not a Kyng of his castle. Failed patriarch Mr. Stark (Jim Backus) cannot protect his son when pranksters call him a chicken in *Rebel without a Cause* (1955). (Author's collection.)

department. In Jim's eyes, the "rebel" wasn't himself but his dad, who agrees to conform to the standards of fatherhood and masculinity.

Stark's being "torn apart" morbidly paralleled the real-life death of James Dean shortly before the film's release, which enshrined him as a symbol of youth rebellion. But postwar youth angst had precedence since 1945. The story arcs of Christopher Blake, Paul Kyng, and Johnny Holiday reflected the anxieties from the Great Depression, which Stark reworked as a yearning for patriarchy and conformity. Stark and his girlfriend retreat to an abandoned Hollywood estate to re-create an idealized nuclear family; Stark and the audience partake in make-believe in a secure, safe family unit—all the more poignant since his "house" came from the ticket sales of millions of moviegoers in the dark.

Moviegoers also fondly looked back, although they risked receiving a rude wake-up call. In 1957, one fan told Hedda Hopper how he and his generation grew up on wholesome film families like the Hardys: "How well I remember the laughs, the tears, the sheer delight these films have me and millions of others back in the not-so-happy days of depression and pre-war times."[42] Selective nostalgia glorified the silver screen as escapism, strongly contrasting with the gloomy hard times outside theaters. Anticipating the revived Hardys in *Andy Hardy Comes*

Home (1958), this fan expressed a "longing for a return of those movie years when the stars really had talent and one seldom saw on the screen the sordidness, depravity, and evil our children see on it today." One can imagine the disappointment; coming home to Carvel meshed a rocking and rolling Rooney with awkward flashback moments from previous installments. The jarring comparison between then and now revealed how artificial the Hardy mythos was in 1937 and its irrelevancy as a historic relic twenty years later. Andy Hardy's hyperwholesomeness had no place in the nation's new teen culture. Nevertheless, even as Andy's short resurrection demonstrated how times had changed, the memory of the Depression and World War II shadowed the 1950s, as anxieties symbolically threatened to tear postwar youths *and* their parents apart. The Deanlinquents offered nothing new. They echoed older concerns about youth and family, masculinity and maturity, and the formation and projection of national identity, stemming from the past several decades of American history.[43]

Postscript: Sixty Years Later

Rock and roll and delinquent teens aside, the construction of boyhood became part of the Cold War consensus, as "normal" as the Cleavers appeared on *Leave It to Beaver* (1957–1963). The end of the Cold War—and even the "end of history"—characterized the United States in another transitional moment. During the 1990s, having kicked the so-called Vietnam Syndrome in the first Gulf War and prior to the War on Terror, Americans turned inward, calling the construction of childhood into question. Scholars, notably Carol Gilligan and Peggy Orenstein, championed girlhood, which they perceived as under attack by a dominant masculinity—the hardened Cold Warrior persona that grew out from the patriotic efforts of fathers and sons like the Cvetics.[44] Defenders of the fractured Cold Warrior consensus decried the so-called feminist war against boyhood, claiming that the "natural" masculine standards during the fifties were the way things always have been.[45]

This debate over childhood, gender, and biological sex has evolved since the 1990s. Scholars have inaugurated masculinity studies, deconstructing how manhood—and boyhood—reflected changes in the American landscape, past and present. Over a decade into the War on Terror, the balkanization of gender terminology continues, with micro categories asserting their identities by contrasting themselves against others. This search for personal security reflects the ongoing negotiation between children and societal norms, parental expectations, and private/public memory of the past. Parents surely want their kids to grow up as upstanding citizens, filling the large shoes of their forefathers on the domestic and world stages. However, Americans disagree on the best way to do that—just as they did back then.

Popular culture, with Hollywood at the forefront, continues to navigate the murky waters of childhood. Audiences can see children grow up before their eyes, from the multi-epic Harry Potter franchise (2001–2011) to recent one-offs like *Boyhood* (2014), *Growing Up Smith* (2015), and *Good Boys* (2019), in which filmmakers and filmgoers not only depict how children mature but construct what it means to grow up. Gillette's controversial "We Believe: The Best Men Can Be" (2019) advertisement blurs the line between commercialism and progressivism, while #MeToo, LGBTQ activists, and their critics wage gender wars over the definitions of "toxic masculinity," "alpha masculinities," and the "naturalness" of each to pass on to sons, on and off the screen. Tapping into the zeitgeist of the times, and befitting his showmanship background, Donald Trump trumpeted a mandate to make America "great again." With all the fanfare of a Hollywood tagline, this ready-made ballyhoo fondly recalled the 1950s and appealed to a constituency of so-called angry white men whom social progressives have derisively labeled "boomers."[46] This name-calling evokes a generation gap that references Cold Warriors who came of age alongside Christopher Blake, Johnny Holiday, and their peers, who themselves were responses to the wild boys of the Depression. In moving forward, Americans seek security and stability in uncertain times and, not unlike the youths who transitioned from dead ends to Cold Warriors, must grapple with the past. Otherwise, we doom ourselves to repeat the darker days we thought we had forever entombed in celluloid.

Acknowledgments

Hollywood's many names—Tinsel Town, the Dream Factory—speak to the film industry's glamour and status as the entertainment capital of the world. Writing a book about Hollywood can be anything but glamorous, but aside from the films themselves—which are still enormously entertaining, even on multiple viewings—friends, associates, and colleagues have made the research, the writing, and the rewriting a joy. Without further ado, roll credits:

This book started as a dissertation, and my committee, James Carter, Angie Kirby-Calder, and Shakti Jaising, gave immense support every step of the way, served as critics, and provided invaluable feedback and support that guided this rocky production from inception to reception.

Special thanks go to the starring players—the artists whose feedback, insight, and encouragement vastly informed the behind-the-scenes activity of the studio system. Ted Donaldson, Richard Eyer, Ron Hagerthy, Darryl Hickman, and Claude Jarman were generous with their time, recollections, and thoughts. To my regret, some of their films and commentary did not make it into the book's final cut.

Many archivists, institutions, and private collectors made their holdings available, without which none of this would have been possible. Thanks go to Jenny Romero and the staff at the Academy of Motion Picture Arts and Sciences; Mary Huelsback and her staff at the Wisconsin Historical Society; Sandra Garcia-Myers, Edward Comstock, and the staff at the Cinema Television Arts Library, USC and the Warner Bros. Archives; the staff at the Charles E. Young Research Library at UCLA; Lynda Claassen and her staff at the Mandeville Special Collections, UC San Diego Library; Amanda Leinberger at the United Nations Archives and Records Management; the Media History Digital Library and Lantern; Bob Young and Robert Connors for making their stills and film collections available' Richard B. Jewell for assistance on *Berlin Express*, and John

McElwee for timely information on *The Search*. Their support was invaluable, the errors are all mine.

At Rutgers University Press, Nicole Solano and Maggie Tibbett, with assistance from Dayna Hedgewood and Malaika Jawed, were a pleasure to work with, guiding the manuscript into the presses. They more than once steered me away from the abyss of late-night reformatting, and I am grateful this study on postwar filmic boyhood has a home with Rutgers's growing scholarship on film and childhood studies and American history.

Deep thanks to my peers and associates: the German Historical Institute's Bosch Summer School program, especially Mischa Honeck and Karin Hilck, for opening my eyes to new source material and archives; coworkers Daniel Zhao, Jacob Hallman, Keyu Miao, Ning Kang, Maruko Hikawa, Terri Beth Miller, and Leigh Morgan for accommodating my workload while I pace back and forth; the Greenwood Gang for being there; and my brothers, Alexander and Nicholas Lee, who don't mind an occasional old movie now and then.

My parents, James and Theresa Lee, encouraged, then tolerated, then accepted my obsession with classic films. They're happy I found a line of work that keeps me energized. They read every word, questioned my ideas, and have already asked for a sequel.

Finally, Dino Bello merits a special "mwah," which, while untranslatable, says more than words convey.

Notes

Introduction

1 *The Wild One*, directed by László Benedek (Stanley Kramer Productions, 1953), DVD (Sony Pictures Home Entertainment, 1998).

2 Alan Nadel, *Containment Culture: American Narratives, Postmodernism, and the Atomic Age* (Durham, NC: Duke University Press, 1995).

3 Quoted in Andrew E. Kersten, *Labor's Home Front: The American Federation of Labor during World War II* (New York: New York University Press, 2006), 194–195.

4 Conrad Blyth, *American Business Cycles, 1945–50* (New York: Routledge, 1969), 67.

5 "Double Danger," *CSM*, March 12, 1948, 22.

6 Stephen Kemp Bailey, *Congress Makes a Law: The Story behind the Employment Act of 1946* (New York: Columbia University Press, 1950), 228.

7 Curt Caldwell, *NSC 68 and the Political Economy of the Early Cold War* (Cambridge: Cambridge University Press, 2011); Thomas C. Mills, *Post-war Planning on the Periphery: Anglo-American Economic Diplomacy in South America, 1939–1945* (Edinburgh: Edinburgh University Press, 2012), 3, 48–52. Policy makers pointed to the postwar depression in 1920–1921 after World War I as precedence. They blamed this slump on overproduction and falling demand when the Great War ended.

8 Lizabeth Cohen, *A Consumers' Republic: The Politics of Mass Consumption in Postwar America* (New York: Knopf, 2003); Greg Castillo, *Cold War on the Home Front: The Soft Power of Midcentury Design* (Minneapolis: University of Minnesota Press, 2010), chap. 1.

9 Laura Haddock, "Family Held Cornerstone of Strong, Stable Society," *CSM*, April 25, 1946, 4.

10 John Mason Brown, *Morning Faces: A Book of Children and Parents* (New York: Whittlesey House, 1949), 59.

11 Ibid., 60.

12 For a history of the oft-cited Payne Fund Studies, see Garth S. Jowett, Ian C. Jarvie, and Kathryn H. Fuller, *Children and the Movies: Media Influences and the Payne Fund Studies* (Cambridge: Cambridge University Press, 1996).

13 F. Scott Fitzgerald, *The Damned and the Beautiful* (New York: Scribner's, 1922).

14 William M. Tuttle, *"Daddy's Gone to War": The Second World War in the Lives of America's Children* (New York: Oxford University Press, 1995); Ralph LaRossa, *Of War and Men: World War II in the Lives of Fathers and Their Families* (Chapel Hill: University of North Carolina Press, 2011); Lisa K. Ossian, *The Forgotten Generation: American Children and World War II* (Columbia: University of Missouri Press, 2011).

15 James Gilbert, *A Cycle of Outrage: America's Reaction to the Juvenile Delinquent of the 1950s* (New York: Oxford University Press, 1988); Robert L. Griswold, *Fatherhood in America: A History* (New York: Basic Books, 1993); Anthony M. Platt, *The Child Savers: The Invention of Delinquency*, expanded ed. (New York: Oxford University Press, 2009); David B. Wolcott, *Cops and Kids: Policing Juvenile Delinquency in Urban America, 1890–1940* (Columbus: Ohio State University Press, 2005).

16 David M. Potter, *People of Plenty: Economic Abundance and the American Character* (Chicago: University Press of Chicago, 1958). See also Laura A. Belmonte, *Selling the American Way: U.S. Propaganda and the Cold War* (Philadelphia: University of Pennsylvania Press, 2008).

17 For a historical analysis of postwar prosperity and its impact on the family, the standard references are Elaine Tyler May, *Homeward Bound: American Families in the Cold War Era* (New York: Basic Books, 1988) and Kenneth T. Jackson, *Crabgrass Frontier: The Suburbanization of the United States* (New York: Oxford University Press, 1987). Historians have long noted Americans did not fully subscribe to domestic containment; see, for instance, Wini Breines, *Young, White, and Miserable: Growing Up Female in the Fifties* (Chicago: University of Chicago Press, 2001).

18 James Gilbert, *Men in the Middle: Searching for Masculinity in the 1950s* (Chicago: University of Chicago Press, 2005). For general works on fatherhood, see Griswold, *Fatherhood in America*; Ralph LaRossa, *Modernization of Fatherhood: A Social and Political History* (Chicago: University of Chicago Press, 1997); Michael Kimmel, *Manhood in America*, 3rd ed. (New York: Oxford University Press, 2011); E. Anthony Rotundo: *American Manhood: Transformations in Masculinity from the Revolution to the Moon* (New York: Basic Books, 1994), chaps. 2–4.

19 Dale Kramer and Madeline Karr, *Teen-Age Gangs* (New York: Popular Library, 1954); Albert K. Cohen, *Delinquent Boys: The Culture of the Gang* (Glencoe, IL: Free Press, 1955); Eric C. Scheider, *Vampires, Dragons, and Egyptian Kings: Youth Gangs in Postwar New York* (Princeton, NJ: Princeton University Press, 2001), chaps. 3–6; Mariah Adin, *The Brooklyn Thrill-Kill Gang and the Great Comic Book Scare of the 1950s* (Santa Barbara, CA: Praeger, 2014).

20 Margaret Peacock, *Innocent Weapons: The Soviet and American Politics of Childhood in the Cold War* (Chapel Hill: University of North Carolina Press, 2014), 39; Jennifer Helgren, *American Girls and Global Responsibility: A New Relation to the World during the Early Cold War* (New Brunswick, NJ: Rutgers University Press, 2017). On the prominence of girlhood from the silent to midcentury, see Gaylyn Studlar, *Precocious Charms: Performing Girlhood in Classic Hollywood Cinema* (Berkeley: University of California Press, 2013); Ilana Nash, *American Sweethearts: Teenage Girls in Twentieth-Century Popular Culture* (Indianapolis: Indiana University Press, 2005).

21 See Philip Wylie, *Generation of Vipers* (New York: Farrar & Rhinehart, 1942); see also Rebecca Jo Plant, *Mom: The Transformation of Motherhood in Modern America* (Chicago: University of Chicago Press, 2010). On motherhood in postwar movies,

see Michael Rogin, "Kiss Me Deadly: Communism, Motherhood, and Cold War Movies," *Representations* 6 (Spring 1984): 1–36; Mike Chopra-Gant, "Hollywood's 'Moms' and Postwar America," in *Motherhood Misconceived: Representing the Maternal in U.S. Films*, eds., Heather Addison, Mary Kate Goodwin-Kelly, and Elaine Roth (New York: State University of New York Press, 2009): 125–138.

22 *The Boy with Green Hair*, directed by Joseph Losey (RKO-Radio Pictures, 1948), DVD (Warner Home Video, 2010).

23 Victor D. Brooks, *Boomers: The Cold-War Generation Grows Up* (Chicago: Ivan R. Dee, 2009), 177.

24 Sidney Skolsky, "The New Look in Hollywood Men," *Photoplay*, July 1957, 41–43, 111–112.

25 "Children Play Their Parts," *NYT*, July 15, 1956, 153.

26 Hedda Hopper, "Eyer, 11, Will Costar with Clint Walker," *LAT*, July 3, 1957, 11.

27 In 1946, Margaret O'Brien led the polls with "No Favorite Child Actor" following. Jackie "Butch" Jenkins, O'Brien's closest rival, garnered 6 percent of the vote, with Peggy Ann Garner, Roddy McDowall, and "other" making up the rest. See Leo A. Handel, *Hollywood Looks at Its Audience: A Report of Film Audience Research* (Urbana: University of Illinois Press, 1950), 144. In 1950, O'Brien became a teenager and after her *The Secret Garden* (1949) flopped, she and MGM mutually ended her contract. *The Secret Garden* lost $840,000. See E. J. Mannix ledger, Howard Strickling papers, MHL, AMPAS. On O'Brien's termination with six months left on her contract, see "Margaret O'Brien Stays at Metro Till September," *DV*, June 9, 1949, 1. "Margaret O'Brien, MGM Sever Pact," *HR*, June 1, 1949, 1.

28 David Dye, *Child and Youth Actors: Filmographies of Their Entire Careers, 1914–1985* (Jefferson, NC: McFarland, 1988), xi.

29 Industry representative Arch Reeve conceded many "juvies" cited the movies as their inspiration to commit crimes, but he refuted them: "It's common practice for poor cornered kids to shift their blame." The Motion Picture Association of America issued a pamphlet titled *Exploding a Myth: Motion Pictures ARE NOT Responsible for Juvenile Delinquency* to outline their views, and cited works such as Eleanor and Sheldon Glueck, *Unraveling Juvenile Delinquency* (New York: Commonwealth Fund, 1950); D. H. Stott, *Delinquency and Human Nature* (Dunfermline, Scotland: Carnegie United Kingdom Trust, 1950); Paul Tappen, *Juvenile Delinquency* (New York: McGraw-Hill, 1949). The association "strongly recommend[ed]" Tappen's work and quoted the National Probation and Parole Association's announcement: "The parent who feels a sense of guilt about his own role in the family and his own responsibility is sometimes only too glad to find a scapegoat in Hollywood or on the radio." See "A Symposium of Opinion Concerning Causation through Dramatized Entertainment—Motion Pictures and Radio Programs," September 1948, "Juvenile Delinquency—Statements 1947–1956," 27.f.270, AMPTP records, MHL, AMPAS.

30 "Hollywood Against Communism," n.d. Essays, 12-f.126, AMPTP records, MHL, AMPAS.

31 Thomas Doherty, *Teenagers and Teenpics: The Juvenilization of American Movies in the 1950s* (Boston: Unwin Hyman, 1988).

Chapter 1 The Family in Trouble, 1920–1945

1 "Dreams of 1946," *Life*, November 25, 1946, 57.

2 Ibid., 57.

3 Ibid., 58–60.
4 Glen H. Elder Jr., *Children of the Great Depression: Social Change in Life Experiences* (Chicago: University of Chicago Press, 1974); Kathleen W. Jones, *Taming the Troublesome Child: American Families, Child Guidance, and the Limits of Psychiatric Authority* (Cambridge, MA: Harvard University Press, 1999), chaps. 4–5; Glen H. Elder Jr. and Richard C. Rockwell, "Economic Depression and Postwar Opportunity in Men's Lives: A Study of Life Patterns and Health," in *Research in Community and Mental Health*, ed. Roberta G. Simmons (Greenwich, CT: JAI, 1979), 249–303; John A. Clausen, *American Lives: Looking Back at the Children of the Great Depression* (Berkeley: University of California Press, 1993).
5 Clausen, *American Lives*, 284–285, 504–505.
6 Robert S. Lynd and Helen Merrell Lynd, *Middletown: A Study in Modern American Culture* (1929; New York: Harcourt Brace Jovanovich, 1956), 266.
7 Hamilton Cravens, *Great Depression: People and Perspectives* (Santa Barbara, CA: ABC-CLIO, 2009), 46.
8 Mirra Komarovsky, *The Unemployed Man and His Family: The Effect of Unemployment upon the Status of the Man in Fifty-Nine Families* (New York: Dryden Press, 1940).
9 Grace Abbott, "Children and the Depression: A National Study and Warning," *NYT*, December 18, 1932, XX5; see also Errol Lincoln Ulys, *Riding the Rails: Teenagers on the Move during the Great Depression* (New York: Routledge, 2004), 10.
10 James Wingate to J. L. Warner, letter, June 10, 1933, "Wild Boys of the Road [W.B. 1933]," Motion Picture Association of America, PCA records, MHL, AMPAS. The studio cut the line.
11 Ibid.
12 James Wingate to J. L. Warner, letter, August 9, 1933. "Wild Boys of the Road [W.B. 1933]," Motion Picture Association of America, PCA records, MHL, AMPAS. Jack Warner thanked Wingate, saying he and producer Hal Wallis were "gratified" for releasing a picture "with good taste." Jack Warner to James Wingate, letter, August 10, 1933, "Wild Boys of the Road [W.B. 1933]," Motion Picture Association of America, PCA records, MHL, AMPAS.
13 Censor Report, December 3, 1933, "Wild Boys of the Road [W.B. 1933]," Motion Picture Association of America, PCA records, MHL, AMPAS. British Columbia censors included a long, poetic, sentimental paragraph deploring the living conditions of homeless boys and men, mourning that boys of the dominion are "fast returning from the higher standard to the level of the coolie and untouchable of the Yangtse-Kiang and other great rivers of the sorrowful earth." At the same time, the censors excised the picture's tagline from the trailer: "See this picture and weep for the forgotten youth."
14 Censor Report, January 18, 1934, "Wild Boys of the Road [W.B. 1933]," Motion Picture Association of America, PCA records, MHL, AMPAS.
15 Nancy Beck Young, William D. Pederson, Byron W. Daynes, eds., *Franklin D. Roosevelt and the Shaping of American Political Culture* (London: M.E. Sharpe, 2001).
16 Maurine H. Beasley, *Eleanor Roosevelt and the Media: A Public Quest for Self-Fulfillment* (Urbana: University of Illinois Press, 1987), 167.
17 Robert Cohen, ed., *Dear Mrs. Roosevelt: Letters from Children of the Great Depression* (Chapel Hill: University of North Carolina Press, 2002); Robert S. McElvaine, ed., *Down and Out in the Great Depression: Letters from the Forgotten Man* (Chapel Hill: University of North Carolina Press, 2012).

18 A. G. to Federal Emergency Relief, letter, December 12, 1934, in McElvaine, *Down and Out in the Great Depression*, 59–60.
19 John Kasson, *The Little Girl Who Fought the Great Depression: Shirley Temple and 1930s America* (New York: Norton, 2014).
20 Kathrine Brush, "The Perennial Hardy Family," *WP*, June 15, 1941, L1.
21 Ibid., L1.
22 Ibid., L1.
23 Agnes Christine Johnson, "Andy Hardy's Blonde Trouble (1944)," A-868, Turner/MGM scripts, MHL, AMPAS.
24 "100 Years of Marriage and Divorce Rates Statistics: United States, 1867–1967," *National Vital Statistics System* 21, no. 24 (1973), https://www.cdc.gov/nchs/data/series/sr_21/sr21_024.pdf; "The Depression and Alimony," *NYT*, September 30, 1931, 20.
25 Robert S. Lynd and Helen Merrell Lynd, *Middletown in Transition: A Study in Cultural Conflicts* (New York: Harcourt, Brace, 1937), 152–153.
26 *Let's Try Again*, directed by Worthington Miner (RKO-Radio Pictures, 1934), personal collection, courtesy of Robert Connors.
27 Joseph I. Breen to L. B. Mayer, letter, April 18, 1938, "Love Finds Andy Hardy [MGM, 1938]," Motion Picture Association of America, PCA records, MHL, AMPAS.
28 Islin Auster, "Memorandum for the Files," "Love Finds Andy Hardy [MGM 1938]," Motion Picture Association of America, PCA records, MHL, AMPAS.
29 Production Code Administration to L. B. Mayer, letter, November 25, 1941, "The Courtship of Andy Hardy [MGM, 1942]," Motion Picture Association of America, PCA records, MHL, AMPAS.
30 Production Code Administration to L. B. Mayer, letter, December 4, 1941, "The Courtship of Andy Hardy [MGM, 1942]," Motion Picture Association of America, PCA records, MHL, AMPAS.
31 Joseph I. Breen to L. B. Mayer, letter, April 30, 1941, "Life Begins for Andy Hardy [MGM, 1941]," Motion Picture Association of America, PCA records, MHL, AMPAS.
32 Joseph I. Breen to L. B. Mayer, letter, May 12, 1941, "Life Begins for Andy Hardy [MGM, 1941]," Motion Picture Association of America, PCA records, MHL, AMPAS.
33 "Showmen's Review," *MPH*, August 16, 1941, 35.
34 "NBC Good News of 1939," *Internet Archive*, September 22, 2012, https://archive.org/details/100OtrThanksgivingHolidayShows/1938-11-24NbcGoodNewsOf1939-ThanksgivingProgramWithAndyHardyMovieCast.mp3.
35 Bosley Crowther, "The Screen," *NYT*, August 2, 1940, 12.
36 Herbert Blumer and Philip M. Hauser, *Movies, Delinquency, and Crime* (New York: Macmillan, 1933). See also David E. Ruth, *Inventing the Public Enemy: The Gangster in American Culture, 1918–1934* (Chicago: University of Chicago Press, 1996).
37 Colin Schindler, *Hollywood in Crisis: Cinema and American Society, 1929–1939* (New York: Routledge, 1996).
38 John Nichols, *The "S" Word: A Short History of an American Tradition . . . Socialism* (New York: Verso, 2011), 120.
39 *Heroes for Sale*, directed by William A. Wellman (First National Pictures, 1933), DVD (Warner Home Video, 2009).
40 Joseph I. Breen to J. L. Warner, letter, September 3, 1936, "Wild Boys on the Road [W.B. 1933]," Motion Picture Association of America, PCA records, MHL,

AMPAS; H. J. McCord to Joseph Breen, letter, September 21, 1936, "Wild Boys on the Road [W.B. 1933]," Motion Picture Association of America, PCA records, MHL, AMPAS.

41 F. Stinnette, Censor Report, December 12, 1938, "Boy Slaves [RKO 1938]," Motion Picture Association of America, PCA records, MHL, AMPAS.

42 Joseph I. Breen to J. R. McDonough, letter, September 29, 1938, "Boy Slaves [RKO 1938]," Motion Picture Association of America, PCA records, MHL, AMPAS.

43 Joseph I. Breen to J. R. McDonough, letter, October 14, 1938, "Boy Slaves [RKO 1938]," Motion Picture Association of America, PCA records, MHL, AMPAS.

44 Ibid.

45 Joseph I. Breen to J. R. McDonough, letter, December 8, 1938, "Boy Slaves [RKO 1938]," Motion Picture Association of America, PCA records, MHL, AMPAS.

46 Ibid.

47 Joseph I. Breen, "Production Code Certificate #4777," December 17, 1938, "Boy Slaves [RKO 1938]," Motion Picture Association of America, PCA records, MHL, AMPAS.

48 Censor Report, March 12, 1939, "Boy Slaves [RKO 1938," Motion Picture Association of America, PCA records, MHL, AMPAS.

49 J. R. McDonough, "Boy Slaves Censorship Elimination," "Boy Slaves [RKO 1938]," Motion Picture Association of America, PCA records, MHL, AMPAS.

50 Ibid.

51 Frank Nugent, "The Screen," *NYT*, February 9, 1939, 24.

52 "What the Picture Did for Me," *MPH*, May 20, 1939, 52.

53 Mickey Rooney, *Life Is Too Short* (New York: Villiard Books, 1991), 114–116.

54 Bosley Crowther, "A Ruin That Was Rooney," *NYT*, Feb 19, 1939, 127. Rooney had played Pluck in *A Midsummer Night's Dream* (1935) and, among an all-star cast, stole the show. He later confessed he did not understand any of his lines. See Rooney, *Life Is Too Short*, 60.

55 Crowther, "A Ruin That Was Rooney," 127.

56 Thomas Brady, "The No. 1 Boy of Filmdom," *NYT*, January 12, 1941, SM8.

57 Ibid., SM8.

58 Ibid., SM8.

59 Grace Kingsley, "Family Series Adhere to Rigid Laws," *LAT*, December 4, 1938, 2.

60 Agnes C. Johnson, "Andy Hardy's Double Life (1943)," A-877, 7, 9, 11, Turner/MGM scripts, MHL, AMPAS.

61 Ibid., 15.

62 Joseph Schrank and Max Liebman, "Andy Hardy Meets Maisie," "Ziegfeld Follies (1945)," Z-29, Turner/MGM scripts, MHL, AMPAS.

63 Mickey Rooney to Hedda Hopper, letter, June 19, 1940, "Rooney, Mickey f. 2797," Hedda Hopper papers, MHL, AMPAS.

64 Bosley Crowther, "So Long, Andy," *NYT*, Feb 21, 1943, X3.

65 Ibid., X3.

66 Nelson B. Bell, "Ten Pictures Are Chosen for the Asiatic Audiences," *WP*, October 27, 1942, B8.

67 "Andy Hardy Meets Debutante," *DV*, June 28, 1940, 2.

68 Vance King, "Hollywood Reviews," *MPD*, July 2, 1940, 6.

69 Elizabeth Blake, "Andy Hardy Discovers America—Story File 1943," Metro-Goldwyn-Mayer Legal Department collection, MHL, AMPAS.

70 LaRossa, *Of War and Men*, 31.

71 "The Nation," *NYT*, May 28, 1944, 2E.

72 Allen Rivkin, "Joe Smith, American Retakes," November 18, 1941, "Joe Smith, American," f.J-98, Turner/MGM scripts, MPH, AMPAS.
73 Ibid.
74 "Hoover Indorses National Family Week as Means of Combating Juvenile Crime," *CSM*, May 3, 1944, 13.
75 Herm, "Love Laughs at Andy Hardy," *VW*, December 4, 1946, 13.
76 Joseph I. Breen to L. B. Mayer, letter, April 3, 1946, "Love Laughs at Andy Hardy [MGM 1947]," Motion Picture Association of America, PCA records, MHL, AMPAS.
77 Jack Holland, "Are Young Marriages Wise?," *Screenland*, September 1947, 69.
78 "Quick Action Sought on Soldier Bonus," *CSM*, May 12, 1944, 11.
79 Suzanne Mettler, *Soldiers to Citizens: The G.I. Bill and the Making of the Greatest Generation* (New York: Oxford University Press, 2005), 7.
80 *Love Laughs at Andy Hardy*, directed by Willis Goldbeck (Metro-Goldwyn-Mayer, 1946), DVD (Warner Home Video, 2013).
81 Warren B. Francis, "Dewey Says Reds Seizing New Deal," *LAT*, November 2, 1944, 1.
82 Gerald Horne, *The Final Victim of the Blacklist: John Howard Lawson, Dean of the Hollywood Ten* (Berkeley: University of California Press, 2006), 162.
83 "Washington in June," *Life*, June 11, 1945, 98.
84 "Teen-Age Boys," *Life*, June 11, 1945, 91–97.

Chapter 2 Gable Is Able

1 Cornell Woolrich, "The Boy Cried Murder," *Mystery Book Magazine* 18 (March 1947): 50.
2 Pamela Robertson Wojcik, *Fantasies of Neglect: Imagining the Urban Child in American Film and Fiction* (New Brunswick, NJ: Rutgers University Press, 2016).
3 *The Window*, directed by Ted Tetzlaff (RKO-Radio Pictures, 1949), DVD (Warner Home Video, 2011).
4 Ibid.
5 "C.J. Tevlin Ledger," *Historical Journal of Radio, Film, and Television* 14, no. 1 (January 1994): microfiche supplement.
6 See Kenneth C. Davis, *Two-Bit Culture: The Paperbacking of America* (Boston: Houghton Mifflin, 1984), 182; Stephen Whitfield, *The Culture of the Cold War* (Baltimore: Johns Hopkins University Press, 1991), 34–37; K. A. Cuordileone, *Manhood and American Political Culture in the Cold War* (New York: Routledge, 2005), xiii–xv.
7 John Edgar Hoover, "A 'Third Front'—against Juvenile Delinquency," *NYT*, February 27, 1944, SM8.
8 Paula S. Fass and Michael Grossberg, eds., *Reinventing Childhood after World War II* (Philadelphia: University of Pennsylvania Press, 2011); Cuordileone, *Manhood and American Political Culture*, chap. 3; Lois Meek Stolz et al., *Father Relations of War-Born Children* (Stanford: Stanford University Press, 1954). Stolz found that forceful fathers "immediately resulted in alienation of their first-borns, whose attitudes became more rejecting of their fathers than were the attitudes of the non-separated group" (319).
9 Benjamin Spock, *The Common Sense Book of Baby and Child Care* (New York: Duell, Sloan, and Pearce, 1946), 254. In 1950, Spock stated, "Twentieth-century Americans has no stable family traditions about how children should be reared. In

fact, it has traditions against traditions." See Benjamin Spock, "Children Need Sensible Parents," *Parents*, December 1950, 41.

10 Karl Claudius Garrison, *Psychology of Adolescence* (New York: Prentice Hall, 1951), 137.

11 Ibid., 321.

12 Philip D. Beidler, *The Victory Album: Reflections on the Good Life after the Good War* (Tuscaloosa: University of Alabama Press, 2010), 17.

13 Hanson W. Baldwin, "Greatest Peril for U.S.," *NYT*, December 1, 1950, 4.

14 Ibid., 4.

15 Fulton John Sheen, *Communism and the Conscience of the West* (Indianapolis: Bobbs-Merrill, 1948), 149.

16 T. Jeremy Gunn, *Spiritual Weapons: The Cold War and the Forging of an American National Religion* (Westport, CT: Praeger, 2009); Jonathan P. Herzog, *The Spiritual-Industrial Complex: America's Religious Battle Against Communism in the Early Cold War* (New York: Oxford University Press, 2011); Steven P. Miller, *Billy Graham and the Rise of the Republican South* (Philadelphia: University of Pennsylvania Press, 2009).

17 Belmonte, *Selling the American Way*, 151.

18 Dianne Suzette Harris, ed., *Second Suburb: Levittown, Pennsylvania* (Pittsburgh: University of Pittsburgh Press, 2010).

19 Roderick Phillips, *Untying the Knot: A Short History of Divorce* (New York: Cambridge University Press, 1991), 212; see also Glenda Riley, *Divorce: An American Tradition* (New York: Oxford University Press, 1991).

20 Joseph I. Breen to Jack Warner, letter, September 9, 1943, "My Reputation [Warner Bros., 1943]," Motion Picture Association of America, PCA records, MHL, AMPAS. *My Reputation* was completed in 1944, but Warner Bros. delayed its general release to clear its backlog of frontline combat stories lest they become obsolete once the war ended. The studio added a short title card explaining to 1946 audiences that the film took place two years earlier.

21 *My Reputation*, directed by Curtis Bernhardt (Warner Bros., 1946), DVD (Warner Home Video, 2007).

22 Malvina Lindsay, "'Decline' of the Home," *WP*, September 3, 1946, 12.

23 Ibid., 12.

24 "The Family: In Western Civilization It is Seriously Threatened and Needs Material and Moral Help," *Life*, March 24, 1947, 36.

25 Ibid., 36. See Carle C. Zimmerman, *Family and Civilization* (New York: Harper & Bros., 1947).

26 Joseph Kirk Folsom, *The Family and Democratic Society* (New York: John Wiley, 1948).

27 "100 Years of Marriage and Divorce Rates Statistics: United States, 1867–1967." Quote from "Divorce Recession," *WP*, October 21, 1948, 8.

28 "Boy Loses Divorce Fight," *NYT*, October 21, 1949, 22; "Boy, 9, Runs Off to Reno to Divorce Folks," *LAT*, June 25, 1947, 1.

29 Frank Walsh, *Sin and Censorship: The Catholic Church and the Motion Picture Industry* (New Haven, CT: Yale University Press, 1996), 268.

30 Ibid., 169, 195.

31 Child of Divorce-Synopsis, "Child of Divorce [RKO, 1945]," Motion Picture Association of America, PCA records, MHL, AMPAS.

32 "Hayward, Flesicher in Auspicious Blows," *HR*, October 15, 1946, 3. See also "Trade Showing," *DV*, October 15, 1946, 3.

33 "C.J. Tevlin Ledger," *Historical Journal of Radio, Film, and Television* 14, no. 1 (January 1994): microfiche supplement.

34 See John R. Rice, *What Is Wrong with the Movies?* (Grand Rapids, MI: Zondervan, 1938); John Carrara, *Enemies of Youth* (Grand Rapids, MI: Zondervan, 1939); Dan Gilbert, *Hell over Hollywood: The Truth about the Movies!* (Grand Rapids, MI: Zondervan, 1942); John R. Rice, *What Is Wrong with the Movies?*, 15th ed. (1938; Grand Rapids, MI: Zondervan, 1954).

35 U. E. Harding, *Movie Mad America: An Utterly Frank and Revealing Expose of the American Movie* (Grand Rapids, MI: Zondervan, 1952), 9–10.

36 "What Does Your Church Say about . . . Divorce in Hollywood," *Motion Picture Magazine*, March 1947, 99.

37 Mrs. Robert Baker, letter, *Motion Picture Magazine*, June 6, 1947, 16. See also Alma Books, letter, *Motion Picture Magazine*, June 6, 1947, 16.

38 John Garfield, "To the Fans," *Motion Picture Magazine*, June 6, 1947, 14. Garfield was perhaps not the best person to make such a defense. Garfield, one of the more prominent Hollywoodite leftists in the public eye, would later suffer a fatal heart attack at age thirty-nine after being hounded by HUAC. Garfield also did not help Hollywood's precarious situation. One industry representative noted that *Motion Picture Magazine* ended the divorce article advertising a future issue featuring a "big, hard-hitting article on 'Politics in Hollywood' by John Garfield. We'll have another problem on our hands then, no doubt." Ernie Foster to Arch Reeve, interoffice memo, February 27, 1947, AMPTP, AMPAS.

39 "Religious Figures Flay Morals of Film Colony," *LAT*, February 18, 1947, 1.

40 Arch Reeve to Publicity Directors, letter, June 17, 1947; "Script Used by Erskine Johnson—Hollywood Commentator and Columnist," March 7, 1947, AMPTP, AMPAS.

41 Industry rep Arch Reeve recalled *Motion Picture Magazine* editor Maxwell Hamilton begging forgiveness. Hamilton cited dwindling circulating numbers and claimed his publication carried a tone "above the ordinary level" of journalism. Arch Reeve to Charley Schlaifer, letter, September 1, 1947, AMPTP, AMPAS. For the industry's perspective, see Arch Reeve to W. H. Fawcett Jr., letter, March 17, 1947, AMPTP, AMPAS. See also Mary Desjardins, "'Fan Magazine Trouble': The AMPP, Studio Publicity Directors, and the Hollywood Press, 1945–1952," *Film History: An International Journal* 26, no. 3 (2014): 38–41; Arch Reeve to Kenneth Clark and Glen Allvine, letter, February 25, 1947; "Fan Magazines-Motion Picture Magazine," f.139, AMPTP, AMPAS; Perry W. Lieber to Arch Reeve, letter, June 17, 1947; Charley Schlaifer to Arch Reeve, August 25, 1947, AMPTP, AMPAS; Perry W. Lieber to Arch Reeve, letter, June 17, 1947; Charley Schlaifer to Arch Reeve, August 25, 1947, AMPTP, AMPAS.

42 "'Too Many' Monitors of Pic Industry Hit by Schary at SPG Dinner," *Weekly Variety*, November 26, 1947, 5, 21.

43 Ibid., 5, 21.

44 William T. Walker, ed., *McCarthyism and the Red Scare: A Reference Guide* (Santa Barbara, CA: ABC-CLIO, 2011), 136–137.

45 L. Ka Torre to Eric Johnston, letter, March 12, 1946, "Sex, divorce, 1946," 14-f.16, Motion Picture Association of America Hollywood office files, MHL, AMPAS.

46 L.A. Savidge to Eric Johnston, letter, March 1947, "Sex, divorce 1946," 14-f.16, Motion Picture Association of America Hollywood office files, MHL, AMPAS.

47 Steven Bach, *Dazzler: The Life and Times of Moss Hart* (New York: Knopf, 2001), 272; Brooks Atkinson, "Hart's Desire," *NYT*, December 8, 1946, 85.

48 Moss Hart, *Christopher Blake* (New York: Random House, 1947), 17.
49 Actor Richard Tyler, a child of divorced parents, played Chris, albeit Tyler told the press he had "none of this trouble" featured in the play. See "Young Tyler Likes Acting and Bugs," *Life*, January 13, 1947, 101; Lester Bernstein, "The Rules and Richard Tyler," *NYT*, January 26, 1947, X1 and X3.
50 Jared Brown, *Moss Hart: A Prince of the Theater* (New York: Backstage Books, 2006), 277–278.
51 Ibid., 278. *Variety* reported the screen rights sold for $400,000. See "'Christopher Blake' Goes to WB," *DV*, December 23, 1946, 1. Hart wanted $500,000 for the rights; the final sale price reflected the play's failure.
52 Ranald MacDougall to Steve Trilling, interoffice communication, November 7, 1947, "The Decision of Christopher Blake" Files, WBA.
53 Ranald MacDougall to Steve Trilling, interoffice communication, July 12, 1947, "The Decision of Christopher Blake" Files, WBA.
54 Ranald MacDougall, "Decision of Christopher Blake," May 22, 1947, "The Decision of Christopher Blake" Files, WBA.
55 "Christopher Blake," folder 12678B, "The Decision of Christopher Blake" Files, WBA.
56 Mrs. Robert Baker, letter, *Motion Picture Magazine*, June 1947, 16. See also "Divorce Called 'Burglar,'" *NYT*, September 30, 1946, 42.
57 Ranald MacDougall, "Decision of Christopher Blake," February 25, 1947—folder Notes 1813A, WBA.
58 Ibid.
59 Hart, *Christopher Blake*, 63.
60 Ranald MacDougall, "Decision of Christopher Blake," February 25, 1947—folder Notes 1813A, WBA.
61 Alma Books, letter, *Motion Picture Magazine*, June 1947, 16. See also "Jean Parker Asks Divorce; Blames Work," *LAT*, July 1, 1949, 2; Jack Harrison Pollack, "The Real Causes of Divorce," *LAT*, January 8, 1956, L8, L9, and L10.
62 *The Decision of Christopher Blake*, directed by Peter Godfrey (Warner Bros., 1948), DVD (Personal Collection Courtesy of Robert Connors).
63 Ranald MacDougall to Steve Trilling, interoffice communication, February 20, 1947, Story File 416/565 1813A, "The Decision of Christopher Blake" Files, WBA.
64 Ibid.
65 Marty Weiser to Alex Evelove, interoffice communication, September 12, 1947, "The Decision of Christopher Blake—correspondence 1948," f. 142, Marty Weiser papers, AMPAS.
66 Cast and Credits, "The Decision of Christopher Blake [Warner Bros. 1948]," CCF, AMPAS.
67 In considering her son's plan for world peace, Mrs. Blake offers to write a "nasty letter to [Soviet Minister of Affairs Vyacheslav] Molotov," ordering the hardened diplomat to cooperate. The studio worried, "Is this good for international relations?" Ranald MacDougall to S. Hetta George, interoffice communication, June 9, 1947, WBA. Chris originally replies, "Let's see what happens," and they laugh. As tensions escalated throughout 1947, Chris's line changed to "I don't think that'll help." Ranald MacDougall, "The Decision of Christopher Blake Screenplay," May 22, 1947, WBA. The film deleted the "nasty" and gave Chris a pessimistic response: "Naw, he'll only say no."
68 Joseph Breen to Jack Warner, letter, July 28, 1947, "The Decision of Christopher Blake [WB 1947]," Motion Picture Association of America, PCA records, MHL, AMPAS.

69 "The Decision of Christopher Blake," folder 1012 12772A, The Decision of Christopher Blake Files, WBA. A school chum also insinuates Mrs. Blake has a "friend as well." See Ranald MacDougall, "The Decision of Christopher Blake," screenplay, April 7, 1947, 135–143, WBA.
70 Ted Donaldson, email to author, August 5, 2017.
71 Ibid.
72 Richard L. Coe, "Small Chris Has Wooden Parents," *WP*, December 17, 1948, B3. See also H. R., "Moss Hart's Play Adapted to the Screen," *CSM*, December 20, 1948, 5; Bosley Crowther, "The Screen in Review," *NYT*, December 11, 1948, 12; John McCarter, *New Yorker*, December 18, 1948, "The Decision of Christopher Blake [Warner Bros. 1948]," CCF, AMPAS; Herbert B. Alexander, "A Child Is as Good as His Neighborhood," *Parents*, April 1950, 26; "Your Guide to Current Films," *Screenland*, December 1948, 54; "'Quotes' What Newspaper Critics Say about New Films," *Independent Exhibitors Film Bulletin*, December 20, 1948, 22.
73 "The Decision of Christopher Blake," *Modern Screen*, January 1949, 96. Warner Bros. employed the same "trick" Chris uses in an earlier divorce-centered film, *Never Say Goodbye* (1946). This picture, however, played for laughs among the misunderstood swanks of Fifth Avenue, complete with dueling Santa Clauses. Leading actor Errol Flynn also had greater box office pull than Alexis Smith.
74 "Exploitips," *BOBG* supplement, *BO*, December 4, 1948, 16.
75 Cast and credits, "The Decision of Christopher Blake [Warner Bros. 1948]," CCF, AMPAS. The film's debut in Chicago grossed a "tragic $6000." See "'Hurry Up, Santa,' Shouts First Run as Take Dips to 186G," *DV*, December 12, 1948, 3; "Chi Biz Blitzed by Pre-Yule Call & Snow Strom," *DV*, December 21, 1948, 4.
76 "Boxoffice Barometer," *BOBG* supplement, *BO*, February 26, 1949, 1.
77 "The Exhibitor Has His Say about Pictures," *BOBG* supplement, *BO*, March 18, 1950, 4.
78 Eric Hodgins, "What's with the Movies?," *Life*, May 16, 1949, 105–106.
79 "Comparison of Negative Costs and Gross Income," [William Schaefer Ledger], William Schaefer Collection, WBA.
80 "'Judge Hardy' Fearful of Role as Gambler," *Any Number Can Play* press book, author's collection.
81 Ibid.
82 Joseph Breen to L. B. Mayer, letter, November 22, 1948, "Any Number Can Play [MGM 1948]," Motion Picture Association of America, PCA records, MHL, AMPAS.
83 Ernest Evred Blanche, *You Can't Win: Facts and Fallacies about Gambling* (Washington, DC: Public Affairs Press, 1949), 11. For contemporary headlines, see "Gambling Expose," *WP*, March 27, 1949, B4; Edwin Goldenthal, "Gambling Contradiction," *WP*, September 5, 1949, 6. Gambling addiction leads to marital ruin in the movie *The Lady Gambles* (1949).
84 Joseph Breen to Harold Melniker, letter, September 11, 1947, "The Window [RKO, 1947]," Motion Picture Association of America, PCA records, MHL, AMPAS.
85 Howard Strickling, "Clark Gable Feature," *Follow Up Promotion Campaign*, "Any Number Can Play [MGM 1948]," CCF, AMPAS.
86 Aaron M. Duncan, *Gambling with the Myth of the American Dream* (New York: Routledge, 2015), 11; Rita Barnard, *The Great Depression and the Culture of Abundance: Kenneth Fearing, Nathanael West, and Mass Culture in the 1930s* (New York: Cambridge University Press, 1995), 116; Reuven Brenner and Gabrielle A. Brenner, *Gambling and Speculation: A Theory, a History, and a Future of Some*

Human Decisions (New York: Cambridge University Press, 1990), 83; James Worthen, *Governor James Rolph and the Great Depression in California* (Jefferson, NC: McFarland, 2006); 32–39, 162–166. Movie houses also partook in gambling to attract patrons, using ticket stubs as raffle tickets for free sets of dishes during certain "Bank Nights."

87 *Any Number Can Play*, directed by Mervyn LeRoy (Metro-Goldwyn-Mayer, 1949), DVD (Warner Home Video, 2011). Censors in Ohio cut this line. Local Censor Report, Ohio, June 18, 1949, "Any Number Can Play [MGM 1948]," Motion Picture Association of America, PCA records, MHL, AMPAS.

88 Clipping, *Newsweek*, July 11, 1949, "Any Number Can Play [MGM 1948]," CCF, AMPAS. The notion of a model citizen extended to Gable. One gossip columnist noted MGM hired professional card shark Sammy Lande to teach the star the art of "card-riffing, chip stacking, and maybe dealing off the bottom." Gable was tough, but honest, and needed to learn the dirty tricks of the trade. See Florabel Muir, "Just for Variety," *DV*, January 5, 1949, 4.

89 Florabel Muir, "Just for Variety," *DV*, February 2, 1949, 4.

90 On film noir and postwar American culture, see Sheri Chinen Biesen, *Blackout: World War II and the Origins of Film Noir* (Baltimore: Johns Hopkins University Press, 2005), chap. 3; James Naremore, *More Than Night: Film Noir in Its Contexts* (Berkeley: University of California Press, 1998), chap. 1; Vivian Sobchack, "Lounge Time: Postwar Crises and the Chronotope of Film Noir," in *Refiguring American Film Genres: History and Theory*, ed. Nick Browne (Berkeley: University of California Press, 1998), 130–136.

91 Eric Avila, *Popular Culture in the Age of White Flight: Fear and Fantasy in Suburban Los Angeles* (Berkeley: University of California Press, 2004), 65–105.

92 Richard Brooks, "Any Number Can Play," script 1, Composite Screenplay, November 4, 1948, A1, Richard Brooks papers, AMPAS.

93 Ibid., 43.

94 *Any Number Can Play* (1949).

95 Ibid.

96 Ibid.

97 *Any Number Can Play* (1949).

98 "Mary Haworth's Mail," *WP*, February 22, 1948, S2.

99 Gladys Gardner Jenkins, Helen Shacter, and William W. Bauer, *These Are Your Children: How They Develop and How to Guide Them* (Chicago: Scott, Foresman, 1949), 66–67.

100 Benjamin Spock, *Common Sense Book*, 253.

101 Richard Brooks, "Any Number Can Play," script 1, Composite Screenplay, November 5, 1948, 83, Richard Brooks papers, AMPAS.

102 William R. Weaver, "Review," *MPD*, April 7, 1953; Darr Smith, "Film Review," *Los Angeles Daily News*, July 23, 1949, "Any Number Can Play [MGM 1948]," Motion Picture Association of America, PCA records, MHL, AMPAS.

103 Herm, "Film Review," *VW*, June 8, 1948, 18; Richard L. Coe, "Lavish Gambling Has Pious Payoff," *WP*, August 12, 1949, 24. Kyng's heart troubles compensated for any glorification of vice.

104 "'Number,' 'Skip' Name Can't Help Confused Script," *HR*, June 1, 1949. Another exhibitor commented, "This picture isn't bad. In fact, I thought it above average, but it is certainly not a picture for a town that has a church on every corner." See "The Exhibitor Has His Say about Pictures," *BOBG* supplement, *BO*, May 6, 1950, 2.

105 "The Exhibitor Has His Say about Pictures," *BOBG* supplement, *BO*, December 3, 1949, 2.
106 The bad guys sneak in thanks to Paul's jealous uncle, Robin Elcott (Wendell Corey), whom the film depicts as a failed man. Elcott and his wife, Mrs. Kyng's sister, live with the Kyngs because Elcott cannot hold a job. Charley Kyng sees him as dependent, a coward, and a parasite. Paul says Elcott lacks morals.
107 Richard Brooks, "Any Number Can Play," script 1, Composite Screenplay, November 5, 1948, 134, Richard Brooks papers, AMPAS.
108 F. B. Kopp, "Content Analysis Chart," "Any Number Can Play [MGM, 1948]," Motion Picture Association of America, PCA records, MHL, AMPAS.
109 Ibid.
110 "Film Daily Reviews of New Features," *FD*, June 2, 1949, 10.
111 "E. J. Mannix ledger, 1924–1963," Howard Stickling papers, MHL, AMPAS.
112 Jenkins, Shacter, and Bauer, *These Are Your Children*, 130.
113 Bosley Crowther, "It's Only Money," *NYT*, July 10, 1949, X1.
114 Spock, *Common Sense Book*, 295.
115 Dick Moore, *Twinkle, Twinkle, Little Star: But Don't Have Sex or Take the Car* (New York: Harper & Row, 1984), 169–170. Hickman added Gable wished he had a son and often roughhoused with him, like a father would.
116 "'Blake' Film Offers Drama," *Los Angeles Examiner*, December 18, 1948, "The Decision of Christopher Blake [Warner Bros. 1948]," CCF, AMPAS; see also Philip K. Scheuer, "Child Seen as Victim of Divorce," *LAT*, December 18, 1948, 7.
117 *The Decision of Christopher Blake* (1948).
118 "Decision on 'Christopher Blake' Proves Negative," *HR*, December 16, 1948, 6, "The Decision of Christopher Blake [Warner Bros. 1948]," CCF, AMPAS.
119 See Dore Schary, *Case History of a Movie* (New York: Random House, 1950), 227, 237. His book, a tie-in to promote his upcoming feature *The Next Voice You Hear* (1950), called Hollywood "a place where normal, likeable people work had and well at intelligent trades." See "Notes on Sales Promotion, July 12, 1950, Dore Schary: Next Voice Making of a Movie Corresp 1950 Oct–Dec 18," Dore Schary papers, US Mss 37, box 46, WHS.
120 Charlotte Eaton, "What Future for Pia?," *Modern Screen*, June 1950, 27. For accounts of the actresses' divorce, see their autobiographies: Shirley Temple Black, *Child Star: An Autobiography* (New York: McGraw-Hill, 1988); Ingrid Bergman and Alan Burgess, *My Story* (New York: Bantam, 1981).
121 Jack Vizzard, *See No Evil: Life Inside a Hollywood Censor* (New York: Simon & Schuster, 1970), 145–148.
122 "Movie Clean-Up Bill Offered in Senate," *LAT*, March 15, 1950, 1.
123 "900 Hear Hurley at Citizen Camp," *WP*, July 4, 1930, 5; John Garry Clifford, *The Citizen Soldiers: The Plattsburg Training Camp Movement, 1913–1920* (Lexington: University Press of Kentucky, 1972), 297.
124 "Pershing Appeals for Preparedness," *NYT*, June 13, 1936, 12.

Chapter 3 Curbing Delinquency

1 John Otto Reinemann, "Juvenile Delinquency and the Community," *Juvenile Delinquency (Philadelphia, PA): Hearing before the Subcommittee to Investigate Juvenile Delinquency of the Committee on the Judiciary, United States Senate, Eighty-Third Congress*, 2nd ed. (Washington, DC: Government Printing Office, 1954), 178.

2 Susan L. Carruthers, *Cold War Captives: Imprisonment, Escape, and Brainwashing* (Berkeley: University of California Press, 2009).
3 "Delinquency Fight Starts as War Ends," *WP*, August 13, 1945, 5; "Fifth Horseman," *WP*, April 12, 1953, B4; Gilbert, *Cycle of Outrage*, 79.
4 "Testimony of Hazel H. Brown, President Judge, Philadelphia Municipal Court," in *Juvenile Delinquency (Philadelphia, PA)*, 102.
5 Ibid., 102.
6 Geoffrey M. Shurlock to J. L. Warner, letter, December 14, 1954, "The Bad Seed [W.B. 1956]," Motion Picture Association of America, PCA records, MHL, AMPAS. Shurlock cited this clause to Jack Warner, warning that the plot of *The Bad Seed* violated the code's statute on child criminality.
7 Joseph I. Breen to J. R. McDonough, letter, September 29, 1938, "Boy Slaves [RKO 1939]," Motion Picture Association of America, PCA records, MHL, AMPAS.
8 J. R. McDonough, "Boy Slaves Censorship Eliminations," n.d., "Boy Slaves [RKO 1939]," Motion Picture Association of America, PCA records, MHL, AMPAS.
9 Margaret Guroff, *The Mechanical Horse: How the Bicycle Reshaped American Life* (Austin: University of Texas Press, 2015); Robert J. Turpin, "'Our Best Bet Is the Boy': A Cultural History of Bicycle Marketing and Consumption in the United States, 1880–1960" (PhD diss., University of Kentucky, 2013.
10 Michael A. Bernstein, *The Great Depression: Delayed Recovery and Economic Change in America, 1929–1939* (New York: Cambridge University Press, 1989), 60.
11 David Weissman, "The Bicycle Comes Back to Life," *LAT*, June 27, 1937, I8.
12 Mildred Adams, "Flashing Symbol of Our Changing Life," *NYT*, November 3, 1935, SM9.
13 Edwin T. Hamilton, "The World's Greatest Amateur Race," *Boys' Life*, May 1936, 12.
14 Ibid., 12.
15 John L. Jacobs, *The Fisher Body Craftsman's Guild: An Illustrated History* (Jefferson, NC: McFarland, 2005).
16 "Boys Strip Auto Fixtures to Equip a Car of Their Own," *NYT*, November 12, 1924, 25; Al G. Waddell, "Speed Racing Costs Money," *LAT*, March 26, 1922, 7.
17 "Thrill Seekers Admit They Stole 77 Autos," *NYT*, March 3, 1930, 52; "Chase Nets Boy Suspects," *LAT*, January 19, 1932, 10.
18 "Patrolman Kills 17-Year-Old Auto Thief; Boy and Comrades Stole Car for Joy Ride," *NYT*, October 17, 1929, 1; "Police Bullet Hits Boy in Auto Chase," *NYT*, March 19, 1934, 4.
19 Walt, "Andy Hardy's Private Secretary," *Variety*, February 26, 1941, 16.
20 "Pointers on Soap-Box," *Popular Mechanics*, April 1947, 202.
21 Andrew Hamilton, "Racing the Hot Rod," *Popular Mechanics*, January 1947, 244.
22 American Automobile Association, *Teacher's Manual for Sportsmanlike Driving* (Washington, DC: American Automobile Association, 1948), 169.
23 "Traffic with the Devil," directed by Gunther von. Fritsch (Metro-Goldwyn-Mayer, 1946), YouTube, August 11, 2015, https://www.youtube.com/watch?v=2Uorwb6M-9A.
24 Gary Cross, *Machines of Youth: America's Car Obsession* (Chicago: University of Chicago Press, 2018), 102–103.
25 "Reviews of New Films," *FD*, January 27, 1947, 7.
26 *The Devil on Wheels*, directed by Crane Wilbur (Producers Releasing Corporation, 1947), DVD (Alpha Home Video, 2010).
27 Joseph I. Breen to David Stephenson, letter, August 7, 1946, "The Devil on Wheels [Eagle Lion, 1946]," Motion Picture Association of America, PCA records, MHL, AMPAS.

28 *Devil on Wheels* (1947).
29 Ibid.
30 Ibid.
31 Edith O. Cignoni to Eric Johnston, letter, May 20, 1946, "Drinking," 8-f.112, Motion Picture Association of America, Hollywood Office files, MHL, AMPAS.
32 Mrs. Esther Horst to Eric Johnston, letter, March 22, 1946, "Drinking," 8-f.112, Motion Picture Association of America, Hollywood Office files, MHL, AMPAS.
33 Joseph I. Breen to Mary W. Robinson, letter, October 15, 1946, "Responses 13-f.154," Motion Picture Association of America, Hollywood Office files, MHL, AMPAS.
34 Joseph I. Breen to E. R. Freeman, letter, November 2, 1946, "Responses 13-f.154," Motion Picture Association of America, Hollywood Office files, MHL, AMPAS.
35 Joseph I. Breen to Mrs. Cynthia A. Dawe, letter, November 14, 1946, "Responses 13-f.154," Motion Picture Association of America, Hollywood Office files, MHL, AMPAS.
36 Joseph I. Breen to Mrs. Richard Felber, letter, February 2, 1947, "Responses 13-f.156," Motion Picture Association of America, Hollywood Office files, MHL, AMPAS.
37 *Devil on Wheels* (1947).
38 Ibid.
39 Ibid.
40 "Feature Reviews," *DV*, January 22, 1947, "The Devil on Wheels," CCF, MHL, AMPAS.
41 Irving Kaplan, "Review: 'The Devil on Wheels," *MPD*, January 22, 1947, 6.
42 *Hot Rod*, directed by Lewis D. Collins (Monogram Pictures, 1950), DVD (Warner Home Video, 2010).
43 Ibid.
44 Andrew Hamilton, "Racing the Hot Rods," *Popular Mechanics*, January 1947, 248.
45 *Hot Rod* (1950).
46 Hot Rod, Production Sheet, September 14, 1950, "Hot Rod [Thomas, 1950]," Motion Picture Association of America, PCA records, MHL, AMPAS.
47 *Hot Rod* (1950).
48 "The Exhibitor Has His Say about Pictures," *BOBG* supplement, *BO*, August 11, 1951, 1.
49 C. R. Metzger, "The Devil Drives—Eagle Lion," August 7, 1946, "The Devil on Wheels [Eagle Lion, 1946]," Motion Picture Association of America, PCA records, MHL, AMPAS.
50 *Hot Rod* (1950).
51 Borg, "Feature Reviews," *DV*, October 18, 1950, 3.
52 "The Exhibitor Has His Say about Pictures," *BOBG* supplement, *BO*, August 25, 1951, 1.
53 "U.S. Traffic Fatalities Drop to Record Low," *CSM*, August 23, 1948, 6. See "Hot Rod Strips Reduce Citations, Officers Say," *LAT*, October 30, 1955, B3.
54 "Hot-Rod Club Teaches Youths Traffic Safety," *LAT*, December 22, 1952, 23.
55 "Speedsters May Be in Civil Defense Setup," *LAT*, September 1, 1950, 2. See also "Police Say Hot Rod Race Supervision Pays Off," *LAT*, November 5, 1950, 43; "Youngsters' Auto Club Aids Defense," *LAT*, December 4, 1952, A10.
56 United States Congress, Senate, Committee on the Judiciary, *Juvenile Delinquency, Comic Books Motion Pictures, Obscene and Pornographic Materials, Television Programs* (New York: Greenwood, 1955), 54–55.
57 Bernard Williams, *Jailbait: The Story of Juvenile Delinquency* (New York: Greenberg, 1949), 84.

58 Angela F. Keaton, "Unholstered and Unquestioned: The Rise of Post–World War II American Gun Cultures" (PhD diss., University of Tennessee–Knoxville, 2006); Richard Slotkin, *Gunfighter Nation: The Myth of the Frontier in Twentieth-Century America* (New York: Atheneum, 1992).

59 Viviana A. Zelizer, *Pricing the Priceless Child: The Changing Social Value of Children* (New York: Basic Books, 1985), 77–81; Platt, *Child Savers*; Wolcott, *Cops and Kids*; Kenneth B. Kidd, *Making American Boys: Boyology and the Feral Tale* (Minneapolis: University of Minnesota Press, 2004).

60 Kevin Brownlow, *Behind the Mask of Innocence* (New York: Knopf, 1990), chaps. 5 and 11; Steven J. Ross, *Working-Class Hollywood: Silent Film and the Shaping of Class in America* (Princeton, NJ: Princeton University Press, 1998), 51–54; Sidney Sheldon to Dore Schary, interdepartment communication, January 4, 1946, "Juvenile Delinquency: A Treatment," Dore Schary papers, US Mss 37, box 46, WHS.

61 *The Lights of New York*, directed by Brian Foy (Warner Bros., 1928), DVD (Warner Home Video, 2018).

62 Indiana Boys' School, *The Second Century: A Look at the Present, a Search for the Future: Indiana Boys' School, Plainfield, Indiana* (Plainfield: Indiana Boys' School, 1973).

63 G. Stanley Hall, *Adolescence: Its Psychology and Its Relations to Physiology, Anthropology, Sociology, Sex, Crime, Religion, and Education*, vol. 1 (New York: D. Appleton, 1904), 223.

64 See H. S. Kay, "A Dangerous Plaything," *NYT*, November 8, 1914, C2; "'Cops and Gangsters' New Game for Youngsters," *LAT*, September 1, 1931, 9; Alexander DeConde, *Gun Violence in America: The Struggle for Control* (Boston: Northeastern University Press, 2001), chap. 9; Gary Cross, *The Cute and the Cool: Wondrous Innocence and Modern American Children's Culture* (New York: Oxford University Press, 2004), 166–167.

65 Harry L. Wilson, *Guns, Gun Control, and Elections: The Politics and Policy of Firearms* (Lanham, MD: Rowman & Littlefield, 2007), 87.

66 Gregory D. Black, *Hollywood Censored: Morality Codes, Catholics, and the Movies* (New York: Cambridge University Press, 1994), 110.

67 Blumer and Hauser, *Movies, Delinquency, and Crime*; Courtney Riley Cooper, *Designs in Scarlet* (Boston: Little, Brown, 1939). See Ruth, *Inventing the Public Enemy*; Jonathan Munby, *Public Enemies, Public Heroes: Screening the Gangster from* Little Creaser *to* Touch of Evil (Chicago: University of Chicago Press, 2009); Jowett, Jarvie, and Fuller, *Children and the Movies*.

68 "War Toys?," *Rotarian*, December 1940, 19.

69 "G-Man Is Donor of Shirley's Gun," *WP*, October 29, 1937. See also Kenneth O'Reilly, "A New Deal for the FBI: The Roosevelt Administration, Crime Control, and National Security," *Journal of American History* 69, no. 3 (December 1982): 638–658.

70 Athan G. Theoharis, ed., *The FBI: A Comprehensive Reference Guide* (Phoenix, AZ: Oryx Press, 1999), 272–279; Bob Herzberg, *The FBI and the Movies: A History of the Bureau on Screen and Behind the Scenes in Hollywood* (Jefferson, NC: McFarland, 2007), chap. 2.

71 In 1944, actor Huntz Hall looked back at his "Dead End" films and faulted them for contributing to wartime delinquency and for criticizing social institutions. Hall, discharged due to poor eyesight, cited reports of the Nazis' editing of movies to show "the degradation of youth in 'decadent democracies,' especially America." Hedda Hopper, "'Dead End Kid' Rues Past," *LAT*, October 8, 1944, B1.

72 Melissa Bingmann, *Prep School Cowboys: Ranch Schools in the American West* (Santa Fe: University of New Mexico Press, 2015). Space prohibits a deeper examination of postwar films featuring the Boy Scouts. Like *Johnny Holiday*, pictures like *Boys Ranch* (1946), *Room for One More* (1952), and *Mister Scoutmaster* (1953) rehabilitated delinquents in the great outdoors. While reviewing *The Bride Goes Wild* (1948), Joseph Breen wanted parodist references to the Boy Scouts removed to prevent a public backlash. See Joseph I. Breen to L. B. Mayer, letter, August 2, 1946, "The Bride Goes Wild [MGM, 1947]," Motion Picture Association of America, PCA records, MHL, AMPAS. The script changed the Boy Scouts to the fictitious "Junior Woodmen."

73 Quoted in Ulys, *Riding the Rails*, 233–235.

74 "War Dominates Children's Desire for Toys; Many Ask Santa to Send Machine Guns," *NYT*, December 9, 1942, 34.

75 "President Praises Boys' War Effort," *CSM*, April 8, 1943, 3.

76 Winchester Repeating Arms Company, "Every Boy Has His Hero," advertisement, *Boys' Life*, August 1944, 31.

77 Michael Hogan, *A Cross of Iron: Harry S. Truman and the Origins of the National Security State, 1945–1954* (Cambridge: Cambridge University Press, 2000), 119–158; Marilyn Irvin Holt, *Cold War Kids: Politics and Childhood in Postwar America, 1945–1960* (Lawrence: University Press of Kansas, 2014).

78 William A. Taylor, *Every Citizen a Soldier: The Campaign for Universal Military Training after World War II* (Austin: Texas A&M University Press, 2014), 29.

79 Speaking from his fifty-acre ranch, General Henry Harley "Hap" Arnold of the Army Air Force wanted a "youth camp movement—country wide—something that would use the fullest our vast string of national and State parks and recreation areas." The reporter noted Arnold was California's fish and game commissioner. See James D. White, "'Hap' Has a Delinquency Cure," *WP*, July 27, 197, B2. For a similar view, see "Juvenile Delinquency Offset by Gardening," *WP*, April 26, 1949, B2.

80 John Sager, "Universal Military Training and the Struggle to Define American Identity during the Cold War," *Federal History* 5 (January 2013): 57–74. See Michael S. Neiberg, *Making Citizen-Soldiers: ROTC and the Ideology of American Military Service* (Cambridge, MA: Harvard University Press, 2001), chap. 2. On the stigma of universal military training as government overreach and a misuse of tax dollars, see Hogan, *Cross of Iron*, chap. 4.

81 Louis Bromfield et al., *Militarism in Education* (Washington, DC: National Council Against Conscription, 1950), 39. See also Albert E. Kahn, *The Game of Death: Effects of the Cold War on Our Children* (New York: Cameron & Kahn, 1953), chap. 3.

82 Taylor, *Every Citizen a Soldier*, 86. One critic noted Franklin Roosevelt specifically directed the War Department not to train CCC enlistees in military tactics. The CCC comprised lower class boys and, "in event of war, those who had the CCC camp training would be the first to be exposed to the danger," while upper-class youths "would have their battle experience postponed." Military training in the CCC was "a discriminatory attitude against the poor." Arthur Rock, "In the Nation," *NYT*, October 30, 1947, C24.

83 See "U.S. Aid Vital to China, Mission Head Asserts," *LAT*, February 29, 1948, 9; "U.S. Arms to China Urged by Dr. Tsiang," *NYT*, December 23, 1948, 3; "U.S. Aid to China Is Urged by Legion," *WP*, September 1, 1949, 3; Walter Lippmann, "U.S. Lost China When F.D.R. Bowed to Chiang," *LAT*, September 14, 1949, A4.

84 Jenkins, Shacter, and Bauer, *These Are Your Children*, 6; George J. Hecht, "Top Priority for Children," *Parents*, March 1951, 26; Naoko Wake, "The Military, Psychiatry, and 'Unfit' Soldiers, 1939–1942," *Journal of the History of Medicine and Allied Sciences* 62, no. 4 (October 2007): 462–494.

85 Hanson W. Baldwin, "Need of Training Revealed in Korea," *NYT*, November 3, 1950, 4.

86 Robert L. Besiner, *Dean Acheson: A Life in the Cold War* (New York: Oxford University Press, 2006), 305. Ironically, Acheson was born in Middletown, Connecticut—the town had the same name the Lynds used to characterize the "average" American town, its inhabitants, and their character.

87 Spock, *Common Sense Book*, 252–253.

88 Richard L. Coe, "One on the Aisle," *WP*, June 22, 1950, 12; R. W. Alcorn to Greyson Bautzer, letter, June 24, 1949, "Alcorn Prod.-1949-June-Aug ('Johnny Holiday')," George L. Bagnall Papers, box 1, WHS. Alcorn recalled, "I was bored stiff in the plane on a wheat-buying trip" to Brazil, "so I just began to write." A. H. Weiler, "Assorted Notes About People and Pictures," *NYT*, January 15, 1950, X7.

89 "United to Release First by Alcorn," *LAT*, July 24, 1949, D3.

90 Clipping, *HR*, December 12, 1947, "The Dangerous Years [Wurtzel-1947]," Motion Picture Association of America, PCA records, MHL, AMPAS.

91 Dore Schary to Eugene W. Biscailuz, letter, January 4, 1946, "Juvenile Delinquency, a Treatment," Dore Schary papers, US Mss 37AN, box 43, WHS.

92 David Palfreyman to Dore Schary, letter, January 29, 1946, "Juvenile Delinquency, a Treatment," Dore Schary papers, US Mss 37AN, box 43, WHS.

93 Alcorn proudly noted, "The school and its inmates have been placed completely at my disposal for the picture." R. W. Alcorn to Greyson Bautzer, letter, June 24, 1949, "Alcorn Prod.-1949-June-Aug ('Johnny Holiday')," George L. Bagnall Papers, box 1, WHS. In 1950, sociologist Albert Deutsch noted Indiana Boys' School had improved in recent years. Deutsch originally observed conditions in the reformatory in 1947 and found them deplorable. The superintendent, a former dairy man, believed in corporal punishment, downplayed education, and wanted "military training here," which meddling social workers opposed: "These boys could use it. If we keep 'em at it all the time, it keeps 'em out of mischief. We could get them neat-cut uniforms, like the new army ones. The boys would love it." Deutsch noted conditions improved in 1948, when Governor Henry F. Schricker, who appeared in *Johnny Holiday*, entered office and replaced the superintendent with a staff of child welfare workers (presumably those seen in the movie), and "introduced many heartening reforms." See Albert Deutsch, *Our Rejected Children* (Boston: Little, Brown, 1950), 47, 54.

94 "Feature Reviews," *DV*, November 18, 1949, 3.

95 "Feature Reviews," *VW*, December 14, 1949, 8. *Johnny Holiday*'s first run market earned an average 101 percent. See "Barometer," *BOBG* supplement, *BO*, July 8, 1950, 1. One Nebraskan exhibitor sighed, "We missed the boat by not plugging it more. Don't be afraid to recommend it. However, it isn't big enough for top billing." "The Exhibitor Has His Say about Pictures," *BOBG* supplement, *BO*, October 21, 1950, 4. Alcorn provided a signed testimonial for his movie posters: "I was this boy! I was born to vice and violence . . . on the other side of the tracks . . . where to be good is to be *good* and dead! This is my story!" Alcorn's name carried more weight in agribusiness than the movies, and reviewers did not believe his statement would draw patrons. See "Feature Reviews," *BOBG* supplement, *BO*, November 26, 1949, 15.

96 A. S. L., letter, "The Reader Writes," *CSM*, July 23, 1951, 16.

97 Pat Shepard, "Ornery Youngster Rises to Assistant Police Chief," *LAT*, October 28, 1945, A1.

98 Joseph I. Breen to Frank Parminter, letter, June 7, 1949, "Johnny Holiday [Alcorn, 1949]," Motion Picture Association of America, PCA records, MHL, AMPAS. Breen had the same complaint about *Boys' Ranch* (1946), a picture about another rural rehabilitation home. He objected to a shot of one boy aiming a gun at another: "Accordingly, we urge that you seriously consider omitting this detail." See Joseph I. Breen to L. B. Mayer, letter, 9 November 1945; letter, November 20, 1945, "Boys Ranch [MGM 1945]," Motion Picture Association of America, PCA records, MHL, AMPAS.

99 M. E. Hohenfield, "Memo for the Files," June 16, 1949, "Johnny Holiday [Alcorn, 1949]," Motion Picture Association of America, PCA records, MHL, AMPAS. Many "J.D." films feature knife fights for their "rumbles" rather than depict street shootings.

100 The school is not an idealized haven. Alcorn captures the rivalry between teachers (the shoe shop instructor resents his low rank in the chain of command). In the film, boys also have their own form of justice; when one runaway returns and the adults punish the entire school, the boys corner the offender in the shower and pummel him. Breen allowed the sequence, but warned against showing nudity in the shower room.

101 "A View of Life in a Reform School," *NYT*, May 17, 1950, 36.

102 Stanley Pashko, "This Should Happen to a Dog," *Boys' Life*, February 1947, 17.

103 Ibid., 37.

104 Lillian Culver, Screen Synopsis, June 25, 1945, "The Yearling [MGM, 1945]," Motion Picture Association of America, PCA records, MHL, AMPAS.

105 *Johnny Holiday*, directed by Willis Goldbeck (Alcorn Productions, 1949), VHS (Republic Entertainment, 1998).

106 "Group to Plan Conservation Corps Revival," *WP*, August 14, 1944, 7.

107 Ibid., 7.

108 "$15.00 Gun Only $4.95," advertisement, *Boys' Life*, December 1948, 45.

109 Ann Kordas, "Wally Cleaver Goes to War: The Boy Citizen-Solider on the Cold War Classroom Scenes," *Thymos: Journal of Boyhood Studies* 5, no. 2 (Fall 2011): 163–173; Cynthia J. Miller and A. Bowdin Van Riper, eds., *1950s "Rocketman" TV Series and Their Fans: Cadets, Rangers, and Junior Space Men* (New York: Palgrave Macmillan, 2012), 97–114.

110 *Johnny Holiday* (1949).

111 Johnny did not react as violently as the British. British censors, stricter than the PCA, ordered several cuts, including the "whole incident showing punishment of boy by other boys in the shower," Eddie's attempt to kill Walker, and Nellie's death—this last cut removed the motivation for Holiday's break with Walker. Local Censor Report, Great Britain, May 30, 1958, "Johnny Holliday [Alcorn 1949]," Motion Picture Association of America, PCA records, MHL, AMPAS. The public relations department in England told distributor United Artists the "name of the Governor of Indiana means nothing in this country" and recommended removing his honor's speech in the parade grounds. Arthur Kelly to Fred Meyers, letter, May 15, 1950, "Arthur Kelly File, 1946–1951, Kelly-Alcorn productions, Ltd," United Artists Corporation Collection, series 6B, box 1, WHS.

112 *Johnny Holiday* (1949).

113 Joseph I. Breen to Frank Parminter, letter, June 7, 1949, "Johnny Holiday [Alcorn, 1949]," Motion Picture Association of America, PCA records, MHL, AMPAS.

114 *Johnny Holiday* (1949).
115 M. E. Hohenfield, "Memo for the Files," June 16, 1949, "Johnny Holiday [Alcorn, 1949]," Motion Picture Association of America, PCA records, MHL, AMPAS.
116 Ibid.
117 *Johnny Holiday* (1949).
118 See "Denied Gun, Boy Starts Collection," *LAT*, March 23, 1940, 8; "Boys to Face Court on Car Theft Charge," *LAT*, March 20, 1941, A1.
119 Gerald Walker, "Should Small Fry Carry Small Arms?" *NYT*, June 29, 1958, SM40.
120 See Will Wright, *The Wild West: The Mythical Cowboy and Social Theory* (Thousand Oaks, CA: Sage, 1983); David Hamilton Murdoch, *The American West: The Invention of a Myth* (Las Vegas: University of Nevada Press, 2001); Joy S. Kasson, *Buffalo Bill's Wild West: Celebrity, Memory, and Popular Culture* (New York: Hill & Wang, 2000); Janet M. Davis, *The Circus Age: Culture and Society under the American Big Top* (Chapel Hill: University of North Carolina Press, 2002), chap. 6; Matthew Carter, *Myth of the Western: New Perspectives on Hollywood's Frontier Narrative* (Edinburgh: Edinburgh University Press, 2014).
121 The "singing cowboy," in particular, emphasized the gunslinger's grassroots through his folk tunes. See Peter Stanfield, *Horse Opera: The Strange History of the 1930s Singing Cowboy* (Urbana: University Press of Illinois, 2002), Douglas B. Green, *Singing in the Saddle: The History of the Singing Cowboy* (Nashville, TN: Vanderbilt University Press, 2005).
122 Francis M. Nevins, "Through the Great Depression on Horseback: Legal Themes in Western Films of the 1930s," in *Legal Realism: Movies as Legal Texts*, ed. John Denvir (Urbana: University of Illinois Press, 1996), 44–69; R. Philip Loy, *Westerns and American Culture, 1930–1955* (Jefferson, NC: McFarland, 2001), 159; Jeremy Agnew, *The Creation of the Cowboy Hero: Fiction, Film, and Fact* (Jefferson, NC: McFarland, 2014), 139; Michael Duchemin, *New Deal Cowboy: Gene Autry and Public Diplomacy* (Oklahoma City: University of Oklahoma Press, 2016).
123 The Old West was a popular, cheap B-movie setting throughout motion picture history. By the 1950s, the "superwestern" launched John Wayne's popularity into various "top-ten" lists for the rest of the decade. Television also cashed in; as many as thirty-seven westerns aired simultaneously in the late 1950s. See Jim Collins, "Faces without Names," in *Back in the Saddle: Essays on Western Film and Television Actors*, ed. Gary A. Yoggy (Jefferson, NC: McFarland, 1998), 145. MGM spoofed the craze in *Callaway Went Thataway* (1951), with producers milking a TV cowboy. Fortunately, during a weeklong Boys Week in Los Angeles, the code of the west prevailed. The studio inserted a closing title card: "This picture was made in the spirit of fun, and was meant in no way to detract from the wholesome influence, civic mindedness, and the many charitable contributions of Western idols of our American youth, or to be a portrayal of any of them." *Callaway Went Thataway*, directed by Melvin Frank (Metro-Goldwyn-Mayer, 1951), DVD (Warner Home Video, 2015).
124 On the cowboy image as a role model for delinquents, see Bingmann, *Prep School Cowboys*, 173–175.
125 "The Westerns Preferred," *MPH*, November 25, 1950, 40. On the postwar western, see Stanley Corkin, *Cowboys as Cold Warriors: The Western and U.S. History* (Philadelphia: Temple University Press, 2004), 6–12; Slotkin, *Gunfighter Nation*, chaps. 7–10; John V. H. Dippel, *War and Sex: A Brief History of Men's Urge for Battle* (New York: Prometheus Books, 2010), 249. The "West" also played out among East and West Germans re-creating their identity. See Pawel Goral, *Cold*

War Rivalry and the Perception of the American West (New York: Palgrave Macmillan, 2014).

126 Jeremy Agnew, *The Old West in Fact and Film: History versus Hollywood* (Jefferson, NC: McFarland, 2012). 63.

127 Leonard Spinrad, "Boots and Saddles," *NYT*, June 8, 1947, X4.

128 "Daniel Boone Target Shoot," *Boys' Life*, June 1950, 4.

129 For examples, see "Two Boys Held in Shooting," *LAT*, October 16, 1946, 12; "Town Terrorized by 2 Boys, 8 and 10," *NYT*, November 8, 1947, 30; "'Gun Wasn't Loaded,' Parent Sobs," *LAT*, May 21, 1949, A1; "Boys Invade Home and Slug Woman," *LAT*, September 4, 1949, 11.

130 "Boys' Leader Traces Delinquency Trends," *NYT*, May 20, 1947, 22.

131 Ibid., 22.

132 Vera Emanuel, "Are We Making Gunmen of Our Children?," *Parents*, May 1952, 48–50. The magazine identified Emanuel as a visitor from a "foreign country." Presumably, her nationality and gender prevented her from understanding the appeal guns held for American boys. See also "Chicago Toy Pistol Ban Hits Small Fry," *LAT*, February 19, 1950, 3; Lazarus Monfried, "To Ban Toy Pistols," letter, *NYT*, April 12, 1954, 28. Monfried proposed banning one "source of evil": the "cruel fighting, shooting or murder" in the movies. One reader replied Monfried needed to look at the lack of family togetherness, not toys. See Vincent Bryan, "Play and Potential Delinquents," letter, *NYT*, April 17, 1954, 12.

133 "Adapted Cap Pistols Can Kill, County Police Warn Parents," *WP*, July 3, 1952, 23; "Probe Told of Juvenile Gang Wars in New York," *WP*, November 21, 1953, 1; "Cowgirls" were also a problem: see "Girl with Cap Gun Arrested for Holdup," *LAT*, May 6, 1954, A1.

134 Some films, notably *Gun Crazy* (1950), had mixed messages. Without a father, Bart Tare lands in juvenile court for stealing a firearm. He later falls under the charms of a woman and the two "gun crazy" youths go on a rampage. In the end, rather than murder a childhood friend turned cop, Tare shoots his partner and dies in a hail of police bullets. The obligatory message against firearms indicates the boy's gun craziness came from the lack of a male role model and a domineering female accomplice.

135 Harry Brand, synopsis of *The Gun Fighter*, "The Gun Fighter [20th C-Fox, 1949]," Motion Picture Association of America, PCA records, MHL, AMPAS.

136 Bosley Crowther, "The Screen: Three Features Have Premieres" *NYT*, June 24, 1950.

137 On the "sophistication" of westerns, see Hubbard Keavy, "And the Villain Still Pursued Him," *WP*, March 1, 1942, L1.

138 Darryl Zanuck to Nunnally Johnson, letter, June 14, 1949, "Gun Fighter—corr. #382," Gregory Peck Collection, 36 Peck B34, Gregory Peck papers, MHL, AMPAS.

139 Harry Brand, synopsis of *The Gun Fighter*, "The Gun Fighter [20th C-Fox, 1949]," Motion Picture Association of America, PCA records, MHL, AMPAS.

140 Ibid.

141 Darryl Zanuck to Nunnally Johnson, letter, June 14, 1949, "Gun Fighter—corr. #382," Gregory Peck Collection, 36 Peck B34, Gregory Peck papers, MHL, AMPAS. Despite the message, Zanuck urged Johnson to focus on "riproaring entertainment" rather than preachment. He wanted to avoid a repeat of *The Ox-Bow Incident* (1943), an antilynching picture that he derided as "probably the only Western in the history of motion pictures that ended up in the red," even with a low cost. Zanuck believed audiences found message pictures "entirely too intellectual,

too morbid, and the ending was total futility." The studio's press book also complicated the message with stories of Gregory Peck's two sons "forcing" their father to wear Ringo's gun around the house and play cowboy with them. Another story bragged how Twentieth Century-Fox housed over fifteen thousand firearms in the studio arsenal, from flintlocks to flamethrowers, that could thwart an invasion should "some hostile national should attempt a surprise raid on the California coast." "'Gunfighter' Studio Owns Largest Private Armory," *The Gunfighter* press book, CCF, MHL, AMPAS.

142 Edwin Schallert, "'Gunfighter' Vital Old West Subject," *LAT*, June 24, 1950, 9.

143 Richard Griffith, "'Gunfighter's' Novel Idea Surprises Critics," *LAT*, July 4, 1950, 8.

144 Quoted in Rudy Behlmer, ed., *Memo from Darryl F. Zanuck: The Golden Years at Twentieth Century-Fox* (New York: Grove Press, 1993), 190.

145 Quoted in Gerald Molyneaux, *Gregory Peck: A Bio-bibliography* (Westport, CT: Greenwood, 1995), 103. Producer Nunnally Johnson, who contributed to the screenplay, called the story about Peck's mustache "nonsense." He denied any intention to revise the western myth, although Zanuck's correspondence suggests otherwise. See Tom Stempel, *Recollections of Nunnally Johnson* (Berkeley: University of California Press, 1969), 280. Stempel's biography of Johnson, based on this interview, asserted, "Audiences brought up on *Jesse James* [1939; a very popular Depression-era biopic Johnson wrote, glamorizing the western outlaw] were put off by the relatively realistic description of Ringo, especially since *The Gunfighter* was one of the first films to begin to dismantle the popular myths of the West." Tom Stempel, *Screenwriter: The Life and Times of Nunnally Johnson* (San Diego: S.A. Barnes, 1990), 129.

146 Corkin, *Cowboys as Cold Warriors*, 96. Film scholar Stephen McVeigh characterizes *The Gunfighter* as "an approaching apocalypse," with Ringo "like a Cold War superpower," running a mental countdown as his death draws near. However, 1950s Americans saw guns in a different light than Ringo. For the public, a forceful show of arms would push the communists out of Korea and win the war. See Stephen McVeigh, *The American Western* (Edinburgh: Edinburgh University Press, 2007), 81.

147 *The Gunfighter*, directed by Henry King (Twentieth Century-Fox Film, 1950), DVD (Twentieth Century Fox Home Entertainment, 2008).

148 Red Kann, "Review: The Gunfighter," *MPD*, April 26, 1950, 3.

149 "Boxoffice Barometer," *BOBG* supplement, *BO*, July 22, 1950, 1. *The Gunfighter* cost $1.42 million to produce and earned $1.95 million in domestic rentals. Aubrey Solomon, *Twentieth Century-Fox: A Corporate and Financial History* (Lanham, MD: Scarecrow Press, 2002), 222–223, 245. One optimistic report in 1950 noted a reversal in the box office slump and listed *The Gunfighter* as one of example. The author added, "The International Crisis [i.e., Korea] was given little credit for the better business." See "Definite Trend in Film Income Rise," *MPD*, August 15, 1950, 5.

150 Darryl Zanuck to Nunnally Johnson, letter, July 13, 1950, Henry King Collection, folder 15: The Gunfighter, Henry King papers, MHL, AMPAS.

151 Behlmer, *Memo from Darryl F. Zanuck*, 189–190.

152 T. A. W., "The Theatre," *WSJ*, June 28, 1950. 12.

153 Joseph I. Breen to Eleanor O. Curtiss, letter, February 7, 1947, "Responses 1947," 13-f.156," Motion Picture Association of America Hollywood Office files, MHL, AMPAS.

154 "The Exhibitor Has His Say about Pictures," *BOBG* supplement, *BO*, November 4, 1950, 3.

155 "The Exhibitor Has His Say about Pictures," *BOBG* supplement, *BO*, January 13, 1951, 3.
156 "The Exhibitor Has His Say about Pictures," *BOBG* supplement, *BO*, March 31, 1951, 4.
157 Quoted in Kahn, *Game of Death*, 115.
158 Ibid., 115.
159 Sidney Green, "Are We Making Gunmen of Our Children?," *Parents*, May 1952, 50, 100.
160 Ibid., 100.
161 House Committee on Un-American Activities, "100 Things You Should Know about Communism and Education," in *100 Things You Should Know about Communism*, 2nd ed. (Washington, DC: House Committee on Un-American Activities, 1949), 53.
162 Vincent Bryan, "Play and Potential Delinquents," *NYT*, April 17, 1954, 1.
163 The communists recognized the cowboy image as uniquely American. In 1958, the *Christian Science Monitor* reported East German deputy minister president Walter Ulbricht told a group of youth leaders not to wear cowboy shirts "and if they must wear clothes with pictures they should show North Viet Nam—not Texas." See "Cowboy Shirt Trend Irks Communist Chief," *CSM*, September 18, 1958, 4. See also "Swiss Act to Expel 40 Americans in Rodeo after Cowboys and Cowgirls Engage in Riot," *NYT*, October 26, 1948, 33.
164 "Loyalty Pledged for ROTC Negroes," *NYT*, April 3, 1948, 3.
165 Ibid., 3. See also "Equal Opportunity is Sought for Negroes in College Training as Reserve Officers," *NYT*, October 21, 1949, 5.

Chapter 4 Whitewashing the Race Cycle in 1949

1 Thomas F. Brady, "The Hollywood Wire," *NYT*, November 14, 1948, X5; Charles Palmer to Arthur Mayer, letter, November 19, 1948, folder 35, Charles Palmer papers, MHL, AMPAS; A. H. Weiler, "By Way of Report," *NYT*, May 15, 1949, X4.
2 Charles Palmer, "Lost Boundaries," undated, folder 21, Charles Palmer papers, MHL, AMPAS.
3 Joseph I. Breen to Eugene Ling, letter, January 17, 1949, "Lost Boundaries [Film Classics, 1949]," Motion Picture Association of America, PCA records, MHL, AMPAS.
4 Joseph I. Breen to Borden Mace, letter, June 22, 1949, "Lost Boundaries [Film Classics, 1949]," Motion Picture Association of America, PCA records, MHL, AMPAS.
5 "'Boundaries' Suit to Test Power of the Censors," *DV*, November 21, 1949, 10.
6 "MPAA May Join with De Rochemont to Fight Southern 'Boundaries' Ban," *DV*, August 31, 1949, 20.
7 See Matty Brescia, "Tenn. Supreme Court Rules Binford Has 'No Authority' to Censor Curley," *VW*, December 21, 1949, 4.
8 "State Censorship Upheld in Supreme Court in 'Boundaries,'" *HR*, October 17, 1950, 5.
9 Vincent Lowery, "Preparing the Next Generation for Massive Resistance: The Historical Pageantry of the Children of the Confederacy, 1955–1965," in *Children and Youth during the Civil War Era*, ed. James Marten (New York: New York University Press, 2012), 209.

10 Bernard F. Dick, *The Star-Spangled Screen: The American World War II Film* (Lexington: University Press of Kentucky, 1985); Jeanine Basinger, *The World War II Combat Film: Anatomy of a Genre* (Middleton, CT: Wesleyan University Press, 1986); Clayton R. Koppes and Gregory D. Black, *Hollywood Goes to War: How Politics, Profits, and Propaganda Shaped World War II* (Berkeley: University of California Press, 1990); Thomas Doherty, *Projections of War: Hollywood, American Culture, and World War II* (New York: Columbia University Press, 1993); Robert L. McLaughlin and Sally E. Parry, *We'll Always Have the Movies: American Cinema during World War II* (Lexington: University Press of Kentucky, 2006); Wendy L. Wall, *Inventing the "American Way": The Politics of Consensus from the New Deal to the Civil Rights Movement* (New York: Oxford University Press, 2008), pt. 2; Thomas A. Bruscino, *A Nation Forged in War: How World War II Taught Americans to Get Along* (Nashville: University of Tennessee Press, 2010).

11 See Donald Bogle, *Toms, Coons, Mulattoes, Mammies, and Bucks: An Interpretive History of Blacks in American Films* (New York: Continuum, 2000), 143–158; Thomas Cripps, *Making Movies Black: The Hollywood Message Movie from World War II to the Civil Rights Era* (New York: Oxford University Press, 1993).

12 Cheryl Greenberg, *"Or Does It Explode?" Black Harlem in the Great Depression* (New York: Oxford University Press, 1991); H. Viscount Nelson, *Black Leadership's Response to the Great Depression in Philadelphia* (Lewiston, NY: Edwin Mellen Press, 2006).

13 Jeff R. Woods, *Black Struggle, Red Scare: Segregation and Anti-communism in the South, 1948–1968* (Baton Rouge: Louisiana State University Press, 2004), 22.

14 Elizabeth Kirkpatrick Dilling, *The Roosevelt Red Record and Its Background* (Kenilworth, IL: self-published, 1936), 162.

15 Ibid., 229.

16 Robin D. G. Kelley, *Hammer and Hoe: Alabama Communists during the Great Depression* (Chapel Hill: University of North Carolina Press, 1990), 75.

17 Clarence Taylor, *Reds at the Blackboard: Communism, Civil Rights, and the New York City Teachers Union* (New York: Columbia University Press, 2013); John Noakes, "Radicalizing Subversion: The FBI and the Depiction of Race in Early Cold War Movies," *Ethnic and Racial Studies* 26, no. 4 (July 2003): 728–749. For contemporary accounts, see George S. Schuyler, *The Communist Conspiracy Against the Negroes* (New York: Catholic Information Society, 1947).

18 Woods, *Black Struggle, Red Scare*, 28.

19 Whitfield, *Culture of the Cold War*, 21.

20 Leonard Malton, *The Little Rascals: The Life and Times of* Our Gang (New York: Crown, 1992), 108. The child camaraderie did not mean full racial equality. Black adults often appeared as primitive, superstitious, and aped animalistic behavior. See Julia Lee, *Our Gang: A Racial History of* The Little Rascals (Minneapolis: University of Minnesota Press, 2014), 134–135.

21 J. R. McDonough, "Boy Slaves Censorship Elimination," "Boy Slaves [RKO 1938]," Motion Picture Association of America, PCA records, MHL, AMPAS.

22 Bogle, *Toms, Coons, Mulattoes, Mammies, and Bucks*, 136; Thomas Cripps, *Slow Fade to Black: The Negro in American Film, 1900–1942* (Oxford: Oxford University Press, 1977), 388. See "Better Breaks for Negroes in H'wood," *Weekly Variety*, March 25, 1942, 1.

23 Fred Stanley, "Hollywood Takes a Hint from Washington," *NYT*, February 7, 1943, X3. See John Beaufort, "Move Marquees Shed light into Darkness of Racial Prejudice," *CSM*, July 15, 1949, 9.

24 Moviegoers were not as surprised as the Hardys to see a professional person of color, as Lee had a supporting role in MGM's medical series *Dr. Gillespie*. This crossover reflected the wartime spirit of inclusiveness and provided MGM with an opportunity to promote its other films.

25 Wounded Ex-GI to Sirs, letter, January 28, 1946, "Racism 1946–1947," 12-f.141, Motion Picture Association of America, Hollywood Office Files, MHL, AMPAS.

26 William McKane to Sir, letter, April 5, 1946, "Racism 1946–1947," 12-f.141, Motion Picture Association of America, Hollywood Office Files, MHL, AMPAS.

27 Joseph Losey based *The Lawless* (1950) on the Sleepy Lagoon case and allegorized HUAC. See Doug Dissen, "The Violent Poetry of the Times: The Politics of History in Daniel Mainwaring and Joseph Losey's *The Lawless*," in *"Un-American" Hollywood: Politics and Film in the Blacklist Era*, edited by Frank Krutnik, Steve Neale, Brian Neve, and Peter Stanfield (New Brunswick, NJ: Rutgers University Press, 2007), 97–112.

28 Frances Stonor Saunders, *The Cultural Cold War: The CIA and the World of Arts and Letters* (New York: Free Press, 2013), 66. For examples, see "Teen Agers Deplore Prejudice," *CSM*, October 22, 1949, 7; "Hands across the Color Line," *Parents*, August 1948, 34.

29 "Noted Negro Actor Has Big Role in Gable Film," *Any Number Can Play* press book, author's collection.

30 Roi Ottley, "Harlem Is Confident, but Cautious," *NYT*, June 1, 1947, SM20.

31 *Home of the Brave* (1949) and *Lost Boundaries* (1949) had initial northern runs to generate positive word of mouth before their studios distributed them in southern circuits. Studios also produced different trailers; the northern trailer for *Intruder in the Dust* (1949) featured more brutality and coarse language. See "Intruder in the Dust Trailer (Northern Version)," November 8, 1949; "Intruder in the Dust Trailer (Southern Version)," October 21, 1949, Intruder in the Dust, f.1–675, Turner/MGM scripts, MHL, AMPAS.

32 Mary Elizabeth Vroman, who penned the original story, declared, "I didn't want to prove anything. I didn't want to agitate anything. I merely thought—if people could now these children as I do, they would be certain to love them all." Producer Al Gilks confirmed the film "makes no protest; it makes no complaint." See Al Gilks, "See How They Run," *International Photographer*, December 1952, 11–12. Producer Sol Baer Fielding predicted, "The Negro audience will just about pay for the cost of the picture. If it has enough quality to attract a segment of the white audience, it will make a profit." He hoped the low budget and fast shoot compensated for the risky subject. Bob Thomas, "MGM Doing Offbeat Film with an All Negro Cast," *Hollywood Citizen-News*, August 28, 1952, 18. MGM lost $263,000 on the project. "E. J. Mannix Ledger," Howard Strickling papers, AMPAS.

33 "'Amateur' Film at Dupont Moving," *WP*, September 24, 1949, B7.

34 Hattie McDaniel, "What Hollywood Means to Me," *HR*, September 29, 1947, reprinted in Tichi Wilkerson and Marcia Borie, eds., *The Hollywood Reporter: The Golden Years* (New York: Coward-McCann, 1984), 210–211. When asked why she accepted roles of maids throughout her career, McDaniel replied she would rather play maids for high payouts than become a real maid working for pittance. See Al Young, "I'd Rather Play a Maid Than Be One," *NYT*, October 15, 1989, BR13.

35 Gerald Horne, *Class Struggle in Hollywood, 1930–1950: Moguls, Mobsters, Stars, Reds, and Trade Unionists* (Austin: University of Texas Press, 2001), 32.

36 On race and the Hollywood Ten, see Horne, *Final Victim of the Blacklist*, xix and 10; John J. Gladchuk, *Hollywood and Anticommunism: H.U.A.C. and the Evolution*

of the Red Menace, 1935–1950 (New York: Routledge, 2013), 101–102; Jennifer Frost, *Hedda Hopper's Hollywood: Celebrity Gossip and American Conservatism* (New York: New York University Press, 2011), chap. 6; John Sbardellati, *J. Edgar Hoover Goes to the Movies: The FBI and the Origins of Hollywood's Cold War* (Ithaca, NY: Cornell University Press, 2012), 170–173.

37 Regina K. Fadiman, *Faulkner's* Intruder in the Dust*: Novel into Film* (Knoxville: University of Tennessee Press, 1978), 28.

38 Schary recalled Mayer thought the project unwholesome and, therefore, unsalable. Mayer preferred stories about motherhood. See Fadiman, *Faulkner's* Intruder in the Dust, 28. Schary added Mayer did not think highly of the finished film and faulted Hernandez as "too uppity. He ought to take off his hat when he talks to the white man—and he didn't say thank you to the lawyer." Dore Schary, *Heyday* (Boston: Little, Brown, 1979), 213.

39 Gene D. Phillips, *Fiction, Film, and Faulkner: The Art of Adaptation* (Knoxville: University of Tennessee Press, 1988), 100.

40 "The Exhibitor Has His Say about Pictures," *BOBG* supplement, *BO*, October 21, 1950, 2.

41 Irma E. Lowe, "Synopsis of Novel," May 20, 1946, "Intruder in the Dust" 1444-f.1-667, Turner/MGM scripts, MHL, AMPAS. Faulkner presents this view in the novel. Lawyer Gavin Stevens lectures, "We must resist the North: not just to preserve ourselves . . . [but] the privilege of setting him free ourselves: which we will have to do for the reason that nobody else can since going on a century ago now the North tried it and have been admitting for seventy-five years now that they failed." William Faulkner, *Intruder in the Dust* (1948; New York: Vintage, 1991), 151.

42 Philip K. Scheuer, "Brown Champions Work on Location," *LAT*, October 30, 1949, D1. Brown told the newspaper of his own southern heritage "by adoption," stating he "went south when I was 12."

43 Irma E. Lowe, "Synopsis of Novel," May 20, 1946, "Intruder in the Dust" 1444-f.1-667, Turner/MGM scripts, MHL, AMPAS.

44 Woods, *Black Struggle, Red Scare*, 37.

45 Quoted in Phillips, *Fiction, Film, and Faulkner*, 92.

46 Fadiman, *Faulkner's* Intruder in the Dust, 29. Jarman recalled that, by the time he and the MGM crew arrived in Oxford, the residents welcomed them: "Oxford rolled out the red carpet to black and white alike, thrilled that Hollywood had descended on their community," despite the picture's theme. See Claude Jarman Jr., *My Life and the Final Days of Hollywood* (Murrells Inlet, SC: Covenant Books, 2018), 72.

47 "MGM Going All Out on 'Dust' Tri-State Bow," *HR*, September 9, 1949, 4; "Memphis Censor OKs M-G-M's 'Intruder,'" *MPD*, September 9, 1949, 2.

48 "Binford Bows to Court Ruling, Ends 'Racial' Bans," *Independent Exhibitors Film Bulletin*, January 2, 1950, 8.

49 After its Oxford premiere on October 10, MGM planned to open the film in two theaters in Tennessee by the twelfth. See "'Dust' into Memphis," *DV*, October 4, 1949, 7.

50 "'Intruder' Pulls Year-High $2,300 on Memphis Opening," *DV*, November 10, 1949, 7.

51 One black newspaper predicted, "Hollywood will probably adopt this part in toto." Gertrude Martin, "Movies of 3 Novels to Show Race Problems," *CD*, March 19, 1949, 7.

52 See "Memphis Approves Film," *NYT*, September 10, 1949, 11; "'Intruder in Dust' Gets Miss. Preem," *HR*, October 12, 1949, 9; "'Intruders [*sic*] in the Dust' Okayed for Memphis," *DV*, September 9, 1949, 1; "Jarman to 'Dust,'" *DV*, October 13, 1949, 10.

53 Matty Brescia, "Tenn. Supreme Court Rules Binford Has 'No Authority' to Censor *Curley*," *VW*, December 21, 1949, 4, 18.

54 "Case of Made-to-Order Type-Casting," "Even Drafted the Mayor!" Intruder in the Dust press book, Cinematic Arts Library, USC; John N. Popham, "Film Unit Tastes Real Southern Hospitality," *NYT*, April 10, 1949, X5. One local said, "It was just like a picnic. We spent more time watching the movie or helping make it than we did at our jobs." See "Faulkner and Oxford Helped," *Life*, December 12, 1949, 153. Professional actors later dubbed over the Oxford residents' voices.

55 Ad 308 and 212, Intruder in the Dust press book, USC. One radio spot read, "You'll see the seething fury in the hearts of men . . . you'll know the fear that stalks the night . . . the hate that walks Main Street!," without specifying race.

56 *Intruder in the Dust*, directed by Clarence Brown (Metro-Goldwyn-Mayer, 1949), DVD (Warner Home Video, 2011).

57 Ibid.

58 In one scene, Beauchamp sends a white boy with molasses for Chick, which Chick says made his debt worse. According to studio reader Frances B. Kopp, Beauchamp's dignity came from "white blood in his veins," which made him "'uppity' and arrogant." His "pride came to him from his white great grandfather" who had passed down Beauchamp's land. Frances B. Kopp, "Synopsis of the Complete Okay Script, dated December 8, 1948 from Ben Maddow," December 29, 1948, Intruder in the Dust files, Cinematic Arts Library, USC. The film mentions Beauchamp's ancestry in passing. He inherited his land from his grandfather, who was a slave and cousin to a white landowner, thereby distancing Beauchamp's lineage from miscegenation concerns and the possibility of the white boy as a blood relative. In lieu of white relatives as a source of a black man's strength, Chick says that Beauchamp is a strong black man because he happens to own his own land and family farm.

59 One treatment visualized Mallison's demons, showing Beauchamp's "face and naked arms hanging upside down, not even Lucas Beauchamp but someone already anonymous, already effused by flame, by pride watered by gasoline, by leaves of fire shooting up from below." Ben Maddow, Intruder in the Dust Treatment, October 1, 1948, "Intruder in the Dust," 1444.f.1–668, Turner/MGM scripts, MHL, AMPAS.

60 Irma E. Lowe, "Synopsis of Novel," May 20, 1946, "Intruder in the Dust," 1444-f.1-667, Turner/MGM scripts, MHL, AMPAS.

61 *Intruder in the Dust* (1950).

62 Ibid.

63 Ibid.

64 Ibid.

65 Hernandez recalled his accent-free diction: "One thing I learned very soon [after arriving from Puerto Rico] was that if you speak English with any kind of accent, people are inclined to laugh at you." See Gladwin Hill, "Man of Character," *NYT*, May 28, 1950, 51.

66 Ben Maddow, Intruder in the Dust, December 8–16, 1948, "Intruder in the Dust," 1444.f.1–642, Turner/MGM scripts, MHL, AMPAS.

67 "Family Movie Guide," *Parents*, December 1949, 111–112. For more laudatory notices, see Bosley Crowther, "The Screen in Review," *NYT*, November 23, 1949, 19;

"Movie of the Week," *Life*, December 12, 1949, 149; "'Intruder,' Lynching Story, Is Dynamic Screen Fare," *HR*, October 11, 1949, 3; John Huston to Clarence Brown, interoffice communication, June 17, 1949, "Correspondence—B-Miscellaneous, 93-f.887, John Huston papers, AMPAS; Dorothy B. Jones, "Program Notes on the film Intruder in the Dust," Jones, Dorothy B. 1943–1957, 1-f.10. Motion Picture Industry Council records, MHL, AMPAS.

68 Walter White, "Columnist Walter White Sees Brighter Side of Negro Life," *CD*, January 7, 1950, 7. The "odor" refers to a cultural stigma concerning African Americans lacking "facilities to wash properly or often or even to wash bathe often even without the facilities to do it with; that it was a little to be preferred that they did not." Faulkner, *Intruder in the Dust*, 11.

69 Jennifer Ritterhouse, *Growing Up Jim Crow: How Black and White Southern Children Learned Race* (Chapel Hill: University of North Carolina Press, 2006).

70 Lowell E. Redelings, "'Intruder in the Dust' Realistic Photoplay of Racial Prejudice," *Hollywood Citizen-News*, "Intruder in the Dust [MGM 1949]," CCF, MHL, AMPAS.

71 Ezra Goodman, "Film Review," *Los Angeles Daily News*, November 12, 1949, "Intruder in the Dust [MGM 1949]," CCF, MHL, AMPAS. See Brog, "Intruder in the Dust," *VW*, October 12, 1949, 12.

72 Joel Williamson, *William Faulkner and Southern History* (New York: Oxford University Press, 1993), 330.

73 Ibid., 330.

74 Quoted in Roger Biles, *Memphis in the Great Depression* (Knoxville: University of Tennessee Press, 1986), 86.

75 Darryl Zanuck to Joseph Mankiewicz, interoffice correspondence, June 14, 1950, "Production Files-Produced," 31.f-363, Joseph L. Mankiewicz papers, MHL, AMPAS.

76 Quoted in Fadiman, *Faulkner's* Intruder in the Dust, 36. Brown also spooked Emanuel with white sheets and "ghost wailings" throughout the scene. In contrast, Hernandez praised the cast and crew during his stay in Oxford, telling *Ebony* the racial tensions in Oxford were no different than in New York. See ibid., 35.

77 "Inside Stuff Pictures," *VW*, August 23, 1950, 2.

78 Bert Briller, "Radio Indies Like the New Tricks to Lure Business," *DV*, November 7, 1949, 335.

79 "The Exhibitor Has His Say about Pictures," *BOBG* supplement, *BO*, December 9, 1950, 3.

80 "MGM's Intruder Draws Critics Praise and Censure," *Independent Exhibitors Film Bulletin*, January 2, 1950, 20.

81 John M. Howard, letter, "Comment in the Mail," *NYT*, December 4, 1949, X8.

82 Richard L. Coe, "One of the Aisle," *WP*, March 14, 1950, B9.

83 See Bruscino, *Nation Forged in War*.

84 Greenberg, *"Or Does It Explode?,"* chap. 5.

85 Ken Fones-Wolf and Elizabeth Fones-Wolf, *Struggle for the Soul of the Postwar South: White Evangelical Protestants and Operation Dixie* (Urbana: University of Illinois Press, 2015), 180.

86 Ibid., 179.

87 Hanson W. Baldwin, "Need of Training Revealed in Korea," *NYT*, November 3, 1950, 4.

88 "The Exhibitor Has His Say," *BOBG* supplement *BO*, November 25, 1950, 2.

89 Tom Goldrup and Jim Goldrup, *Growing Up on the Set: Interviews with 39 Former Child Actors of Classic Film and Television* (Jefferson, NC: McFarland, 2002), 166.

90 Claude Jarman, Jr., interview with author, February 6, 2015.

91 One exhibitor screened a reissue of *Guadalcanal Diary* (1943) in 1950, noting, "If the war in Korea is helping your boxoffice with war pictures, this is one of the best." He implied new and old pictures about the "good war" appealed to audiences tired about the stalemate in Korea. "The Exhibitor Has His Say about Pictures," *BOBG* supplement, *BO*, December 2, 1950, 4.

92 Aside from flashback sequences or films with a wartime setting (e.g., espionage pictures, home front traumas), the studios released one combat film in 1946, none in 1947, two in 1948, five in 1949, and in increasing numbers as the Cold War heated up. See Basinger, *World War II Combat Film*, 278–283. Hollywood released the first Korean War movie, *The Steel Helmet*, in early 1951, although newsreels of the conflict, such as *Cassino to Korea*, premiered earlier.

93 Ivan Spear, "The Big War Cycle On," *BO*, February 24, 1951, 20–21, 24, 26.

94 Michael Wilson, "Conditioning the American Mind: War Films Show Vicious Over-All Policy," *Hollywood Review* 1, no. 1 (January 1953): 3. Wilson later cowrote *Bridge on the River Kwai* (1957).

95 Ibid., 3.

96 *Battleground*, directed by William A. Wellman (Metro-Goldwyn-Mayer, 1950), Blu-ray (Warner Home Video, 2017).

97 Walter White, "Movies' 'Social Content' Covers Multitude of Sins," *CD*, August 19, 1950, 7.

98 Ibid., 7. Zanuck, who produced *The Grapes of Wrath*, commented to Schary he made the film "with the best intentions in the world and it was used by the communists to bolster communism and expose the plight of the American farmer in the dust bowl. *Pinky* was also exploited by the Communists, as was *No Way Out*." Darryl Zanuck to Dore Schary, letter, January 1, 1956, U.S. Mss 37AN, Schary, Blackboard Jungle 1954–1956, Dore Schary papers, 1920–1980, box 33, Wisconsin Center for Film & Theater Research, University of Wisconsin–Madison.

99 White, "Movies' 'Social Content' Covers Multitude of Sins," 7.

100 "E. J. Mannix Ledger," Howard Strickling papers, MHL, AMPAS. Schary insisted films helped African Americans. "More vital stories are being written and made into motion pictures which treat honestly and objectively of America and the peoples of every nationality, race, and creed who, together, have contributed to the fiber and substance of our democracy." Mayer and the studio's marketers clearly disagreed. See A. S. "Doc" Young, "MGM Studio Head Predicts Bright Future for Negroes in Hollywood," *CD*, February 25, 1950, 21.

101 "Boxoffice Barometer," *BO*, February 25, 1950, 111.

102 "Atlanta Censor Is Putrid Explaining Why 'Pinky' Is Nixed," *CD*, April 8, 1950, 21.

103 Ibid., 21.

104 "Feature Reviews," *BO*, October 15, 1949, 117.

105 "Exploitips," *BO*, October 15, 1949, 118.

106 "Intruder Pulls Year-High $2,300 on Memphis Opening," *DV*, November 10, 1949, 7.

107 "Hollywood Inside," *DV*, July 19, 1949, 2.

108 Ibid., 2.

109 "First Run Stumble to Weak $249,400 Holiday Weekend," *DV*, November 15, 1949, 3.

110 See "Three Big Houses Go Dark; 1st Run B.O. Weak $200,200," *DV*, November 22, 1949, 3; "Local First Runs Top '48; 'Foxes' Leads Pack," *DV*, December 13, 1949, 7; "'. . . Before Xmas and All thru the House-' Sigh L.A. First Runs," *DV*, December 20, 1949, 3.
111 "Mayer, Schenck, and Rodgers Discuss Divorce," *DV*, November 1, 1949, 12. The article claimed Louis B. Mayer was initially "enthused" over the *Intruder in the Dust*'s smash opening in Memphis. However, the picture's ultimate reception surely confirmed his convictions the public disliked social messages in the movies.
112 H. R., "'Intruder in the Dust,'" *CSM*, December 15, 1949, 4.
113 Edwin Schallert, "'Intruder in the Dust' Grimly Courageous," *LAT*, November 12, 1949, 11.
114 "The Exhibitor Has His Say about Pictures," *BOBG* supplement *BO*, June 24, 1950, 3.
115 "The Exhibitor Has His Say about Pictures," *BOBG* supplement, *BO*, October 14, 1950, 3.
116 "What the Picture Did for Me," *MPH*, October 7, 1950, 41.
117 Lillian Scott, "'Intruder in the Dust' Puts Hernandez in 'The Tops' Class," *CD*, November 26, 1949, 27.
118 Comer Van Woodward, *The Origins of the New South, 1877–1913* (New Orleans: Louisiana State University Press, 1951).
119 Nash K. Burger, "Books of the Times," *NYT*, July 17, 1951, 25.
120 "E. J. Mannix ledger," Howard Strickling papers, MHL, AMPAS. Phillips erroneously states the film's "box office returns were satisfactory." See Phillips, *Fiction, Film, and Faulkner*, 99.
121 Stars in My Crown press book, Cinematic Arts Library, USC.
122 Ibid.
123 Ibid.
124 Alice Goodman, "*Stars in My Crown* by Joe David Brown," May 28, 1947, *Stars in My Crown* Files, Cinematic Arts Library, USC.
125 Edith Lindeman, "A Lesson to Producers," *DV*, August 17, 1950, 12.
126 Ibid., 12.
127 Chris Fujiwara, *Jacques Tourneur: The Cinema of Nightfall* (Jefferson, NC: McFarland, 1998), 167.
128 Margaret Fitts, "Stars in My Crown—Inc. Script, March 3, 1948," *Stars in My Crown* Files, Cinematic Arts Library, USC.
129 David W. Blight, *Beyond the Battlefield: Race, Memory, and the American Civil War* (Amherst: University of Massachusetts Press, 2002), 137.
130 Richard Abel, *Americanizing the Movies and "Movie-Mad" Audiences, 1910–1914* (Berkeley: University of California Press, 2006), chap. 4.
131 Bruce Chadwick, *The Reel Civil War: Mythmaking in American Film* (New York: Knopf Doubleday, 2001), chaps. 9 and 10; Brian Steel Willis, *Gone with the Glory: The Civil War in Cinema* (Lanham, MD: Rowman & Littlefield, 2007), chap. 3.
132 Jon Wiener, "Civil War, Cold War, Civil Rights: The Civil War Centennial in Context, 1960–1965," in *The Memory of the Civil War in American Culture*, ed. Alice Fahs and Joan Waugh (Chapel Hill: University of North Carolina Press, 2004), 247.
133 Margaret Fitts, "Stars in My Crown—Inc. Script, May 21, 1948," *Stars in My Crown* Files, Cinematic Arts Library, USC.
134 Ibid.

135 Margaret Fitts, "Stars in My Crown—CP Script, June 9, 1948," *Stars in My Crown* Files, Cinematic Arts Library, USC.
136 Alice Goodman, "*Stars in My Crown* by Joe David Brown," May 28, 1947, *Stars in My Crown* Files, Cinematic Arts Library, USC.
137 David Mark Chambers, *Hooded Americanism: The History of the Ku Klux Klan* (Durham, NC: Duke University Press, 1987); Douglas Field, "Passing as a Cold War Novel: Anxiety and Assimilation in James Baldwin's *Giovanni's Room*," in *American Cold War Culture*, ed. Douglas Field (Edinburgh: Edinburgh University Press, 2005), 93; Thomas Borstelmann, *The Cold War and the Color Line: American Race Relations in the Global Arena* (Cambridge, MA: Harvard University Press, 2001), 215; Rick Bowers, *Superman versus the Ku Klux Klan: The True Story of How the Iconic Superhero Battled the Men of Hate* (Washington, DC: National Geographic Books, 2012).
138 Wyn Craig Wade, *The Fiery Cross: The Ku Klux Klan in America* (New York: Oxford University Press, 1998), 305.
139 In the novel, the story arc is the first major plot point and ends in chapter 2. The Night Riders then disappear, but Backett (named "Lon Hamilton" in the novel) blames African Americans for the climactic typhoid.
140 Margaret Fitts, "Stars in My Crown Retakes," October 6, 1949, "Stars in My Crown," 2782-f.S-2374, Turner/MGM scripts, MHL, AMPAS.
141 *Stars in My Crown*, directed by Jacques Tourneur (Metro-Goldwyn-Mayer, 1950), DVD (Warner Home Video, 2011).
142 Margaret Fitts, "Stars in My Crown O/K Composite Script," May 4, 1949, *Stars in My Crown* Files, Cinematic Arts Library, USC.
143 *Stars in My Crown* (1950).
144 Margaret Fitts, "Stars in My Crown—DC, August 31, 1948," *Stars in My Crown* Files, Cinematic Arts Library, USC.
145 Fujiwara, *Jacques Tourneur*, 167. The novel ends with Kenyon as a soldier leaving for World War I. Filming this coda would require leaving the small town, while adding to production costs.
146 Joseph Breen to L. B. Mayer, letter, April 4, 1949, "Stars in My Crown [MGM 1949]," Motion Picture Association of America, PCA records, MHL, AMPAS.
147 Robert M. Vogel to Joseph Breen, letter, April 25, 1949, "Stars in My Crown [MGM 1949]," Motion Picture Association of America, PCA records, MHL, AMPAS.
148 Mrs. Dan Fankhauser, letter, December 4, 1950, "Stars in My Crown [MGM 1949]," Motion Picture Association of America, PCA records, MHL, AMPAS.
149 "'Stars' Inspiring Drama; 'Girl' Action in Sea Story," *HR*, March 1, 1950, 3; "Stars in My Crown," *DV*, March 1, 1950, 3; *Time*, January 8, 1951; "B.O. Paradox for M-G's McCrea 'Stars,'" *VW*, October 11, 1950, 3; "Stars in My Crown," *MPH*, March 4, 1950, 19.
150 "What the Picture Did for Me," *MPH*, October 7, 1950, 41. The picture's Protestant preacher generated buzz from pressure groups eager to mimic the powerful Legion of Decency's influence. See William D. Romanowski, *Reforming Hollywood: How American Protestants Fought for Freedom at the Movies* (New York: Oxford University Press, 2008), 120–121.
151 "What the Picture Did for Me," *MPH*, November 4, 1950, 39.
152 "The Exhibitor Has His Say about Pictures," *BOBG* supplement, *BO*, January 20, 1951, 2.
153 "Juan Hernandez Scores in 'Stars in My Crown,'" *CD*, April 29, 1950, 20.

154 See Catherine Silk and John Silk, *Racism and Anti-racism in American Popular Culture: Portrayals of African-Americans in Fiction and Film* (New York: Manchester University Press, 1990), chap. 2.
155 "White Texan," "Song of the South," *WP*, January 18, 1947, 4. See also Jason Sperb, *Disney's Most Notorious Film: Race, Convergence, and the Hidden Histories of* Song of the South (Austin: University of Texas Press, 2012), chaps. 1–3.
156 "'Song of South' Picketed," *NYT*, December 14, 1946, 18.
157 George Gleason to Eric Johnston, letter, February 27, 1947, "Racism 1946–1947," 12-f.141, Motion Picture Association of America, Hollywood Office Files, MHL, AMPAS.
158 Hedda Hopper, "Screen and Stage," *LAT*, December 14, 1947, H3. See Jim Korkis, *Who's Afraid of the* Song of the South*? And Other Forbidden Disney Stories* (New York: Theme Park Press, 2012), 17–107; Maurice Berger, *For All the World to See: Visual Culture and the Struggle for Civil Rights* (New Haven, CT: Yale University Press, 2010), 36–41.
159 "Foundation Presents More Than 800 Prizes," *CSM*, February 23, 1951, 13; "Metro's 'Stars' Cited by Freedom Foundation," *VW*, February 21, 1951, 4.
160 William G. Weart, "Bradley Predicts Liberty's Victory," *NYT*, February 23, 1951, 11. MGM had nominated *Intruder in the Dust* for the same award a year earlier, but the film did not win. See "Freedom Foundation Awards," *CSM*, November 10, 1950, WM19.
161 *A Town Solves a Problem* (U.S. Army, 1950), uploaded by Vermont Historical Society, https://archive.org/details/ATownSolvesAProblem.
162 *Storm Warning* (1951), released one year after *Stars in My Crown* and set in contemporary America, featured the KKK as gangsters, but avoided race altogether.
163 "The Exhibitor Has His Say about Pictures," *BOBG* supplement, *BO*, June 16, 1951, 2.
164 "E. J. Mannix Ledger," Howard Strickling papers, AMPAS. *Stars in My Crown* cost $1.175 million, about $200,000 more than *Intruder in the Dust*. In terms of sheer grosses, Tourneur's movie earned $2.146 million while Brown's film grossed $0.837 million.
165 Jarman, *My Life*, 76.
166 "Race Segregation 'Natural' Here, Newell Tells Citizens," *WP*, October 15, 1947, 11.
167 Ibid., 11.
168 "Movies and the Negro," *NYT*, November 25, 1949, 30.
169 Philip K. Scheuer, "Brown Champions Work on Location," *LAT*, October 30, 1949, D1.
170 Edwin Schallert, "Two-Gun Pastor Conquers Village," *LAT*, April 18, 1950, A7. See Richard L. Coe, "One of the Aisle," *WP*, March 14, 1950, B9.
171 Bosley Crowther, "Trouble Enough," *NYT*, January 18, 1959, X1.
172 A. S. "Doc" Young, "Hollywood Digs 'Black Gold,'" *CD*, December 17, 1949, 1.
173 A. S. "Doc" Young, "What Is Hollywood's Real Attitude toward Negroes?," *CD*, May 20, 1950, 21.
174 "When Hollywood Had Courage," *CD*, January 12, 1957, 9.
175 *The Phenix City Story* (1955), a docudrama about the sanitation of "Sin City, USA," starts with the murder of a black girl as a warning for white reformers to desist. *Desperate Search* (1952) features a gentle black convict who befriends a white boy and saves him in a plane crash. The educational short "Duck and Cover" (1952) shows an integrated classroom with black children front and center to participate in civil defense.

176 Edwin Schallert, "Metro May Have Uncle Tom in Grooming Stage; Williams Bid for Italy," *LAT*, April 22, 1949, A7.
177 "The Breaking Point," Synopsis, "The Breaking Point [W.B. 1949]," Motion Picture Association of America, PCA records, MHL, AMPAS.
178 One critic called the ending "not only a fine evidence of racial feeling, but it is the one of the most moving factors in the film." See Bosley Crowther, *NYT*, October 7, 1950, 10. *Variety* singled out the "eloquently silent bit of a small Negro boy waking in solitary terror on the deck for his father." Hebe, "The Breaking Point," *VW*, September 13, 1950, 6.
179 Roger C. Foss to Darryl Zanuck, letter, September 12, 1950, "Production Files-Produced," 31.f-363, Joseph L. Mankiewicz papers, MHL, AMPAS.
180 Ibid.
181 "Picture-of-the-Year Award Ceremony," Hollywood Foreign Correspondents Association, July 27, 1950, Dore Schary papers, GA 114, WHS.
182 E. J. Mannix ledger, Howards Strickling papers, MHL, AMPAS.
183 Lowell E. Redelings, "The Hollywood Scene," *Hollywood Citizen-News*, October 4, 1950.
184 S. F. Seadler to Dore Schary, letter, August 22, 1950; John Joseph to Dore Schary, letter, August 25 1950, "Dore Schary Papers: Correspondence, *The Next Voice You Hear*: 1950 Aug–September 29," Dore Schary papers, US Mss 37, box 46, WHS.
185 "The Exhibitor Has His Say," *BOBG* supplement, *BO*, September 29, 1951, 1.

Chapter 5 The International Picture

1 "Strengthen the Arm of Liberty," *Boys' Life*, February 1949, 3.
2 See David Reynolds, *From World War to Cold War: Churchill, Roosevelt, and the International History of the 1940s* (New York: Oxford University Press, 2006).
3 Caldwell, *NSC 68*.
4 Wall, *Inventing the "American Way,"* chap. 8.
5 John Gunther, *Inside U.S.A.* (New York: Harper & Brothers, 1947), xii. *Inside U.S.A.*'s popularity led it to become a Broadway musical. See O. Spurgeon English and Constance J. Foster, "A Challenge to Mothers," *Parents*, September 1948, 30.
6 Ronald E. Powaski, *Toward an Entangling Alliance: American Isolationism, Internationalism, and Europe, 1901–1950* (Westport, CT: Greenwood, 1991), 27.
7 "Way of Peace Sought on War Anniversary," *CSM*, April 6, 1937, 1.
8 Ibid., 4.
9 Melvyn P. Leffler, "American Policy Making and European Stability, 1921–1933," *Pacific Historical Review* 46, no. 2 (1977): 209.
10 "Buell Warns Against Return to Isolationism," *CSM*, December 3, 1942, 1.
11 "Midwest Isolationism Gone, Kansas Institute Discovers," *CSM*, June 27, 1942, 7.
12 The literature on Hollywood and Hitler is vast. See Michael E. Birdwell, *Celluloid Soldiers: Warner Bros.'s Campaign against Nazism* (New York: New York University Press, 1999), chap. 5; Thomas Doherty, *Hollywood and Hitler, 1933–1939* (New York: Columbia University Press, 2013). The industry went out of its way to maintain an open German market. See Ben Urwand, *The Collaboration: Hollywood's Pact with Hitler* (Cambridge, MA: Harvard University Press, 2013).
13 Ruth Sarles and Bill Kauffman, *A Story of America First: The Men and Women Who Opposed U.S. Intervention in World War II* (Westport, CT: Praeger, 2003).

14 *December 7th*, directed by John Ford and Gregg Toland (1943), https://archive.org/details/December7th.

15 March of Dimes, advertisement, *Life*, February 17, 1947, 115.

16 Beth B. Cohan, "The Last Remnant of the Holocaust: The Representation and Reality of Child Survivors' Lives," in *Children, Childhood, and Cultural Heritage*, ed. Kate Darian-Smith and Carla Pascoe (New York: Routledge, 2013), 175–189.

17 Bess M. Wilson, "Family Life Conferees Vision Postwar Woes," *LAT*, April 4, 1943, A10.

18 Ibid., A10.

19 Jaimey Fisher, *Disciplining Germany: Youth, Reeducation, and Reconstruction after the Second World War* (Detroit: Wayne State University Press, 2007); Jennifer Fay, *Theaters of Occupation: Hollywood and the Reeducation of Postwar Germany* (Minneapolis: University of Minnesota Press, 2008), chap. 1.

20 "Boxoffice Barometer," *BO*, May 19, 1945, 40; "Boxoffice Barometer," *BO*, June 2, 1945, 35. See Phil M. Daly, "Among the Rialto," *FD*, January 24, 1945, 10; Bernie Kreisler, "Cowan Film Builds," *HR*, January 23, 1945, 1; Harry Brandt and Lou Brandt, "An Open Letter to Lester Cowan," advertisement, *MPD*, February 1, 1945, 11.

21 See Shannon Lynn Sturm, "Spies, Lies, and Intrigue: Anti-German Sentiment in West Central Texas during World War I" (PhD diss., Angelo State University, 2010); Ron Theodore Robin, *The Barbed-Wire College: Re-educating German POWs in the United States during World War II* (Princeton, NJ: Princeton University Press, 1995); Rebecca L. Boerhling, "The Effects of Anti-German Sentiment on Planning and Policy-Making for Post-war Germany, 1943–1947" (MA thesis, University of Wisconsin–Madison, 1980).

22 *Tomorrow, the World!*, directed by Leslie Fenton (Lester Cowan Productions, 1944), DVD (Image Entertainment, 2001).

23 Lewis Nichols, "Post-War Planning," *NYT*, April 25, 1943, X1. See also Wilella Waldorf, "Two on the Aisle," *New York Post*, stage files, f-1.19: "Tomorrow the World—Script 1943–1946," Edit Angold papers, MHL, AMPAS; Bosley Crowther, "Measuring Two New Films," *NYT*, January 7, 1945, X1; Kahn, Review, *DV*, October 20, 1944, 8; *HR*, December 15, 1944, 3; "Product Digest," *MPH*, December 23, 1944, 2237; *The Exhibitor*, December 27, 1944.

24 *Hollywood Writers Mobilization Premiere and Town Meeting for Tomorrow, the World*, "Political Material—Hollywood Writers Mobilization 1945, Undated," subject files-general, 46-f.815, Howard Estrabrook papers, MHL, AMPAS.

25 *The Democratic versus the Nazi Way of Life*, Vertical File, 3-f.37: Report 1945, 588. Bureau for Intercultural Education report on TOMORROW THE WORLD, AMPAS. Another student clarified, "Everyone has equal rights to get ahead (except negroes who should have these rights if Jews can)" (600).

26 Ibid., 563.

27 Richard Goldstein, *Helluva Town: The Story of New York City during World War II* (New York: Free Press, 2010), 137.

28 Lewis Nichols, "Post-War Planning," *NYT*, April 25, 1943, X1.

29 "Exploiting the New Films," *MPH*, February 10, 1945, 58. He reiterated the same message in Minneapolis. See "Skippy Not a Brat," *BO*, December 16, 1944, 130. For the war effort, Homeier served as master of ceremonies at the "American Children's" festival, which paid tribute to Russian orphans from the Battle of Stalingrad. See "Soviet Actor Hailed at Reception Here," *NYT*, September 18, 1943, 20.

30 "What the Picture Did for Me," *MPH*, July 14, 1945, 36.

31 "OWI Nixes Cowan Pic for Freed Lands," *HR*, January 18, 1945, 1.
32 "Cowan Asks Review of 'Tomorrow' Ban," *HR*, January 25, 1945, 6; "Cowan to Appeal to OWI on 'Tomorrow,'" *MPD*, January 25, 1945, 2; "OWI Re-examining Tomorrow the World," *FD*, February 6, 1945, 1, 8.
33 "OWI Kayoes 'Tomorrow, the World': Seen as 'Too Sympathetic' to the Nazis," *VW*, January 24, 1945, 1.
34 William L. Peirce Jr. to Al Margolies, letter, April 13, 1945, "G.I. Joe—Margolies, Albert, 1945," production files-produced, 8-f.96, Lester Cowan papers, MHL, AMPAS.
35 "'World' in $2300 Day," *HR*, February 8, 1945, 1; "OWI Again Refuses to Sponsor 'World,'" *HR*, February 8, 1945, 4; "'Tomorrow the World' Fails to Get OWI Okay," *FD*, February 8, 1945, 1, 7.
36 "Cowan Dissatisfied with Returns on 'Tomorrow the World,' May Hold Up Release," *VW*, February 14, 1945, 3.
37 Rheinhold Wagnleitner, *Coca-Colinization: The Cultural Mission of the United States after the Second World War* (Chapel Hill: University of North Carolina Press, 1994).
38 Tony Shaw, *Hollywood's Cold War* (Boston: University of Massachusetts Press, 2007), 26.
39 Edward T. Folliard, "Truman Asks Freer Trade to Aid Peace," *WP*, March 7 1947, 1; see also "Austin Stresses World Economics," *NYT*, May 7, 1947, 41; "Henderson Scores 'New Isolationism,'" *NYT*, October 28, 1947, 10.
40 Wendell L. Willkie, "One World," *Life*, April 26, 1943, 81; Wendell L. Willkie, *One World* (New York: Simon & Schuster, 1943).
41 Simon & Schuster, "Questions and Answers about Wendell Willkie's book *One World*," *Life*, July 12, 1943, 9.
42 "Willkie Is Named to High Film Post," *NYT*, April 10, 1942, 19; "Willkie Again Heads Film Company Board," *NYT*, May 19, 1943, 35.
43 "20th Eyes Rights for Willkie's 'One World,'" *DV*, April 16, 1943, 1; "Willkie's 'One World' to 20th," *DV*, July 20, 1943, 1; "Movie Rights of 'One World' by Willkie Bought by Fox for Reported $100,000," *NYT*, July 21, 1943, 17; Fred Stanley, "How 'One World' Will Be Filmed," *NYT*, October 10, 1943, X3; "Anti-trust Head Clark Has Confidential Sessions Here to Film One World in Eight Languages," *DV*, July 26, 1943, 1..
44 "Wary of Willkie," *VW*, August 4, 1943, 3.
45 "Catholic Dioceses Blast Adds New Hazard to Willkie Book Filming," *VW*, October 20, 1943, 1, 16. The Catholic diocese summarized Willkie's book as "a curious compend[ium] of sophistical reasoning" and could serve a logics class as a "repertorium of bad examples."
46 Zanuck produced *Wilson* (1944), a lengthy extravaganza paying tribute to Woodrow Wilson's ideals of internationalism and the League of Nations and supporting Roosevelt's fourth term. The film flopped badly. Even Zanuck's old family doctor refused to see the movie: "Why should they pay seventy-five cents to see Wilson on the screen when they wouldn't pay ten cents to see him alive?" See Thomas J. Knock, "History with Lightning: The Forgotten Film *Wilson* (1944)," in *Hollywood as Historian: American Film in a Cultural Context*, ed. Peter C. Rollins (Lexington: University Press of Kentucky, 1983), 88–108. Proceeds from *Tomorrow, the World!*'s premiere went to a memorial fund for Willkie. See "Wendell Willkie Memorial Outlined in Premiere," *FD*, December 15, 1944, 2; "Freedom House will Sponsor 'World' Bow," *MPD*, December 13, 1944, 3; "To Premiere 'World' for Willkie Tonight," *MPD*, December 21, 1944, 2.

47 "A.F. of L. Introduces Program for Speeding up Reconversion," *CSM*, August 7, 1945, 12. To assert its protectionist agenda, the AFL withdrew from the International Federation of Trade Unions. According to the article, without AFL pressure, the International Federation of Trade Unions welcomed its rival, the leftist Congress of Industrial Organizations, and the Soviet Trade Unions.

48 Gunther, *Inside U.S.A.*, ix.

49 Ibid., 287.

50 "Referendum on the Marshall Plan Urged by Republican Whip in House," *NYT*, November 26, 1947, 12. Short did not think the Soviets would not risk war with the United States.

51 Cass Warner Sperling, Cork Millner, and Jack Warner Jr., *Hollywood Be Thy Name: The Warner Brothers Story* (Lexington: University Press of Kentucky, 1998), 256. Other studio chiefs echoed this statement. See Jo Fox, *Film Propaganda in Britain and Nazi Germany* (New York: Berg, 2007), 278.

52 Albert Margolies to Bill Perice, letter, April 6, 1945, "G.I. Joe—Margolies, Albert, 1945," production files-produced, 8-f.96, Lester Cowan papers, MHL, AMPAS. On Lippmann, see Barry D. Russo, *Walter Lippmann: Odyssey of a Liberal* (New Brunswick, NJ: Transaction, 1996), 146–147.

53 Bill Peirce Jr. to Albert Margolies, letter, March 28, 1945, "G.I. Joe—Margolies, Albert, 1945," production files-produced, 8-f.96, Lester Cowan papers, MHL, AMPAS.

54 For *The Boy with Green Hair*, see Peter W. Lee, "A Green Peace Tinted Red: Cold War America in *The Boy with Green Hair*," in *Learning the Left: Popular Culture, Liberal Politics, and Informal Education from 1900 to the Present*, ed. Paul J. Ramsey (Charlotte, NC: Info Age, 2015), 49–70.

55 An early publicity report boasted the United Nations held charity screenings of the "semi-documentary" to help "destitute children in the Philippines [who] will be among the chief beneficiaries." "Manilla" [*sic*], "The Search—clippings and reviews 1948," production files-produced, 57-f.775, Fred Zinnemann papers, MHL, AMPAS.

56 For an overview of *The Search*'s production, see Jörg Thuecke, "Flotsam and Jetsam: Fred Zinnemann's Film *The Search* (1948) and the Problem of 'Unaccompanied Children' at the End of World War II," *Modern Austrian Literature* 32, no. 4 (1999): 271–288; J. E. Smyth, "Fred Zinnemann's Search (1945–48): Reconstructing the Voices of Europe's Children," *Film History* 23, no. 1 (2011): 75–92; J. E. Smyth, *Fred Zinnemann and the Cinema of Resistance* (Jackson: University Press of Mississippi, 2014), chap. 2.

57 Doug McClelland, *Forties Film Talk: Oral Histories of Hollywood, with 120 Lobby Posters* (Jefferson, NC: McFarland, 1992), 274.

58 Henry Gonshank, *Hollywood and the Holocaust* (Lanham, MD: Rowman & Littlefield, 2015), 79–80.

59 William L. Shirer, "The Big Four Are Reminded that the German Peril Remains," n.d., "The Search—research (clippings) 1946–1947," production files-produced, 58-f.796, Fred Zinnemann papers, MHL, AMPAS.

60 Bill Davidson, *Germany, What Now?* (London: Frederick Muller, 1950), 247.

61 Fred Zinnemann, "The Story of the Search," *Screen Writer* 4, no. 2 (August 1948): 12.

62 Fred Zinnemann, *The World Is a Stage*, "The Search—Publicity 1948," production files-produced, 58-f.794, Fred Zinnemann papers, MHL, AMPAS.

63 Praesens-Film handled the production through UNRRA, including casting the children and extras (they "must conform with existing Information Control,

Military Government, and German Denazification Regulations"), attaining clearance for location shoots and technical equipment, and processing the film. "Public Information—HPI/IS3/1/ND—Liaison with MGM (Zinnemann) re: Proposed Film," S-0425-0036-10, ARMS.

64 Fred Zinnemann, *The World Is a Stage*, "The Search—Publicity 1948," production files-produced, 58-f.794, Fred Zinnemann papers, MHL, AMPAS.

65 Peter Viertel to Lazar Wechsler, letter, June 22, 1946, "The Search—Correspondence 1946," production files-produced, 57-f.779, Fred Zinnemann papers, MHL, AMPAS.

66 Ibid.

67 Fred Zinnemann to Lazar Wechsler, letter, December 2, 1946, "The Search—Correspondence 1946," production files-produced, 57-f.779, Fred Zinnemann papers, MHL, AMPAS.

68 Fred Zinnemann to Peter Viertel, letter, December 2, 1946, "The Search—Correspondence 1946," production files-produced, 57-f.779, Fred Zinnemann papers, MHL, AMPAS.

69 Anonymous, undated, "The Search—Correspondence 1946," production files-produced, 57-f.779, Fred Zinnemann papers, MHL, AMPAS. Brian C. Etheridge attributes the note to Zinnemann but the authorship is not clear. See Etheridge, "In Search of Germans: Contested Germany in the Production of *The Search*," *Journal of Popular Film and Television* 34 (2006): 40.

70 Unsigned, undated, "The Search—Correspondence 1946," production files-produced, 57-f.779, Fred Zinnemann papers, MHL, AMPAS.

71 Claudia Sternberg, "Real-Life References in Four Fred Zinnemann Films," in *The Films of Fred Zinnemann: Critical Perspectives*, ed. Arthur Nolletti Jr. (New York: State University of New York Press, 1999), 203.

72 Katharine A. Wills, letter, "Sifting the Departmental Mail," *NYT*, April 11, 1948.

73 Richard Patterson, "The UN in Hollywood: A Lesson in Public Relations," *Hollywood Quarterly* 5, no. 4 (1951): 329.

74 George Woodbridge, *UNRRA: The History of the United Nations Relief and Rehabilitation Administration*, vol. 1 (New York: Columbia University Press, 1950), 282.

75 Ibid., 282.

76 Ibid., 285.

77 McClelland, *Forties Film Talk*, 297.

78 "Movie of the Week," *Life*, April 5, 1948, 75.

79 *The Search*, directed by Fred Zinnemann (Praesens-Film, 1948), DVD (Warner Home Video, 2009).

80 Gene D. Phillips, *Exiles in Hollywood: Major European Film Directors in America* (Cranbury, NJ: Associated University Presses, 1998), 148. Phillips notes Zinnemann originally approved of the narration because he thought it set the tone. He later changed his mind a year later when Italian neorealism showed Hollywood audiences did not need outside introductions to evoke the atmosphere.

81 Arthur Hornblow Jr. to Arthur M. Loew, letter, January 13, 1948, "The Search—Correspondence (Congratulatory) 1947–1948," production files-produced, 58-f.787, Fred Zinnemann papers, MHL, AMPAS.

82 Ibid.

83 Tara Zahra, *The Lost Children: Reconstructing Europe's Families after World War II* (Cambridge, MA: Harvard University Press, 2011), 179; see also Andrea Orzoff, *Battle for the Castle: The Myth of Czechoslovakia in Europe, 1914–1948* (New York: Oxford University Press, 2009), chap. 1.

84 United Nations Relief and Rehabilitation Administration, Office of Public Information, *In the Wake of the Armies: Raw Material for Writers, Directors, Producers, Story Editors*, December 1945, 10–12, "UNRRA—Office of the Historian—Monographs, Documents and Publications," S-1021-0143-09, ARMS.

85 *The Search* (1948).

86 David Moldon to Fred Zinnemann, letter, undated, "The Search—Correspondence 1949–1990," production files-produced, 58-f.786, Fred Zinnemann papers, MHL, AMPAS.

87 Ibid.

88 Ibid. American-occupied countries adopted Disney names into their languages. See Reinhold Wagnleitner, "The Irony of American Culture Abroad," in *Recasting America: Culture and Politics in the Age of the Cold War*, ed. Lary May (Chicago: University of Chicago Press, 1989), 291. By 1952 Disney's *Bambi* "already had half as many fans as the long-time [German] cartoon favorite 'Max and Moritz' in the age group of six to ten years." Zinnemann's catering to American sentiment turned off foreign preview audiences. One preview card read, "I was very tired of all the American propaganda and being told what marvelous people the Yanks are—this spoilt an otherwise perfect film." Peter Loftus, "The Search Opinions—Adverse Criticism," 3, "The Search—Screenings (London) 1949," production files-produced, 59-f.806, Fred Zinnemann papers, MHL, AMPAS.

89 Fred Zinnemann to Lazar Wechsler, letter, July 3, 1947, "The Search—Correspondence [July–August] 1947," production files-produced, 58-f.782, Fred Zinnemann papers, MHL, AMPAS.

90 Viertel served as an Office of Strategic Services correspondent, but Zinnemann considered the writer's experience outdated. Germany was "like an express train moving at full speed without an engineer." Fred Zinnemann to Peter Viertel, letter, April 3, 1947, "The Search—Correspondence [January–April] 1947," production files-produced, 57-f.780, Fred Zinnemann papers, MHL, AMPAS. Zinnemann softened Viertel's harsh anti-Nazi tone to accommodate the Allies' efforts to woo West Germany from the Soviet sphere. Viertel worried that his dismissal would hamper his career. See Etheridge, "In Search of Germans," 41–44.

91 Paul Jarrico to Fred Zinnemann, letter, June 10, 1947, 3, "The Search—Correspondence [May-June] 1947," production files-produced, 58-f.781, Fred Zinnemann papers, MHL, AMPAS.

92 Patricia Bosworth, *Montgomery Clift: A Biography* (New York: Harcourt Brace Jovanovich, 1978), 127–130. Wechsler referred to Clift as a "stupid actor." Many of Clift's changes made it into the picture.

93 Lazar Wechsler, "Re: Mr. Clift's Suggestions," September 8, 1947, "The Search—Correspondence [September] 1947," production files-produced, 58-f.783, Fred Zinnemann papers, MHL, AMPAS.

94 Lazar Wechsler, "Notes on Mr. Zinnemann's Alterations to the Dialogue of the Concluding Scenes," September 17, 1947, "The Search—Correspondence [September] 1947," production files-produced, 58-f.783, Fred Zinnemann papers, MHL, AMPAS. Jandl's father informed Zinnemann the sentimental ending prevented the picture from winning prizes in European film festivals. He was happy, however, that his son was a hit and was carried away on crowds' shoulders. Klement Jandl to Fred Zinnemann, letter, August 8, 1949, "The Search—Jandl, Ivan 1947–1949," production files-produced, 58-f.790, Fred Zinnemann papers, MHL, AMPAS.

95 Fred Zinnemann to Lazar Wechsler, letter, September 18, 1947; Fred Zinnemann, "Regarding Mr. Wechsler's notes on alterations of dialogue of concluding scenes,"

"The Search—Correspondence [September] 1947," production files-produced, 58-f.783, Fred Zinnemann papers, MHL, AMPAS. Wechsler and Schweizer shared the Academy Award for best motion picture story. The film uses children to rebuild nationalities, notably Zionism. In a subplot, a harassed Jewish-German orphan bonds with a group of youngsters who head to Palestine. The kids march off in matching uniforms and song. Despite the controversies over the founding of the Israel, no movie critic called attention to it. Zinnemann proposed a picture to "repeat in the Holy Land the technique he used on making M-G's 'The Search' in Germany." The project never materialized. "Zinnemann's Lion Film a la 'Search' for RKO," *VW,* May 12, 1948, 2.

96 On Wyler's documentaries, see Mark Harris, *Five Came Back: A Story of Hollywood and the Second World War* (New York: Penguin, 2014); *Thunderbolt*, directed by William Wyler (1947), www.youtube.com/watch?v=tWD4ITJGdTw.

97 Hubert M. Humphrey, Speech, "Promotion Flashes," 619, September 9, 1948, "The Search—Clippings and Reviews 1948," production files-produced, 57-f.775, Fred Zinnemann papers, MHL, AMPAS.

98 "Editorial" [clipping], April 25, 1948, "The Search—Clippings and Reviews 1948," production files-produced, 57-f.775, Fred Zinnemann papers, MHL, AMPAS.

99 "Exploitips," *BO*, March 20, 1948, 126.

100 Gertrude Samuels, "DP's in America: 'We Have Become Alive,'" *NYT,* March 28, 1948, SM12.

101 "Movie of the Week," *Life*, April 5, 1948, 75.

102 Ibid., 75.

103 Quoted in Lawrence Baron, *Projecting the Holocaust into the Present: The Changing Focus of Contemporary Holocaust Cinema* (Lanham, MD: Rowman & Littlefield, 2005), 33.

104 Henry S. Hayward, "Europe's 'Little People' Count on U.S. Aid," *CSM*, May 29, 1948, 13.

105 Henry Cantril and Mildred Strunk, *Public Opinion, 1935–1946* (Princeton, NJ: Princeton University Press, 1951), 456.

106 *Tomorrow Is Forever,* directed by Irving Pichel (International Pictures, 1946), Blu-ray (Classicflix, 2017).

107 William H. Stringer, "United States' Role in a Ruined World," *CSM*, February 27, 1947, 18.

108 Ibid., 18; Virgil Pinkley, "Need Seen for Lengthy Occupation of Germany," *LAT,* October 17, 1945, 7.

109 Zahra, *Lost Children*, 74.

110 Ivo K. Feierabend, "The Communist Infiltration of Czechoslovakia" (PhD diss., University of California, 1953), 17. For a typical headline, see "Czechoslovakia Seized by Reds," *LAT,* February 25, 1948, 1.

111 Abrams, "'The Search' Touching Realistic Drama of War-Torn Germany," *Independent Exhibitors Film Bulletin*, April 12, 1948, 10.

112 Aline MacMahon to Fred Zinnemann, letter, February 22, 1948, "The Search—Correspondence (Congratulatory) 1947–1948" production files-produced, 58-f.787, Fred Zinnemann papers, MHL, AMPAS.

113 R. Barton Palmer, *Shot on Location: Postwar American Cinema and the Exploration of Real Place* (New Brunswick, NJ: Rutgers University Press, 2016), 161. Journalist Jay Comody commented how the "authentic German background" in the movies had a dramatic effect that "does not diminish with repetition." Even three years after the war ended, "its effect is the same, the mind left grasping for a deeper

meaning in these appalling vistas of ruin." Jay Carmody, "Settings by Bomb," *Washington Sunday Star*, May 30, 1948, 6.

114 "Berlin Express Preview Cards," "Berlin Express, Preview Comments," f.6, Bert Granet papers, MHL, AMPAS.

115 Producer Bert Granet notes Toporow stole the show in the previews by portraying a Russian as an individual rather than a caricature. Granet noted *Berlin Express* explicitly refuted nationalism, adding, "I'll probably be lynched for saying this, but I believe all national monuments should be destroyed—and hospitals built instead." See Philip K. Scheuer, "Granet Makes Picture in Berlin Despite Reds," *LAT*, April 8, 1948, C3.

116 Ibid., C3.

117 Ibid., C3.

118 Ibid., C3.

119 Richard B. Jewel, email to author, August 29, 2016.

120 "U.S. Film Execs Frown on Idea of Plunging into British Production," *VW*, May 5, 1948, 15.

121 "Metro's Yankee-Doodle Bally on 'Search' to Offset Foreign Pix Hex," *VW*, April 14, 1948, 19.

122 Erskine Johnson, "In Hollywood," *Portsmouth Herald*, May 6, 1948, 14. Johnson's syndicated column appeared across the country, including in the *Bakersfield Californian*, May 8, 1948, 14, and *Kingsport Times*, May 14, 1948, 4.

123 Walter Brooks, "Managers' Round Table," *MPH*, May 8, 1948, 55. The magazine asserts agents are merely exaggerators: "Showmanship is the art of leading the burned child back to the fire."

124 Evelyn Dotson, letter, *Life*, July 18, 1949, 6. A more bizarre advertising stunt occurred in Rhode Island, where one exhibitor held a contest for newspaper readers to "search" for misspelled words in an article. See "Round Table," *MPH*, November 27, 1948, 43. Another promoted war bonds, corsages, and complimentary dinners for a written contest, "The Bravest Mother in Hartford." See "Showmen in Action," *MPH*, December 4, 1948, 43.

125 Aline MacMahon to Fred Zinnemann, letter, May 2, 1948, "The Search—Correspondence (Congratulatory) 1947–1948," production files-produced, 58-f.787, Fred Zinnemann papers, MHL, AMPAS.

126 Joseph L. Mankiewicz, letter, *MPH*, August 6, 1949, 8. MGM's exhibitor contact, Mike Simons, said the same thing, urging exhibitors to use "special promotional efforts" for smaller pictures such as *Boys' Ranch* and *The Search*. He stated if exhibitors did not make the effort, these movies "might go through your mills without any attention." See "Urge Showmanship, 'TV,' at Mo. Meet," *FD*, November 9, 1949, 6. Zanuck disagreed, advocating pictures with "popular, mass-appeal," his *The Gunfighter* (released a year later) notwithstanding. See "Zanuck Takes Exhibitor Side on Film Theme," *FD*, July 1, 1949, 1.

127 "The Exhibitor Has His Say about Pictures," *BO*, n.d., "The Search—Clippings and Reviews 1948–1951," production files-produced, 57-f.776, Fred Zinnemann papers, MHL, AMPAS.

128 "What the Picture Did for Me," *MPH*, September 3, 1949, 41.

129 "Inside Pictures," *VW*, July 6, 1949, 20. "The Search—Clippings and Reviews 1948–1951," production files-produced, 57-f.776, Fred Zinnemann papers, MHL, AMPAS.

130 William H. Wells to Richard Mockler, letter, December 30, 1946, "The Search—Clippings and Reviews 1948–1951," production files-produced, 57-f.776, Fred Zinnemann papers, MHL, AMPAS.

131 William H. Wells to Fred Zinnemann, letter, March 4, 1947. "The Search—Correspondence [January–April] 1947," production files-produced, 57-f.780, Fred Zinnemann papers, MHL, AMPAS.
132 Ralph W. Collins, letter, March 3, 1947, "The Search—Correspondence [January–April] 1947," production files-produced, 57-f.780, Fred Zinnemann papers, MHL, AMPAS.
133 Leo. J. Margolin to Fred Zinnemann, letter, April 3, 1947, "The Search—Correspondence [January–April] 1947," production files-produced, 57-f.780, Fred Zinnemann papers, MHL, AMPAS.
134 Herbert H. Meyer, *Report Yearly for 1948*, January 1949, "The Search Correspondence 1949–1990," production files-produced, 58-f.786, Fred Zinnemann papers, MHL, AMPAS.
135 William Wells to Fred Zinnemann, Telegram, January 9, 1948, "The Search—Correspondence (Congratulatory) 1947–1948," production files-produced, 58-f.787, Fred Zinnemann papers, MHL, AMPAS.
136 Fred Zinnemann to Herbert H. Meyer, letter, May 5, 1949, "The Search—Correspondence (Congratulatory) 1947–1948," production files-produced, 58-f.787, Fred Zinnemann papers, MHL, AMPAS.
137 Ibid.
138 Herbert Meyer to Zinnemann, letter, May 20, 1949, "The Search—Correspondence 1949–1990," production files-produced, 58-f.786, Fred Zinnemann papers, MHL, AMPAS.
139 Gil Loescher and John A. Scanlan, *Calculated Kindness: Refugees and America's Half-Opened Door* (New York: Free Press, 1998), 20–24.
140 Carruthers, *Cold War Captives*, 69.
141 "Box-Office Performances," *Harrison's Reports*, October 30, 1948, 176.
142 Barnet Novar, "Return of 1918," *WP*, January 1, 1944, 8.
143 William Henry Chamberlain, "Stalin Replaces Hitler," *WSJ*, March 10, 1948, 6.
144 Drew Middleton, "Berlin Receives Its Millionth Ton of Supplies under Western Airlift," *NYT*, February 19, 1949, 1; see also James Reston, "U.S. Air Lift Educates Germans and Russians," *NYT*, September 19, 1948, E4.
145 "Berlin Airlift Pilots Drop Candy, Gum for the Children in Germany," *NYT*, September 16, 1948, 14. See Roger G. Miller, *To Save a City: The Berlin Airlift, 1948–1949* (Austin: Texas A&M University Press, 2000), 103–107.
146 Bess Furman, "Truman Tells D.A.R. Security Is Objective of All U.S. Policies," *NYT*, April 19, 1949, 6.
147 *The Big Lift*, directed by George Seaton (Twentieth Century-Fox Film, 1950), https://archive.org/details/TheBigLift1950complete.
148 Ibid.
149 Clift's character naïvely romances a Nazi sympathizer who uses him to find her SS husband in the United States. In contrast, Clift's buddy, a former POW in a concentration camp, seeks revenge but becomes enamored with a "good" German woman who adopts democracy and memorizes the Constitution. The movie supports a "middle" position where the Allies forgive, but not forget, the legacies of Nazism.
150 Drew Pearson, "An Airlift 'Pearl Harbor' Feared," *WP*, November 14, 1948, B5.
151 Walter H. Waggoner, "Airlift, Though Costly, Pays Off in Experience," *NYT*, October 3, 1948, E4.
152 "Reds Open Campaign to Free Germany of Occupation Troops," *WP*, November 25, 1948, 4; "Occupation of Germany to Continue," *LAT*, May 8, 1949, 11.

153 Fraser J. Harbutt, *The Iron Curtain: Churchill, America, and the Origins of the Cold War* (New York: Oxford University Press, 1988), 210; James W. Muller, ed., *Churchill's "Iron Curtain" Speech Fifty Years Later* (Columbia: University of Missouri Press, 1999).
154 Denise M. Bostdroff, *Proclaiming the Truman Doctrine: The Cold War Call to Arms* (College Station: Texas A&M University Press, 2008), chap. 3.
155 Patrick Wright, *Iron Curtain: From Stage to Cold War* (New York: Oxford University Press, 2007), 375.
156 Joachim Joesten, *Germany, What Now?* (Chicago: Ziff-Davis, 1948), 314.
157 Ibid., 205–206.
158 Thomas W. Devine, *Henry Wallace's 1948 Presidential Campaign and the Future of Postwar Liberalism* (Chapel Hill: University of North Carolina Press, 2013), 169.
159 J. A. Livingston, "Business Outlook: The Bear Comes Closer and Closer," *WP*, February 29, 1948, C3.
160 Ibid., C3.
161 Victoria M. Grieve, *Little Cold Warriors: American Childhood in the 1950s* (New York: Oxford University Press, 2018); Helgren, *American Girls and Global Responsibility*.
162 W. W. Crofton, "The Search Opinions," 6, "The Search—Screenings (London) 1949," production files-produced, 59-f.806, Fred Zinnemann papers, MHL, AMPAS.
163 W. Levant, "The Search Opinions," 23. "The Search—Screenings (London) 1949," production files-produced, 59-f.806, Fred Zinnemann papers, MHL, AMPAS.
164 "Aid to Europe Underlined in Winning Peace," *CSM*, March 5, 1948, 2.
165 Ibid., 2.
166 The "Omaha" ad continued in newspapers a year after Johnson's criticism. See *The North Adams Transcript*, May 26, 1949, 18; *Mason City Globe-Gazette*, November 8, 1949, 10.
167 "What the Picture Did for Me," *MPH*, December 10, 1949, 45.
168 "Inside Stuff Pictures," *VW*, July 13, 1949, 20.
169 Ibid., 20.
170 Ibid., 20.
171 Ibid., 20.
172 *The Search*'s actual box office figures are elusive. The film is not listed in MGM's E. J. Mannix ledger, possibly because MGM distributed the picture. Film historian John McElwee, citing a source who worked at MGM, provided the total gross and profit margins. John McElwee, "Metro Takes a Bold Postwar Step," *Greenbriar Picture Shows*, June 27, 2014, http://greenbriarpictureshows.blogspot.com/2014/06/metro-takes-bold-postwar-step.html; John McElwee to author, email, May 6, 2017.
173 Jarrico was a proud card-carrying communist. See his interview in Patrick McGilligan and Paul Buhle, eds., *Tender Comrades: A Backstory of the Hollywood Blacklist* (New York: St. Martin's, 1997), 325–350. See also Paul Buhle and Dave Wagner, *Radical Hollywood: The Untold Story behind America's Favorite Movies* (New York: Free Press, 2002), 179–180, 259n64. Zinnemann did not testify before HUAC, but one account says he went to the American Legion to prove his loyalty. See Smyth, *Fred Zinnemann and the Cinema of Resistance*, 256n16.
174 Ivan Jandl to Fred Zinnemann, letter, September 19, 1948, "The Search—Jandl, Ivan 1947–1949," production files-produced, 58-f.790, Fred Zinnemann papers, MHL, AMPAS; John Holmstrom, ed., *The Moving Picture Boy: An International Encyclopedia, 1895–1995*, 2nd ed. (Wilby, UK: Michael Russell, 1998), 202.
175 Florabel Muir, "Just for Variety," *DV*, April 2, 1948, 4.
176 "'Search' Moppet Stays in Czechoslovakia," *VW*, May 12, 1948, 2.

177 "Metro Stymied on Importing Moppet," *DV*, May 7, 1948, 1.
178 "The Boy Wonder of the Search'" *NYT*, April 25, 1948. See also "From Behind the Iron Curtain, No Reply from Boy Oscar Winner," *DV*, March 29, 1949, 3.
179 "Jandl Sends His Thanks for Award," *DV*, April 1, 1949, 8.
180 Ibid., 8. Jandl cabled, "Dear Mr. Zinnemann, I thank you very much. You deserved well for the trophy which you wire. I enjoy on it very much."
181 "From Behind the Iron Curtain, No Reply from Boy Oscar Winner," *DV*, March 29, 1949, 3.
182 Ivan Jandl to Fred Zinnemann, letter, August 8, 1949, "The Search—Jandl, Ivan 1947–1949," production files-produced, 58-f.790, Fred Zinnemann papers, MHL, AMPAS.
183 "Presents Award to Czech," *FD*, May 2, 1949, 2; "Boy Actor's Oscar Given Czech Envoy," *LAT*, May 15, 1949, 10; "Presents Award to Czech," *MPD*, May 17, 1949, 2; Ivan Jandl to Fred Zinnemann, letter, October 14, 1949, "The Search—Jandl, Ivan 1947–1949," production files-produced, 58-f.790, Fred Zinnemann papers, MHL, AMPAS.
184 "From Behind the Iron Curtain, No Reply from Boy Oscar Winner," *DV*, March 29, 1949, 3.
185 Ivan Jandl to Fred Zinnemann, letter, September 19, 1948, "The Search—Jandl, Ivan 1947–1949," production files-produced, 58-f.790, Fred Zinnemann papers, MHL, AMPAS.
186 Alta Durant, "Just For Variety," *DV*, November 28, 1949, 4.
187 "Walter Wanger Also Given Special Award," *DV*, March 25, 1949, 3; Mike Connolly, "Just for Variety," *DV*, August 4, 1950, 4.
188 Oskar Reif to Fred Zinnemann, letter, n.d., "Jandl, Ivan 1985–1991," correspondence, b.105, Fred Zinnemann papers, MHL, AMPAS.
189 Fred Zinnemann to Oskar Reif, letter, December 19, 1985, "Jandl, Ivan 1985–1991," correspondence, b.105, Fred Zinnemann papers, MHL, AMPAS.
190 Fred Zinnemann to David Lini, letter, August 20, 1991, "Jandl, Ivan 1985–1991," correspondence, b.105, Fred Zinnemann papers, MHL, AMPAS.
191 Dagmar Mackova Smržová to Zinnemann, letter, February 2, 1990, "The Search—Correspondence 1949–1990," production files-produced, 58-f.786, Fred Zinnemann papers, MHL, AMPAS.
192 Thomas F. Brady, "Hollywood Split by Hearings," *NYT*, October 26, 1947, X5. Corey's statement contradicted Zinnemann's assertion early in the film's production that he was not aiming for an "artistic achievement."
193 G. Muchnic to Wendell Corey, letter, October 30, 1947, "The Search—Correspondence [October–December] 1947," production files-produced, 58-f.784, Fred Zinnemann papers, MHL, AMPAS.
194 Ibid.
195 Wendell Corey to G. Muchnic, letter, November 12, 1947, "The Search—Correspondence [October–December] 1947," production files-produced, 58-f.784, Fred Zinnemann papers, MHL, AMPAS.
196 Ibid.
197 Thomas M. Pryor, "History of 'The Search,'" *NYT*, March 14, 1948, X5.
198 James Agee, "Films," *Nation*, April 24, 1948, 449 (reprinted in James Agee, *Agee on Film: Criticism and Comments on the Movies* [New York: McDowell, Obolensky, 1950], 302).
199 "Strengthen the Arm of Liberty," *Boys' Life*, February 1949, 3.
200 Ibid., 3.
201 Ibid., 3.

Conclusion

1 "Life under Communism in Soviet Russia," *Junior Review*, February 18, 1952, 4–5.
2 *The Son of Rusty*, directed by Lew Landers (Columbia Pictures, 1947), VHS (Columbia Tri Star Home Video, 1995).
3 "Says Stalin Alone Wants Slump Here," *NYT*, May 28 1947, 37. Secretary of State George Marshall told President Truman the Russians hoped for an American depression to strengthen the Soviet position in Europe and Asia. See Drew Pearson, "The Washington Merry-Go-Round," *WP*, May 3, 1947, 7.
4 "Panel Discussions of the Cultural Conference Delegates Cover a Wide Range of Subjects," *NYT*, March 27, 1949, 44. The Cultural and Scientific Conference for World Peace took place at the Waldorf Astoria, New York. The newspaper paraphrased statements from Grace F. Marcus, a social worker at the University of Pittsburgh. Outside the hotel, picketers carried signs featuring slogans such as "American, not Commie Culture."
5 Fritz Sternberg, "Why You Won't Sell Applies in 1949," *LAT*, October 3, 1948, G5.
6 Ibid., G28.
7 Ibid., G28.
8 N. S. B. Gras, "Behavior of Business Men in a Changing World," *Bulletin of the Business Historical Society* 23, no.1 (March 1949): 65.
9 Quoted in Lary May, "Cultural Conversion and the Hollywood Red Scare," in *Recasting America: Culture and Politics in the Age of Cold War*, ed. Lary May (Chicago: University of Chicago Press, 1989), 145. Nunnally Johnson, the screen-writer for *The Grapes of Wrath* and *Tobacco Road*, also produced *The Gunfighter*.
10 Robert L. Sumner, *Hollywood Cesspool: A Startling Survey of Movieland Lives and Morals, Pictures, and Results* (Wheaton, IL: Sword of the Lord, 1955), 120.
11 Daniel J. Leab, *I Was a Communist for the F.B.I.: The Unhappy Life and Times of Matt Cvetic* (University Park: Pennsylvania State University Press, 2000).
12 "Cast of Characters," folder 143, "I Was a Communist for the F.B.I.," 13-f.145, Leo "K" Kuter papers, MHL, AMPAS.
13 "I Was a Communist for the FBI Script," December 30, 1950, Part I Rev. Final, 3, 13-f.143, Leo "K" Kuter papers, MHL, AMPAS.
14 *I Was a Communist for the F.B.I.*, directed by Gordon Douglas (Warner Bros., 1951), DVD (Warner Home Video, 2009). Several moviegoers criticized the picture's anti-Semitism: the Reds exploit American prejudice and showcase the free world as intolerant. See Julie S. Newman to Jack Warner, letter, May 12, 1951; Mr. and Mrs. L. Berher to Jack Warner, May 13, 1951; Mrs. L. Cohen to Jack Warner, letter, n.d., Story-Memos & Correspondence 1 of 2, "I Was a Communist for the F.B.I." files, WBA.
15 Censor Jack Vizzard recalled working on *Trial* to remove any suggestion of producer Dore Schary being a fellow traveler. Schary, branded a liberal for his advocating social reform, claimed that when he takes the "side of the underdog, I'm afraid I may have let my enthusiasms carry me too far." Vizzard, *See No Evil*, 188.
16 "Cast of Characters," folder 143, "I Was a Communist for the F.B.I.," 13-f.145, Leo "K" Kuter papers, MHL, AMPAS.
17 *I Was a Communist for the F.B.I.* (1951).
18 Ibid.
19 One viewer spotted Jackie's father as an extra during the film's communist rally. He criticized Warner Bros. for giving one actor "two parts in the picture. That's what spoiled it. People notice things like that." He did not consider another possibility:

Jackie's father—who protected baseball and his son—was perhaps a dupe. George Willis to Warner Bros., letter, January 28, 1952, "I Was a Communist for the F.B.I." files, WBA.

20 "I Was a Communist for the F.B.I." script, Part II, Rev. Final, January 2, 1951, 28, 13-f.143, Leo "K" Kuter papers, MHL, AMPAS.

21 *I Was a Communist for the F.B.I.* (1951).

22 Crane Wilbur, "I Was a Communist for the FBI," story-Revised Final Draft, 34, December 30, 1950, "I Was a Communist for the F.B.I." files, WBA. Actor Frank Lovejoy was looking at images of his own son, not a child actor. See "Representative Press Comment on Warner Bros.'s 'I Was a Communist for the F.B.I.'—Publicity-misc 65B, "I Was a Communist for the F.B.I." files, WBA.

23 Crane Wilbur, "I Was a Communist for the FBI," story-Revised Final Draft, 120.

24 *I Was a Communist for the F.B.I.* (1951).

25 "Warners Documenting 'Communist Expose,'" *Daily Variety* August 8, 1950, 1.

26 Ibid., 1.

27 Mandel Herbstman, review, *MPD*, April 19, 1951, 6; *HR*, April 19, 1951, 3, "I Was a Communist for the F.B.I. [W.B. 1951]," Core Collection Files, Margaret Herrick Library, AMPAS; "Representative Press Comment on Warner Bros.'s I Was a Communist for the FBI," I was a Communist for the FBI—Publicity-misc 65B, "I Was a Communist for the F.B.I." files, WBA.

28 Jack Warner to Henry Luce, telegram, April 6, 1951, Story-Memos & correspondence 1 of 2; Mr. Howson to Mr. Shernow, November 1, 1951, "I Was a Communist for the F.B.I." files, WBA. In 1956, Washington still had leases on five prints.

29 John Parlow to Warner Bros., letter, October 1, 1950, Story-Memos & Correspondence 1 of 2, "I Was a Communist for the F.B.I." files, WBA. Parlow's sentiment was reiterated by Nancy Olivine to W.B., June 9, 1951, and Bernice Mertes to W.B., September 20, 1951, Story-Memos & Correspondence 1 of 2, "I Was a Communist for the F.B.I." files, WBA.

30 John S. Battle, n.d. Story-Memos & Correspondence 2 of 2, "I Was a Communist for the F.B.I." files, WBA.

31 "The Exhibitor Has His Say about Pictures," *BOBG* supplement, *BO*, September 15, 1951, 2.

32 *Bad Boy*, directed by Roy Neumann (Monogram Pictures, 1949), DVD (Warner Home Video, 2016).

33 "The Exhibitor Has His Say about Pictures," *BOBG* supplement, *BO*, September 2, 1950, 3.

34 Hedda Hopper, "'Red Badge of Courage' to Star Audie Murphy," *LAT*, August 4, 1950, A6.

35 Ibid., A6.

36 Ibid., A6. Claude Jarman, Jr. recalled he badly wanted the part, but Huston was intent on casting Murphy. Jarman, *My Life*, 86.

37 Borden Chase, "I Posed as a Communist for the FBI Outline," October 21, 1950, "I Was a Communist for the F.B.I." files, WBA. Using newsreel footage enhanced the "authenticity" and cut production costs.

38 Borden Chase, "I Posed as a Communist for the FBI," Story-Screenplay, 131, November 1, 1950, "I Was a Communist for the F.B.I." files, WBA.

39 Bill L. Hendricks, "Representative Press Comment on Warner Bros.'s 'I Was a Communist for the FBI,'" September 12, 1951, Publicity-misc 65B, "I Was a Communist for the F.B.I." files, WBA.

40 William Schaefer Ledger, WBA. The near tripling of the costs indicates a profit.

41 *Rebel without a Cause*, directed by Nicholas Ray (Warner Bros., 1955), Blu-ray (Warner Home Video, 2013).

42 Paul Johnson to Hedda Hopper, letter, September 9, 1957, "Rooney, Mickey," f.2797, Hedda Hopper papers, MHL, AMPAS.

43 Actor John Ashley, a veteran of American International Pictures movies, the studio that most successfully exploited the post–James Dean "delinquency" genre, commented, "I personally felt that the kids never took those pictures seriously." He explained, "I think they went to those pictures and laughed at them. They didn't really get that involved because the pictures were not well made. They were written by men who were in their late thirties and forties." Mark Thomas McGee and R. J. Robertson, *The J.D. Films: Juvenile Delinquency in the Movies* (Jefferson, NC: McFarland, 1982), 61.

44 Carol Gilligan, *In a Different Voice: Psychological Theory and Women's Development* (Cambridge, MA: Harvard University Press, 1993); Peggy Orenstein, *Schoolgirls: Young Women, Self-Esteem, and the Confidence Gap* (New York: Anchor House, 1995).

45 Christina Hoff Sommers, *The War Against Boys: How Misguided Feminism Is Harming Our Young Men* (New York: Simon & Schuster, 2000). Boys themselves also spoke out about their varied experiences. See John Nikkah, ed., *Our Boys Speak: Adolescent Boys Write about Their Inner Lives* (New York: St. Martin's Griffith, 2000).

46 On the grievances of white working- and middle-class men, see Michael Kimmel, *Angry White Men: American Masculinity at the End of an Era* (New York: Nation Books, 2013).

Bibliography

Archives and Collections

Cinema Arts Collection, Doheny Memorial Library, University of Southern California
Intruder in the Dust
Stars in My Crown
Margaret Herrick Library, Academy of Motion Picture Arts and Sciences
Association of Motion Picture and Television Producers records
Bert Granet papers
Bureau for Intercultural Education report on *TOMORROW THE WORLD*
Charles Palmer papers
Core Collection Files
Edith Angold papers
Fred Zinnemann papers
Gregory Peck papers
Hedda Hopper papers
Henry King papers
Howard Estrabrook papers
Howard Strickling papers
John Huston papers
Joseph L. Mankiewicz papers
Leo "K" Kuter papers
Lester Cowan papers
Marty Weiser papers
Metro-Goldwyn-Mayer Legal Department collection
Motion Picture Association of America: Hollywood Office files
Motion Picture Association of America: Production Code Administration records
Motion Picture Industry Council records
Richard Brooks papers
Turner/MGM scripts
United Nations Archives and Records Management Section
Warner Bros. Archives, University of Southern California
The Decision of Christopher Blake

I Was a Communist for the F.B.I.
William Schafer Collection
Wisconsin Historical Society
Dore Schary papers
George L. Bagnall papers
United Artists Corporation collection

Newspapers, Magazines, and Trade Journals

Boxoffice
Boys' Life
Chicago Defender
Christian Science Monitor
Daily Variety
Film Daily
Harrison's Reports
Hollywood
Hollywood Citizen-News
Independent Exhibitors Film Bulletin
Junior Review
Life
Los Angeles Examiner
Los Angeles Times
Mason City Globe-Gazette
Modern Screen
Motion Picture Daily
Motion Picture Herald
Motion Picture Magazine
New York Herald-Tribune
New York Times
North Adams Transcript
Parents
Photoplay
Popular Mechanics
Portsmouth Herald
Rotarian
Screenland
Wall Street Journal
Washington Post
Variety Weekly

Interviews and Correspondence

Ted Donaldson, August 5, 2017
Claude Jarman, February 6, 2015

Print Sources

"100 Years of Marriage and Divorce Rates Statistics: United States, 1867–1967." *National Vital Statistics System* 21, no. 24 (1973). https://www.cdc.gov/nchs/data/series/sr_21/sr21_024.pdf.

Abel, Richard. *Americanizing the Movies and "Movie-Mad" Audiences, 1910–1914*. Berkeley: University of California Press, 2006.

Adin, Mariah. *The Brooklyn Thrill-Kill Gang and the Great Comic Book Scare of the 1950s*. Santa Barbara, CA: Praeger, 2014.

Agee, James. *Agee on Film: Criticism and Comments on the Movies*. New York: McDowell, Obolensky, 1950.

Agnew, Jeremy. *The Creation of the Cowboy Hero: Fiction, Film, and Fact*. Jefferson, NC: McFarland, 2014.

———. *The Old West in Fact and Film: History versus Hollywood*. Jefferson, NC: McFarland, 2012.

Alexander, Ruth M. *The Girl Problem: Female Sexual Delinquency in New York, 1900–1930*. Ithaca, NY: Cornell University Press, 1998.

Allen, Frederick Lewis. *Only Yesterday: An Informal History of the 1920s*. New York: Harper & Row, 1931.

Alvarez, Luis. *Power of the Zoot*. Berkeley: University of California Press, 2009.

American Automobile Association. *Teacher's Manual for Sportsmanlike Driving.* Washington, DC: American Automobile Association, 1948.

Atkinson, Ted. *Faulkner and the Great Depression: Aesthetics, Ideology, and Cultural Politics*. Athens: University of Georgia Press, 2006.

Avila, Eric. *Popular Culture in the Age of White Flight: Fear and Fantasy in Suburban Los Angeles*. Berkeley: University of California Press, 2004.

Bach, Steven. *Dazzler: The Life and Times of Moss Hart*. New York: Knopf, 2001.

Bailey, Stephen Kemp. *Congress Makes a Law: The Story behind the Employment Act of 1946*. New York: Columbia University Press, 1950.

Barnard, Rita. *The Great Depression and the Culture of Abundance: Kenneth Fearing, Nathanael West, and Mass Culture in the 1930s*. New York: Cambridge University Press, 1995.

Baron, Lawrence. *Projecting the Holocaust into the Present: The Changing Focus of Contemporary Holocaust Cinema*. Lanham, MD: Rowman & Littlefield, 2005.

Basinger, Jeanine. *I Do and I Don't: A History of Marriage in the Movies*. New York: Knopf, 2014.

———. *The World War II Combat Film: Anatomy of a Genre*. Middleton, CT: Wesleyan University Press, 1986.

Beasley, Maurine H. *Eleanor Roosevelt and the Media: A Public Quest for Self-Fulfillment*. Urbana: University of Illinois Press, 1987.

Behlmer, Rudy, ed. *Memo from Darryl F. Zanuck: The Golden Years at Twentieth Century-Fox*. New York: Grove Press, 1993.

Beidler, Philip D. *The Victory Album: Reflections on the Good Life after the Good War.* Tuscaloosa: University of Alabama Press, 2010.

Bellesiles, Michael A. *Arming America: The Origins of a National Gun Culture*. New York: Knopf, 2000.

Belmonte, Laura A. *Selling the American Way: U.S. Propaganda and the Cold War.* Philadelphia: University of Pennsylvania Press, 2008.

Bendersky, Joseph W. *"The Jewish Threat": Anti-Semitic Politics of the U.S. Army*. New York: Basic Books, 2008.

Berger, Maurice. *For All the World to See: Visual Culture and the Struggle for Civil Rights*. New Haven, CT: Yale University Press, 2010.

Bergman, Ingrid, and Alan Burgess. *My Story*. New York: Bantam, 1981.

Bernstein, Matthew, ed. *Controlling Hollywood: Censorship and Regulation in the Studio Era*. New Brunswick, NJ: Rutgers University Press, 2000.

Bernstein, Michael A. *The Great Depression: Delayed Recovery and Economic Change in America, 1929–1939*. New York: Cambridge University Press, 1989.

Besiner, Robert L. *Dean Acheson: A Life in the Cold War.* New York: Oxford University Press, 2006.

Biesen, Sheri Chinen. *Blackout: World War II and the Origins of Film Noir.* Baltimore: Johns Hopkins University Press, 2005.

Biles, Roger. *Memphis in the Great Depression*. Knoxville: University of Tennessee Press, 1986.

Bingmann, Melissa. *Prep School Cowboys: Ranch Schools in the American West.* Santa Fe: University of New Mexico Press, 2015.

Birdwell, Michael E. *Celluloid Soldiers: Warner Bros.'s Campaign against Nazism*. New York: New York University Press, 1999.

Black, Gregory D. *The Catholic Crusade against the Movies, 1940–1975*. New York: Cambridge University Press, 1998.

———. *Hollywood Censored: Morality Codes, Catholics, and the Movies*. New York: Cambridge University Press, 1994.
Black, Shirley Temple. *Child Star: An Autobiography*. New York: McGraw-Hill, 1988.
Blanche, Ernest Evred. *You Can't Win: Facts and Fallacies about Gambling*. Washington, DC: Public Affairs Press, 1949.
Blight, David W. *Beyond the Battlefield: Race, Memory, and the American Civil War*. Amherst: University of Massachusetts Press, 2002.
Blumer, Herbert, and Philip M. Hauser, *Movies, Delinquency, and Crime*. New York: Macmillan, 1933.
Blyth, Conrad. *American Business Cycles, 1945–50*. New York: Routledge, 1969.
Boerhling, Rebecca L. "The Effects of Anti-German Sentiment on Planning and Policy-Making for Post-War Germany, 1943–1947." Master's thesis, University of Wisconsin–Madison, 1980.
Bogle, Donald. *Toms, Coons, Mulattoes, Mammies, and Bucks: An Interpretive History of Blacks in American Films*. New York: Continuum, 2000.
Borstelmann, Thomas. *The Cold War and the Color Line: American Race Relations in the Global Arena*. Cambridge, MA: Harvard University Press, 2001.
Bostdroff, Denise M. *Proclaiming the Truman Doctrine: The Cold War Call to Arms*. College Station: Texas A&M University Press, 2008.
Bosworth, Patricia. *Montgomery Clift: A Biography*. New York: Harcourt Brace Jovanovich, 1978.
Bowers, Rick. *Superman versus the Ku Klux Klan: The True Story of How the Iconic Superhero Battled the Men of Hate*. Washington, DC: National Geographic Books, 2012.
Breines, Wini. *Young, White, and Miserable: Growing Up Female in the Fifties*. Chicago: University of Chicago Press, 2001.
Brenner, Reuven, and Gabrielle A. Brenner. *Gambling and Speculation: A Theory, a History, and a Future of Some Human Decisions*. New York: Cambridge University Press, 1990.
Brinkley, Alan. *Voices of Protest: Huey Long, Father Coughlin, and the Great Depression*. New York: Knopf Doubleday, 1983.
Bromfield, Louis, et al. *Militarism in Education*. Washington, DC: National Council Against Conscription, 1950.
Brooks, Victor D. *Boomers: The Cold-War Generation Grows Up*. Chicago: Ivan R. Dee, 2009.
Brown, Jared. *Moss Hart: A Prince of the Theater*. New York: Backstage Books, 2006.
Brown, Joe David. *Stars in My Crown*. New York: Pocket Books, 1949.
Brown, John Mason. *Morning Faces: A Book of Children and Parents*. New York: Whittlesey House, 1949.
Brownlow, Kevin. *Behind the Mask of Innocence*. New York: Knopf, 1990.
Bruscino, Thomas A. *A Nation Forged in War: How World War II Taught Americans to Get Along*. Nashville: University of Tennessee Press, 2010.
Buhle, Paul, and Dave Wagner, *Radical Hollywood: The Untold Story behind America's Favorite Movies*. New York: Free Press, 2002.
Burrows, Jack. *John Ringo: The Gunfighter Who Never Was*. Phoenix: University of Arizona Press, 1987.
Caldwell, Curt. *NSC 68 and the Political Economy of the Early Cold War*. New York: Cambridge University Press, 2011.
Cantril, Henry, and Mildred Strunk. *Public Opinion, 1935–1946*. Princeton, NJ: Princeton University Press, 1951.

Caplair, Larry, and Steven Englund. *The Inquisition in Hollywood: Politics in the Film Community, 1930–1960*. New York: Doubleday, 1980.

Carrara, John. *Enemies of Youth*. Grand Rapids, MI: Zondervan, 1939.

Carruthers, Susan L. *Cold War Captives: Imprisonment, Escape, and Brainwashing*. Berkeley: University of California Press, 2009.

Carter, Matthew. *Myth of the Western: New Perspectives on Hollywood's Frontier Narrative*. Edinburgh: Edinburgh University Press, 2014.

Castillo, Greg. *Cold War on the Home Front: The Soft Power of Midcentury Design*. Minneapolis: University of Minnesota Press, 2010.

Chadwick, Bruce. *The Reel Civil War: Mythmaking in American Film*. New York: Knopf Doubleday, 2001.

Chambers, David Mark. *Hooded Americanism: The History of the Ku Klux Klan*. Durham, NC: Duke University Press, 1987.

Chopra-Gant, Mike. *Hollywood Genres and Postwar America: Masculinity, Family and Nation in Popular Movies and Film Noir*. London: I.B. Tauris, 2005.

———. "Hollywood's 'Moms' and Postwar America." In *Motherhood Misconceived: Representing the Maternal in U.S. Films*, edited by Heather Addison, Mary Kate Goodwin-Kelly, and Elaine Roth, 125–138. New York: State University of New York Press, 2009.

"C.J. Tevlin Ledger." *Historical Journal of Radio, Film, and Television* 14, no. 1 (January 1994).

Clausen, John A. *American Lives: Looking Back at the Children of the Great Depression*. Berkeley: University of California Press, 1993.

Clifford, John Garry. *The Citizen Soldiers: The Plattsburg Training Camp Movement, 1913–1920*. Lexington: University Press of Kentucky 1972.

Cohan, Beth B. "The Last Remnant of the Holocaust: The Representation and Reality of Child Survivors' Lives." In *Children, Childhood, and Cultural Heritage*, edited by Kate Darian-Smith and Carla Pascoe, 175–189. New York: Routledge, 2013.

Cohen, Albert K. *Delinquent Boys: The Culture of the Gang*. Glencoe, IL: Free Press, 1955.

Cohen, Lizabeth. *A Consumers' Republic: The Politics of Mass Consumption in Postwar America*. New York: Knopf, 2003.

Cohen, Robert, ed. *Dear Mrs. Roosevelt: Letters from Children of the Great Depression*. Chapel Hill: University of North Carolina Press, 2002.

Collins, Jim. "Faces without Names." In *Back in the Saddle: Essays on Western Film and Television Actors*, edited by Gary A. Yoggy, 145–160. Jefferson, NC: McFarland, 1998.

Cooper, Courtney Riley. *Designs in Scarlet*. Boston: Little, Brown, 1939.

Corkin, Stanley. *Cowboys as Cold Warriors: The Western and U.S. History*. Philadelphia: Temple University Press, 2004.

Couvares, Francis G. *Movie Censorship and American Culture*. 2nd ed. Amherst: University of Massachusetts Press, 2006.

Cravens, Hamilton. *Great Depression: People and Perspectives*. Santa Barbara, CA: ABC-CLIO, 2009.

Crawford, Miki, Karie Kaori Hayashi, and Shizuko Suenaga. *Japanese War Brides in America: An Oral History*. New York: Greenwood, 2010.

Cripps, Thomas. *Making Movies Black: The Hollywood Message Movie from World War II to the Civil Rights Era*. New York: Oxford University Press, 1993.

———. *Slow Fade to Black: The Negro in American Film, 1900–1942*. New York: Oxford University Press, 1977.

Cross, Gary. *The Cute and the Cool: Wondrous Innocence and Modern American Children's Culture*. New York: Oxford University Press, 2004.

———. *Machines of Youth: America's Car Obsession*. Chicago: University of Chicago Press, 2018.
Cunningham, Dean P. *American Politics in the Postwar Sunbelt: Conservative Growth in the Battleground Region*. New York: Cambridge University Press, 2014.
Cuordileone, K. A. *Manhood and American Political Culture in the Cold War*. New York: Routledge, 2005.
Currell, Susan. *The March of Spare Time: The Problem and Promise of Leisure in the Great Depression*. Philadelphia: University of Pennsylvania Press, 2010.
Davidson, Bill. *Germany, What Now?* London: Frederick Muller, 1950.
Davis, Janet M. *The Circus Age: Culture and Society under the American Big Top*. Chapel Hill: University of North Carolina Press, 2002.
Davis, Kenneth C. *Two-Bit Culture: The Paperbacking of America*. Boston: Houghton Mifflin, 1984.
DeConde, Alexander. *Gun Violence in America: The Struggle for Control*. Boston: Northeastern University Press, 2001.
Desjardins, Mary. "'Fan Magazine Trouble': The AMPP, Studio Publicity Directors, and the Hollywood Press, 1945–1952." *Film History: An International Journal* 26, no. 3 (2014): 29–56.
Deutsch, Albert. *Our Rejected Children*. Boston: Little, Brown, 1950.
Devine, Thomas W. *Henry Wallace's 1948 Presidential Campaign and the Future of Postwar Liberalism*. Chapel Hill: University of North Carolina Press, 2013.
Dick, Bernard F. *The Star-Spangled Screen: The American World War II Film*. Lexington: University Press of Kentucky, 1985.
Dilling, Elizabeth Kirkpatrick. *The Roosevelt Red Record and Its Background*. Kenilworth, IL: self-published, 1936.
Dippel, John V. H. *War and Sex: A Brief History of Men's Urge for Battle*. New York: Prometheus Books, 2010.
Dissen, Doug. "The Violent Poetry of the Times: The Politics of History in Daniel Mainwaring and Joseph Losey's The Lawless." In *"Un-American" Hollywood: Politics and Film in the Blacklist Era*, edited by Era Frank Krutnik, Steve Neale, Brian Neve, and Peter Stanfield, 97–112. New Brunswick, NJ: Rutgers University Press, 2007.
Doherty, Thomas. *Hollywood and Hitler, 1933–1939*. New York: Columbia University Press, 2013.
———. *Hollywood's Censor: Joseph I. Breen and the Production Code Administration*. New York: Columbia University Press, 2009.
———. *Projections of War: Hollywood, American Culture, and World War II*. New York: Columbia University Press, 1993.
———. *Teenagers and Teenpics: The Juvenilization of American Movies in the 1950s*. Boston: Unwin Hyman, 1988.
Duchemin, Michael. *New Deal Cowboy: Gene Autry and Public Diplomacy*. Oklahoma City: University of Oklahoma Press, 2016.
Dudziak, Mary L. *Cold War, Civil Rights: Race and the Image of American Democracy*. Princeton, NJ: Princeton University Press, 2000.
Dumenil, Lynn, ed. *The Modern Temper: American Culture and Society in the 1920s*. New York: Macmillan, 1995.
Duncan, Aaron M. *Gambling with the Myth of the American Dream*. New York: Routledge, 2015.
Dye, David. *Child and Youth Actors: Filmographies of Their Entire Careers, 1914–1985*. Jefferson, NC: McFarland, 1988.
Eastman, Max. "Let's Close the Muscle Gap." *Readers' Digest*, November 1961, 124.

Elder, Glen H., Jr. *Children of the Great Depression: Social Change in Life Experiences.* Chicago: University of Chicago Press, 1974.

Elder, Glen H., Jr., and Richard C. Rockwell. "Economic Depression and Postwar Opportunity in Men's Lives: A Study of Life Patterns and Health." In *Research in Community and Mental Health*, edited by Roberta G. Simmons, 249–303. Greenwich, CT: JAI, 1979.

Englehardt, Tom. *The End of Victory Culture: Cold War America and the Disillusioning of a Generation.* Amherst: University of Massachusetts Press, 1995.

Etheridge, Brian C. "In Search of Germans: Contested Germany in the Production of *The Search.*" *Journal of Popular Film and Television* 34 (2006): 34–45.

Fadiman, Regina K. *Faulkner's* Intruder in the Dust*: Novel into Film.* Knoxville: University of Tennessee Press, 1978.

Fass, Paula S. *The Damned and the Beautiful: American Youth in the 1920s.* New York: Oxford University Press, 1979.

Fass, Paula S., and Michael Grossberg, eds. *Reinventing Childhood after World War II.* Philadelphia: University of Pennsylvania Press, 2011.

Faulkner, William. *Intruder in the Dust.* New York: Vintage, 1991.

Fay, Jennifer. *Theaters of Occupation: Hollywood and the Reeducation of Postwar Germany.* Minneapolis: University of Minnesota Press, 2008.

Feierabend, Ivo K. "The Communist Infiltration of Czechoslovakia." PhD dissertation, University of California, 1953.

Field, Douglas. "Passing as a Cold War Novel: Anxiety and Assimilation in James Baldwin's *Giovanni's Room.*" In *American Cold War Culture*, edited by Douglas Field, 88–105. Edinburgh: Edinburgh University Press, 2005.

Fisher, Jaimey. *Disciplining Germany: Youth, Reeducation, and Reconstruction after the Second World War.* Detroit, MI: Wayne State University Press, 2007.

Fitzgerald, F. Scott. *The Damned and the Beautiful.* New York: Scribner's, 1922.

Folsom, Joseph Kirk. *The Family and Democratic Society.* New York: John Wiley, 1948.

Fones-Wolf, Ken, and Elizabeth Fones-Wolf. *Struggle for the Soul of the Postwar South: White Evangelical Protestants and Operation Dixie.* Urbana: University of Illinois Press, 2015.

Forman, Harry James. *Our Movie Made Children.* New York: Macmillan, 1933.

Fosler-Lussier, Danielle. *Music in America's Cold War Diplomacy.* Berkeley: University of California Press, 2015.

Fox, Jo. *Film Propaganda in Britain and Nazi Germany.* New York: Berg, 2007.

Frost, Jennifer. *Hedda Hopper's Hollywood: Celebrity Gossip and American Conservatism.* New York: New York University Press, 2011.

Fujiwara, Chris. *Jacques Tourneur: The Cinema of Nightfall.* Jefferson, NC: McFarland, 1998.

Fuller-Seeley, Kathryn H., ed. *Hollywood in the Neighborhood: Historical Case Studies of Local Moviegoing.* Berkeley: University of California Press, 2008.

Garrison, Karl Claudius. *Psychology of Adolescence.* New York: Prentice Hall, 1951.

Gilbert, Dan. *Hell over Hollywood: The Truth about the Movies!* Grand Rapids, MI: Zondervan, 1942.

Gilbert, James. *A Cycle of Outrage: America's Reaction to the Juvenile Delinquent of the 1950s.* New York: Oxford University Press, 1988.

———. *Men in the Middle: Searching for Masculinity in the 1950s.* Chicago: University of Chicago Press, 2005.

Gilks, Al. "See How They Run." *International Photographer*, December 1952, 11–12.

Gilligan, Carol. *In a Different Voice: Psychological Theory and Women's Development.* Cambridge, MA: Harvard University Press, 1993.

Gladchuk, John J. *Hollywood and Anticommunism: H.U.A.C. and the Evolution of the Red Menace, 1935–1950*. New York: Routledge, 2013.
Glueck, Eleanor, and Sheldon Glueck. *Unraveling Juvenile Delinquency*. New York: Commonwealth Fund, 1950.
Goldrup, Tom, and Jim Goldrup. *Growing Up on the Set: Interviews with 39 Former Child Actors of Classic Film and Television*. Jefferson, NC: McFarland, 2002.
Goldstein, Richard. *Helluva Town: The Story of New York City during World War II*. New York: Free Press, 2010.
Gonshank, Henry. *Hollywood and the Holocaust*. Lanham, MD: Rowman & Littlefield, 2015.
Goodwin, E. Marvin. *Black Migration in America from 1915 to 1960: An Uneasy Exodus*. Lewiston, NY: E. Mellen Press, 1990.
Goral, Pawel. *Cold War Rivalry and the Perception of the American West*. New York: Palgrave Macmillan, 2014.
Gras, N. S. B. "Behavior of Business Men in a Changing World." *Bulletin of the Business Historical Society* 23, no. 1 (March 1949): 65.
Green, Douglas B. *Singing in the Saddle: The History of the Singing Cowboy*. Nashville, TN: Vanderbilt University Press, 2005.
Greenberg, Cheryl. *"Or Does It Explode?" Black Harlem in the Great Depression*. New York: Oxford University Press, 1991.
Greig, Christopher. *Ontario Boys; Masculinity and the Ideas of Boyhood in Postwar Ontario, 1945–1960*. Waterloo, Canada: Wilfred Laurier University Press, 2014.
Grieve, Victoria M. *Little Cold Warriors: American Childhood in the 1950s*. New York: Oxford University Press, 2018.
Griswold, Robert L. *Fatherhood in America: A History*. New York: Basic Books, 1993.
Gunn, T. Jeremy. *Spiritual Weapons: The Cold War and the Forging of an American National Religion*. Westport, CT: Praeger, 2009.
Gunther, John. *Inside U.S.A.* New York: Harper & Brothers, 1947.
Guroff, Margaret. *The Mechanical Horse: How the Bicycle Reshaped American Life*. Austin: University of Texas Press, 2015.
Hall, G. Stanley. *Adolescence: Its Psychology and Its Relations to Physiology, Anthropology, Sociology, Sex, Crime, Religion, and Education*. Vol. 1. New York: D. Appleton, 1904.
Handel, Leo A. *Hollywood Looks at Its Audience: A Report of Film Audience Research*. Urbana: University of Illinois Press, 1950.
Hantover, Jeffrey P. "The Boy Scouts and the Validation of Masculinity." *Journal of Social Issues* 34, no. 1 (January 1978): 184–195.
Hapke, Laura. *Daughters of the Great Depression: Women, Work, and Fiction in the American 1930s*. Athens: University of Georgia Press, 1997.
Harbutt, Fraser J. *The Iron Curtain: Churchill, America, and the Origins of the Cold War*. New York: Oxford University Press, 1988.
Harding, U. E. *Movie Mad America: An Utterly Frank and Revealing Expose of the American Movie*. Grand Rapids, MI: Zondervan, 1952.
Harris, Dianne Suzette, ed. *Second Suburb: Levittown, Pennsylvania*. Pittsburgh: University of Pittsburgh Press, 2010.
Harris, Mark. *Five Came Back: A Story of Hollywood and the Second World War*. New York: Penguin, 2014.
Hart, Moss. *Christopher Blake*. New York: Random House, 1947.
Hartman, Andrew. *Education at the Cold War: The Battle for the American School*. New York: Palgrave Macmillan, 2008.

Hatch, Kristen. *Shirley Temple and the Performance of Girlhood*. New Brunswick, NJ: Rutgers University Press, 2015.

Hawes, Joseph M. *Children between the Wars: American Childhood, 1920–1940*. New York: Twayne, 1997.

Hayes, David, and Brent Walker. *The Films of the Bowery Boys*. New York: Citadel Press, 1984.

Haytok, Jennifer. *The Middle Class in the Great Depression: Popular Women's Novels of the 1930s*. New York: Palgrave Macmillan, 2013.

Helgren, Jennifer. *American Girls and Global Responsibility: A New Relation to the World during the Early Cold War*. New Brunswick, NJ: Rutgers University Press, 2017.

Helleiner, Eric. *Forgotten Foundations of Bretton Woods: International Development and the Making of the Postwar Order*. Ithaca, NY: Cornell University Press, 2014.

Herzberg, Bob. *The FBI and the Movies: A History of the Bureau on Screen and Behind the Scenes in Hollywood*. Jefferson, NC: McFarland, 2007.

Herzog, Jonathan P. *The Spiritual-Industrial Complex: America's Religious Battle Against Communism in the Early Cold War*. New York: Oxford University Press, 2011.

Hochman, Barbara. *Uncle Tom's Cabin and the Reading Revolution: Race, Literary, Childhood, and Fiction, 1851–1911*. Amherst: University of Massachusetts Press, 2011.

Hogan, Michael. *A Cross of Iron: Harry S. Truman and the Origins of the National Security State, 1945–1954*. New York: Cambridge University Press, 2000.

Holmstrom, John. *The Moving Picture Boy: An International Encyclopedia, 1895–1995*. 2nd Ed. Wilby, UK: Michael Russell, 1998.

Holt, Marilyn Irvin. *Cold War Kids: Politics and Childhood in Postwar America, 1945–1960*. Lawrence: University Press of Kansas, 2014.

Honey, Maureen. *Creating Rosie the Riveter: Class, Gender, and Propaganda during World War II*. Boston: University of Massachusetts Press, 1985.

Horne, Gerald. *Class Struggle in Hollywood, 1930–1950: Moguls, Mobsters, Stars, Reds, and Trade Unionists*. Austin: University of Texas Press, 2001.

———. *The Final Victim of the Blacklist: John Howard Lawson, Dean of the Hollywood Ten*. Berkeley: University of California Press, 2006.

House Committee on Un-American Activities. "100 Things You Should Know about Communism and Education." In *100 Things You Should Know about Communism*, 2nd ed. Washington, DC: House Committee on Un-American Activities, 1949.

———. "100 Things You Should Know about Communism and Religion." In *100 Things You Should Know about Communism*, 2nd ed. Washington, DC: House Committee on Un-American Activities, 1949.

Indiana Boys' School. *The Second Century: A Look at the Present, a Search for the Future: Indiana Boys' School, Plainfield, Indiana*. Plainfield: Indiana Boys' School, 1973.

Jackson, Kenneth T. *Crabgrass Frontier: The Suburbanization of the United States*. New York: Oxford University Press, 1987.

Jacobs, John L. *The Fisher Body Craftsman's Guild: An Illustrated History*. Jefferson, NC: McFarland, 2005.

Jacobson, Lisa. *Raising Consumers: Children and the Mass Market in the Early Twentieth Century*. New York: Columbia University Press, 2005.

Jarman, Claude, Jr. *My Life and the Final Days of Hollywood*. Murrells Inlet, SC: Covenant Books, 2018.

Jenkins, Gladys Gardner, Helen Shacter, and William W. Bauer. *These Are Your Children: How They Develop and How to Guide Them*. Chicago: Scott, Foresman, 1949.

Joesten, Joachim. *Germany, What Now?* Chicago: Ziff-Davis, 1948.

Jones, Kathleen W. *Taming the Troublesome Child: American Families, Child Guidance, and the Limits of Psychiatric Authority*. Cambridge, MA: Harvard University Press, 1999.

Jowett, Garth S., Ian C. Jarvie, and Kathryn H. Fuller. *Children and the Movies: Media Influence and the Payne Fund Controversy*. New York: Cambridge University Press, 2007.

Juvenile Delinquency, California: Hearings before the Subcommittee to Investigate Juvenile Delinquency of the Committee on the Judiciary. Washington, DC: U.S. Government Printing Office, 1955.

Juvenile Delinquency (Philadelphia, PA): Hearing before the Subcommittee to Investigate Juvenile Delinquency of the Committee on the Judiciary, United States Senate, Eighty-Third Congress. 2nd ed. Washington, DC: Government Printing Office, 1954.

Kahn, Albert E. *The Game of Death: Effects of the Cold War on Our Children*. New York: Cameron & Kahn, 1953.

Kasson, John. *The Little Girl Who Fought the Great Depression: Shirley Temple and 1930s America*. New York: Norton, 2014.

Kasson, Joy S. *Buffalo Bill's Wild West: Celebrity, Memory, and Popular Culture*. New York: Hill & Wang, 2000.

Keaton, Angela F. "Unholstered and Unquestioned: The Rise of Post–World War II American Gun Cultures." PhD dissertation, University of Tennessee–Knoxville, 2006.

Kelley, Robin D. G. *Hammer and Hoe: Alabama Communists during the Great Depression*. Chapel Hill: University of North Carolina Press, 1990.

Kersten, Andrew E. *Labor's Home Front: The American Federation of Labor during World War II*. New York: New York University Press, 2006.

Kidd, Kenneth B. *Making American Boys: Boyology and the Feral Tale*. Minneapolis: University of Minnesota Press, 2004.

Kimmel, Michael. *Angry White Men: American Masculinity at the End of an Era*. New York: Nation Books, 2013.

———. *Manhood in America*. 3rd ed. New York: Oxford University Press, 2011.

Knock, Thomas J. "History with Lightning: The Forgotten Film *Wilson* (1944)." In *Hollywood as Historian: American Film in a Cultural Context*, edited by Peter C. Rollins, 88–108. Lexington: University Press of Kentucky, 1983.

Komarovsky, Mirra. *The Unemployed Man and His Family: The Effect of Unemployment upon the Status of the Man in Fifty-Nine Families*. New York: Dryden Press, 1940.

Koppes, Clayton R., and Gregory D. Black. *Hollywood Goes to War: How Politics, Profits, and Propaganda Shaped World War II*. Berkeley: University of California Press, 1990.

Kordas, Ann. "Wally Cleaver Goes to War: The Boy Citizen-Solider on the Cold War Classroom Scenes." *Thymos: Journal of Boyhood Studies* 5, no. 2 (Fall 2011): 163–173.

Korkis, Jim. *Who's Afraid of the* Song of the South*? And Other Forbidden Disney Stories*. New York: Theme Park Press, 2012.

Kramer, Dale, and Madeline Karr. *Teen-Age Gangs*. New York: Popular Library, 1954.

LaRossa, Ralph. *The Modernization of Fatherhood: A Social and Political History*. Chicago: University of Chicago Press, 1997.

———. *Of War and Men: World War II in the Lives of Fathers and Their Families*. Chapel Hill: University of North Carolina Press, 2011.

Lasky, Betty. *RKO: The Biggest Little Major of Them All*. Santa Monica, CA: Round Table, 1989.

Leab, Daniel J. *I Was a Communist for the F.B.I.: The Unhappy Life and Times of Matt Cvetic*. University Park: Pennsylvania State University Press, 2000.

Lee, Julia. *Our Gang: A Racial History of* The Little Rascals. Minneapolis: University of Minnesota Press, 2014.

Lee, Peter W. "A Green Peace Tinted Red: Cold War America in *The Boy with Green Hair*." In *Learning the Left: Popular Culture, Liberal Politics, and Informal Education from 1900 to the Present*, edited by Paul J. Ramsey, 49–69. Charlotte, NC: Info Age, 2015.

Leffler, Melvyn P. "American Policy Making and European Stability, 1921–1933." *Pacific Historical Review* 46, no. 2 (1977): 207–228.

Lindenmeyer, Kristie. *The Greatest Generation Grows Up: American Childhood in the 1930s*. Chicago: Ivan R. Dee, 2007.

———. *"A Right to Childhood": The U.S. Children's Bureau and Child Welfare*. Chicago: University of Illinois Press, 1997.

Lipsitz, George, ed. *Rainbow at Midnight: Labor and Culture in the 1940s*. Chicago: University of Illinois Press, 1994.

Loescher, Gil, and John A. Scanlan. *Calculated Kindness: Refugees and America's Half-Opened Door*. New York: Free Press, 1998.

Lowery, Vincent. "Preparing the Next Generation for Massive Resistance: The Historical Pageantry of the Children of the Confederacy, 1955–1965." In *Children and Youth during the Civil War Era*, edited by James Marten, 209–224. New York: New York University Press, 2012.

Loy, R. Philip. *Westerns and American Culture, 1930–1955*. Jefferson, NC: McFarland, 2001.

Luke, Carmen. *Constructing the Child Viewer: A History of the American Discourse on Television and Children, 1950–1980*. New York: Praeger, 1990.

Lynd, Robert S., and Helen Merrell Lynd. *Middletown in Transition: A Study in Cultural Conflicts*. New York: Harcourt, Brace, 1937.

———. *Middletown: A Study in Modern American Culture*. 1929. New York: Harcourt Brace Jovanovich, 1956.

Macleod, David I. *Building Character in the American Boy: The Boys Scouts, YMCA, and Their Forerunners, 1870–1920*. Madison: University of Wisconsin Press, 1983.

Maher, Neil M. *Nature's New Deal: The Civilian Conservation Corps and the Roots of the American Environmental Movement*. New York: Oxford University Press, 2009.

Malton, Leonard. *The Little Rascals: The Life and Times of* Our Gang. New York: Crown, 1992.

May, Elaine Tyler. *Homeward Bound: American Families in the Cold War Era*. New York: Basic Books, 1988.

———. "Rosie the Riveter Gets Married." In *The War in American Culture: Society and Consciousness during World War II*, edited by Lewis A. Erenberg and Susan E. Hirsch, 128–143. Chicago: University of Chicago Press, 1996.

May, Lary. *The Big Tomorrow: Hollywood and the Politics of the American Way*. Chicago: University of Chicago Press, 2000.

———. "Cultural Conversion and the Hollywood Red Scare." In *Recasting America: Culture and Politics in the Age of Cold War*, edited by Lary May, 125–153. Chicago: University of Chicago Press, 1989.

———. "Making the American Consensus: The Narrative of Conversion and Subversion in World War II Films." In *The War in American Culture: Society and Consciousness during World War II*, edited by Lewis A. Erenberg and Susan E. Hirsh, 71–104. Chicago: University of Chicago Press, 1996.

———. *Screening Out the Past: The Birth of Mass Culture and the Motion Picture Industry*. Chicago: University of Chicago Press, 1983.

McClelland, Doug. *Forties Film Talk: Oral Histories of Hollywood, with 120 Lobby Posters*. Jefferson, NC: McFarland, 1992.
McDaniel, Hattie. "What Hollywood Means to Me." In *The Hollywood Reporter: The Golden Years*, edited by Tichi Wilkerson and Marcia Borie, 210–211. New York: Coward-McCann, 1984.
McElvaine, Robert S., ed. *Down and Out in the Great Depression: Letters from the Forgotten Man*. Chapel Hill: University of North Carolina Press, 2012.
McElwee, John. "Metro Takes a Bold Postwar Step." *Greenbriar Picture Shows*, June 27, 2014. http://greenbriarpictureshows.blogspot.com/2014/06/metro-takes-bold-postwar-step.html.
McGee, Mark Thomas, and R. J. Robertson. *The J.D. Films: Juvenile Delinquency in the Movies*. Jefferson, NC: McFarland, 1982.
McGilligan, Patrick, and Paul Buhle, eds. *Tender Comrades: A Backstory of the Hollywood Blacklist*. New York: St. Martin's, 1997.
McLaughlin, Robert L., and Sally E. Parry. *We'll Always Have the Movies: American Cinema during World War II*. Lexington: University Press of Kentucky, 2006.
McNally, Karen. *When Frankie Went to Hollywood: Frank Sinatra and American Male Identity*. Urbana: University of Illinois Press, 2008.
McVeigh, Stephen. *The American Western*. Edinburgh: Edinburgh University Press, 2007.
Mechling, Jay. *On My Honor: Boy Scouts and the Making of American Youth*. Chicago: University of Chicago Press, 2001.
Mettler, Suzanne. *Soldiers to Citizens: The G.I. Bill and the Making of the Greatest Generation*. New York: Oxford University Press, 2005.
Meyer, Alan. *Weekend Pilots: Technology, Masculinity, and Private Aviation in Postwar America*. Baltimore: Johns Hopkins University Press, 2015.
Meyerowitz, Joanne, ed. *Not June Cleaver: Women and Gender in Postwar America, 1945–1960*. Philadelphia: Temple University Press, 1994.
Mickenberg, Julia L. *Learning from the Left: Children's Literature, the Cold War, and Radical Politics in the United States*. New York: Oxford University Press, 2006.
Miller, Cynthia J., and A. Bowdin Van Riper, eds. *1950s "Rocketman" TV Series and Their Fans: Cadets, Rangers, and Junior Space Men*. New York: Palgrave Macmillan, 2012.
Miller, Roger G. *To Save a City: The Berlin Airlift, 1948–1949*. Austin: Texas A&M University Press, 2000.
Miller, Steven P. *Billy Graham and the Rise of the Republican South*. Philadelphia: University of Pennsylvania Press, 2009.
Mills, Thomas C. *Post-war Planning on the Periphery: Anglo-American Economic Diplomacy in South America, 1939–1945*. Edinburgh: Edinburgh University Press, 2012.
Molyneaux, Gerald. *Gregory Peck: A Bio-bibliography*. Westport, CT: Greenwood, 1995.
Moore, Dick. *Twinkle, Twinkle, Little Star: But Don't Have Sex or Take the Car*. New York: Harper & Row, 1984.
Motion Picture Association of America. *Exploding a Myth: Motion Pictures ARE NOT Responsible for Juvenile Delinquency*. New York: Motion Picture Association of America, 1950.
Muller, James W., ed. *Churchill's "Iron Curtain" Speech Fifty Years Later*. Columbia: University of Missouri Press, 1999.
Munby, Jonathan. *Public Enemies, Public Heroes: Screening the Gangster from* Little Creaser *to* Touch of Evil. Chicago: University of Chicago Press, 2009.
Murdoch, David Hamilton. *The American West: The Invention of a Myth*. Las Vegas: University of Nevada Press, 2001.

Nadel, Alan. *Containment Culture: American Narratives, Postmodernism, and the Atomic Age*. Durham, NC: Duke University Press, 1995.

Naremore, James. *More Than Night: Film Noir in Its Contexts*. Berkeley: University of California Press, 1998.

Nash, Ilana. *American Sweethearts; Teenage Girls in Twentieth-Century Popular Culture*. Indianapolis: Indiana University Press, 2005.

Navasky, Victor S. *Naming Names*. New York: Viking, 1980.

Neiberg, Michael S. *Making Citizen-Soldiers: ROTC and the Ideology of American Military Service*. Cambridge, MA: Harvard University Press, 2001.

Nelson, H. Viscount. *Black Leadership's Response to the Great Depression in Philadelphia*. Lewiston, NY: Edwin Mellen Press, 2006.

Nevins, Francis M. "Through the Great Depression on Horseback: Legal Themes in Western Films of the 1930s." In *Legal Realism: Movies as Legal Texts*, edited by John Denvir, 44–69. Urbana: University of Illinois Press, 1996.

Nichols, John. *The "S" Word: A Short History of an American Tradition . . . Socialism*. New York: Verso, 2011.

Nikkah, John, ed. *Our Boys Speak: Adolescent Boys Write about Their Inner Lives*. New York: St. Martin's Griffith, 2000.

Noakes, John. "Radicalizing Subversion: The FBI and the Depiction of Race in Early Cold War Movies." *Ethnic and Racial Studies* 26, no. 4 (July 2003): 728–749.

Oddian, Lisa. *The Forgotten Generation: American Children and World War II*. Columbia: University of Missouri Press, 2011.

O'Reilly, Kenneth. "A New Deal for the FBI: The Roosevelt Administration, Crime Control, and National Security." *Journal of American History* 69, no. 3 (December 1982): 638–658.

Orenstein, Peggy. *Schoolgirls: Young Women, Self-Esteem, and the Confidence Gap*. New York: Anchor House, 1995.

Orzoff, Andrea. *Battle for the Castle: The Myth of Czechoslovakia in Europe, 1914–1948*. New York: Oxford University Press, 2009.

Ossian, Lisa K. *The Forgotten Generation: American Children and World War II*. Columbia: University of Missouri Press, 2011.

Osteen, Mark. *Nightmare Alley: Film Noir and the American Dream*. New York: Johns Hopkins University Press, 2012.

Palmer, R. Barton. *Shot on Location: Postwar American Cinema and the Exploration of Real Place*. New Brunswick, NJ: Rutgers University Press, 2016.

Patterson, Richard. "The UN in Hollywood: A Lesson in Public Relations." *Hollywood Quarterly* 5, no. 4 (1951): 326–333.

Peacock, Margaret. *Innocent Weapons: The Soviet and American Politics of Childhood in the Cold War*. Chapel Hill: University of North Carolina Press, 2014.

Phillips, Gene D. *Exiles in Hollywood: Major European Film Directors in America*. Cranbury, NJ: Associated University Presses, 1998.

———. *Fiction, Film, and Faulkner: The Art of Adaptation*. Knoxville: University of Tennessee Press, 1988.

Phillips, Roderick. *Untying the Knot: A Short History of Divorce*. New York: Cambridge University Press, 1991.

Pipher, Mary. *Reviving Ophelia: Saving the Selves of Adolescent Girls*. New York: Penguin, 1994.

Plant, Rebecca Jo. *Mom: The Transformation of Motherhood in Modern America*. Chicago: University of Chicago Press, 2010.

Platt, Anthony M. *The Child Savers: The Invention of Delinquency*. Expanded ed. New York: Oxford University Press, 2009.
Potter, David M. *People of Plenty: Economic Abundance and the American Character*. Chicago: University Press of Chicago, 1958.
Powaski, Ronald E. *Toward an Entangling Alliance: American Isolationism, Internationalism, and Europe, 1901–1950*. Westport, CT: Greenwood, 1991.
Prime, Rebecca. *Hollywood Exiles in Europe: The Blacklist and Cold War Film Culture*. New Brunswick, NJ: Rutgers University Press, 2014.
Putney, Clifford. *Muscular Christianity: Manhood and Sports in Protestant America*. Cambridge, MA: Harvard University Press, 2001.
Ramsay, Debra. *American Media and the Memory of World War II*. New York: Routledge, 2015.
Renner, Karen J., ed. *The "Evil Child" in Literature, Film, and Popular Culture*. New York: Routledge, 2013.
Reynolds, David. *From World War to Cold War: Churchill, Roosevelt, and the International History of the 1940s*. New York: Oxford University Press, 2006.
Rice, John R. *What Is Wrong with the Movies?* Grand Rapids, MI: Zondervan, 1938.
———. *What Is Wrong with the Movies?* 15th ed. 1938. Grand Rapids, MI: Zondervan, 1954.
Riley, Glenda. *Divorce: An American Tradition*. New York: Oxford University Press, 1991.
Ritterhouse, Jennifer. *Growing Up Jim Crow: How Black and White Southern Children Learned Race*. Chapel Hill: University of North Carolina Press, 2006.
Robin, Ron Theodore. *The Barbed-Wire College: Re-educating German POWs in the United States during World War II*. Princeton, NJ: Princeton University Press, 1995.
Rogin, Michael. "Kiss Me Deadly: Communism, Motherhood, and Cold War Movies." *Representations* 6 (Spring 1984): 1–36.
Romanowski, William D. *Reforming Hollywood: How American Protestants Fought for Freedom at the Movies*. New York: Oxford University Press, 2008.
Rooney, Mickey. *Life Is Too Short*. New York: Villard Books, 1991.
Rose, Kenneth. *Myth and the Greatest Generation: A Social History of Americans in World War II*. New York: Routledge, 2008.
Rosenzweig, Roy, and Elizabeth Blackmar. *The Park and the People: A History of Central Park*. Ithaca, NY: Cornell University Press, 2002.
Ross, Steven J. *Hollywood Left and Right: How Movie Stars Shaped American Politics*. New York: Oxford University Press, 2011.
———. *Working-Class Hollywood: Silent Film and the Shaping of Class in America*. Princeton, NJ: Princeton University Press, 1998.
Rotundo, E. Anthony. *American Manhood: Transformations in Masculinity from the Revolution to the Moon*. New York: Basic Books, 1994.
Rudolph, John L. *Scientists in the Class Room: The Cold War Reconstruction of American Science Education*. New York: Palgrave Macmillan, 2002.
Russo, Barry D. *Walter Lippmann: Odyssey of a Liberal*. New Brunswick, NJ: Transaction, 1996.
Ruth, David E. *Inventing the Public Enemy: The Gangster in American Culture, 1918–1934*. Chicago: University of Chicago Press, 1996.
Sager, John. "Universal Military Training and the Struggle to Define American Identity during the Cold War." *Federal History* 5 (January 2013): 57–74.
Sammond, Nicholas. *Babes in Tomorrowland: Walt Disney and the Making of the American Child, 1930–1960*. Durham, NC: Duke University Press, 2005.

Sarles, Ruth, and Bill Kauffman. *A Story of America First: The Men and Women Who Opposed U.S. Intervention in World War II.* Westport, CT: Praeger, 2003.

Saunders, Frances Stonor. *The Cultural Cold War: The CIA and the World of Arts and Letters.* New York: Free Press, 2013.

Sbardellati, John. *J. Edgar Hoover Goes to the Movies: The FBI and the Origins of Hollywood's Cold War.* Ithaca, NY: Cornell University Press, 2012.

Schary, Dore. *A Case History of a Movie.* New York: Random House, 1950.

———. *Heyday.* Boston: Little, Brown, 1979.

Schatz, Thomas. *Boom and Bust: American Cinema in the 1940s.* Berkeley: University of California Press, 1999.

Scheider, Eric C. *Vampires, Dragons, and Egyptian Kings: Youth Gangs in Postwar New York.* Princeton, NJ: Princeton University Press, 2001.

Schindler, Colin. *Hollywood in Crisis: Cinema and American Society, 1929–1939.* New York: Routledge, 1996.

Schrum, Kelly. *Some Wore Bobby Sox: The Emergence of Teenage Girls' Culture, 1920–1945.* New York: Palgrave Macmillan, 2004.

———. "'Teena Means Business': Teenage Girls' Culture and *Seventeen Magazine,* 1944–1950." In *Delinquent Daughters: Twentieth-Century American Girls' Culture,* edited by Sherrie Inness, 134–163. New York: New York University Press, 1998.

Schuyler, George S. *The Communist Conspiracy Against the Negroes.* New York: Catholic Information Society, 1947.

Scott, Ellen Christine. "Race and the Struggle for Cinematic Meaning: Film Production, Censorship, and African American Reception, 1940–1960." PhD dissertation, University of Michigan, 2007.

Shary, Timothy. *Teen Movies: American Youth on Screen.* New York: Columbia University Press, 2005.

Shaw, Tony. *Hollywood's Cold War.* Boston: University of Massachusetts Press, 2007.

Sheen, Fulton John. *Communism and the Conscience of the West.* Indianapolis: Bobbs-Merrill, 1948.

Silk, Catherine, and John Silk. *Racism and Anti-racism in American Popular Culture: Portrayals of African-Americans in Fiction and Film.* New York: Manchester University Press, 1990.

Slocum, J. David, ed. *Rebel Without a Cause: Approaches to a Maverick Masterpiece.* Albany: State University of New York Press, 2005.

Slotkin, Richard. *Gunfighter Nation: The Myth of the Frontier in Twentieth-Century America.* New York: Atheneum, 1992.

Smyth, J. E. *Fred Zinnemann and the Cinema of Resistance.* Jackson: University Press of Mississippi, 2014.

———. "Fred Zinnemann's Search (1945–48): Reconstructing the Voices of Europe's Children." *Film History* 23, no. 1 (2011): 75–92.

Sobchack, Vivian. "Lounge Time: Postwar Crises and the Chronotope of Film Noir." In *Refiguring American Film Genres: History and Theory,* edited by Nick Browne, 129–170. Berkeley: University of California Press, 1998.

Solomon, Aubrey. *Twentieth Century-Fox: A Corporate and Financial History.* Lanham, MD: Scarecrow Press, 2002.

Sommers, Christina Hoff. *The War Against Boys: How Misguided Feminism Is Harming Our Young Men.* New York: Simon & Schuster, 2000.

Sperb, Jason. *Disney's Most Notorious Film: Race, Convergence, and the Hidden Histories of Song of the South.* Austin: University of Texas Press, 2012.

Sperling, Cass Warner, Cork Millner, and Jack Warner Jr. *Hollywood Be Thy Name: The Warner Brothers Story*. Lexington: University Press of Kentucky, 1998.
Spock, Benjamin. "Children Need Sensible Parents." *Parents*, December 1950, 40–41, 131–132.
———. *The Common Sense Book of Baby and Child Care*. New York: Duell, Sloan, and Pearce, 1946.
Stanfield, Peter. *Horse Opera: The Strange History of the 1930s Singing Cowboy*. Urbana: University Press of Illinois, 2002.
Stempel, Tom. *Recollections of Nunnally Johnson*. Berkeley: University of California Press, 1969.
———. *Screenwriter: The Life and Times of Nunnally Johnson*. San Diego: S.A. Barnes, 1990.
Sternberg, Claudia. "Real-Life References in Four Fred Zinnemann Films." In *The Films of Fred Zinnemann: Critical Perspectives*, edited by Arthur Nolletti Jr., 199–218. New York: State University of New York Press, 1999.
Stewart, Jacqueline. *Migrating to the Movies: Cinema and Black Urban Modernity*. Berkeley: University of California Press, 2005.
Stolz, Lois Meek, et al. *Father Relations of War-Born Children*. Stanford, CA: Stanford University Press, 1954.
Stott, D. H. *Delinquency and Human Nature*. Dunfermline, Scotland: Carnegie United Kingdom Trust, 1950.
Studlar, Gaylyn. *Precocious Charms: Performing Girlhood in Classic Hollywood Cinema*. Berkeley: University of California Press, 2013.
Sturm, Shannon Lynn. "Spies, Lies, and Intrigue: Anti-German Sentiment in West Central Texas during World War I." PhD dissertation, Angelo State University, 2010.
Sumner, Robert L. *Hollywood Cesspool: A Startling Survey of Movieland Lives and Morals, Pictures, and Results*. Wheaton, IL: Sword of the Lord, 1955.
Tappen, Paul. *Juvenile Delinquency*. New York: McGraw-Hill, 1949.
Taylor, Clarence. *Reds at the Blackboard: Communism, Civil Rights, and the New York City Teachers Union*. New York: Columbia University Press, 2013.
Taylor, Quintard. *The Forging of a Black Community: Seattle's Central District from 1870 through the Civil Rights Era*. Seattle: University of Washington Press, 1994.
Taylor, William A. *Every Citizen a Soldier: The Campaign for Universal Military Training after World War II*. Austin: Texas A&M University Press, 2014.
Theoharis, Athan G., ed. *The FBI: A Comprehensive Reference Guide*. Phoenix, AZ: Oryx Press, 1999.
Thuecke, Jörg. "Flotsam and Jetsam: Fred Zinnemann's Film *The Search* (1948) and the Problem of 'Unaccompanied Children' at the End of World War II." *Modern Austrian Literature* 32, no. 4 (1999): 271–288.
Trumpbour, John. *Selling Hollywood to the World: U.S. and Europeans Struggles for Mastery of the Global Film Industry, 1920–1950*. New York: Cambridge University Press, 2002.
Turpin, Robert J. "'Our Best Bet Is the Boy': A Cultural History of Bicycle Marketing and Consumption in the United States, 1880–1960." PhD dissertation, University of Kentucky, 2013.
Tuttle, William M. *"Daddy's Gone to War": The Second World War in the Lives of America's Children*. New York: Oxford University Press, 1995.
Ulys, Errol Lincoln. *Riding the Rails: Teenagers on the Move during the Great Depression*. New York: Routledge, 2004.
United States Congress, Senate, Committee on the Judiciary. *Juvenile Delinquency, Comic Books Motion Pictures, Obscene and Pornographic Materials, Television Programs*. New York: Greenwood, 1955.

Urwand, Ben. *The Collaboration: Hollywood's Pact with Hitler.* Cambridge, MA: Harvard University Press, 2013.

Van Woodward, Comer. *The Origins of the New South, 1877–1913.* New Orleans: Louisiana State University Press, 1951.

Vizzard, Jack. *See No Evil: Life Inside a Hollywood Censor.* New York: Simon & Schuster, 1970.

Wade, Wyn Craig. *The Fiery Cross: The Ku Klux Klan in America.* New York: Oxford University Press, 1998.

Wagnleitner, Reinhold. *Coca-Colinization: The Cultural Mission of the United States after the Second World War.* Chapel Hill: University of North Carolina University Press, 1994.

———. "The Irony of American Culture Abroad." In *Recasting America: Culture and Politics in the Age of the Cold War,* edited by Lary May, 285–301. Chicago: University of Chicago Press, 1989.

Wake, Naoko. "The Military, Psychiatry, and 'Unfit' Soldiers, 1939–1942." *Journal of the History of Medicine and Allied Sciences* 62, no. 4 (October 2007): 462–494.

Walker, William T., ed. *McCarthyism and the Red Scare: A Reference Guide.* Santa Barbara, CA: ABC-CLIO, 2011.

Wall, Wendy L. *Inventing the "American Way": The Politics of Consensus from the New Deal to the Civil Rights Movement.* New York: Oxford University Press, 2008.

Walsh, Frank. *Sin and Censorship: The Catholic Church and the Motion Picture Industry.* New Haven, CT: Yale University Press, 1996.

Weier, Jonathan. "The Building of Boys for War: The Militarization of Boys' Work in the Canadian and American YMCAs." In *Children's Literature and Culture of the First World War,* edited by Lissa Paul and Rosemary R. Johnston, 162–178. New York: Routledge, 2015.

Whitfield, Stephen. *The Culture of the Cold War.* Baltimore: Johns Hopkins University Press, 1991.

Wiener, Jon. "Civil War, Cold War, Civil Rights: The Civil War Centennial in Context, 1960–1965." In *The Memory of the Civil War in American Culture,* edited by Alice Fahs and Joan Waugh, 237–257. Chapel Hill: University of North Carolina Press, 2004.

Williams, Bernard. *Jailbait: The Story of Juvenile Delinquency.* New York: Greenberg, 1949.

Williamson, Joel. *William Faulkner and Southern History.* New York: Oxford University Press, 1993.

Willis, Brian Steel. *Gone with the Glory: The Civil War in Cinema.* Lanham, MD: Rowman & Littlefield, 2007.

Willkie, Wendell L. *One World.* New York: Simon & Schuster, 1943.

Wilson, Harry L. *Guns, Gun Control, and Elections: The Politics and Policy of Firearms.* Lanham, MD: Rowman & Littlefield, 2007.

Wilson, Michael. "Conditioning the American Mind: War Films Show Vicious Over-All Policy." *Hollywood Review* 1, no. 1 (January 1953): 3.

Wojcik, Pamela Robertson. *Fantasies of Neglect: Imagining the Urban Child in American Film and Fiction.* New Brunswick, NJ: Rutgers University Press, 2016.

Wojcik-Andrews, Ian. *Children's Films: History, Ideology, Pedagogy, Theory.* New York: Garland, 2000.

Wolcott, David B. *Cops and Kids: Policing Juvenile Delinquency in Urban America, 1890–1940.* Columbus: Ohio State University Press, 2005.

Woodbridge, George. *UNRRA: The History of the United Nations Relief and Rehabilitation Administration.* Vol. 1. New York: Columbia University Press, 1950.

Woods, Jeff R. *Black Struggle, Red Scare: Segregation and Anti-communism in the South, 1948–1968*. Baton Rouge: Louisiana State University Press, 2004.
Woolrich, Cornell. "The Boy Cried Murder." *Mystery Book Magazine* 18 (March 1947): 50–83.
Worthen, James. *Governor James Rolph and the Great Depression in California*. Jefferson, NC: McFarland, 2006.
Wright, Patrick. *Iron Curtain: From Stage to Cold War*. New York: Oxford University Press, 2007.
Wright, Will. *The Wild West: The Mythical Cowboy and Social Theory*. Thousand Oaks, CA: Sage, 1983.
Wylie, Philip. *Generation of Vipers*. New York: Farrar & Rhinehart, 1942.
Young, Nancy Beck, William D. Pederson, Byron W. Daynes, eds. *Franklin D. Roosevelt and the Shaping of American Political Culture*. London: M.E. Sharpe, 2001.
Zahra, Tara. *The Lost Children: Reconstructing Europe's Families after World War II*. Cambridge, MA: Harvard University Press, 2011.
Zelizer, Viviana A. *Pricing the Priceless Child: The Changing Social Value of Children*. New York: Basic Books, 1985.
Zimmerman, Carle C. *Family and Civilization*. New York: Harper & Bros., 1947.
Zinnemann, Fred. *An Autobiography: A Life in the Movies*. New York: Scribner's Sons, 1992.
———. "The Story of the Search." *Screen Writer* 4, no. 2 (August 1948): 12–13, 30.

Filmography and Media Sources

And Baby Makes Three. Directed by Henry Levin. Columbia Pictures, 1949.
Andy Hardy Comes Home. Directed by Howard W. Koch. Metro-Goldwyn-Mayer, 1958.
Andy Hardy Gets Spring Fever. Directed by W. S. Van Dyke. Metro-Goldwyn-Mayer, 1939.
Andy Hardy Meets Debutante. Directed by George B. Seitz. Metro-Goldwyn-Mayer, 1940.
Andy Hardy's Blonde Trouble. Directed by George B. Seitz. Metro-Goldwyn-Mayer, 1944.
"Andy Hardy's Dilemma: A Lesson in Mathematics—and Other Things." Directed by George B. Seitz. Metro-Goldwyn-Mayer, 1940.
Andy Hardy's Double Life. Directed by George B. Seitz. Metro-Goldwyn-Mayer, 1942.
Andy Hardy's Private Secretary. Directed by George B. Seitz. Metro-Goldwyn-Mayer, 1941.
Any Number Can Play. Directed by Mervyn LeRoy. Metro-Goldwyn-Mayer, 1949.
The Atomic City. Directed by Jerry Hopper. Paramount Pictures, 1952.
Babes in Arms. Directed by Busby Berkeley. Metro-Goldwyn-Mayer, 1939.
Babes on Broadway. Directed by Busby Berkeley. Metro-Goldwyn-Mayer, 1941.
"Baby Blues." *Our Gang*. Directed by Edward L. Cahn. Metro-Goldwyn-Mayer, 1941.
Back to Bataan. Directed by Edward Dmytryk. RKO-Radio Pictures, 1945.
Bad Boy. Directed by Roy Neumann. Monogram Pictures, 1949.
Bataan. Directed by Tay Garnett. Metro-Goldwyn-Mayer, 1943.
Battleground. Directed by William A. Wellman. Metro-Goldwyn-Mayer, 1950.
The Beloved Brat. Directed by Arthur Lubin. Warner Bros., 1938.
Ben-Hur. Directed by B. Reeves Eason. Metro-Goldwyn-Mayer, 1925.
Berlin Express. Directed by Jacques Tourneur. RKO-Radio Pictures, 1948.
The Best Years of Our Lives. Directed by William Wyler. Samuel Goldwyn Company, 1946.
The Big House. Directed by George Hill. Metro-Goldwyn-Mayer, 1930.
The Big Lift. Directed by George Seaton. Twentieth Century-Fox Film, 1950.
Blonde Comet. Directed by William Beaudine. Producers Releasing Corporation, 1941.
Born to Speed. Directed by Edward L. Cahn. Producers Releasing Corporation, 1947.

The Boy from Stalingrad. Directed by Sidney Salkow. Columbia Pictures, 1943.
A Boy, a Girl, and a Dog. Directed by Herbert Kline. W. R. Frank Productions, 1946.
Boyhood. Directed by Richard Linklater. IFC Productions, 2014.
A Boy of Flanders. Directed by Jack Coogan, Sr. Metro-Goldwyn, 1924.
Boy Slaves. Directed by P. J. Wolfson. RKO-Radio Pictures, 1939.
The Boy with Green Hair. Directed by Joseph Losey. RKO-Radio Pictures, 1948.
Boys' Ranch. Directed by Roy Rowland. Metro-Goldwyn-Mayer, 1946.
Boys' Town. Directed by Norman Taurog. Metro-Goldwyn-Mayer, 1938.
The Breaking Point. Directed by Michael Curtiz. Warner Bros., 1950.
The Bride Goes Wild. Directed by Noram Taurog. Metro-Goldwyn-Mayer, 1948.
Bright Road. Directed by Gerald Mayer. Metro-Goldwyn-Mayer, 1953.
Buck Privates Come Home. Directed by Charles T. Barton. Universal International Pictures, 1947.
Bullets or Ballots. Directed by William Keighley. Warner Bros., 1936.
Cabin in the Sky. Directed by Vincent Minnelli. Metro-Goldwyn-Mayer, 1943.
Callaway Went Thataway. Directed by Melvin Frank. Metro-Goldwyn-Mayer, 1951.
Cassino to Korea. Directed by Edward P. Genock. Paramount Pictures, 1950.
Cause for Alarm! Directed by Tay Garnett. Metro-Goldwyn-Mayer, 1951.
The Champ. Directed by King Vidor. Metro-Goldwyn-Mayer, 1931.
Chicken Every Sunday. Directed by George Seaton. Twentieth Century-Fox Film, 1949.
Child of Divorce. Directed by Richard Fleischer. RKO-Radio Pictures, 1946.
China's Little Devils. Directed by Monta Bell. Monogram Pictures, 1945.
Close to My Heart. Directed by William Keighley. Warner Bros., 1951.
"Coffin on Wheels." *Crime Does Not Pay*. Directed by Joseph M. Newman. Metro-Goldwyn-Mayer, 1941.
The Courtship of Andy Hardy. Directed by George B. Seitz. Metro-Goldwyn-Mayer, 1942.
The Cowboys. Directed by Mark Rydell. Warner Bros., 1972.
Crossfire. Directed by Edward Dmytryk. RKO-Radio Pictures, 1947.
The Crowd Roars. Directed by Howard Hawks. Warner Bros., 1932.
The Cry of the City. Directed by Robert Siodmak. Twentieth Century-Fox Film, 1948.
Curley. Directed by Bernard Carr. Hal Roach Studios, 1947.
Danger! Women at Work. Directed by Sam Newfield. Jack Schwartz Productions, 1943.
Dead End. Directed by William Wyler. Samuel Goldwyn Company, 1937.
December 7th. Directed by John Ford and Gregg Toland. Navy Department, U.S. War Department, 1943.
The Decision of Christopher Blake. Directed by Peter Godfrey. Warner Bros., 1948.
Desperate Search. Directed by Joseph H. Lewis. Metro-Goldwyn-Mayer, 1952.
The Devil on Wheels. Directed by Crane Wilbur. Producers Releasing Corporation, 1947.
Dial 1119. Directed by Gerald Mayer. Metro-Goldwyn-Mayer, 1950.
The Divorcee. Directed by Robert Z. Leonard. Metro-Goldwyn-Mayer, 1930.
Divorce in the Family. Directed by Norman Taurog. Metro-Goldwyn-Mayer, 1932.
A Dog of Flanders. Directed by Edward Sloman. RKO-Radio Pictures, 1935.
The Doughgirls. Directed by James V. Kern. Warner Bros., 1944.
"Education for Death." Directed by Clyde Geronimi. Walt Disney Productions, 1943.
A Family Affair. Directed by George B. Seitz. Metro-Goldwyn-Mayer, 1937.
Fighting Father Dunne. Directed by Ted Teztlaff. RKO-Radio Pictures, 1948.
The Fighting Sullivans. Directed by Lloyd Bacon. Twentieth Century-Fox Film, 1944.
The First Auto. Directed by Roy Del Ruth. Warner Bros., 1927.
Footlight Parade. Directed by Lloyd Bacon. Warner Bros., 1933.
A Foreign Affair. Directed by Billy Wilder. Paramount Pictures, 1948.

Fury. Directed by Fritz Lang. Metro-Goldwyn-Mayer, 1936.
Gabriel over the White House. Directed by Gregory La Cava. Metro-Goldwyn-Mayer, 1933.
The Gay Divorcee. Directed by Mark Sandrich. RKO-Radio Pictures, 1934.
Gentleman's Agreement. Directed by Elia Kazan. Twentieth Century-Fox Film, 1947.
"Give Us the Earth!" Directed by Gunther V. Fritsch. Metro-Goldwyn-Mayer, 1947.
The Godless Girl. Directed by Cecil B. DeMille. Paramount Pictures, 1929.
Gone with the Wind. Directed by Victor Fleming. Selznick International Pictures, 1939.
Good Boys. Directed by Gene Stupnitsky. Universal Pictures, 2019.
Good-bye, My Lady. Directed by William A. Wellman. Batjac Productions, 1956.
"Good News of 1939." Sponsored by Maxwell House Coffee, broadcast November 24, 1938.
The Grapes of Wrath. Directed by John Ford. Twentieth Century-Fox Film, 1940. (Released in Europe under the name *This American Paradise!*)
Growing Up Smith. Directed by Frank Lotito. Brittany House Pictures, 2015.
Gun Crazy. Directed by Joseph H. Lewis. King Brothers Production, 1950.
The Gunfighter. Directed by Henry King. Twentieth Century-Fox Film, 1950.
Gun for a Coward. Directed by Abner Biberman. Universal Pictures, 1957.
The Hardys Ride High. Directed by George B. Seitz. Metro-Goldwyn-Mayer, 1939.
Hell's Highway. Directed by Rowland Brown. RKO-Radio Pictures, 1932.
Hell's Kitchen. Directed by Lewis Seiler and E. A. Dupont. Warner Bros., 1939.
Here Comes the Groom. Directed by Frank Capra. Paramount Pictures, 1951.
Heroes for Sale. Directed by William A. Wellman. First National Pictures, 1933.
High Gear. Directed by Leigh Jason. Majestic Pictures, 1933.
High Noon. Directed by Fred Zinnemann. Stanley Kramer Productions, 1952.
Hitler's Children. Directed by Edward Dmytryk. RKO-Radio Pictures, 1943.
Home of the Brave. Directed by Mark Robeson. Stanley Kramer Productions, 1949.
Hot Rod. Directed by Lewis D. Collins. Monogram Pictures, 1950.
"The House I Live In." Directed by Mervyn LeRoy. Frank Ross Productions, 1945.
I Am a Fugitive from a Chain Gang. Directed by Mervyn LeRoy. Warner Bros., 1932.
Intruder in the Dust. Directed by Clarence Brown. Metro-Goldwyn-Mayer, 1949.
I Was a Communist for the F.B.I. Directed by Gordon Douglas. Warner Bros., 1951.
Imitation of Life. Directed by John M. Stahl. Universal Pictures, 1934.
Imitation of Life. Directed by Douglas Sirk Universal-International Pictures, 1959.
Jesse James. Directed by Henry King. Twentieth Century-Fox Film, 1939.
Joe Smith, American. Directed by Richard Thorpe. Metro-Goldwyn-Mayer, 1942.
Johnny Holiday. Directed by Willis Goldbeck. Alcorn Productions, 1949.
Journey for Margaret. Directed by W. S. Van Dyke. Metro-Goldwyn-Mayer, 1942.
Judge Hardy and Son. Directed by George B. Seitz. Metro-Goldwyn-Mayer, 1939.
Judge Hardy's Children. Directed by George B. Seitz. Metro-Goldwyn-Mayer, 1938.
Kim. Directed by Victor Saville. Metro-Goldwyn-Mayer, 1951.
Lassie Come Home. Directed by Fred M. Wilcox. Metro-Goldwyn-Mayer, 1943.
Let's Try Again. Directed by Worthington Miner. RKO-Radio Pictures, 1934.
Life Begins for Andy Hardy. Directed by George B. Seitz. Metro-Goldwyn-Mayer, 1941.
Lifeboat. Directed by Alfred Hitchcock. Twentieth Century-Fox Film, 1944.
The Lights of New York. Directed by Brian Foy. Warner Bros., 1928.
Little Boy Lost. Directed by George Seaton. Paramount Pictures, 1953.
The Little Colonel. Directed by David Butler. Fox Film, 1935.
Little Fugitive. Directed by Ray Ashley, Morris Engel, and Ruth Orkin. Little Fugitive Production Company, 1953.
Love Finds Andy Hardy. Directed by George B. Seitz. Metro-Goldwyn-Mayer, 1938.
Love Laughs at Andy Hardy. Directed by Willis Goldbeck. Metro-Goldwyn-Mayer, 1947.

A Man for All Seasons. Directed by Fred Zinnemann. Highland Films, 1966.
Manhattan Melodrama. Directed by W. S. Van Dyke. Metro-Goldwyn-Mayer, 1934.
The Marrying Kind. Directed by George Cukor. Columbia Pictures, 1952.
The Mayor of Hell. Directed by Archie Mayo. Warner Bros., 1933.
Memphis Belle: The Story of a Flying Fortress. Directed by William Wyler. U.S. War Department, 1944.
Mission to Moscow. Directed by Michael Curtiz. Warner Bros., 1943.
Mister Scoutmaster. Directed by Henry Levin. Twentieth Century-Fox Film, 1953.
Mokey. Directed by Wells Root. Metro-Goldwyn-Mayer, 1942.
The More the Merrier. Directed by George Stevens. Columbia Pictures, 1943.
Mr. Belevedere Goes to College. Directed by Elliot Nugent. Twentieth Century-Fox Film, 1949.
Mr. Blandings Builds His Dream House. Directed by H. C. Potter. RKO-Radio Pictures, 1948.
Mr. Smith Goes to Washington. Directed by Frank Capra. Columbia Pictures, 1939.
My Brother Talks to Horses. Directed by Fred Zinnemann. Metro-Goldwyn-Mayer, 1947.
My Foolish Heart. Directed by Mark Robeson. Samuel Goldwyn Company, 1949.
My Friend Flika. Directed by Harold D. Schuster. Twentieth Century-Fox Film, 1943.
My Reputation. Directed by Curtis Bernhardt. Warner Bros., 1946.
My Son John. Directed by Leo McCarey. Rainbow Productions, 1952.
The Naked City. Directed by Jules Dassin. Universal-International Pictures, 1948.
National Velvet. Directed by Clarence Brown. Metro-Goldwyn-Mayer, 1945.
Navajo. Directed by Norman Foster. Bartlett-Foster Productions, 1952.
The Next Voice You Hear. Directed by William A. Wellman. Metro-Goldwyn-Mayer, 1950.
Night Passage. Directed by James Neilson. Universal Pictures, 1957.
Ninotchka. Directed by Ernst Lubitsch. Metro-Goldwyn-Mayer, 1939.
The North Star. Directed by Lewis Miletsone. Samuel Goldwyn Company, 1944.
No Way Out. Directed by Joseph L. Mankiewicz. Twentieth Century-Fox Film, 1950.
The Nun's Story. Directed by Fred Zinnemann. Warner Bros., 1959.
Old Yeller. Directed by Robert Stevenson. Walt Disney Productions, 1957.
On Our Merry Way. Directed by Leslie Fenton and King Vidor. Benedict Bogeaus Production, 1948.
Our Daily Bread. Directed by King Vidor. Viking Productions, 1934.
The Ox-Bow Incident. Directed by William A. Wellman. Twentieth Century-Fox Film, 1943.
Payment on Demand. Directed by Curtis Bernhardt. Warner Bros., 1951.
Penrod and Sam. Directed by William McGann. Warner Bros., 1937.
Personal Maid's Secret. Directed by Arthur Greville Collins. Warner Bros., 1935.
The Phenix City Story. Directed by Phil Karlson. Allied Artists Pictures, 1955.
The Pied Piper. Directed by Irving Pichel. Twentieth Century-Fox Film, 1942.
Pinky. Directed by Eliza Kazan. Twentieth Century-Fox Film, 1949.
The Plastic Age. Directed by Wesley Ruggles. Preferred Pictures, 1925.
The President Vanishes. Directed by William A. Wellman. Walter Wanger Productions, 1935.
Public Enemy. Directed by William A. Wellman. Warner Bros., 1931.
The Quiet One. Directed by Sidney Meyers. Film Documents, 1948.
Rebel without a Cause. Directed by Nicholas Ray. Warner Bros., 1955.
The Red Badge of Courage. Directed by John Huston. Metro-Goldwyn-Mayer, 1951.
The Red Stallion. Directed by Lesley Selander. Ben Stoloff Productions, 1947.
Rocky Mountain. Directed by William Keighley. Warner Bros., 1950.
The Romance of Rosy Ridge. Directed by Roy Rowland. Metro-Goldwyn Mayer, 1947.
Room for One More. Directed by Norman Taurog. Warner Bros., 1952.

Sahara. Directed by Zoltan Korda. Columbia Pictures, 1943.
The Search. Directed by Fred Zinnemann. Praesens-Film, 1948.
Secret Command. Directed by Eddie Sutherland. Terneen Productions, 1944.
Shane. Directed by George Stevens. Paramount Pictures, 1953.
Show Boat. Directed by Snub Pollard. Universal Pictures, 1929.
Show Boat. Directed by James Whale. Universal Pictures, 1936.
Show Boat. Directed by George Sidney. Metro-Goldwyn-Mayer, 1951.
Since You Went Away. Directed by John Cromwell. Selznick International, 1944.
Skippy. Directed by Norman Taurog. Paramount Pictures, 1931.
Song of Russia. Directed by Gregory Ratoff. Metro-Goldwyn-Mayer, 1944.
Song of the South. Directed by Wilfred Jackson and Harve Foster. Walt Disney Pictures, 1946.
The Son of Rusty. Directed by Lew Landers. Columbia Pictures, 1947.
Speedway. Directed by Harry Beaumont. Metro-Goldwyn-Mayer, 1929.
Stablemates. Directed by Sam Wood. Metro-Goldwyn-Mayer, 1938.
Stars in My Crown. Directed by Jacques Tourneur. Metro-Goldwyn-Mayer, 1950.
The Steel Helmet. Directed by Samuel Fuller. Deputy Corp, 1951.
Storm Over Tibet. Directed by Andrew Marton. Summit Productions, 1952.
Storm Warning. Directed by Stuart Heisler. Warner Bros., 1951.
Stormy Weather. Directed by Andrew Stone. Twentieth Century-Fox Film, 1943.
The Story of Seabuscuit. Directed by David Butler. Warner Bros., 1949.
Suddenly. Directed by Lewis Allen. Libra Productions, 1954.
The Sun Comes Up. Directed by Richard Thorpe. Metro-Goldwyn-Mayer, 1949.
Talk about a Stranger. Directed by David Bradley. Metro-Goldwyn-Mayer, 1952.
They Came to Blow Up America. Directed by Edward Ludwig. Twentieth Century-Fox Film, 1943.
They Won't Forget. Directed by Mervyn LeRoy. Warner Bros., 1937.
Thoroughbreds Don't Cry. Directed by Alfred E. Green. Metro-Goldwyn-Mayer, 1937.
Thunderbolt. Directed by William Wyler. Carol Krueger Productions and U.S. War Department, 1947.
To Be or Not to Be. Directed by Ernst Lubitsch. Romaine Film Corporation, 1942.
Tomorrow Is Forever. Directed by Irving Pichel. International Pictures, 1946.
Tomorrow's a Wonderful Day. Directed by Helmar Lerski. Children to Palestine, Inc., 1949.
Tomorrow, the World! Directed by Leslie Fenton. Lester Cowan Productions, 1944.
To Please a Lady. Directed by Clarence Brown. Metro-Goldwyn-Mayer, 1950.
"A Town Solves a Problem." Directed by U.S. Army. United States Army, 1950.
"Traffic with the Devil." Directed by Gunther von Fritsch. Metro-Goldwyn-Mayer, 1946.
Trial. Directed by Mark Robson. Metro-Goldwyn-Mayer, 1955.
The Trouble with Harry. Directed by Alfred Hitchcock. Paramount Pictures, 1955.
Washington Merry-Go-Round. Directed by James Cruze. Columbia Pictures, 1932.
Watch on the Rhine. Directed by Herman Shumlin. Warner Bros., 1943.
Wednesday's Child. Directed by John Robertson. RKO-Radio Pictures, 1934.
What Becomes of the Children? Directed by Walter Shumway. Sentinel Productions, 1936.
When Worlds Collide. Directed by George Pal. Paramount Pictures, 1951.
Where Are Your Children? Directed by William Nigh. Monogram Pictures, 1944.
Where the Red Fern Grows. Directed by Norman Tokar. Doty-Dayton Production, 1974.
Wild Boys of the Road. Directed by William A. Wellman. First National Pictures, 1933.
The Wild One. Directed by László Benedek. Stanley Kramer Productions, 1953.
Wilson. Directed by Henry King. Twentieth Century-Fox Film, 1944.
The Window. Directed by Ted Tetzlaff. RKO-Radio Pictures, 1949.

The Women. Directed by George Cukor. Metro-Goldwyn-Mayer, 1939.
Yankee Doodle Dandy. Directed by Michael Curtiz. Warner Bros., 1942.
The Yearling. Directed by Clarence Brown. Metro-Goldwyn-Mayer, 1947.
Yellow Sky. Directed William A. Wellman. Twentieth Century-Fox Film, 1948.
You're Only Young Once. Directed by George B. Seitz. Metro-Goldwyn-Mayer, 1937.
Youth Runs Wild. Directed by Mark Robson. RKO-Radio Pictures, 1944.
Zenobia. Directed by Gordon Douglas. Hal Roach Studios, 1939.

Index

Page numbers in *italics* refer to figures

About the Author

PETER W. Y. LEE is an independent historian specializing in modern American history and youth culture. He completed his doctorate at Drew University. He has published widely on comic books, film, and television. His most recent edited volume is *Peanuts and American Culture: Essays on Charles M. Schulz's Iconic Comic Strip.*